PE🌎PLE
in Time and Place

COMPARING REGIONS

AUTHORS

Dr. W. Frank Ainsley, Jr.
Professor of Geography
University of North Carolina
Wilmington, NC

Dr. Gary S. Elbow
Professor of Geography
Texas Tech University
Lubbock, TX

Dr. Linda L. Greenow
Assistant Professor of Geography
SUNY — The College at New Paltz
New Paltz, NY

Dr. Gail S. Ludwig
Geographer-in-Residence
National Geographic Society
Geography Education Program
Washington, D.C.

SERIES CONSULTANTS

Dr. James F. Baumann
Professor and Head of the Department
of Reading Education, College of Education
The University of Georgia
Athens, GA

Dr. Theodore Kaltsounis
Professor of Social Studies Education
University of Washington
Seattle, WA

LITERATURE CONSULTANTS

Dr. Ben A. Smith
Assistant Professor of Social Studies Education
Kansas State University
Manhattan, KS

Dr. John C. Davis
Professor of Elementary Education
University of Southern Mississippi
Hattiesburg, MS

Dr. Jesse Palmer
Assistant Professor, Department of Curriculum and Instruction
University of Southern Mississippi
Hattiesburg, MS

SILVER BURDETT & GINN

MORRISTOWN, NJ • NEEDHAM, MA
Atlanta, GA • Cincinnati, OH • Dallas, TX • Deerfield, IL • Menlo Park, CA

SERIES AUTHORS

Dr. W. Frank Ainsley, Professor of Geography, University of North Carolina, Wilmington, NC

Dr. Herbert J. Bass, Professor of History, Temple University, Philadelphia, PA

Dr. Kenneth S. Cooper, Professor of History, Emeritus, George Peabody College for Teachers, Vanderbilt University, Nashville, TN

Dr. Gary S. Elbow, Professor of Geography, Texas Tech University, Lubbock, TX

Roy Erickson, Program Specialist, K–12 Social Studies and Multicultural Education San Juan Unified School District, Carmichael, CA

Dr. Daniel B. Fleming, Professor of Social Studies Education, Virginia Polytechnic Institute and State University, Blacksburg, VA

Dr. Gerald Michael Greenfield, Professor and Director, Center for International Studies, University of Wisconsin — Parkside, Kenosha, WI

Dr. Linda Greenow, Assistant Professor of Geography, SUNY — The College at New Paltz, New York, NY

Dr. William W. Joyce, Professor of Education, Michigan State University, East Lansing, MI

Dr. Gail S. Ludwig, Geographer-in-Residence, National Geographic Society, Geography Education Program, Washington, D.C.

Dr. Michael B. Petrovich, Professor Emeritus of History, University of Wisconsin, Kenosha, WI

Dr. Arthur Roberts, Professor of Education, University of Connecticut, Storrs, CT

Dr. Christine L. Roberts, Professor of Education, University of Connecticut, Storrs, CT

Parke Rouse, Jr., Virginia Historian and Retired Executive Director of the Jamestown-Yorktown Foundation, Williamsburg, VA

Dr. Paul C. Slayton, Jr., Distinguished Professor of Education, Mary Washington College, Fredericksburg, VA

Dr. Edgar A. Toppin, Professor of History and Dean of the Graduate School, Virginia State University, Petersburg, VA

GRADE-LEVEL WRITERS/CONSULTANTS

Connie K. Christiansen, Teacher, Easterly Parkway School, State College, PA

Gloria J. Ebbe, Teacher, Torey J. Sabatini Elementary School, Madison, NJ

Carolyn Hopp, Teacher, Mohawk Trail Elementary School, Carmel, IN

Margaret Love, Teacher, King Elementary School, Akron, OH

ACKNOWLEDGEMENTS

Page 29: From *The Little Prince* by Antoine de Saint-Exupery. © 1962 and renewed 1971 by Harcourt Brace Jovanovich, Inc. Reprinted by permission of the publisher.

Page 53: From *The Home Planet*. Conceived and edited by Kevin W. Kelley for the Association of Space Explorers. Addison-Wesley Publishing Company. © 1988 by Kevin W. Kelley. Used by permission.

Page 54: From *Last Flight* by Amelia Earhart. Used by kind permission of Margaret H. Lewis.

Page 61: From *Tales of the Elders* by Carol Ann Bales. Copyright 1977 by Carol Ann Bales. Reprinted by permission of Modern Curriculum Press, Inc.

Page 116: From *The House on Spruce Street* by John L. Loeper. Reprinted by permission of Atheneum Publishers, an imprint of Macmillan Publishing Company. Copyright © 1982 by John L. Loeper. Used by permission.

Page 138: From *Chesapeake* by James Michener. Copyright © 1978 by Random House, Inc. Used by permission of Random House, Inc.

Page 157: From *By the Shores of Silver Lake* by Laura Ingalls Wilder. Text copyright 1939 by Laura Ingalls Wilder. Copyright renewed 1967 by Roger L. MacBride. Used by permission of Harper & Row, Publishers, Inc.

Page 175: From *Farmer Boy* by Laura Ingalls Wilder. © 1961, renewed. Harper & Row. Reprinted by permission of the publisher.

Pages 187 and 237: From *Complete Book of Marvels* by Richard Halliburton. Copyright 1937, 1938, 1941, 1960 (copyright renewed) by the Bobbs-Merrill Company, Inc. Reprinted by permission of Macmillan Publishing Company, a Division of Macmillan Inc.

Page 241: From "Mt. St. Helens: The Volcano Explodes" by Prof. Leonard Palmer. Used courtesy of KOIN-TV, Portland, OR.

Page 280: From *Yagua Days* by Cruz Martel. Text copyright © 1976 by Cruz Martel. Pictures by Jerry Pinkney. Pictures copyright © 1976 by Jerry Pinkney. Reprinted/reproduced by permission of the publisher, Dial Books for Young Readers.

Page 296: From *Uncle Fonzo's Ford* by Miska Miles. © 1968 Miska Miles. Used by permission of Ruth Cohen Agent. All rights reserved. Illustration copyright © 1968 by Wendy Watson. Used by permission of Curtis Brown Ltd.

Page 346: From *In Coal Country* by Judith Hendershot. © 1987 by Judith Hendershot. Reprinted by permission of Alfred A. Knopf, Inc.

Contents

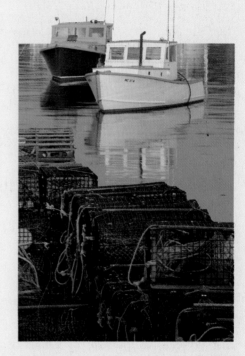

MAP SKILLS HANDBOOK   **2–25**
Learning About the Earth
Using Maps to Find Your Way
Using Latitude and Longitude
Using Symbols and Scale
Kinds of Maps
Map Skills Handbook Review

CHAPTER 1 **GEOGRAPHY: A WONDERFUL ADVENTURE**   **28–51**
What Is Geography?
The World We Live In
Earning a Living in Our World
CHAPTER REVIEW: PUTTING IT ALL TOGETHER

CHAPTER 2 **LEARNING ABOUT REGIONS** **52–66**
Discovering What a Region Is
The United States in the World
USING SOURCE MATERIAL
An Interview with Abraham Gamberg   **61**
CHAPTER REVIEW: PUTTING IT ALL TOGETHER

UNIT 1 REVIEW: COOPERATIVE LEARNING 67

Reading a Temperature Map   **68–69**
Reading to Learn   **70–71**

UNIT 2 REGIONS OF THE UNITED STATES

CHAPTER 3 THE NEW ENGLAND
REGION   **74–97**

Land and Climate in the New England Region
Farming in New England
Natural Resources and Industry in the New
England Region
Communities in the New England Region
State Charts: New England Region   **94–95**
CHAPTER REVIEW: PUTTING IT ALL TOGETHER

CHAPTER 4 THE MIDDLE ATLANTIC
REGION   **98–123**

The Lands and Waters of the Middle Atlantic
Region
Farming in the Middle Atlantic Region
Earning a Living in the Middle Atlantic Region
People and Cities of the Middle Atlantic Region

 LITERATURE *The House on
Spruce Street* by John L. Loeper **116**
State Charts: Middle Atlantic
Region   **120–121**
CHAPTER REVIEW: PUTTING IT ALL TOGETHER

CHAPTER 5 THE SOUTHEAST REGION

Old and New in the Southeast
Climate and Farming in the Southeast

CITIZENSHIP AND AMERICAN VALUES
George Washington Carver:
Why Do We Remember Him? **136–137**
Industries in the Southeast
Cities and Vacationlands of the Southeast
State Charts: Southeast Region   **150–153**
CHAPTER REVIEW: PUTTING IT ALL TOGETHER

CHAPTER 6 THE NORTH CENTRAL
REGION   **156–185**

The Heartland of the United States
Climate and Crops of the North Central Region
Natural Resources and Industries
Living in the North Central Region

LITERATURE *Farmer Boy*
by Laura Ingalls Wilder   **175**
State Charts: North Central Region   **180–183**
CHAPTER REVIEW: PUTTING IT ALL TOGETHER

CHAPTER 7   THE SOUTHWEST REGION **186–209**
The Land of the Southwest
Farms and Ranches of the Southwest
Natural Resources of the Southwest Region
The Three Cultures of the Southwest
State Charts: Southwest Region   **206–207**
CHAPTER REVIEW: PUTTING IT ALL TOGETHER

CHAPTER 8   THE MOUNTAIN WEST
REGION   **210–235**
Getting to Know the Mountain West
Earning a Living in the Mountain West
Mining and Manufacturing in the Mountain West
Cities of the Mountain West
State Charts: Mountain West Region **232–233**
CHAPTER REVIEW: PUTTING IT ALL TOGETHER

CHAPTER 9   THE PACIFIC WEST REGION
A Land of Great Variety
Climate and Farms of the Pacific West
USING SOURCE MATERIAL
The Eruption of Mount St. Helens **241**
CITIZENSHIP AND AMERICAN VALUES
Sharing the Harvest in the
Pacific West   **248–249**
Natural Resources of the Pacific West
Ways of Life in the Pacific West
State Charts: Pacific West Region   **261–262**
CHAPTER REVIEW: PUTTING IT ALL TOGETHER
UNIT 2 REVIEW: COOPERATIVE LEARNING **265**

SKILLBUILDER

Reading a Mileage Chart   **266–267**
Writing a Report   **268–269**

UNIT 3 CONNECTIONS — THE UNITED STATES AND THE WORLD

CHAPTER 10 CONNECTIONS WITH DISTANT LANDS — 272–291

American Citizens in Faraway Lands

Some Islands of the Caribbean Sea

 LITERATURE *Yagua Days* by Cruz Martel — 280

Some Islands in the Pacific Ocean

CHAPTER REVIEW: PUTTING IT ALL TOGETHER

CHAPTER 11 MOVING PEOPLE AND GOODS — 292–311

People and Transportation

LITERATURE *Uncle Fonzo's Ford* by Miska Miles — 296

How Trade Began

The Importance of International Trade

CHAPTER REVIEW: PUTTING IT ALL TOGETHER

CHAPTER 12 FARMING AROUND THE WORLD — 312–335

Land from the Sea

Farming in an African Rain Forest

Rice Farming in East Asia

Ranching Down Under

CHAPTER REVIEW: PUTTING IT ALL TOGETHER

CHAPTER 13 ENERGY SOURCES AROUND US — 336–355

Energy That Comes from Wells

Energy That Comes from Mines

LITERATURE *In Coal Country* by Judith Hendershot — 346

CITIZENSHIP AND AMERICAN VALUES
You Decide: How Can We Stop Polluting the Air? — 348–349

Renewable Energy Resources

CHAPTER REVIEW: PUTTING IT ALL TOGETHER

CHAPTER **14** LIVING IN
OTHER LANDS   **356–376**

Food from the Sea
Forest Resources
Mineral Riches in the Americas
Japan — A Country with Few Natural Resources
CHAPTER REVIEW: PUTTING IT ALL TOGETHER

UNIT 3 REVIEW: COOPERATIVE LEARNING   **377**

SKILLBUILDER

Understanding Cause and Effect   **378–379**
Identifying Main Ideas   **380–381**

RESOURCE SECTION

Atlas	**382–399**	Glossary	**410–417**
Gazetteer	**400–409**	Index	**418–423**

MAPS

The Earth: Oceans and Continents	**5**	The New England Region: Physical	**78**
North America: Political	**6**	New England: Yearly Snowfall	**80**
The United States: National Parks	**9**	The Middle Atlantic Region: Political	**98**
Compass Directions	**10**	The Erie Canal, 1825	**102**
Latitude Lines	**11**	The Middle Atlantic Region: Physical	**103**
Longitude Lines	**12**	The United States: Census Regions	**113**
Using Latitude and Longitude	**13**	The United States: Population Density	**114**
Georgia: Using a Grid	**14**	The Southeast Region: Political	**124**
Oregon: Two Different Scales	**19**	The Southeast Region: Physical	**128**
From Photograph to Map	**20**	The United States: Rice	**131**
Understanding Contour Lines	**23**	The United States: Citrus Fruits	**132**
Indiana: Political	**32**	The North Central Region: Political	**156**
The World: Average Annual Precipitation	**35**	The North Central Region: Physical	**159**
Pennsylvania: Three Kinds of Regions	**55**	The St. Lawrence Waterway	**160**
The United States: Regions	**63**	The United States: Corn	**165**
The New England Region: Political	**74**	The United States: Wheat	**166**

The Dairy Belt 167
The Southwest Region: Political 186
The Southwest Region: Physical 189
The United States: Cotton 194
The United States: Oil Fields 198
The Mountain West Region: Political 210
The Mountain West Region: Physical 212
The United States: Deserts 215
The United States: Gold 221
The United States: Silver 222
The United States: Copper 222
The United States: Major Highways 228
The Pacific West Region: Political 236
The Pacific West Region: Physical 239
The Trans-Alaska Pipeline 251
Department of Defense Dependents Schools 274
The West Indies 278
Some Islands in the Pacific 286
The United States: Major Railroads 295
The United States: Major Rivers 298
The World: Major Airports 300
The European Community 307
The Netherlands: Building Polders 315
The World: Where Rice Is Grown 322
Australia: Major Highways 326
The World: Where Sheep Are Raised 329
The World: Where Petroleum Is Located 341
The United States and the Soviet Union:
    Two Large Countries 361
The Soviet Union: Vegetation 362
The World: Where Copper Is Located 367
The World: Where Tin Is Located 369

ATLAS

The World: Political 382–383
North America: Political 384
North America: Physical 385
The United States: Political 386–387
The United States: Physical-Political 388–389
South America: Political 390
South America: Physical 391
Africa: Political 392
Africa: Physical 393
Eurasia: Political 394–395
Eurasia: Physical 396–397
Australia and New Zealand:
    Political-Physical 398
The World: Forests 399
The World: Population Density 399

TIME LINES

Events in Connecticut's Whaling History,
    1784–1865 92
The Nation's Capital, 1776–1860 100
Hurricanes in the Southeast, 1928–1989 126
Inventions That Improved Farming,
    1793–1878 176
Construction of Major Dams in the
    Southwest, 1916–1964 201
Events in the Mountain West Region,
    1847–1884 231
National Parks Founded in the Pacific
    West, 1890–1968 257
Events in Australia's History 1770–1851 332

GRAPHS

The Earth's Land Area 7
The United States: Cranberry Production 83
Population of Philadelphia, 1790–1990 117
Leading Growers of Rice 131
Leading Growers of Citrus Fruits 132
Leading Textile-Producing States 139
Leading Coal-Producing States 143
Climograph: Columbus, Ohio 163
Climograph: Omaha, Nebraska 163
Leading Growers of Corn 165
Leading Growers of Wheat 166
Climograph: Phoenix, Arizona 192
Leading Growers of Cotton 194
Leading Producers of Oil 198
Climograph: Denver, Colorado 216
Leading Producers of Gold 221
Leading Producers of Silver 222
Leading Producers of Copper 222
States That Lead in Fish Caught 253
Top Ten Manufacturing States 255
Climograph: San Juan, Puerto Rico 279
The World: Leading Growers of Rice 322
Leading Sheep-Raising Countries 329
The World: Leading Producers of Oil 341
The World: Leading Producers
    of Copper 367
The World: Leading Producers of Tin 369
The World: Countries That Lead in
    Fish Caught 372

TABLES

Immigration to the United States,
 1860–1900   62
Average Water Use   200
Leading Producers of Certain Fruits   245

CHARTS

Understanding Symbols   17
Products of the Menhaden   84
How Paper Is Made   87
New England Region: State Charts   94–95
Middle Atlantic Region: State
 Charts   120–121
Peanuts: From Planting to Shipping   133
Southeast Region: State Charts   150–153
Products That Come from Beef Cattle   168
Milling: From Wheat to Flour   171
North Central Region: State Charts   180–183
Southwest Region: State Charts   206–207
Mountain West Region: State Charts   232–233
Pacific West Region: State Charts   261–262
Slash-and-burn Farming   318–319
How Petroleum Is Refined   339
Products Made from Petroleum   340

DIAGRAMS

Football Field   18
The Four Seasons   37
Fahrenheit and Celsius Thermometers   130
Hydroelectric Power   144
A Cross Section of a Volcano   240
A Fish Ladder   254
Rain Shadow   279
Desalination of Sea Water   284
A Coral Atoll   287
How Coal Is Formed   344
Open-pit Mining   345
Shaft Mining   345
Water Cycle   351

SPECIAL FEATURES

USING SOURCE MATERIAL

An Interview with Abraham Gamberg   61
The Eruption of Mount St. Helens   241

LITERATURE

The House on Spruce Street   116
Farmer Boy   175
Yuaga Days   280
Uncle Fonzo's Ford   296
In Coal Country   346

MUSIC

"Erie Canal"   104
"Shrimp Boats"   140
"I've Been Working on the Railroad"   227
"The House I Live In"   242
"Waltzing Matilda"   331

CITIZENSHIP AND AMERICAN VALUES

George Washington Carver: Why Do
 We Remember Him?   136–137
Sharing the Harvest in the Pacific
 West   248–249
You Decide: How Can We Stop
 Polluting the Air?   348–349

SKILLBUILDER

SOCIAL STUDIES

Reading a Temperature Map   68–69
Reading a Mileage Chart   266–267
Understanding Cause and Effect   378–379

LANGUAGE ARTS

Reading to Learn   70–71
Writing a Report   268–269
Identifying Main Ideas   380–381

MAP SKILLS HANDBOOK

Knowing how to work with maps is a social studies skill that everyone must have. You can't learn geography without being able to read and understand maps. Maps, however, have uses that go beyond what you are learning in school.

Watch the nightly news. How many times are maps used? The next time you are in the library, take a copy of a weekly newsmagazine and count the number of maps that accompany the articles. Are maps used in any of the advertisements in the magazine? Keep a record over a week of all the times you see or use a map.

As you study geography this year, you will be using map skills that you already have. You will also be learning some new map skills. All the map skills you will need appear in this Map Skills Handbook. Study the table of contents on these pages to see what you will learn.

LESSON *1*
Learning About the Earth
page 4

LESSON *2*
Using Maps to Find Your Way
page 8

North Pole

South Pole

LESSON 3
Using Latitude and Longitude page 11

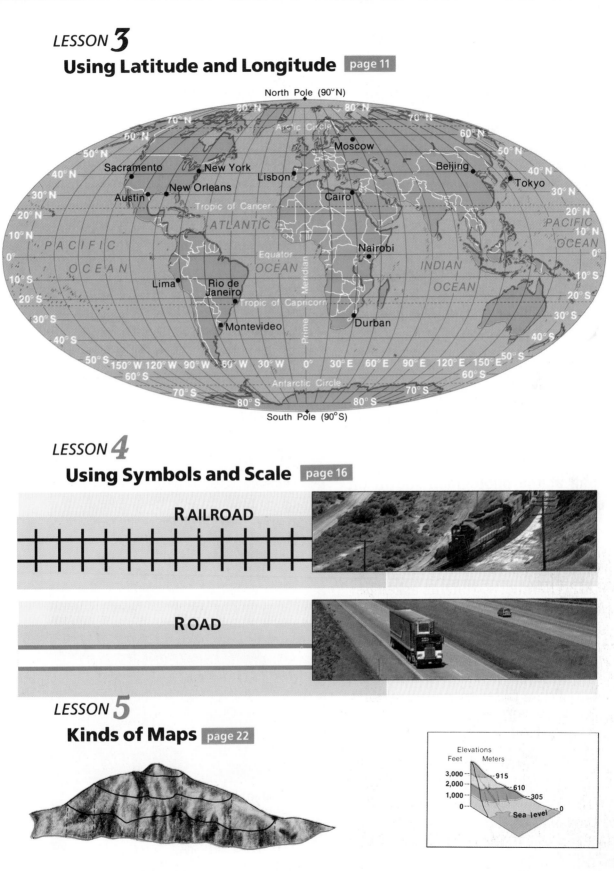

North Pole (90°N)

Moscow

Sacramento · New York · Lisbon · Beijing · Tokyo

New Orleans · Cairo

Austin · Tropic of Cancer

ATLANTIC

PACIFIC OCEAN · PACIFIC OCEAN

OCEAN · Nairobi · INDIAN

Equator · OCEAN · OCEAN

Lima · Rio de Janeiro

Tropic of Capricorn · Durban

Montevideo

150°W 120°W 90°W 60°W 30°W 0° 30°E 60°E 90°E 120°E 150°E

Antarctic Circle

South Pole (90°S)

LESSON 4
Using Symbols and Scale page 16

RAILROAD

ROAD

LESSON 5
Kinds of Maps page 22

Elevations
Feet   Meters
3,000 -- -- 915
2,000 -- -- 610
1,000 -- -- 305
0 -- -- 0
Sea level

Learning About the Earth

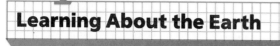

THINK ABOUT WHAT YOU KNOW

Imagine that you are a traveler from another planet. What might you want to learn about the earth?

STUDY THE VOCABULARY

sphere	map
model	continent
globe	ocean
atlas	pie graph

FOCUS YOUR READING

How can a globe and an atlas help us learn about the earth?

A. Looking at the Earth

"Wow! This is a neat photograph of the earth!" exclaimed Kim, a student in Miss Sumner's class. The class was looking at the photograph shown on this page. In the photograph the earth looks like a colorful ball surrounded by darkness. It was taken by an astronaut while on a flight in outer space.

Miss Sumner's students asked her to tell them more about the earth. Miss Sumner began by saying, "Earth, our home in the universe, is one of nine planets that revolve, or move, around the sun. From outer space, astronauts see the earth differently than we see it. They can see the shape of the earth.

"The earth is shaped like a **sphere** (sfihr). A sphere is round, like a ball. Even from outer space, a person can see only half of the earth at one time. The best way for you and me to see what the entire earth looks like is to look at a **model** of the earth.

"A model is a small copy of a real thing. A model of the earth is called a **globe**. Globes come in different sizes. Each globe is shaped like a sphere.

"Another important tool that you can use to learn about the earth," Miss Sumner continued, "is an **atlas**. An atlas is a collection of many **maps**. A map is a special kind of drawing that shows the earth or part of the earth on a flat surface."

Then Miss Sumner said, "Let's use our globe and atlases to learn about the earth. You already know that the earth is divided into land and water. Let's begin by learning more about the land areas of the earth."

This photograph of the earth was taken from space.
► What are the blue areas in the photograph?

B. The Earth's Land Areas

About one third of the earth is made up of land areas. These large land areas are divided into **continents**. There are seven continents — Asia, Africa, North America, South America, Europe, Australia, and Antarctica. Miss Sumner pointed to each continent on a globe.

"Miss Sumner," said Carlos with a puzzled expression, "it looks as though Europe and Asia are one continent."

"You are right, Carlos," Miss Sumner replied. "Europe and Asia look like one large area of land. We sometimes speak of the land area of Europe and Asia as Eurasia. That name combines letters from the words *Europe* and *Asia*."

C. The Earth's Water Areas

About two thirds of the earth is covered by water. Much of that water is in **oceans**. Oceans are the largest areas of water on the earth.

There are four oceans. They are the Pacific, the Atlantic, the Indian, and the Arctic oceans. The Pacific Ocean is the largest ocean, and the Arctic Ocean is the smallest ocean. Find the Indian Ocean and the Arctic Ocean on the map at the bottom of this page.

There are many branches of the oceans. Some of these branches are called seas and bays. Other areas of water are lakes and rivers. You will learn more about the earth's areas of water in Chapter 1.

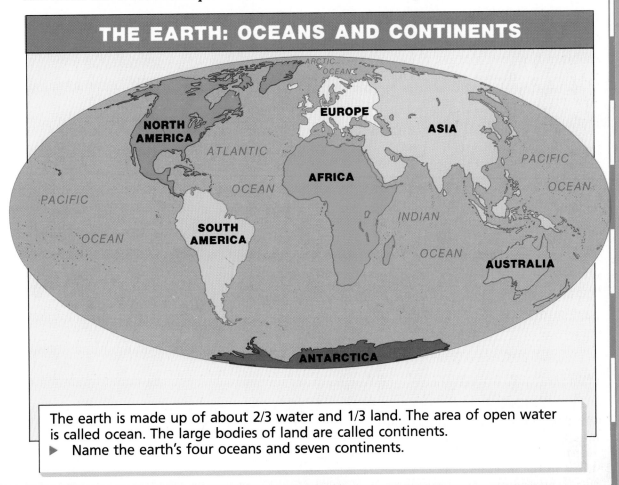

THE EARTH: OCEANS AND CONTINENTS

The earth is made up of about 2/3 water and 1/3 land. The area of open water is called ocean. The large bodies of land are called continents.
▶ Name the earth's four oceans and seven continents.

NORTH AMERICA: POLITICAL

⊛ National capitals
• Cities
▨ State boundaries

0   250   500 miles
0   250   500 kilometers

GREENLAND

ARCTIC OCEAN

Bering Sea

Fairbanks
Anchorage
Juneau

Arctic Circle

C A N A D A

Edmonton
Vancouver
Calgary
Seattle
Portland
Spokane
Columbia River

Lake Winnipeg

Winnipeg

Quebec
Ottawa ⊛   Montreal
Halifax

San Francisco
Great Salt Lake
Denver
Colorado River
Arkansas

Minneapolis   St. Paul

Great Lakes

Detroit   Buffalo   Boston
Chicago   Cleveland   New York
Pittsburgh   Philadelphia
St. Louis   Baltimore
Ohio River   ⊛ Washington, D.C.

Los Angeles
San Diego
Phoenix

Kansas City

U N I T E D   S T A T E S   O F   A M E R I C A

River

Memphis

El Paso   Dallas
Atlanta

ATLANTIC OCEAN

San Antonio
Houston
New Orleans

Mississippi

M E X I C O

Gulf of Mexico

Miami

PACIFIC OCEAN

Mexico City ⊛

Tropic of Cancer

Caribbean Sea

The United States is one country found on the continent of North America.

▶ Name the neighbor of the United States to
6 the south.

S O U T H
A M E R I C A

D. Continents and Countries

Large land areas called continents are usually divided into smaller areas called countries. The United States of America is one country on the continent of North America. If you look on the map on page 6, you can see that the United States has a neighbor to the north. Can you name that neighbor?

People often divide countries into even smaller areas. The United States, for example, is a country that is divided into 50 separate states. Can you think of a reason for dividing a large country into states?

Reading a Pie Graph A graph (graf), like a map, is a special kind of drawing. Graphs use pictures, circles, bars, and lines to compare things.

The graph on this page is called a **pie graph**. A pie graph is used to show the parts of a whole. If you have ever cut a piece of apple pie or another kind of pie, you know how a pie graph works.

In the graph on this page, the entire circle stands for the total land area of the earth. The circle is divided into seven pieces. Each piece stands for a continent. The largest piece is for Asia. Asia is the earth's largest continent. Look at the piece where the name *Australia* appears. What can you learn about Australia from the pie graph?

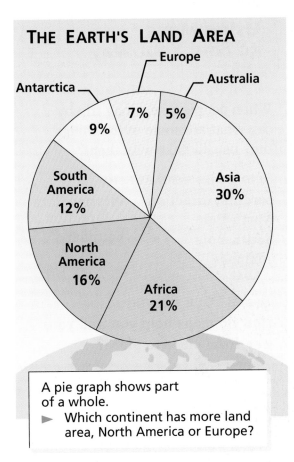

THE EARTH'S LAND AREA

- Europe 7%
- Australia 5%
- Antarctica 9%
- South America 12%
- Asia 30%
- North America 16%
- Africa 21%

A pie graph shows part of a whole.
► Which continent has more land area, North America or Europe?

LESSON *1* REVIEW

THINK AND WRITE
A. How is a map different from a globe?
B. Why are Europe and Asia sometimes called Eurasia?
C. About how much of the earth is covered with water?
D. What is the difference between a continent and a country?

SKILLS CHECK

THINKING SKILL
The Gazetteer, on pages 400–409, has information about places named in this lesson. Use the Gazetteer to find one fact about Asia, one about the Pacific Ocean, and one about Canada.

Using Maps to Find Your Way

THINK ABOUT WHAT YOU KNOW

When people take a long trip by car, what are some of the things they usually take with them?

STUDY THE VOCABULARY

cardinal direction
North Pole
South Pole
compass rose
intermediate direction
boundary

FOCUS YOUR READING

How do maps help you find your way from place to place?

A. Learning About Directions

Joy and Billy had just found out that their family was going to take a trip across the United States during the summer vacation. They had always wanted to visit the Grand Canyon and Yellowstone National Park, but they never really knew where these places were or how to get to them.

The children decided to look at a large map of the United States. Joy pointed to Jacksonville, the city in the state of Florida where she and Billy live. Florida is on the eastern coast of the United States. Billy said, "Look here! On this map you can really see where Jacksonville is and how close it is to the Atlantic Ocean."

To plan a trip, Joy and Billy decided that they needed to learn something about directions. There are different ways to explain where something is located. You can say that something is up or down. You can say that something is to the right or to the left or in front of you or behind you. Something might even be located *inside* something else.

There are four important direction words that you can use to locate places on a map. These four main direction words are *north, south, east,* and *west.* These four directions are called the **cardinal directions**.

North is the direction toward the **North Pole**. The North Pole is the northernmost place on the surface of the earth. The southernmost place on

In 1909 Robert E. Peary led the first expedition to reach the North Pole.
▶ What kinds of transportation did the expedition use?

UNITED STATES: NATIONAL PARKS

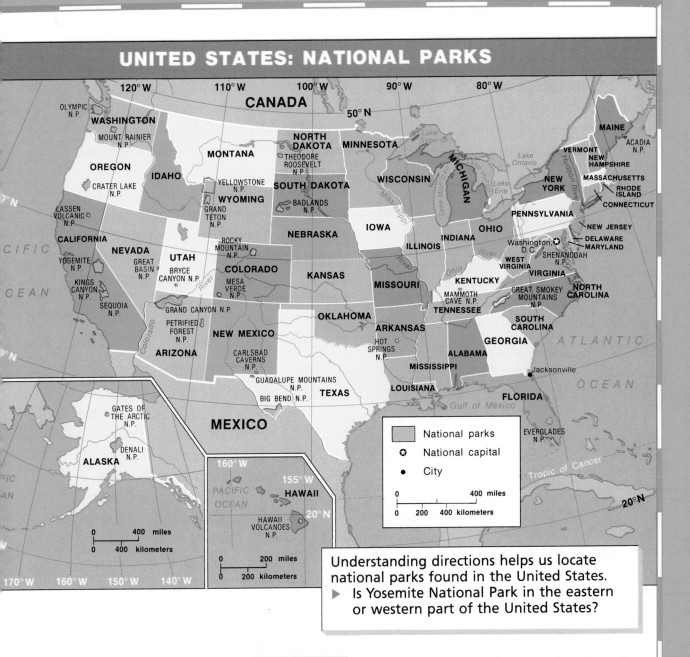

Understanding directions helps us locate national parks found in the United States.
▶ Is Yosemite National Park in the eastern or western part of the United States?

the earth's surface is the **South Pole**. South is the direction toward the South Pole. North and south are opposite each other on a globe.

The other two main directions, east and west, are also opposite each other. If you stand with your right arm extended to the east and your left arm extended to the west, you are facing north. South is directly behind you.

Many maps have a drawing that shows where north, south, east, and west are on the map. The drawing on a map is called a **compass rose**. Some people call it a direction finder. A compass is an instrument that is used to tell direction. On the compass rose, the letters *N*, *S*, *E*, and *W* stand for the cardinal directions which you know are *north*, *south*, *east*, and *west*.

B. Learning About Four Other Important Directions

Sometimes places are located between two of the four main directions. To help us locate those places we can use **intermediate directions**. The intermediate directions are northeast, northwest, southeast, and southwest. The letters *NE* stand for *northeast* on a map. Northeast is between north and east. The letters *NW* stand for *northwest*. Northwest is between north and west. What does *SW* stands for?

Joy drew a line on the map to represent the route they would take on their trip. They figured out that they would have to travel west and north to get to the Grand Canyon from their home in Florida.

C. Boundary Lines

As Joy and Billy were planning the route of their trip, they noticed that the route crossed many lines shown on the road map they were using. These lines are called **boundary** lines. A boundary is a line that separates one state or country from another state or country.

The states of the United States, except for Alaska and Hawaii, border, or touch, one another at boundaries. Can you name the states that border your state? What countries share a boundary with the United States?

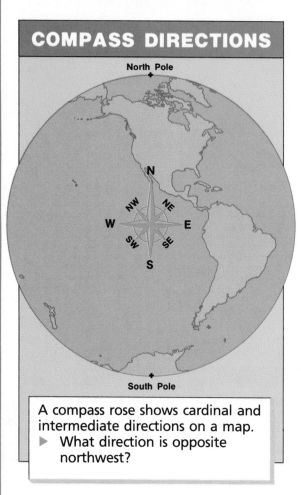

COMPASS DIRECTIONS

North Pole

South Pole

A compass rose shows cardinal and intermediate directions on a map.
▶ What direction is opposite northwest?

LESSON 2 REVIEW

THINK AND WRITE

A. What might a map tell you about the city of Jacksonville?

B. What are the four intermediate directions?

C. What does a boundary line on a map show?

SKILLS CHECK

MAP SKILL

Find the state of Kansas on the map of the United States, on page 9. For each of the following states, use a direction word to give the state's location in relation to Kansas: Florida, Oregon, Ohio, and New Mexico.

Using Latitude and Longitude

THINK ABOUT WHAT YOU KNOW

If you wanted to describe to a friend where your school is, how would you do it?

STUDY THE VOCABULARY

Equator   Prime
latitude   Meridian
hemisphere   grid
longitude

FOCUS YOUR READING

How do latitude and longitude help us to locate places on the earth?

A. Lines of Latitude

To help us locate places on maps, mapmakers draw special lines. One line, called the **Equator**, is located halfway between the North Pole and the South Pole. The Equator runs completely around the earth. All the lines that run around a globe or across a map are called lines of **latitude**.

Lines of latitude measure distances north and south of the Equator. The Equator is the most important line of latitude. It is numbered 0° (read "zero degrees") latitude. The Equator is the starting point for numbering north and south latitude lines.

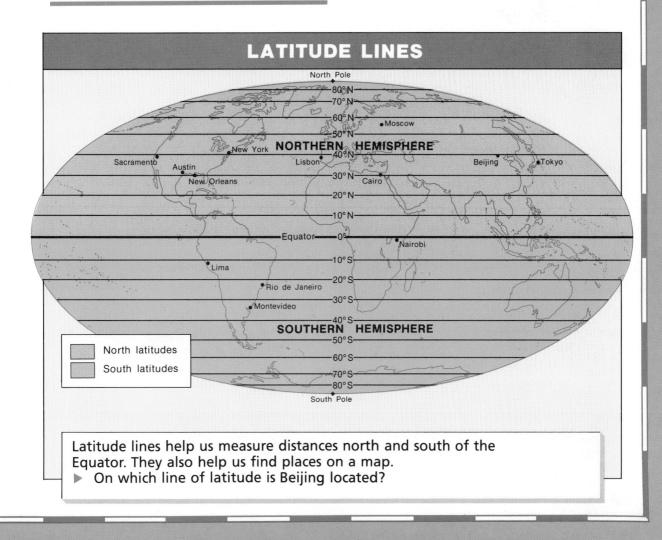

LATITUDE LINES

Latitude lines help us measure distances north and south of the Equator. They also help us find places on a map.
▶ On which line of latitude is Beijing located?

The Equator divides the earth into **hemispheres**, or two equal halves. Remember that the earth is a sphere. Half of a sphere is a hemisphere. Any place north of the Equator is in the Northern Hemisphere. Any place south of the Equator is in the Southern Hemisphere. The lines between the Equator and the North Pole are called lines of north latitude. Lines between the Equator and South Pole are lines of south latitude.

B. Lines of Longitude

Mapmakers also draw lines from north to south on maps. These lines are called lines of **longitude**. They cross the Equator. The most important line of longitude is the **Prime Meridian**. It is numbered 0° (read "zero degrees") longitude.

Look at the map on this page. On the map you can see that the Prime Meridian passes through Greenwich, England. Lines of longitude measure distances east and west of the Prime Meridian. Again, these distances are measured in degrees. Any place located east of the Prime Meridian is in the Eastern Hemisphere. Any place west of the Prime Meridian is in the Western Hemisphere.

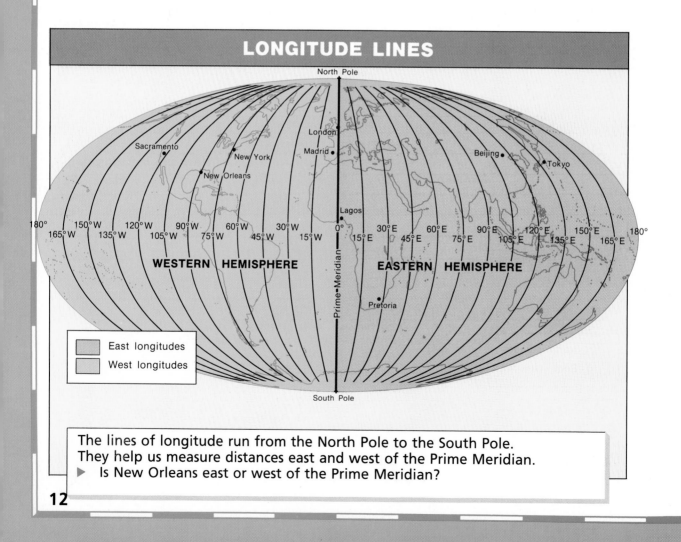

LONGITUDE LINES

The lines of longitude run from the North Pole to the South Pole. They help us measure distances east and west of the Prime Meridian.
▶ Is New Orleans east or west of the Prime Meridian?

C. Lines of Latitude and Lines of Longitude

Lines of latitude and longitude make it possible to find places on a map easily and quickly. Look at the map on this page and find the city of New Orleans. Notice that New Orleans is found at 30° north latitude (read "thirty degrees north latitude").

Look again at the map below. Notice that the city of New Orleans is also found at 90° west longitude (read "ninety degrees west longitude"). To tell someone where New Orleans is, you say it is found at 30° north latitude and 90° west longitude.

Now look at the map below. Find the city of Cairo. It is found at 30° north latitude and 30° east longitude. Find the city of Durban. It is found at 30° south latitude and 30° east longitude. How can you tell that Cairo is at 30° north latitude and Durban is at 30° south latitude?

Sometimes the places you want to find on a map are not exactly at the point where two lines cross. When this is the case, you have to estimate, or figure out about, where those places are located.

On the next page there is a map of Georgia. Find Savannah on the map. It

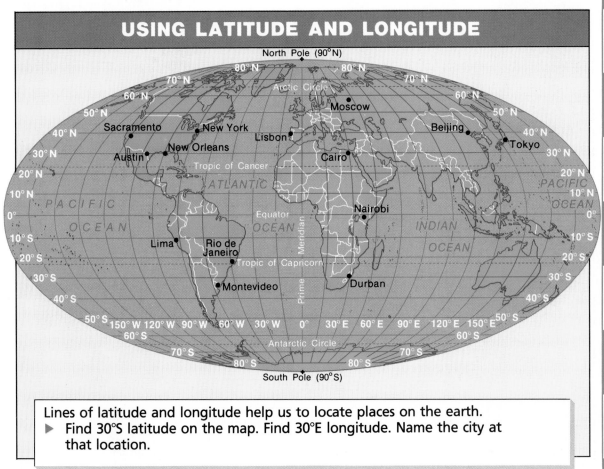

USING LATITUDE AND LONGITUDE

Lines of latitude and longitude help us to locate places on the earth.
▶ Find 30°S latitude on the map. Find 30°E longitude. Name the city at that location.

GEORGIA: USING A GRID

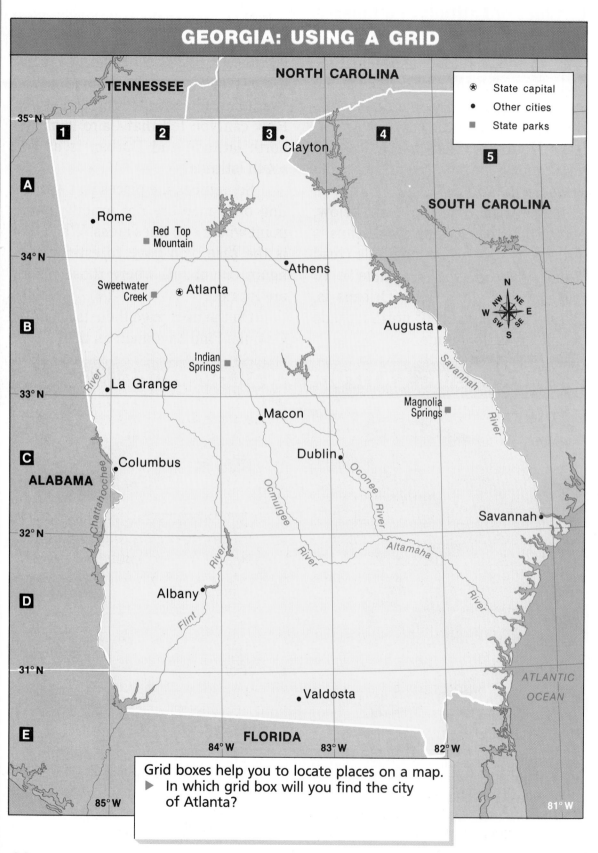

TENNESSEE

NORTH CAROLINA

⊛	State capital
•	Other cities
■	State parks

35° N

1 **2** **3** •Clayton **4**

5

A

SOUTH CAROLINA

•Rome

Red Top
■ Mountain

34° N

•Athens

Sweetwater
Creek ■ ⊛ •Atlanta

B

Augusta•

N
NW NE
W E
SW SE
S

Indian
Springs ■

33° N •La Grange

Magnolia
Springs ■

•Macon

C

Columbus•

Dublin•

ALABAMA

Savannah•

32° N

D

Albany•

31° N

•Valdosta

ATLANTIC
OCEAN

E

FLORIDA

84° W   83° W   82° W

85° W

81° W

Chattahoochee River · Ocmulgee River · Oconee River · Altamaha River · Savannah River · Flint River

Grid boxes help you to locate places on a map.
▶ In which grid box will you find the city
of Atlanta?

14

is not exactly on any line of latitude or longitude. Therefore, you have to estimate its location. You will see that Savannah is very close to 32° north latitude. It is also very close to 81° west longitude. Therefore, you can say that Savannah is located at about 32° north latitude and 81° west longitude. See if you can estimate the latitude and longitude of three other cities in Georgia— La Grange, Dublin, and Athens.

D. Using a Grid

If you know the latitude and longitude of a place, you can find it on a map by using the **grid**. A grid is a system of crossing lines that form boxes on a map. Crossing latitude and longitude lines are a grid.

Look again at the map of Georgia. Near the top of the map, you will see the numbers *1, 2, 3, 4,* and *5.* Along the left-hand side of the map, you will see the letters *A, B, C, D,* and *E.* Put a finger on the letter *B.* Then, put a finger of your other hand on the number *3.* Move both fingers, one down and the other

Savannah is an important city in Georgia. Find it on the map.
► On which river is Savannah located?

across, until they meet. You have found box *B-3.* You will see that the city of Athens and Indian Springs State Park are both in box *B-3.*

LESSON **3** REVIEW

THINK AND WRITE

A. What does it mean to say that a place is at 40° north latitude?
B. What does it mean to say that a place is at 100° west longitude?
C. Why do you have to estimate the location of some places on a map?
D. How do you use the grid on a map to tell where a place is?

SKILLS CHECK

MAP SKILL
Look at the map on page 14. List the following places on a separate sheet of paper: Albany, Clayton, Columbus, Macon, Magnolia Springs, Red Top Mountain, Rome, Sweetwater Creek, and Valdosta. Next to each place tell what grid box it is located in.

Using Symbols and Scale

THINK ABOUT WHAT YOU KNOW

What might you see if you were to take a balloon ride over your community?

STUDY THE VOCABULARY

symbol **legend**
key **scale**

READ FOR THE MAIN IDEA

Why is learning about symbols and scale important in reading a map?

A. Symbols on a Map

A map can show where places or things on the earth are found. Maps use **symbols** to stand for real things and places. Before you can read a map, you have to find out what the symbols on the map mean.

The part of the map that tells what the symbols stand for is called the **key** or **legend**. A map key may contain several symbols. Look at the map on page 14. The box in the top right corner is the key. On page 17 you can see some of the symbols that are used on maps.

B. Scale on a Map

Maps cannot show places and things in their real sizes. To do that, a map would have to be the same size as the place being mapped. Therefore, maps are drawn to **scale**. This means that the places, things, and distances shown on maps are small compared with their real sizes and real distances on the earth's surface.

Perhaps you have put together scale models of airplanes, cars, or boats, or played with dollhouses. If so, then you already have a good idea about what scale is. All of these models are much smaller than the real things.

On every map, a certain number of inches stands for a certain number of feet or yards or miles on the earth's surface. When we show size or distance in this way, we say the map is drawn to a certain scale. The map scale lets us know the real distance from one place to another. A map scale is usually found in the key or legend.

These students are building a model to scale.
► What, do you think, are they building?

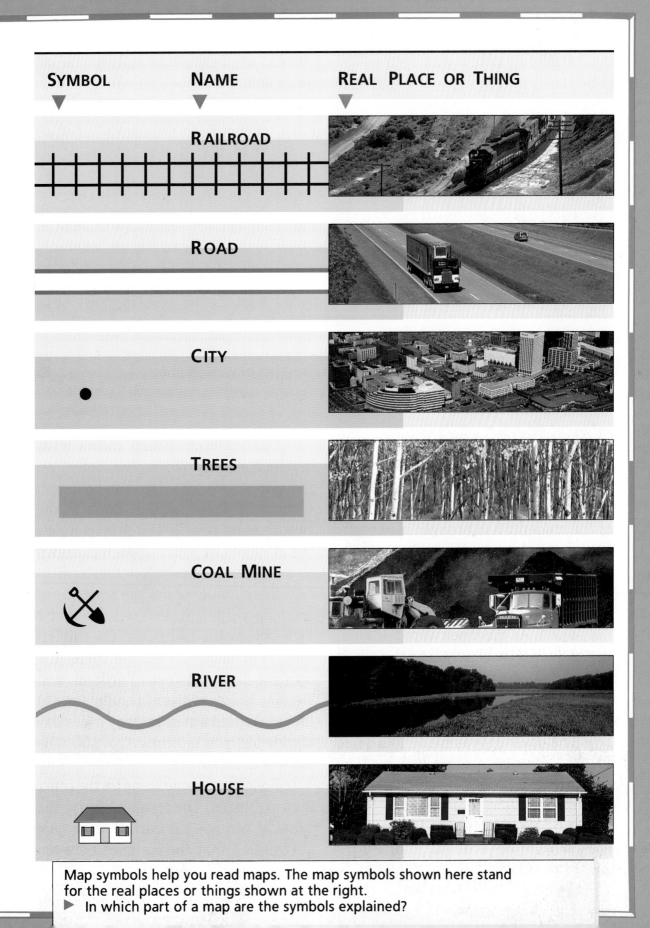

SYMBOL	NAME	REAL PLACE OR THING
	RAILROAD	
	ROAD	
	CITY	
	TREES	
	COAL MINE	
	RIVER	
	HOUSE	

Map symbols help you read maps. The map symbols shown here stand for the real places or things shown at the right.

► In which part of a map are the symbols explained?

On the football field above, 1 inch stands for 20 yards.

► How many yards are there between each pair of vertical lines on the football field?

C. Map Distance and Earth Distance

The students at Chestnut Street School were excited. The father of one of the students had brought his hot-air balloon to the school playground. He was about to give the students a ride in the balloon.

A group of students climbed into the basket. As the ropes were released, the balloon rose slowly into the air. It drifted over the football field. The students looked down and saw the field. It looked much like the drawing above.

The drawing was made to a scale in which 1 inch stands for 20 yards. The drawing is 6 inches long. This means that the total length of the real football field is 6 times 20 yards, or 120 yards, or six groups of 20 yards ($20 + 20 + 20 + 20 + 20 + 20 = 120$).

The scale on a map shows what distance an inch (or a centimeter) on the map stands for. Maps can be drawn to many different scales. Look at the two maps on page 19. Each map shows the state of Oregon, but each is drawn to a different scale.

Place a ruler under the scale line of the map at the left. You will see that 1 inch stands for 100 miles. On the left map, how many inches are there in a straight line between Portland and Bend? Your answer should be $1\frac{1}{4}$ inches. To find out how many miles this stands for, you multiply $1\frac{1}{4} \times 100$. The answer is 125 miles.

Follow the same steps on the other map of Oregon. The result is always the same. If you use the correct scale, you always find that the distance between Portland and Bend is 125 miles.

18

OREGON: TWO DIFFERENT SCALES

Portland
Salem
Eugene
Bend
0
100 miles
0
100 kilometers

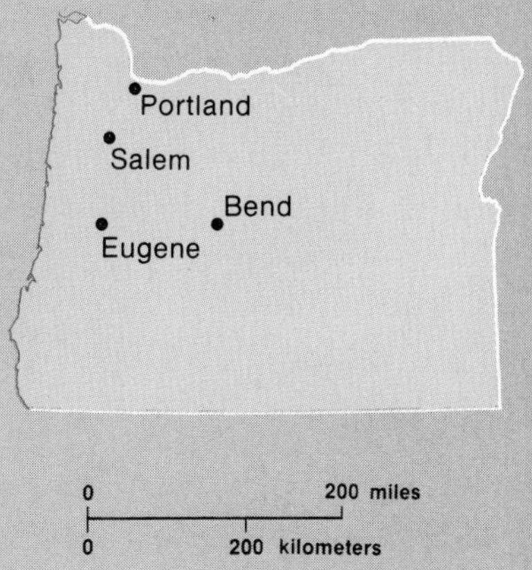

Portland
Salem
Bend
Eugene
0
200 miles
0
200 kilometers

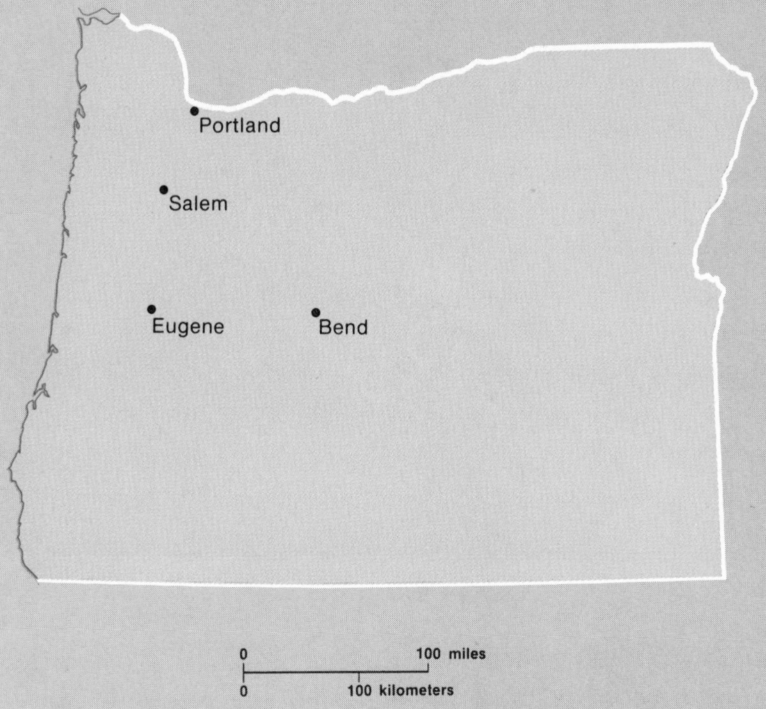

These two maps show the state of Oregon, but each map is drawn to a different scale.

▶ What does 1 inch stand for on the map on the left?

THE METRIC SYSTEM

Notice that there is a scale on each of the maps above. Find the words *miles* and *kilometers* on each scale. Kilometer is a unit of measure in the metric system.

The metric system is a way of measuring area, distance, weight, capacity, and temperature. This system is used in all major countries except the United States. In the future you will be using more of the metric system.

To help you get ready for this change, both customary and metric measurements are given in this book. Each measurement used is followed by the metric measurement that is about equal to it. Miles are changed to kilometers (km), feet or yards to meters (m), inches to centimeters (cm), acres to hectares (ha), pounds to kilograms (kg), and degrees Fahrenheit (°F) to degrees Celsius (°C).

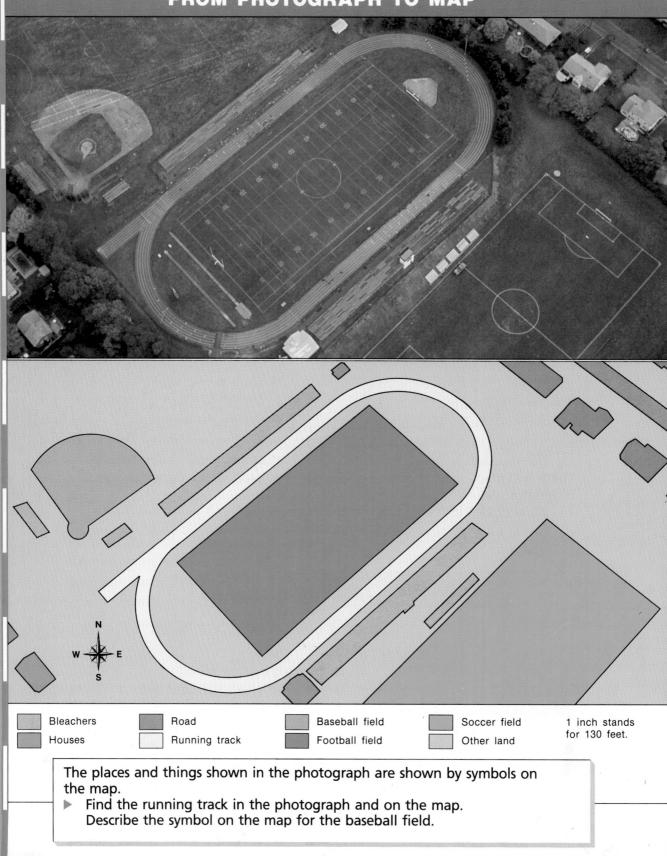

FROM PHOTOGRAPH TO MAP

Bleachers	Road	Baseball field	Soccer field	1 inch stands
Houses	Running track	Football field	Other land	for 130 feet.

The places and things shown in the photograph are shown by symbols on the map.

▶ Find the running track in the photograph and on the map.
Describe the symbol on the map for the baseball field.

D. A Bird's-eye View

As the groups of fourth graders at the Chestnut Street Elementary School drifted in the balloon, they saw how their community looked from straight overhead. The higher they rose, the more of the earth they could see. It was fun to look down and see some of the houses, streets, trees, and playing fields in their community.

One student exclaimed, "Now I know what our community looks like to a bird flying overhead."

Another student said, "You know what? A map is a bird's-eye view of a part of the earth. A map shows what a bird would see if it looked down on the earth from high in the sky."

The photograph on page 20 shows some of the things the students saw from the balloon. Notice the shapes in the photograph. Do you see a baseball diamond, a soccer field, and a running track around a football field? The map below the photograph shows the same place. Notice the shapes on the map. Do you see the same shapes that you see in the photograph?

A hot-air balloon floats over a neighborhood in Alburquerque, New Mexico.
▶ Have you ever seen a hot-air balloon?

LESSON **4** REVIEW

THINK AND WRITE

A. Why does a map need a key?
B. What does map scale tell?
C. If, on a map scale, 1 inch stands for 30 yards, what would 7 inches stand for?
D. How is a map like a bird's-eye view of a part of the earth?

SKILLS CHECK

MAP SKILL
Look at the table of map symbols on page 17. On a separate sheet of paper, list the names of any items that could be added to the table. Draw the symbol next to the name.

Kinds of Maps

LESSON 5

THINK ABOUT WHAT YOU KNOW

Name all the things that you now know about maps.

STUDY THE VOCABULARY

sea level	contour line
elevation	relief map

FOCUS YOUR READING

How do contour lines and physical maps show elevation?

A. Learning About Contour Maps

The surface of the earth is made up of different shapes. For example, land can be flat or hilly. Sometimes it rises to very high peaks. The surface of the sea is level, or flat. The surface of the sea is called **sea level**. Sea level is the base, or starting point, for measuring how high land areas are on the surface of the earth.

To understand this, think about how you measure your own height. You measure from the bottom of your feet, which is your base, to the top of your head. You measure the height of land surfaces in a similar way. You measure from the base level, which is the surface of the sea, to the highest point of land. The height of land is called its **elevation**. In other words, elevation is the distance above sea level.

To show the elevation of land on a map, we use **contour lines**. All points on the earth that have the same height are located along the same contour line. All points on the same contour line are the same level above sea level.

On page 23 you can see three drawings labeled A, B, and C. Find sea level (0 feet or 0 meters) in each of the drawings. Look again at drawing A. Find the contour line for 2,000 feet (610 m). All the points along that line are 2,000 feet (610 m) above sea level. Now look at the other contour lines on drawing A. What elevations do those lines stand for?

The map's key shows that green is used for sea level. Orange is used to show 1,000 feet (600 m) above sea level. Tan is used to show 2,000 feet (1,5000 m) above sea level, and lavender is used to show 5,000 feet (3,000 m) above sea level.

You can see different elevations in this photograph of Hawaii.
▶ Is the elevation of the cliff higher, or lower, than the land along the sea?

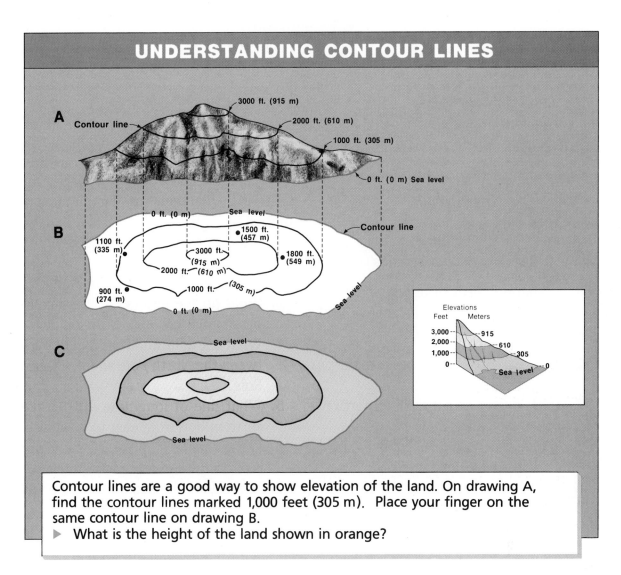

UNDERSTANDING CONTOUR LINES

Contour lines are a good way to show elevation of the land. On drawing A, find the contour lines marked 1,000 feet (305 m). Place your finger on the same contour line on drawing B.

▶ What is the height of the land shown in orange?

B. Understanding a Relief Map

Maps that use different colors to show the range between contour lines are often called **relief maps**. They are also called physical maps. This kind of map shows the elevation of the land.

Look at the physical map of North America in the Atlas. It is a relief map. What does each of the colors in the key stand for? What is the elevation of the land that is along the Atlantic Ocean?

LESSON **5** REVIEW

THINK AND WRITE

A. Why are contour lines used on some maps?

B. What is special about a relief map?

SKILLS CHECK

THINKING SKILL

Why is elevation needed on some maps?

MAP SKILLS HANDBOOK REVIEW

USING THE VOCABULARY

sphere   grid
globe   symbol
compass rose key
latitude   scale
longitude   contour lines

On a separate sheet of paper, write the word or words from the list above that best complete the sentence.

1. The earth, like a basketball, is shaped like a _____.
2. Lines drawn on a map from north to south are called lines of _____.
3. A blue line drawn on a map to show a river is an example of a _____.
4. A _____ is a model of the earth.
5. Lines on a map that show elevation are called _____.
6. Lines drawn across a map are called lines of _____.
7. Another name for a direction finder on a map is a _____.
8. Crossing lines on a map that form boxes are called a _____.
9. _____ is a way of showing size or distance on a map.
10. The part of a map that tells what the symbols stand for is the _____.

REMEMBERING WHAT YOU READ

On a separate sheet of paper, answer the following questions in complete sentences.

1. What is the difference between an ocean and a continent?
2. What are the cardinal directions?
3. What do the letters *SW* on a compass stand for?
4. What line of latitude lies halfway between the North Pole and the South Pole?
5. What line of longitude divides the earth in half from east to west?
6. What does a map use to stand for real things and real places?
7. What does the scale on a map tell you?
8. What do contour lines on a map show?
9. What is the base for all the earth's hills and mountains?
10. Why is color sometimes used between contour lines?

TYING ART TO SOCIAL STUDIES

On a separate sheet of paper, draw a map of the neighborhood around your school. Place the school in the center of your map. Then show roads, buildings, parks, and any other places of interest that surround the school. Be sure to include a map key that shows the different symbols you have used on your map.

THINKING CRITICALLY

On a separate sheet of paper, answer the following questions in complete sentences.

1. How might our lives be different if the earth were flat?
2. Why is it important to know where different places are in the world?
3. How do maps make people's lives easier?
4. What problems might people face if all maps had to be drawn to the same scale?
5. Why, do you think, is it necessary to show elevation on some maps?

SUMMARIZING THE HANDBOOK

Copy this graphic organizer on a separate sheet of paper. Under the main idea in each rectangle, write three phrases that support the idea. The first one for each main idea has been done for you.

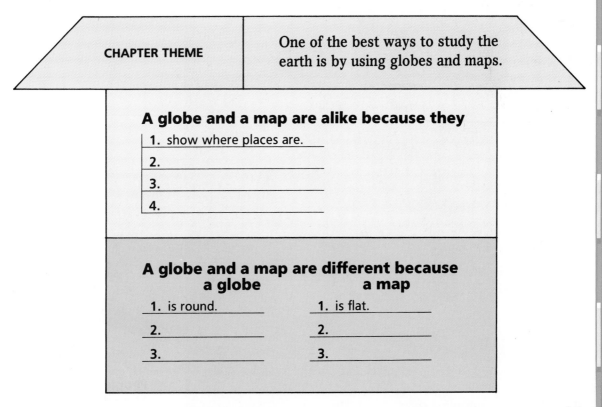

CHAPTER THEME

One of the best ways to study the earth is by using globes and maps.

A globe and a map are alike because they

1. show where places are.
2. _____
3. _____
4. _____

A globe and a map are different because

a globe
1. is round.
2. _____
3. _____

a map
1. is flat.
2. _____
3. _____

Location

▲ **Place**

◀ **People and
Their Environment**

26

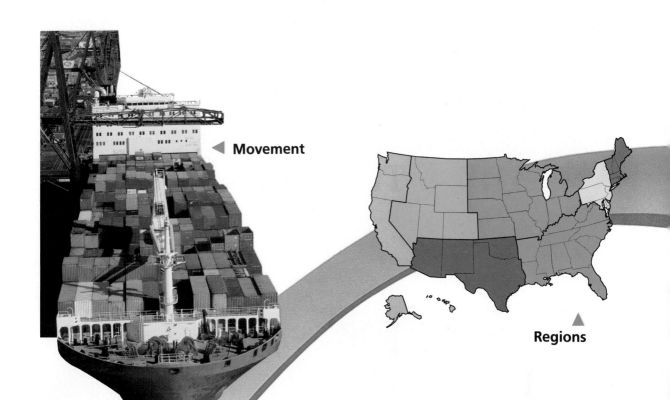

Movement

Regions

1 THE EARTH AND ITS PEOPLE

When we study geography, we use five themes to help us to understand the earth and its people. The themes are given on these pages.

CHAPTER 1

GEOGRAPHY: A WONDERFUL ADVENTURE

The earth is our home. Geography helps us to understand the earth and its people. By studying geography we can discover many interesting things about our home.

What Is Geography?

THINK ABOUT WHAT YOU KNOW

Think about where you live or a place that you have visited. Describe the place you are thinking about.

STUDY THE VOCABULARY

location   desert
geography
environment

FOCUS YOUR READING

How does knowing geography help us in everyday life?

A. Meeting a Geographer

"What is that big book?" asked the little prince. "What are you doing?"

"I am a geographer," said the old gentleman.

"What is a geographer?" asked the little prince.

"A geographer is a person who knows the location of all the seas, rivers, towns, mountains, and deserts."

What you have just read is a part of a book called *The Little Prince*. The book was written many years ago by a man named Antoine de Saint-Exupéry (ahn TWAHN duh san teg zoo pay-REE). In that book a little prince talked with an old gentleman who was a geographer. The old gentleman told the little prince how important geography is.

"Geographies," said the geographer, "are the books which, of all books, are most concerned with matters of consequence. They never become old-fashioned. It is very rarely that a mountain changes its position. It is very rarely that an ocean empties itself of its waters. We write of eternal things."

The geographer explained to the little prince what the nature of eternal things means. He explained that a mountain is eternal because it lasts forever, but a flower does not.

Finally the time came for the little prince to leave. He asked what place the geographer would advise him to visit. The geographer recommended the planet Earth.

These people seem to be standing within a globe.
► Which continent is shown completely on the dome?

To visit the planet Earth, the little prince needed to know the **location** of things. The location of something is where it is on the earth.

Knowing where things are is an important part of geography, but geography is much more than just locating things. It is a way of understanding our world. *Geography* comes from two words in the Greek language. The word *geo* means "earth," and the word *graphein* means "to write about" or "to study." **Geography** then is the study of the earth and how people use it.

Five Themes of Geography Geography has five themes, or main ideas. Locating places is the first of the five themes. Discovering what a place is like is the second theme. How people live in their surroundings is the third theme. The fourth theme is the movement of people and goods from place to place. Regions make up the fifth theme of geography. This chapter is about the first four themes. In Chapter 2 you will learn about regions.

B. Important Questions in Geography

What, Where, and How As you study geography, you will ask many *what*, *where*, and *how* questions. What are mountains? What are the names of our largest cities? Where are all these located? How do people use the earth?

Perhaps the question geographers most often ask is the question *where*. After asking where something is, a geographer tries to explain why that something is where it is.

Where are you right now? That is an easy question to answer. As you are reading this book, you may be seated at your desk in your classroom or you may be at home.

Now let's take a more difficult question. Where is your school? You might answer that your school is on Main Street or in the north part of town or in the city or in the countryside.

The children are playing soccer in the playground of their school.
► How can you tell that the school is in a city?

Some trees stand near the school in the photograph.
▶ How are the surroundings of this school like the surroundings of your school?

Asking Why Let's take the question a step further and ask, "Why is your school located where it is?" There are many possible answers to that question. One answer might be that it is located in a neighborhood where there are many homes. The leaders of your community decided that a school should be close to where children live.

A question that usually follows *where* and *why* is the *what* question. What is the location of your school like? To answer that, you would describe the **environment**, or surroundings, in which your school is located. You might talk about big shade trees over the playground or wide, busy streets in front of your school. You might describe the kinds of homes or stores that you see next to your school.

Location When the little prince arrived on the earth, he landed in the middle of the Sahara, a large **desert** on the continent of Africa. A desert is a place that gets very little rain. The little prince had never heard of the Sahara.

In the Map Handbook at the beginning of this book, you learned that you can locate places on the earth by using the grid system. Let's say the little prince landed at 25° north latitude and 5° east longitude. That's in the middle of the Sahara.

If the little prince had landed at 19° north latitude and 99° west longitude, he would have landed in Mexico City, the world's most populated city. The little prince would have been surrounded by millions of people.

C. Discovering What a Place Is Like

Tom Sawyer Abroad Mark Twain is one of America's best-known writers. In one of his books, called *Tom Sawyer Abroad*, he described an adventure shared by Tom Sawyer and Tom's two friends, Huckleberry Finn and Jim.

The three friends sailed in a balloon across the Atlantic Ocean to the Sahara in Africa. They began their trip in St. Louis, Missouri. Shortly after they set out, Tom Sawyer began to inquire about their location over the land.

Huckleberry Finn remembered something about a map of the United States. He used what he remembered to answer Tom's question. Here is part of the conversation between Huckleberry Finn and Tom Sawyer.

"I know by the color. We're right over Illinois yet. And you can see for yourself that Indiana ain't in sight."

"I wonder what's the matter with you, Huck. You know by the color?"

"Yes, of course I do."

"What's the color got to do with it?"

"It's got everything to do with it. Illinois is green, Indiana is pink. You show me any pink down here, if you can. No, sir; it's green."

"Indiana pink? Why, what a lie!"

"It ain't no lie; I've seen it on a map, and it's pink."

Mixing Things Up Huckleberry Finn had once seen a map on which the state of Indiana was colored pink. So he

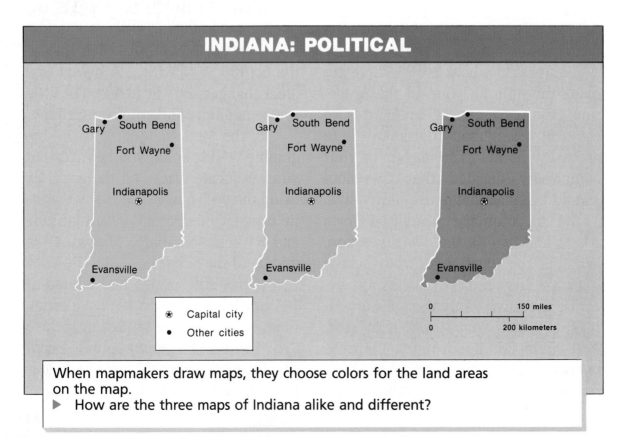

INDIANA: POLITICAL

Gary
South Bend
Fort Wayne
Indianapolis
Evansville

Gary
South Bend
Fort Wayne
Indianapolis
Evansville

Gary
South Bend
Fort Wayne
Indianapolis
Evansville

✹ Capital city
• Other cities

0   150 miles
0   200 kilometers

When mapmakers draw maps, they choose colors for the land areas on the map.
▶ How are the three maps of Indiana alike and different?

thought that everything in Indiana was pink. He did not realize that the person who made the map he saw used the color pink as a symbol to stand for Indiana. Many different colors are part of Indiana. There are green fields where corn grows. The blue waters of the lakes and rivers in Indiana are an important part of the state.

Knowing About Place Geographers like to find out how one place in the world is the same as or different from places around it. What a place is like is another theme of geography.

All of us live in a certain place. We may live in a farm community, a small village, a town, or a city. Most likely there are different styles of homes and kinds of stores where we live. There may be school buildings, a library, a museum, churches, temples, and synagogues (SIHN ih gahgz).

In many ways all communities are alike. Yet every place in the world has something special about it that makes it different from all other places. Just as you have qualities, or traits, that make you a special person, so every place has qualities that make it special.

Indiana has cities, such as Indianapolis, as well as farms.
 What do you think the building with the flag is in the top picture?

LESSON 1 REVIEW

THINK AND WRITE

A. What is geography?
B. What questions do geographers most often ask?
C. Why is every place in the world special?

SKILLS CHECK

THINKING SKILL
You will find a Gazetteer on pages 400–409. Look through the Gazetteer. What kinds of information can you find in the Gazetteer?

The World We Live In

THINK ABOUT WHAT YOU KNOW

Think about where you live. How do the land and weather influence what you and your friends do?

STUDY THE VOCABULARY

landform	axis
weather	growing season
climate	natural vegetation
temperature	diagram
precipitation	

FOCUS YOUR READING

What do we need to know to describe our world?

A. The Natural World

Unexplored Places Try to imagine a place in the world where no human being has ever walked. That may not be an easy thing to do. Why? Because there are not many places left in the world that people have not explored and changed. Still, think about the possibility of a place that nobody has ever been to. What might it be like?

Perhaps you are thinking about a place in the Far North or Far South, such as Greenland or Antarctica. Yes, it's very probable that there are large sections of those ice-covered lands where people have never walked.

Perhaps you are thinking of some of the higher, more rugged mountain ranges in the world. There are many peaks and slopes that no one has ever climbed. You may be thinking that no one has ever explored the depths of the world's oceans. Faraway forests and swampy areas are other parts of the world that you might name.

Landforms The lands of our world are of many different elevations and shapes. We use the word **landform** when we speak of the particular shape or form of the land. On pages 40–43 are pictures and descriptions of different landforms and water forms.

Antarctica is a continent that few people visit.
▶ Why, do you think, do few people visit Antarctica?

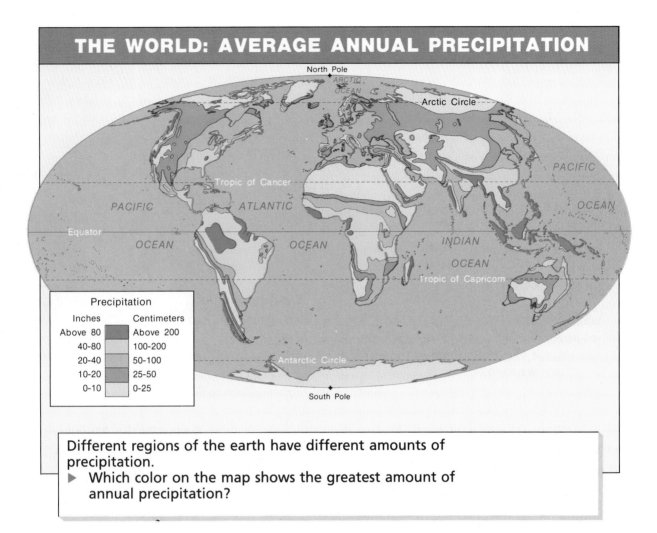

THE WORLD: AVERAGE ANNUAL PRECIPITATION

North Pole
ARCTIC
OCEAN
Arctic Circle

PACIFIC

Tropic of Cancer

PACIFIC   ATLANTIC   OCEAN

Equator

OCEAN   OCEAN   INDIAN

OCEAN

Tropic of Capricorn

Antarctic Circle

South Pole

Precipitation

Inches	Centimeters
Above 80	Above 200
40-80	100-200
20-40	50-100
10-20	25-50
0-10	0-25

Different regions of the earth have different amounts of precipitation.
▶ Which color on the map shows the greatest amount of annual precipitation?

B. Weather, Climate, and Vegetation

Weather Have you ever had a day off from school because of a snowstorm? Or have you ever canceled a trip to the beach because of rain? Snow and rain as well as wind, heat, and cold are all a part of **weather**. Weather is the way the air is at a certain time in a certain place. Weather may change from day to day or even from hour to hour.

Climate We all like to know what the weather is going to be. More important is to know the kind of weather a place

has over a period of years. When certain kinds of weather repeat again and again in an area, it becomes a pattern. We call this pattern **climate**. To understand the entire picture of climate, we must learn about **temperature** and **precipitation**. Temperature tells us how hot or cold the air is. Water that falls to the earth in the form of rain, snow, sleet, or hail is called precipitation. You have probably heard the word precipitation in a weather report.

Not all places on the earth receive the same amount of precipitation. There is a place in Hawaii that receives

35

In many places, leaf-bearing trees change with the seasons.
▶ How is the tree shown in the photograph different in winter than in spring?

about 470 inches (1,194 cm) of rainfall every year. The Atacama Desert in South America receives almost no precipitation at all. Sometimes as many as 15 years go by without a single drop of rainfall there.

The Four Seasons Temperatures and precipitation change during the seasons of the year. A season is a part of the year that has a certain kind of weather. Spring, summer, autumn, and winter are the seasons.

When it is winter in the Northern Hemisphere, it is summer in the Southern Hemisphere. This is because the earth is always tilted on its **axis**. The earth's axis is an imaginary line running through the earth between the North Pole and the South Pole. When the top half of the earth is tilted toward

the sun, it is summer in the Northern Hemisphere. In the Southern Hemisphere, which is then tilted away from the sun, it is winter.

Reading a Diagram A **diagram** is a special kind of drawing. A diagram is not meant to show exactly what something looks like. It is meant to explain how something works or why something happens.

Look at the diagram on page 37. At the right side of the diagram you will see the position of the earth on December 21 or December 22. Follow the arrows from the sun to the earth. The area of the earth where the sun's rays are striking directly is mostly below the Equator, isn't it? Because of the earth's tilt, the Southern Hemisphere is getting more direct sunlight. Therefore the

Southern Hemisphere is receiving more heat at this time of year than the Northern Hemisphere is. Because the Southern Hemisphere is receiving more heat, it is summer there. It is winter in the Northern Hemisphere, which is receiving less heat.

As the earth moves on its path around the sun, it reaches — on June 21 or June 22 — the point shown at the left side of the diagram. Now it is the Southern Hemisphere that is tilted *away* from the direct rays of the sun. The Northern Hemisphere is now tilted *toward* the sun. In which hemisphere is it summer on June 21 or June 22?

Climate and Farming Places in the world with mild temperatures throughout the year allow farmers to have a long **growing season**. A growing season is the length of time that an area is warm enough for crops to grow.

In some hot climates, the growing season lasts all year. Places that have cold winters have a much shorter growing season. Farmers cannot grow crops outside during the winter months.

Natural Vegetation Climate and soil both affect **natural vegetation**. *Natural vegetation* is all the plants that grow in an area without any help from

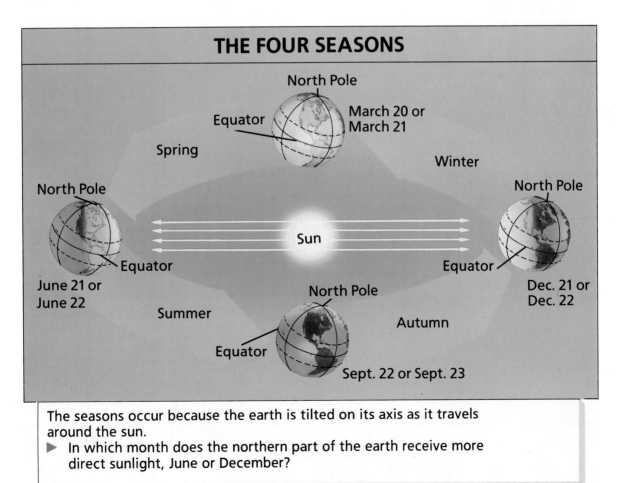

THE FOUR SEASONS

North Pole
Equator
March 20 or March 21
Spring
Winter
North Pole
North Pole
Sun
Equator
Equator
June 21 or June 22
Dec. 21 or Dec. 22
North Pole
Summer
Autumn
Equator
Sept. 22 or Sept. 23

The seasons occur because the earth is tilted on its axis as it travels around the sun.
► In which month does the northern part of the earth receive more direct sunlight, June or December?

people. The most important things that affect natural vegetation are the soil, the amount of rainfall, and the temperature. Every part of the world was once covered by some kind of natural vegetation except for frozen, ice-covered areas, very dry areas, and areas of bare rock where there was no soil.

C. Geography and People

People We know that the world is more than mountains, plains, lakes, and oceans. People are a part of our world, too. In fact, people make up a very special part of our world.

Wildlife are a resource that we should try to protect.
▶ How many of these animals have you seen when you visited a zoo?

Thousands of years ago most people lived in small groups and hunted or fished or gathered nuts and berries to eat. They depended on the world around them to survive. Today, people depend less upon the world around them for daily life. Geography helps us to understand how and why people live and work the way they do in different parts of the world.

Wildlife There is another part of the world. Think of the forests, lakes, and rivers. There is life there, too. It is called wildlife. There are birds and animals in the forests. Lions and zebras roam the vast plains of Africa. All kinds of fish and mammals live in the oceans and rivers of the world.

Many tall buildings now stand in the city of New Orleans.
▶ How might the river have once made the land swampy?

D. Relationship Between People and the Environment

The Way People Live Land and water, soils, weather and climate, wildlife — all of these make up our natural world. The natural world influences what human beings do. The way people live in their environment is another theme of geography.

Most people change their natural surroundings. New Orleans, Louisiana, is a large city. When people first settled there, the land was low swampy marshes. Little by little the marshes were filled in with soil and rock.

Buildings could be constructed there. People changed the land and made a very different-looking environment.

The really important thing to remember is that people and the earth depend on each other. It is like a two-way street. The environment does not completely determine what people in a certain place can do, and people are not able to completely change their environment. Our world sets some limits on what people are able to change. Yet people can change their environment in some ways.

LESSON 2 REVIEW

THINK AND WRITE

A. What kinds of places in our world have people not settled?

B. What two things does climate depend on?

C. What do we mean when we say the world is more than bodies of land and water?

D. How is the relationship between people and their environment like a two-way street?

SKILLS CHECK

MAP SKILL

Find the Equator on the map on page 35. Name the amounts of precipitation that the lands on the Equator receive.

GEOGRAPHICAL DICTIONARY

1. Canyon

A **canyon** is a deep valley with very steep sides. The best-known canyon in the United States is the Grand Canyon in Arizona.

2. Coast

A **coast** is land next to a large body of water. The coast of California stretches along the Pacific Ocean.

3. Delta

A **delta** is land formed by mud and sand that settle from water flowing out of the place where a river ends. Find the Mississippi River delta on the map.

2
Coast

1
Grand Canyon

PACIFIC OCEAN

5
Hawaiian Islands

6
Great Lakes

L. Superior
L. Michigan
L. Huron
L. Ontario
L. Erie

River

Mississippi

3
Delta

4
Gulf of Mexico

ATLANTIC OCEAN

4. Gulf ——————

A **gulf** is a part of an ocean or a sea that pushes inland. The Gulf of Mexico is shown on the map. It is off the southern shore of the United States.

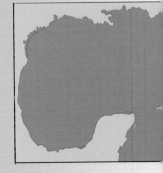

5. Island ——————

An **island** is a body of land that has water all around it. The state of Hawaii is made up of a group of islands in the Pacific Ocean.

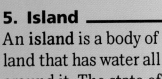

6. Lake ——————

A **lake** is a body of water with land all around it. The map shows five big lakes at the northern border of the United States. They are the Great Lakes.

7. Mountain

A **mountain** is a piece of land that rises sharply from the land that is around it. Mount McKinley, in Alaska, is the highest mountain in the United States.

8. Peninsula

A **peninsula** is a strip of land with water nearly all the way around it. It is connected to a main body of land. The state of Florida is a peninsula.

9. Plain

A **plain** is an almost level, often treeless piece of land that stretches for miles and miles. The state of Kansas lies on a plain.

9
Plain

10
Colorado Plateau

PACIFIC
OCEAN

7
Mount McKinley

10. Plateau

A **plateau** is a raised level piece of land. It covers a large area. Find the Colorado Plateau on the map. It covers parts of Arizona, Colorado, Utah, and New Mexico.

11. Sea

A **sea** is a large body of water, but it is not as large as an ocean. The Caribbean Sea lies between South America, Central America, and the West Indies islands.

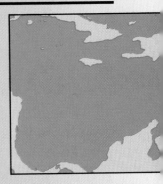

12. Valley

A **valley** is a long low place between hills or mountains. There is often a stream or river in a valley. Find the Shenandoah Valley, in northern Virginia, on the map.

L. Superior

L. Michigan

L. Huron

L. Ontario

L. Erie

River

Mississippi

12
Shenandoah
Valley

*ATLANTIC
OCEAN*

8
Peninsula

11
Caribbean Sea

Earning a Living in Our World

THINK ABOUT WHAT YOU KNOW

Name three kinds of work that people do in your community that they might not be able to do in a different environment.

STUDY THE VOCABULARY

natural resource	industry
manufacture	service
raw material	veterinarian
timber	

FOCUS YOUR READING

What are some ways that people in our world make a living?

A. Earning a Living by Farming

Freedom from Want You know that all human beings need food to survive. People obtain food by farming, fishing, and hunting. Of these three ways of getting food, the most important by far is farming.

Look at the painting on this page. It is called *Freedom from Want*. Norman Rockwell, a famous American artist, painted this scene in 1943.

In Rockwell's painting a family is just about to eat what looks like a Thanksgiving dinner. A woman is placing a large turkey in the center of the table. Can you name the other foods shown in the painting? Pretend that you are a geographer and think about where the various foods on the table come from.

Food from Around Our Country

Let's start with the main attraction of the feast—the turkey. Turkeys are raised by the thousands on farms known as turkey farms. The states that lead in the production of turkeys are North Carolina and Minnesota. Find these states on the map of the United States on page 9.

The apples in the fruit bowl grow best in fairly cool areas. They might have come from the state of Virginia, Washington, or Michigan. The pears more than likely were grown in Washington State or California. The grapes could have come from vineyards in California or New York.

Many people in the United States celebrate Thanksgiving Day with their families.
▶ Which food most reminds you of Thanksgiving?

44

Before cranberries are harvested, the cranberry bog is flooded. A water reel churns up the cranberries, which then float to the surface.

▶ How, do you think, might the worker who is walking in front of the water reel use the pole that he is carrying?

Other foods on the table include sweet potatoes and cranberries. North Carolina is the state that leads in the growing of sweet potatoes. Cranberries grow in cool, wet, swampy regions. New Jersey and Massachusetts are two states that grow cranberries. As you can see, each part of our Thanksgiving dinner comes from a different part of the United States.

Kinds of Farms There are many different kinds of farms and farmers in our country and in the world. Some raise just enough food for their families to survive from year to year. Others operate giant farms and raise enough food to sell to people who do not farm.

B. Using Natural Resources from the Earth

Natural Resources Look around your classroom at the things you use every day. For example, consider your desk. It is probably made of wood and steel. The wood may have came from trees that grow in our forests, and the steel was made from iron that was probably dug from a mountain area somewhere in the world.

Your desk is one of many things that are made from **natural resources**. A natural resource is something that is provided by nature and is useful to people. Land, air, soil, water, forests, and plants are natural resources.

Gathering Resources All over the world there are people who earn their living by gathering the different resources that everyone needs. These people are fishers and loggers, miners, and drillers of oil. You will read about the work of these people in this book.

C. Making Things for a Living

Manufacturing Think for a minute of all the things you use today—the supplies you use in school, the equipment you use at play, the car or bus that takes you to and from school.

Most of the things that we use are **manufactured** in the United States or other parts of the world. *Manufacture* means to make something by hand or by machine.

Raw Materials All around the world, people use **raw materials** to manufacture goods. A raw material is a resource that is gathered and used to make a different kind of product. For example,

Loggers use a huge crane to lift logs onto a flatbed, which is a truck with a body in the form of a platform.
► Why, do you think, do loggers use a flatbed to remove logs from a forest?

The woman is making sure that the leg of the chair is securely in place.
▶ What other things in the workshop are made of wood?

Movement People use the natural resources of the world in different ways to make a living. All kinds of raw materials like timber and finished goods like furniture are moved daily to places where they are needed.

People, too, move from place to place. They travel from home to school or work. Many people travel far distances, either for business or for enjoyment. The movement of people and goods is another important theme of geography. You will learn more about this theme as you read this book.

Automobiles are often moved by railroad cars from where they are made to where they are sold.
▶ How can you tell that this is a large railroad center?

timber is a raw material. Standing trees that are to be cut and used for wood are often called timber.

Most of the things we use are made by people who work in various **industries**. An industry is a kind of business that produces goods for a profit, or gain. For example, the furniture industry turns timber from our forests into the chairs, tables, and desks that you have in school.

D. Providing Services for People

Depending on Others Many people do a special kind of work that helps to make life better for other people. The kind of work that helps people is called a **service**. We all depend on services. Most services are provided by people living in towns and cities. Some service workers are teachers, and some are doctors and nurses. Others work as police officers or firefighers. The following story can give you an idea of how many people in one community perform services.

"Are you ready, Mark?" called Father. "It's time to take Izzy to Dr. Bailey's office for his checkup. We don't want to be late."

It was a short drive from Mark's home to Dr. Bailey's office. Dr. James Bailey is a **veterinarian**. A veterinarian is a doctor who takes care of the health of animals.

Many workers have jobs that provide a service for other people.
▶ What service does each of the workers in these photographs provide?

After Dr. Bailey had thoroughly examined the dog, he turned to Mark and said, "Izzy is healthy and strong for his age. You are doing a very good job of caring for your dog. Keep up the good work."

As Mark and his father left Dr. Bailey's office, Mark said, "I'm hungry. Could we stop at The Breakfast House for muffins and juice?"

"Good idea," his father replied, "but let's take Izzy home first. We can't just leave him in the car."

When they arrived at The Breakfast House, a young man directed Mark and his father to a table and gave them a menu. Soon a waitress came along and took their order. When Mark and his father were ready to leave, they went to the cashier and Mark's father

48

paid for their breakfast. As he and his father walked back to the car, Mark noticed that a police officer was directing traffic at an intersection on Main Street. A postal worker stopped his truck by the corner mailbox and got out to collect the mail.

"I just remembered," Mark's father said. "I need some money to do the food shopping this afternoon and to pick up Aunt Ellen's medicine at the drug store. To the bank!"

"Just one more stop," Mark's father said as they left the bank. "I'd better get some gas." At a nearby service station, an attendant filled the tank, as he was asked to do, and then cleaned the back window and the windshield. Then Mark and his father drove home, where Izzy was waiting for them.

Mark and his father had a busy morning. Many of the people they met were service workers. Find the service workers in the story.

LESSON 3 REVIEW

THINK AND WRITE

A. Why can we say that Thanksgiving should be called an all-American feast?

B. In what way is the work of miners and loggers alike?

C. Why are raw materials needed by people who work in industries?

D. Name some of the ways in which workers who perform services help people.

SKILLS CHECK

THINKING SKILL

Name as many thing in the environment that farmers depend on to earn a living.

49

USING THE VOCABULARY

location	temperature
desert	growing season
landforms	natural vegetation
weather	manufactured
climate	raw materials

On a separate sheet of paper, write the word or words from the list above that best complete the sentence.

1. To know where something is on the earth is to know its _____.
2. Rain, snow, wind, heat, and cold are part of our _____.
3. A region with little rainfall and few plants is a _____.
4. Some things that are _____ in our country have a label that says "Made in the USA."
5. We know how hot or cold something is by its _____.
6. A weather pattern of little or no rain causes a dry _____.
7. An area has _____ if plants grow there without people's help.
8. The length of time an area is warm enough for crops to grow is the _____.
9. Mountains, islands, and plateaus are some of nature's _____.
10. To make products we need _____ from natural resources.

REMEMBERING WHAT YOU READ

1. What do the two words *geo* and *graphein* mean in English?
2. At what latitude and longitude is Mexico City located?
3. What do people and places have in common?
4. Why is it difficult to imagine a place where no person has ever been?
5. What does geography help us to understand?
6. What word do we use to describe rain, snow, sleet, or hail?
7. What are three things that influence natural vegetation?
8. How do we get most of our food — by fishing or by farming?
9. What are natural resources?
10. What do you call the kind of work that people do when they help other people?

TYING LANGUAGE ARTS TO SOCIAL STUDIES

In the book *The Little Prince*, the geographer suggested to the little prince that he take a trip to the earth. Imagine that you have been asked to make a folder describing a place you think the prince would like to visit.

Include in your description what the landscape would be like and what kind of weather the place would have. Describe what makes the place special.

THINKING CRITICALLY

On a separate sheet of paper, answer the following questions in complete sentences.

1. How would you describe the place where you live?
2. Which would you choose to explore — a mountain range or a place in Antarctica? Why?
3. In what way have we made our environment better and in what way have we made it worse? Give one example of each.
4. What makes the place where you live special?
5. Would you prefer to make you living as a farmer or a miner? Explain why.

SUMMARIZING THE CHAPTER

Copy this graphic organizer on a separate sheet of paper. Write a word or phrase on every line to support each main idea. The first one in each lesson has been done for you.

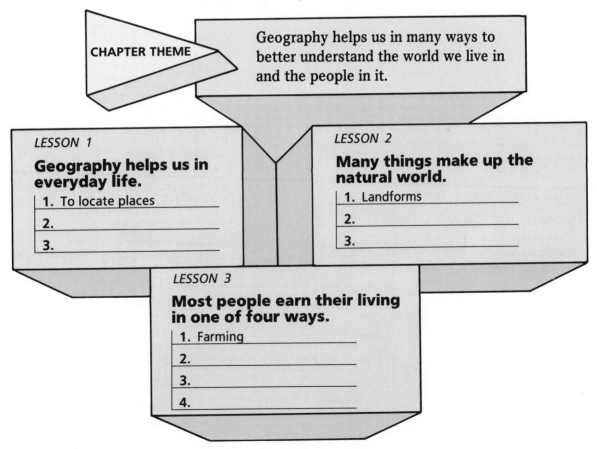

CHAPTER THEME

Geography helps us in many ways to better understand the world we live in and the people in it.

LESSON 1
Geography helps us in everyday life.
1. To locate places
2.
3.

LESSON 2
Many things make up the natural world.
1. Landforms
2.
3.

LESSON 3
Most people earn their living in one of four ways.
1. Farming
2.
3.
4.

2
LEARNING ABOUT REGIONS

*T*he earth is too large to study all at once. So geographers divide the earth into regions, or parts, that are alike in certain ways.

Discovering What a Region Is

THINK ABOUT WHAT YOU KNOW
Imagine that you are an astronaut flying in space above the earth. Describe what you think you might learn about the earth from your spacecraft.

STUDY THE VOCABULARY
mountain range	ancient
region	terrace
wheat belt	

FOCUS YOUR READING
What are some different kinds of regions?

A. Our Earth from Above

We orbit and float in our space gondola and watch the oceans and islands and green hills of the continents pass by at five miles [8 km] per second. We move silently and effortlessly past the ground. I want to say "over the ground" as I write this, but remember that in space your sense of up or down is completely gone. . . . You do not sit before the window to view the passing scene, but rather you float there and look out on the scene, certainly not down upon it. Are you speeding past oceans and continents, or are you just hovering and watching them move beside you?

These were the thoughts of Joseph Allen, an American astronaut, as he flew in his spacecraft hundreds of miles above the earth. He saw things on earth that we cannot see from the ground. He saw the oceans and the continents, the two largest features on the earth. He also saw deserts, forests, and **mountain ranges**. A mountain range is a row of connected mountains.

About 50 years earlier, in 1930, Amelia Earhart became the first woman to fly her own airplane alone across the Atlantic Ocean. She was the first person to fly from California to Hawaii. That flight was longer than the flight across the Atlantic Ocean.

Amelia Earhart piloted this airplane across the Atlantic Ocean.
▶ How can you tell that the photograph was taken many years ago?

53

The port city of Dakar and a tribal campsite in Mali show the great contrasts in Africa.
▶ Which place do you think has more people?

When I was a little girl in Kansas, the adventures of travel fascinated me. With my sister and my cousins I gratified [satisfied] my ambitions [to travel] by make-believe. That was in a barn behind our house in Atchison. There, in an old abandoned carriage, we made imaginary journeys full of fabulous perils [dangers].

Early we discovered the special joys of geography. The maps of far places that fell into our clutches supplemented the hair-raising experiences of the decrepit [worn out] carriage. Map-traveling took its place beside window-shopping as an accepted diversion [pastime]. The map of Africa was a favorite. The very word meant mystery. . . . we rolled on our tongues such names as Senegal, Timbuctu, Ngami [eng-GAHM ee], El Fasher, and Khartoum [kahr TOOM].

While Amelia Earhart was once flying over Africa, she remembered how much she had liked geography when she was a little girl. She wrote about some of the things that she remembered from her childhood. As you read what she wrote, try to picture what Amelia Earhart was remembering.

From her travels Amelia Earhart learned that many distant places are like places in the United States. When she flew over Central Africa, she wrote about the land and plants she saw.

Amelia Earhart thought that the deserts in Central Africa were like the deserts in the southwestern part of the United States. In fact, she wrote that they were so much alike that she almost had to pinch herself to realize how far from Arizona and New Mexico she really was. How far from the southwestern part of the United States do you think Africa is?

B. Understanding Regions

A **region** is an area that has something special that is common to the area. Geographers often divide the earth into many kinds of regions. They create regions based on what they want to study.

Sometimes geographers create regions based on the special kind of farming common in certain places. If they want to study wheat farming, they create a region where a lot of wheat is grown. This region might be called a **wheat belt**. What would you call a region where cotton is raised?

Regions can also be based on climate, vegetation, or landforms. A desert is an example of a climate region. We could also have a region based on the kind of trees or natural vegetation. Plains and mountain areas are examples of landform regions.

Regions can also be based on groups of countries or states that have something in common. We could decide to make a region called the Mediterranean region. All the countries that border the Mediterranean Sea would make up the region.

We could establish a region on the basis of the language spoken by most of the people in a group of countries. If we did this, we might create a region known as Latin America. This region would include all the countries in North America and South America in which Spanish is the major language. Spanish comes from an **ancient**, or very old, language called Latin.

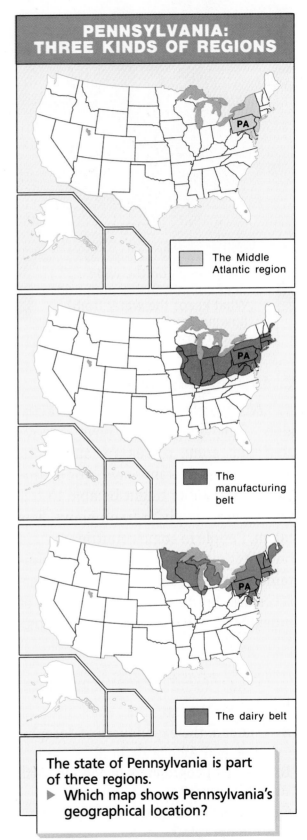

PENNSYLVANIA: THREE KINDS OF REGIONS

The Middle Atlantic region

The manufacturing belt

The dairy belt

The state of Pennsylvania is part of three regions.
▶ Which map shows Pennsylvania's geographical location?

55

Rice is growing on the wide terraces cut into the mountainside.
► What keeps the water from flowing down the mountainside?

C. Looking for Patterns

No two places on earth are exactly alike. Still, geographers have discovered that some places are similar to each other in certain ways. For example, a geographer might be able to tell you where the photograph above was taken. People in some countries in Asia build **terraces** to make steep mountainsides level enough to farm. Terraces are flat areas that are dug out of hillsides and then planted with crops.

Other clues in the photograph even tell which part of Asia is shown. Look at the straw-covered shelter. In the Asian country of Indonesia (ihn-duh NEE shuh), farmers rest in such shelters. Farmers there also wear the kind of hat shown.

There are patterns to the way people live and use the land in different places. When you know these patterns, you can better understand the world. As you read this book, you will learn some of the patterns that are an important part of geography.

LESSON 1 REVIEW

THINK AND WRITE
A. Compare the experiences of Joseph Allen and Amelia Earhart.
B. Why do geographers divide the earth into regions?
C. Why are patterns an important part of geography?

SKILLS CHECK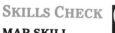

MAP SKILL
Look at the world map on pages 382–383 in the Atlas and name the countries that border the Mediterranean Sea.

The United States in the World

THINK ABOUT WHAT YOU KNOW

Name three things that you already know about the geography of the United States.

STUDY THE VOCABULARY

landscape	mineral
suburb	immigrant
rural area	migration
ore	

FOCUS YOUR READING

What do geographers look at when they study a country like the United States?

A. Location of the United States

Map Study Mrs. Fleener, the fourth-grade teacher at Northside School, was preparing to teach her class about the United States. She asked the students how they might begin to learn about the United States.

Location Sally said, "We could look at a globe or map and find where the United States is in the world."

"Very good," answered Mrs. Fleener. "Let's look at our wall map of the world. What does it tell us about the location of the United States?"

Terry raised his hand and said, "The United States is on the continent of North America."

"That's right," said Mrs. Fleener. "Which two countries are the closest neighbors of the United States?"

The class answered that Canada is the neighbor to the north and Mexico is the neighbor to the south. Mrs. Fleener then asked the class to name the bodies of water that border the United States. The class quickly named the Atlantic Ocean and the Pacific Ocean.

"These two oceans are not the only bodies of water that border the United States," Mrs. Fleener said. "See if you can find the Gulf of Mexico. It borders the southern shore of the United States. The Gulf of Mexico also touches the eastern part of Mexico and the large island of Cuba."

"Now let's find the state of Alaska on the map," Mrs. Fleener said. "It is in the northwestern part of North America. Alaska is bordered by Canada on the east, but it is surrounded by water on the other three sides. The Arctic Ocean is to the north, the Bering Sea to the west, and the Gulf of Alaska is to the south."

A globe is a useful tool for locating places on the earth.
▶ Why, do you think, is a globe round?

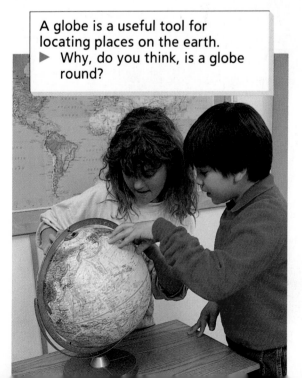

Two Distant States Mrs. Fleener reminded the class that Alaska is one of two states of the United States that are not connected to the rest of the country. Alaska is far distant from the mainland, or principal part of the country.

The other state is Hawaii, which consists of a group of islands in the Pacific Ocean. The Hawaiian Islands are nearly 2,000 miles (3,225 km) from California, the nearest state on the United States mainland.

"Well," said Mrs. Fleener, "I think we have a good idea of the location of the United States. Tomorrow we'll begin to think about some of the things that make the United States a special place. Place, as you remember, is another of the five themes of geography."

This worker in Hawaii is picking orchids.
▶ Have you ever seen an orchid or an orchid plant?

B. The United States: A Special Place

Comparing Places The next day, Mrs. Fleener showed the class several photographs. She explained that the photographs were taken in China, a country on the continent of Asia.

"These places look different from each other and different from the United States," Mrs. Fleener began. "Geographers call the special way a place looks the **landscape**. The landscape is made up of the natural environment and the things people have built on it as they live and work. What do you see in these photographs that make the places different from places in the United States?"

Some of the students said the trees in the photographs were quite different from trees they usually see. Other students mentioned that the homes they live in are different from those in the pictures. Another difference was in the way people dress.

Mrs. Fleener told the class that they would see other differences if they visited the places in the photographs. But since people don't travel to every country, photographs help them to see what the landscapes of other places are like.

Kinds of Communities The landscapes of the United States make it a special country. Many people in the United States live in big cities. The cities of the United States have tall buildings called skyscrapers. These tall buildings are part of the landscape of the city.

Highways are another important part of the landscape of the United States. Large cities in the United States are connected to highways that let cars move rapidly from place to place.

Perhaps you live in a **suburb**. A suburb is a community near a large city. Suburbs are another special part of the landscape around American cities.

The **rural areas** of our country have special landscapes, too. A rural area is one that is out in the country, far away from cities. In most rural areas there are large farms. The barns, silos, and other farm buildings in the United States look different from those in other parts of the world.

C. How Land in the United States Has Been Changed

Our Country Long Ago What, do you suppose, did the United States look like when the first Europeans arrived on its shores? Most of the eastern part of the United States was covered with thick forests. In some places Native Americans had cleared the land to build their villages and to grow food.

The central part of the United States was a huge grassland. Some of the early settlers said the grass blowing in the wind reminded them of the waves in the sea.

Our Country Today Today much of the land in the United States has been changed. The once grassy plains have

Rolling hills and broad fields surround this small community.
▶ Is this kind of community called a rural or suburban community?

The Granger Collection

Many immigrants who came to the United States years ago arrived in New York.
► How might they have felt when they saw the Statue of Liberty?

been plowed up for farms. Those lands are now covered with large fields of corn, soybeans, or wheat. Forests remain, but they are mainly in the areas that are too hilly, mountainous, or swampy for farming.

People also change our land by digging into the earth to obtain **ores**. An ore is a kind of rock from which we get valuable and useful substances called **minerals**. Iron ore, copper ore, gold ore, and many other ores are found in our country.

Throughout the United States, people have built towns and cities. Roads, highways, and railroads crisscross the country. Airports can be found in every state in the United States. People have left their mark across our great land.

D. Movement of People and Goods in the United States

People from Many Lands One day Mrs. Fleener told her class that some people say the United States is a country of **immigrants**. An immigrant is a person who leaves one country to come and live in another.

"Does that mean that everyone in the United States came from somewhere else?" Norma Jean asked.

Mrs. Fleener explained that everyone who lives in the United States now moved here from somewhere else or is descended from people who moved here from somewhere else. The

AN INTERVIEW WITH ABRAHAM GAMBERG

Abraham Gamberg immigrated to the United States from Russia. He didn't bring many possessions with him and he didn't speak English. His father had taught him to work hard and to be generous to others. Today, Abraham Gamberg owns a successful business and has received many honors in his community. When he was interviewed, Mr. Gamberg explained why he came to the United States.

> I came to the United States on January 18, 1913, but had decided to leave Russia long before that. I was only eight or nine years old when we had [trouble] in our city. Mobs of Russians, non-Jewish people, robbed our stores; some Jewish people were killed. I hid in the cellar with my brother for three days without food. . . .
>
> I decided while I was still a child that I would leave such a country. I thought, "The first chance I have, I'm going to go away." And that's the chance that came to me when my cousin sent me a paid passage to the United States.
>
> Of course, I had heard America was a great democracy — that you didn't have to work twenty-four hours a day only to be persecuted, that everyone was equal, that people enjoyed freedom.

Understanding Source Material

1. Why did Mr. Gamberg want to leave Russia?
2. Who helped Mr. Gamberg come to the United States?
3. How might Mr. Gamberg describe a democracy?

movement of people from one place to another is called **migration**.

Migration has been a very important part of the history of our country. People moved here from everywhere in the world—Europe, Asia, Africa, South America, and even from Australia. The only continent that has not contributed people to the United States is Antarctica, and that is because no one lives there.

Reading a Table   A table is a way of presenting facts. The facts are in columns that run down the page and in rows that go from left to right across the page. The facts in a table are often in the form of numbers. A table is useful in answering such questions as How many, How much? How big?

Below is a table of facts about the number of immigrants who came to the United States from four countries between 1860 and 1900. Beneath the title of the table, there are five columns. Each column has a label. The label shows the kind of information found in the column.

To find a fact—for example, the number of immigrants who came to the United States from Ireland in 1860—go to the column labeled *year* and find 1860. Then follow to the right on that line until you come to the column labeled *Ireland*. The table tells you that 48,637 immigrants came to the United States from Ireland in 1860. How many immigrants came to the United States from Italy in 1880? From which country did more immigrants come in 1900, Germany or Russia?

Movement of People   Mrs. Fleener told the class that immigrants are not the only people who leave their homes. Every year many people move from one part of the United States to another. People move for many reasons. Some people move because they have found new jobs. Some people want to live closer to their relatives.

Movement of Goods   Mrs. Fleener then asked the class to think about how they get the food, clothes, books, toys, and other things they have. Every one

IMMIGRATION TO THE UNITED STATES, 1860-1900

Year	Germany	Ireland	Russia	Italy
1860	54,491	48,637	65	1,019
1870	118,225	56,996	907	2,891
1880	84,638	71,603	5,014	12,354
1890	92,427	53,024	35,598	52,003
1900	18,507	35,730	90.787	100,135

Through the years many people have come to the United States from different parts of the world.
► How many people came to the United States from Italy in 1880?

of those things has to be moved from somewhere else. The movement of goods is another kind of movement.

Today the United States depends on countries all over the world to buy the things we produce on our farms and in our factories. We also depend on those countries to sell us things that are grown on their farms or made in their factories. Trading goods helps us to have many kinds of food to eat and products to use.

E. Regions of the United States

A Large Country The United States is the fourth-largest country in the world in area. Only the Soviet Union, Canada, and China are larger. The United States is also the fourth most populated country in the world. Only China, India, and the Soviet Union have more people than the United States.

Studying a Large Country It is easier to study a large country if we divide it

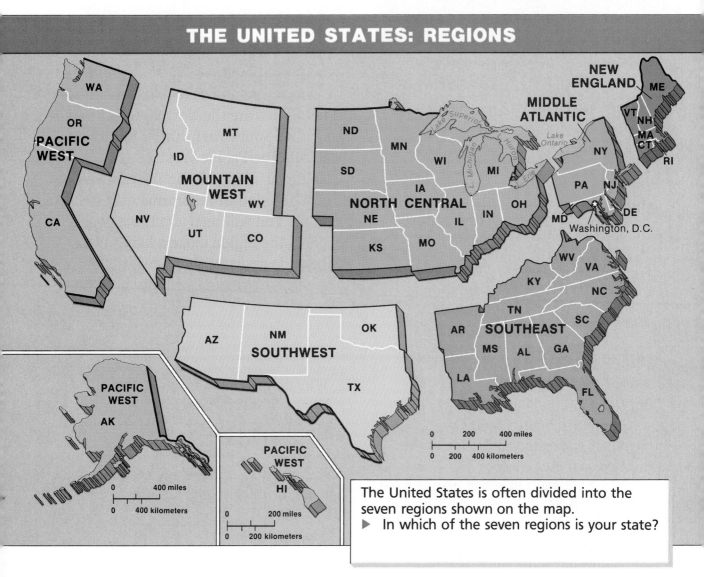

THE UNITED STATES: REGIONS

The United States is often divided into the seven regions shown on the map.
▶ In which of the seven regions is your state?

Although Americans live in different regions and come from many backgrounds, they are alike in many ways.
▶ What are some of these ways?

into regions. There are many different ways of dividing a country into regions. One way is to look for areas that have similar climates, ways of living, and ways of using the land. For example you could look at how people build their houses and towns. You could find out what crops are grown on their farms and what products are made in their factories.

We can divide the United States in many different ways. In this book the United States is divided into seven regions. Three of these regions are called New England, the Middle Atlantic region, and the Southeast.

The other four regions in the United States are the North Central region, the Southwest, the Mountain West, and the Pacific West.

As you read this book, you will learn what kind of landforms each region has. You will read about the ways people in the region make a living. You will also learn how these regions are alike and how they are different.

LESSON 2 REVIEW

THINK AND WRITE

A. What are the bodies of water that border the United States?
B. What makes the landscape of the United States special?
C. What are ways in which people have changed the natural environment of the United States?
D. Why is the movement of goods important to the United States?

E. Why do geographers divide the United States into regions?

SKILLS CHECK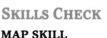

MAP SKILL

Look at the map of the United States on page 63. In which region are Alaska and Hawaii located?

64

USING THE VOCABULARY

mountain range	suburb
region	rural area
ancient	ore
terrace	immigrant
landscape	migration

On a separate sheet of paper, write the word or words from the list above that best complete the sentence.

1. A community near a large city is a _____.
2. A community far away from cities is a _____.
3. An area that has something special that is common to the area is a _____.
4. A row of connected mountains form a _____.
5. Something that is very old is said to be _____.
6. A flat area dug out of hillsides and planted with crops is a _____.
7. The movement of people from one place to another is called _____.
8. The natural environment and the things people have built on it make up a _____.
9. A person who moves from one country to live in another is an _____.
10. A kind of rock from which we get valuable minerals is an _____.

REMEMBERING WHAT YOU READ

On a separate sheet of paper, answer the following questions in complete sentences.

1. What is a region?
2. What is a wheat belt?
3. What kind of regions are plains and mountains?
4. What countries make up Latin America?
5. Which two countries are neighbors of the United States?
6. What body of water borders the United States on the south?
7. Which state in the United States is bordered by the Arctic Ocean?
8. From which continent have we not received any immigrants?
9. Which three countries are larger in land area than the United States?
10. Into how many regions can the United States be divided?

TYING MUSIC TO SOCIAL STUDIES

Many songs have been written about the United States. The words of some of the songs paint a picture of our country. Others tell about our history.

Do you know the songs "America, the Beautiful," "This Land Is Your Land," and "Yankee Doodle"? If you made up a song about the United States, what would you sing about?

THINKING CRITICALLY

On a separate sheet of paper, answer the following questions in complete sentences.

1. Why is the earth divided into regions?
2. If you could have met Amelia Earhart, what questions would you have liked to ask her?
3. What are some things special about the United States?
4. How are people all over the world alike and how are they different?
5. How might the United States be a different country if no immigrants ever came here?

SUMMARIZING THE CHAPTER

Copy this graphic organizer on a separate sheet of paper. Write a phrase on each line to support each main idea. The first one for each main idea has been done for you.

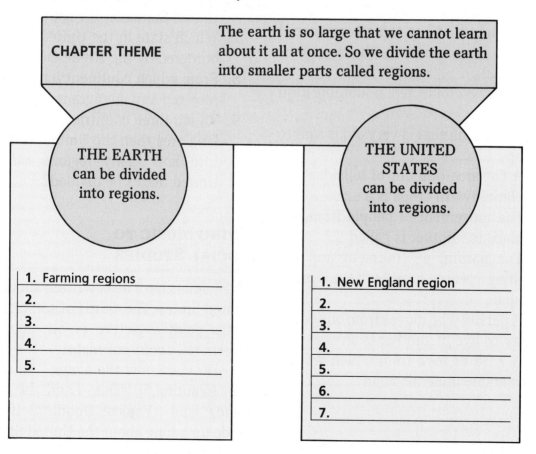

CHAPTER THEME

The earth is so large that we cannot learn about it all at once. So we divide the earth into smaller parts called regions.

THE EARTH can be divided into regions.

1. Farming regions
2.
3.
4.
5.

THE UNITED STATES can be divided into regions.

1. New England region
2.
3.
4.
5.
6.
7.

COOPERATIVE LEARNING

In Unit 1 you learned that geography is the study of the earth's natural features and the ways in which people use the earth. You read that studying geography can be a great adventure. Now you are going to work with some of your classmates to demonstrate to others how geography can be a great adventure. You will do that by making a poster.

REMEMBER TO:
- Give your ideas.
- Listen to others' ideas.
- Plan your work with the group.
- Present your project.
- Discuss how your group worked.

PROJECT

• Working with a small group of classmates, talk about your ideas for the poster. Listen carefully to the suggestions of the group members. Choose someone to record the suggestions.

• Decide how you can carry out the suggestions that you agree on. Assign a task to each member of the group.

• One or two members could make drawings or find pictures for the poster.

• One or two members of the group could print or cut out the letters for the words you need on the poster.

• One member could plan how the words and pictures or drawings will be arranged on the poster.

PRESENTATION AND REVIEW

• Display your group's work on the bulletin board for the class to see.

• Allow time for the class to study the poster.

• Ask your classmates what they like most and what they like least about the poster.

• Meet with your group again and talk about how well you completed your project. Discuss what everyone learned by working together. Ask how well you worked together as a group. Think of ways that might help the group to work better together. Ask what you might do differently if you were going to make another poster.

A. WHY DO I NEED THIS SKILL?

Maps can do many things besides show us where places are and how far apart one place is from another. One of the most helpful things a map can do is tell us about the weather. Knowing what the weather will be each day helps us decide what clothes to wear.

Knowing about the climate in different parts of the United States will help us understand our country better. Climate affects the way in which people live. It also makes a difference in the kinds of foods people grow and eat.

B. LEARNING THE SKILL

The map on page 69 shows the average January temperatures in the United States. Different parts of the United States are shown in different colors. Each color on the map stands for a range of temperatures, shown in degrees Fahrenheit (°F) and degrees Celsius (°C).

Look at the areas on the map that are colored yellow. Then find the color yellow in the key. The key tells you that yellow stands for 20° to 30° on the Fahrenheit scale (°F) and −7° to −1° on the Celsius scale (°C). From this information, you know the average January temperatures in the areas on the map that are colored yellow.

The lowest temperature range in the key is below −10°F (below −23°C). The highest temperature range in the key is 70° to 80°F (21° to 27°C). The lowest average January temperature in the United States is in the northern part of Alaska. The two places in the United States with the highest average January temperature are the southern tip of Florida and Hawaii.

Most states have more than one temperature range. Find Florida on the map. The colors show that there are three temperature ranges in Florida. Find the temperature ranges in the key.

C. PRACTICING THE SKILL

Use the map on page 69 to answer the following questions.

1. How many temperature ranges are there in Oregon in January?
2. Which state has the lower average January temperature, North Dakota or Washington?
3. Which state has the higher average January temperature, Nebraska or Arkansas?
4. What is the range of temperatures in the states between 30°N latitude and 40°N latitude?
5. What is the average January temperature in West Virginia?

D. APPLYING THE SKILL

Watch a weather report on television or look at a weather map in a newspaper. Find the place where you live on the weather map. Compare the temperature in your area with the temperature in another part of the United States.

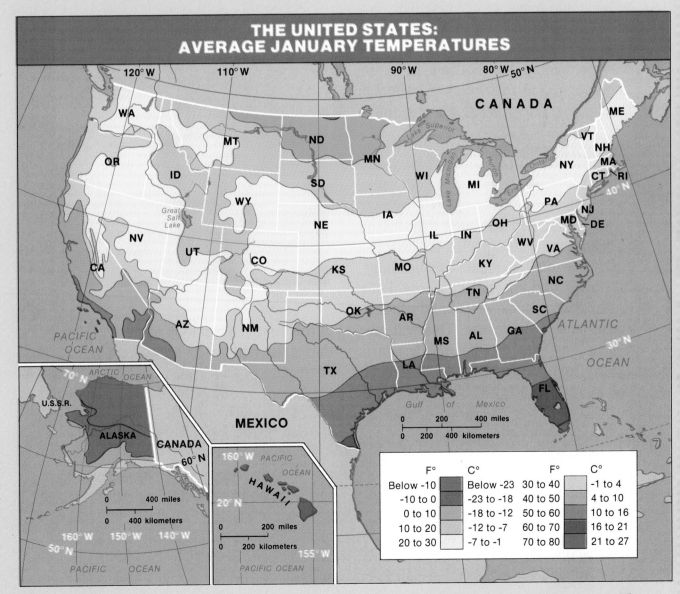

THE UNITED STATES:
AVERAGE JANUARY TEMPERATURES

F°	C°	F°	C°
Below -10	Below -23	30 to 40	-1 to 4
-10 to 0	-23 to -18	40 to 50	4 to 10
0 to 10	-18 to -12	50 to 60	10 to 16
10 to 20	-12 to -7	60 to 70	16 to 21
20 to 30	-7 to -1	70 to 80	21 to 27

A. WHY DO I NEED THIS SKILL?

This social studies book contains a lot of information about people, places, and events. Each lesson contains many ideas to learn and remember. You will do well if you have a plan of action when you study. Survey, Question, Read (SQR) is a study-reading plan that will help you understand and remember the ideas in this book and in other textbooks, too.

B. LEARNING THE SKILL

There are three steps in the SQR strategy. Each step is described below.

The first step is to survey the lesson to get a general idea of what the lesson is about. To do this, read the headings, questions, and vocabulary words. Look at the photographs, maps, and other illustrations in the lesson. This will give you a good idea of what the lesson is about. Then think about what you already know about the topic. Make some guesses about the ideas you think will be in the lesson.

The second step is to think of questions you may have about the lesson. If questions do not come to mind, use the words *what, where, when, how,* and *why* to get you started. Read the Focus Your Reading question at the beginning of the lesson to help you focus on the main idea of the lesson. Then look at the question that goes with each photograph, map, chart, and graph. Read the questions in the Lesson Review. Once you have your list of questions, you're ready to start reading the lesson.

The third step is to read the lesson to find the answers to the questions on your list. As you find the answers, write them next to the questions on your paper. You may find yourself asking other questions as you read. Try to find answers to these questions, too.

70

C. Practicing the Skill

Turn to page 34. Practice the SQR study-reading plan by reading Lesson 2 of Chapter 1. The lesson is called The World We Live In.

Start by surveying the lesson. Follow the directions given on page 70. Think about what you already know about landforms, weather, and climate. What guesses can you make about the ideas in this lesson?

Read the questions in the lesson. Prepare a list of questions of your own. Write your questions on the left-hand side of a sheet of paper.

Then read the lesson carefully to find the answers to the questions. Write the answers to the questions on the right-hand side of the paper.

D. Applying the Skill

Using the SQR study-reading plan can help you when you are studying for a test. If you save your SQR questions and answers, you can use them to help you review what you have studied.

Practice using the SQR study-reading plan as you read Chapter 3. See how it can help you understand and remember the information in the chapter. See how it can help you do well on your next test.

Using SQR

Survey	Look at the questions, vocabulary words, and visuals in the lesson. Think about what you already know about the topic of the lesson. Make predictions about the lesson content.
Question	Note questions already in the lesson. Use vocabulary words and headings to prepare other questions. Write your questions on a sheet of paper or make a mental note of them.
Read	Read the text and then answer your questions. Write your answers or say them to yourself. Ask and answer other questions that come to mind as you read.

The Using SQR chart on this page will help you remember the steps. Make a copy of the chart and use it when you are studying.

2 REGIONS OF THE UNITED STATES

To help us learn about the United States, geographers divide the country into parts called regions.

In this book you will study the seven regions of the United States, shown on the map.

Columbus, Ohio, is one of many manufacturing and trade centers in the United States. ▼

Rich farmland in the United States provides food for our nation. ▶

THE NEW ENGLAND REGION

*W*hen the Pilgrims came to New England in 1620, they farmed the land. Today, New England is a major manufacturing region of the United States.

69° W   67° W   65° W

4

67° W

47° N

CANADA

CANADA

A

75° W   73° W

1   2

45° N

MAINE

● Burlington
Montpelier ⊛
● Barre

VERMONT

Augusta ⊛

B

NEW

HAMPSHIRE

Portland ●

Concord ⊛

ATLANTIC

43° N

Manchester ●

OCEAN

NEW YORK

MASSACHUSETTS

Boston ⊛
● Worcester

C

THE NEW ENGLAND REGION: POLITICAL

Plymouth ●

Providence
⊛ Hartford   ● Pawtucket
Waterbury ● **CONNECTICUT**   ● Warwick
RHODE ISLAND

⊛   State capital

●   Other cities

New Haven   Groton ●

PA

Bridgeport ●

NEW JERSEY

● Stamford

41° N

LONG ISLAND

0		25	50	75	100 miles
0	25	50	75	100	kilometers

Land and Climate in the New England Region

THINK ABOUT WHAT YOU KNOW

What is your favorite outdoor place? How would you describe that place?

STUDY THE VOCABULARY

sound   **promontory**

FOCUS YOUR READING

What are some of the important physical features of the New England region?

A. The *New* in New England

New England is a place of beautiful rocky coastlines, green valleys, many rivers and lakes, and mountains covered with tall trees. The region includes some large cities, such as Boston, Massachusetts, and Providence, Rhode Island. New England also has small towns, busy fishing villages, and peaceful farms.

The name *New England* tells us something about this region. The first European settlers in this area came from England, which is a country in Europe. They arrived at Plymouth Rock on the Atlantic coast of Massachusetts in 1620. They were called Pilgrims.

Many more English settlers came to New England after the Pilgrims arrived. They probably missed their homeland very much. Most people who move to a new place are a little homesick for a while. So to remind themselves of their homeland, the settlers named new places in this country after places they had known in England. This is how the region came to be known as New England.

B. Locating the New England Region

The nicknames of some of the New England states tell us something about the geography of the region. Rhode Island's nickname, the Ocean State, gives us a good idea of that state's location. The Atlantic Ocean forms one of the borders of Rhode Island.

Massachusetts's nickname gives us a clue about the state's location.

CITY INDEX

Cities less than 100,000		
Augusta (ME) B-3	Pawtucket (RI) C-2	New Haven (CT) C-2
Barre (VT) B-2	Plymouth (MA) C-3	Providence (RI) C-2
Burlington (VT) B-1	Portland (ME) B-3	Stamford (CT) C-1
Concord (NH).................. B-2	Warwick (RI) C-2	Waterbury (CT) C-1
Groton (CT) C-2		Worcester (MA) C-2
Manchester (NH) C-2	**Cities 100,000 to 499,999**	
Montpelier (VT) B-2	Bridgeport (CT) C-1	**Cities 500,000 to 999,999**
	Hartford (CT) C-2	Boston (MA) C-2

This map has a grid system. The lines of latitude and longitude form the boxes of the grid. The letters and numbers identify the boxes and help you find the location of a city.

▶ Which capital city is in box B-3?

Waves beat against the rocky shore of the coast of Maine.
► Why, do you think, is there a lighthouse at the edge of the shore?

Massachusetts is called the Bay State. Part of the state's eastern border is located along a section of the Atlantic Ocean called Massachusetts Bay.

The Atlantic Ocean touches all the states of New England except Vermont. Even New Hampshire has a small bit of coastline along the Atlantic Ocean. It's easy to see that the ocean forms the eastern and southern boundaries of the New England region.

Along southern Connecticut the ocean is called the Long Island Sound. A **sound** is a long, wide stretch of water that separates the mainland and an island or that links two large bodies of water. Look at the map on page 78 to find the two pieces of land that the Long Island Sound separates.

The western boundary of New England is drawn by the Green Mountains. This boundary separates Vermont from New York State, which is not a part of the New England region. Vermont's nickname is the Green Mountain State because these mountains cover most of the state.

The northern boundary of New England separates Vermont, New Hampshire, and Maine from Canada. Rivers and lakes form some parts of this boundary. Other parts of the border were decided on by leaders of the United States and Canada.

C. Physical Features of New England

The Atlantic Coastline One of the main physical features of the New England region is the Atlantic coastline. The New England coastline is rocky, with some sandy beaches. In Maine there are many areas of high, rocky land that jut out into the water. They are called **promontories** (PRAHM untor eez). Find a promontory in the picture above.

A River and Its Valley The Connecticut River is the longest river in the New England region. It begins in northern New Hampshire and flows along the whole New Hampshire–Vermont border. The river continues south through Massachusetts and Connecticut until it reaches Long Island Sound.

The Connecticut River valley is the widest and most important valley in the New England region. There are many farms on its flatlands, but there also are good-size cities and towns. Hartford, the capital city of Connecticut, is in the Connecticut River valley.

The Mountains The Appalachian Mountains are another important physical feature of the New England region. This mountain range begins in Canada and then extends south in the United States as far as the state of Alabama.

The Appalachians have different names in different parts of the New England region. In Vermont the Appalachians are called the Green Mountains. In New Hampshire the Appalachians are known as the White Mountains.

Mount Washington, in the White Mountains, is the highest point in the New England region. It reaches an elevation of 6,288 feet (1,917 m). This is high but not high enough to have snow all year-round. The White Mountains are really only white in the winter.

Snowshoeing is a popular activity in New Hampshire's White Mountain National Forest.
▶ Would you like to go snowshoeing?

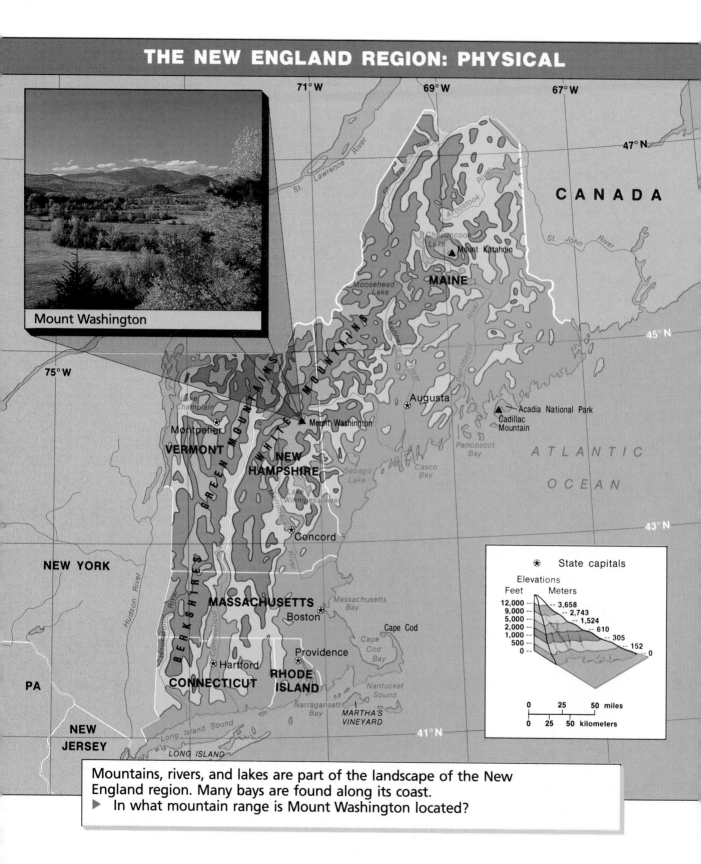

THE NEW ENGLAND REGION: PHYSICAL

Mount Washington

CANADA

MAINE

St. Lawrence River

St. Francis River

Aroostook River

Chesuncook Lake

Mount Katahdin

Moosehead Lake

St. John River

Kennebec River

Penobscot River

Augusta

Acadia National Park
Cadillac Mountain

Penobscot Bay

ATLANTIC OCEAN

Lake Champlain

Montpelier

VERMONT

Mount Washington

NEW HAMPSHIRE

Sebago Lake

Casco Bay

GREEN MOUNTAINS

WHITE MOUNTAINS

Lake Winnipesaukee

Merrimack River

Concord

NEW YORK

Hudson River

Housatonic River

BERKSHIRES

Connecticut River

MASSACHUSETTS

Massachusetts Bay

Boston

Cape Cod

Cape Cod Bay

Providence

Hartford

RHODE ISLAND

CONNECTICUT

Nantucket Sound

Narragansett Bay

MARTHA'S VINEYARD

PA

NEW JERSEY

Long Island Sound

LONG ISLAND

Elevations	
Feet	Meters
12,000	3,658
9,000	2,743
5,000	1,524
2,000	610
1,000	305
500	152
0	0

⊛ State capitals

0   25   50 miles
0   25   50 kilometers

Mountains, rivers, and lakes are part of the landscape of the New England region. Many bays are found along its coast.
▶ In what mountain range is Mount Washington located?

Size and Population The largest state in New England by far is Maine. Its area is 33,215 square miles (86,027 sq km). Rhode Island is the smallest state, not only in New England but in the United States as well. Its area is only 1,052 square miles (2,725 sq km).

In the New England region, the smaller states have more people than the larger states. The smaller states — Massachusetts, Connecticut, and Rhode Island — have nearly 10 million people. The larger states — Maine, New Hampshire, and Vermont — have less than 3 million people.

D. Climates of New England

Interest in Weather Some people are interested in climates because their work depends on having certain kinds of weather. For example, farmers need long, warm summers with plenty of rain so that their crops can grow. Fishers need clear weather, because the ocean is dangerous during storms. Owners of ski resorts hope for plenty of snow in winter.

Changing Seasons New England is famous for its changing seasons. Its most colorful season is fall when the

Canoeing is just one activity that people enjoy on the lakes in Connecticut.
▶ How can you tell that the photograph was taken in autumn?

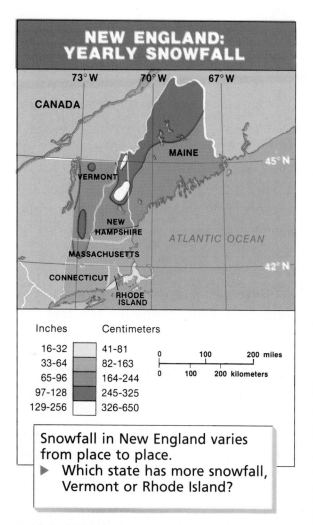

NEW ENGLAND: YEARLY SNOWFALL

Inches	Centimeters
16-32	41-81
33-64	82-163
65-96	164-244
97-128	245-325
129-256	326-650

Snowfall in New England varies from place to place.
▶ Which state has more snowfall, Vermont or Rhode Island?

leaves of the trees turn brilliant colors. The third week in October is usually the peak time. Then many people from the northeastern cities come to see the autumn leaves.

Some parts of the region, especially northern areas, have very cold winters with lots of snow. In some places a winter snowfall can total more than 100 inches (254 cm). The winter skies are often dull and overcast.

Spring in New England is usually short. The apple trees, dogwood trees, and many other plants are in bloom. As the snow melts, the waterfalls become stronger and more beautiful.

Summer is pleasant but fairly cool in northern New England. In the southern part of the region, summers can get hot. The season is short, but people enjoy it while they can. Although the temperatures at most of the lakes, bays, and the Atlantic Ocean are cool, people flock to the beaches.

LESSON 1 REVIEW

THINK AND WRITE

A. How did the New England region get its name?

B. How do the nicknames of some New England states help us learn about the region?

C. In which part of New England do most people live, in the larger states or in the smaller states?

D. If you were to visit Maine in the winter, what kind of clothing would you take along?

SKILLS CHECK

THINKING SKILL

On the map of New England on page 74 find the latitude of the northernmost point in Maine. Then find the latitude of the southernmost point in Connecticut. Use the scale on the map to figure out the distance in miles between the two points.

Farming in New England

THINK ABOUT WHAT YOU KNOW

List three ideas that you think of when you hear or read the word *farming*.

STUDY THE VOCABULARY

bog   bar graph
specialty crop

FOCUS YOUR READING

What are some of the important crops of the New England region?

A. Farming in a Rugged Land

New England's climate is somewhat cooler than many other regions of the United States. The growing season is shorter here than farther to the south. In most parts of New England, the soil is rocky. Yet, in spite of the cool climate, short growing season, and stony soil, there are lots of farms in the New England region.

Many farmers grow a variety of crops for home use. However, some farmers specialize in raising animals and crops that do well in New England. These animals, animal products, and crops are sold for profit.

B. Dairy Farming

Dairy farming is the most important kind of farming in the New England region. Dairy farms are found in all six states, but most dairy farms are in Vermont. Certain kinds of pasture grasses that dairy cattle eat grow very well in the cool, short summer climate of New England.

People in large cities use a great amount of milk every day. Most of New England's dairy farms are located

In New England, where dairy farming is the most important kind of farming, cows are often milked by machine.
▶ Have you ever visited a dairy farm?

Workers gather potatoes that have been dug up by a machine.
▶ What two kinds of containers do these workers use?

within an easy half-day drive of the region's cities. Dairy companies can pick up the fresh milk from the morning's milking on the surrounding farms. Large stainless steel milk trucks carry the milk to the cities. There the milk is processed for sale and some of it is made into cheese, butter, ice cream, and other milk products.

C. Special Farming in New England

Potato Farming Most people like French fries and other foods made from potatoes. Did you know that a good share of the potatoes grown in the United States come from New England? In northern Maine the soils in the Aroostook (uh ROOS tuk) River valley are especially good for this crop.

Maine's short growing season is also good for potatoes. The season is between 90 and 120 days. This is too short a time for many crops to grow, but it is a perfect length of time for potatoes to grow.

Growing Other Crops Tomatoes, corn, and other vegetables are grown in Massachusetts. Cranberries are also grown in Massachusetts.

Cranberries grow in low marshy places called **bogs**. The bogs are spread with a thin layer of sand, and cranberry vine cuttings are set in the sand. As the vines grow, they push through the sand. The bogs are then flooded to keep the vines moist as the berries grow. The cranberries are picked in late September. Some are sold as whole fresh berries, but most are canned as sauce, juice, or jelly.

A special kind of soil, a certain climate, and a lot of care are needed to grow cranberries. Cranberry growers usually get a high price when they sell their crop. We call crops like cranberries **specialty crops**.

Reading a Bar Graph On this page there is a **bar graph** that shows the leading states that grow cranberries. A bar graph uses horizontal or vertical bars to show information.

The bar graph has a title. Along the bottom of the graph are the names of five states. Which state has the tallest bar? This means the most cranberries are grown in that state.

The numbers along the left show how many 100-pound (45-kg) barrels of cranberries are produced in each state. Place a finger at the top of the bar for New Jersey. Move your finger to the left. All the cranberries grown in New Jersey in one year would fill about 280,000 barrels of 100 pounds each.

THE UNITED STATES: CRANBERRY PRODUCTION

This graph shows the five states that grow the most cranberries.

► Which state grows more cranberries, New Jersey or Washington?

LESSON 2 REVIEW

THINK AND WRITE

A. Why is farming difficult in the New England region?

B. Why are there successful dairy farms in the New England region?

C. Why is Maine a good area for potato farming?

SKILLS CHECK

THINKING SKILL

Many people who have never visited New England have tasted New England foods. What foods might they have tasted and how would they have been able to do this?

Natural Resources and Industry in the New England Region

THINK ABOUT WHAT YOU KNOW

Imagine that you were shipwrecked and landed on a deserted island. How might you provide for your food, clothing, and shelter?

STUDY THE VOCABULARY

wood pulp   **textile**
quarry   **high technology**
mill

FOCUS YOUR READING

What are the most important natural resources of the New England region?

A. Fish, an Important Resource

A Good Fishing Region From the earliest settlement of New England, many people earned their living by fishing. One of the best fishing regions in the world is off the coast of Massachusetts. Schools of fish travel to the shallow waters here and in Maine to feed. Thousands of tons of fish each year are caught in these cool ocean waters.

Valuable Fish Menhaden (men HAYD-un), are one of the most valuable kinds of fish caught along the Atlantic coast. They are more valuable as a source of useful products, however, than as a food. Some of the products from menhaden are shown in the drawing at the bottom of this page.

USES OF THE MENHADEN

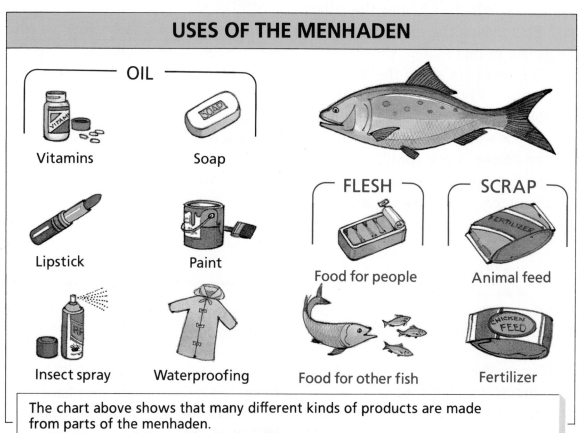

OIL

Vitamins   Soap

Lipstick   Paint

Insect spray   Waterproofing

FLESH

Food for people

Food for other fish

SCRAP

Animal feed

Fertilizer

The chart above shows that many different kinds of products are made from parts of the menhaden.
► Which part of the menhaden has the most uses?

Lobsters are caught in the wide-open waters of the ocean.
▶ How are lobsters caught?

Herring, cod, and haddock are also caught along the Atlantic coast. They are among the most important food fish in the world. Most young herring are canned. If you have ever eaten sardines, you may actually have been eating herring.

Lobsters Maine is famous for its lobsters, which are considered a treat by people who like shellfish. Lobsters, however, are not really fish, and to catch them people use traps called lobster pots. Each lobster pot only holds one lobster, so it takes many traps and many hours to catch enough to sell.

B. Water as a Natural Resource

There are many lakes and rivers in New England. Their use for transportation has been important in developing the region. They have also served as a source of power.

Most of the early industries in New England were located along the rivers that flowed from the mountains toward the Atlantic Ocean. Because of the rocky and hilly landscape, many rivers flow rapidly downhill and tumble over cliffs. At these points the rivers become waterfalls.

The force of falling water was first used to turn water wheels, which created water power. All over New England are old mills and old towns that used falling water as a source of power. Later, the same source was often used to create electric power. Both of these uses of water were important to the success of manufacturing in the New England region. New England grew as an important manufacturing region in the United States.

C. The Forests of New England

Early Use of Timber The forests and woods of New England have long been an important natural resource for the people in the region. When the first English colonists came here, they were thrilled by the many tall, straight trees. These fir trees were perfect to use for the masts of the English sailing ships.

Although New England is today one of the most populated regions of the United States, much of the land is still forested. Many different kinds of trees are found there, including fir, birch, spruce, pine, oak, and maple. Timber became one of the earliest raw materials for New England industry.

The wood-product industry began in New England as early as 1607, when a ship named *Virginia* was built in Maine. That was the beginning of the area's shipbuilding industry, which was the largest source of income in New England for many years.

Later Use of Timber Before 1900, half of the nation's oceangoing ships were built in Maine. Today, ships are made of steel, and New England's shipbuilding industry is not as important as it once was. The timber of New England's forests is now used mostly for **wood pulp**. Wood pulp is wood that has been washed, cut into chips, and boiled. It is the raw material that is used to make paper. The chart on page 87 shows how paper is made.

Another Product from Trees One of the "sweetest" products of New England's forests comes from sugar maple trees. Have you ever had maple syrup? Many people like to pour maple syrup on their pancakes and waffles.

Maple syrup is made from the sap, or the liquid in the stems and roots of certain maple trees, especially sugar maples. In the late winter and early spring, as the days begin to warm, the sap starts to flow in the sugar maple trees. "Sugaring" is the name used by New Englanders to describe the collecting of the sap. The sap is then slowly boiled down to make the rich maple syrup. Vermont is one of the leading producers of maple syrup in the United States.

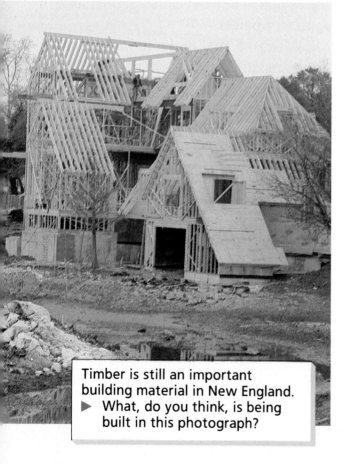

Timber is still an important building material in New England.
▶ What, do you think, is being built in this photograph?

HOW PAPER IS MADE

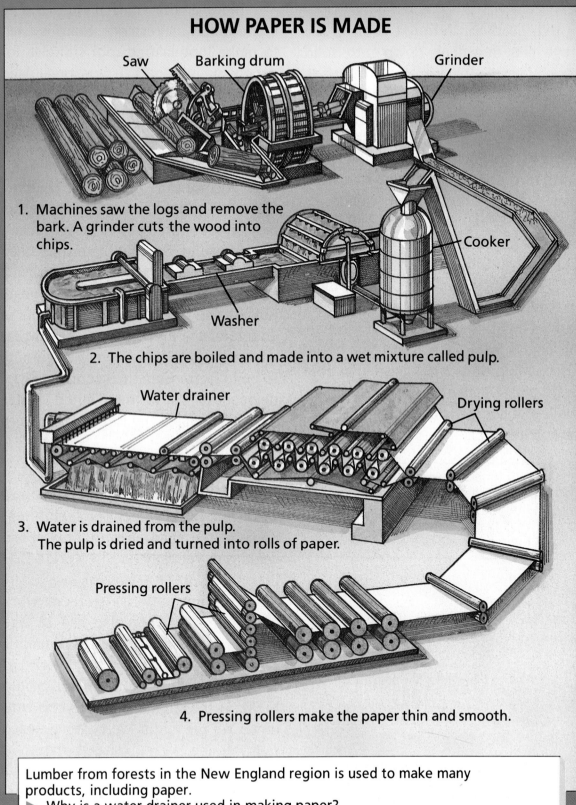

Saw   Barking drum   Grinder

1. Machines saw the logs and remove the bark. A grinder cuts the wood into chips.

Cooker

Washer

2. The chips are boiled and made into a wet mixture called pulp.

Water drainer   Drying rollers

3. Water is drained from the pulp. The pulp is dried and turned into rolls of paper.

Pressing rollers

4. Pressing rollers make the paper thin and smooth.

Lumber from forests in the New England region is used to make many products, including paper.
▶ Why is a water drainer used in making paper?

D. Useful Stones from Vermont

In northern Vermont you can see huge pits dug deep down into solid rock. These pits are stone **quarries** (KWAWR eez), and they are among the largest quarries in the United States. The most important stones found in Vermont are granite, marble, and slate. Granite is a very hard stone that lasts many years, through all kinds of weather. It is used for buildings, statues, and tombstones. Cutting and finishing granite is difficult work.

Vermont leads the United States in marble quarrying. Marble is another kind of building stone. Most of the marble comes from the western side of the Green Mountains. The quarried marble is cut and polished and used mostly for walls and floors of public buildings and on monuments.

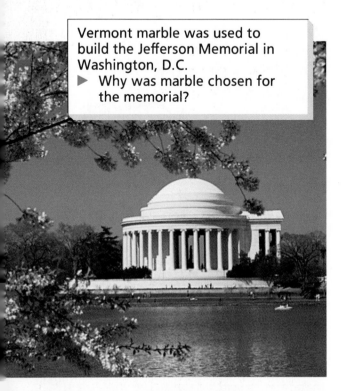

Vermont marble was used to build the Jefferson Memorial in Washington, D.C.
▶ Why was marble chosen for the memorial?

Slate is the third main building stone found in Vermont. Slate is used to make long-lasting roof shingles for expensive buildings. It was once used for chalkboards in almost all the classrooms in the United States.

E. The Early Textile Industry

The Beginning   In 1789, Samuel Slater built the first cotton **mill**, or factory, in the United States in Pawtucket, Rhode Island. Samuel Slater had been born in England. He began to work in a mill there when he was only 14 years old. By the time he was 21, he was in charge of the mill. Then he heard that American companies were beginning to build factories in their country. So he decided to go to the United States where he copied the English machines from memory.

Working Conditions   Soon many other mills were built. Most of the mill workers were women and children. Some of the children were only seven years old, yet they had to work a 72-hour week.

Not only did the workers work long hours but they also had to face terrible conditions in the **textile** mills. *Textile* is another word for "cloth" or "fabric." Because cotton fibers would break in the slightest breeze, the windows of the mills were kept closed tight. Some were boarded over. So there was very little fresh air.

Some mills had booths, like telephone booths, that had small fans in the ceiling. Workers were allowed to sit in a booth and rest for five minutes.

F. Modern Industries

Through the years new industries have appeared in New England to meet new demands. Connecticut has a large defense industry which helps to guard, or protect, our country against attack. Building submarines, tanks, and airplanes is part of the defense industry.

Submarines are built near Groton, Connecticut. Submarines are also built in Bath, Maine, along with steel ships. Jet engines, other airplane parts, and computers are made in the region.

Submarine building is one of the many industries in the New England region that use **high technology**. These industries are often called high-tech industries. They use the most up-to-date knowledge and tools to make things. High-tech industries often make products like computers. Massachusetts is a leading state in the manufacture of high-tech products.

The Granger Collection

In the 1800s many youngsters worked in factories.
▶ What might they be carrying to work in the buckets?

LESSON 3 REVIEW

THINK AND WRITE

A. Why is the New England region an important fishing region?

B. How was water used as a power source for early industries?

C. Why were the forests so important to the early settlers of New England?

D. Why is granite such an important stone?

E. What were working conditions like in the first mills in New England?

F. How have high-tech industries made a difference in your life?

SKILLS CHECK

THINKING SKILL

Make a list of all the things you can think of that might be high-tech products. Choose two of the products and describe how they are used.

89

Communities in the New England Region

THINK ABOUT WHAT YOU KNOW
What historic place have you visited, read, or heard about? What makes it a historic place?

STUDY THE VOCABULARY
metropolitan area   colony

commerce   famine

time line   ethnic neighborhood

FOCUS YOUR READING
What different kinds of communities can you find in New England?

A. Cities and Metropolitan Areas

Large Cities More than 12 million people live in the New England region. Although there are many small towns in the region, about three out of every four people in the region live in larger towns and cities.

A city's **metropolitan area** includes the city itself and all the smaller communities around it. The number of people who live in a metropolitan area is always larger than the number of people who live in the city itself. For example, about 574,000 people live in the city of Boston, Massachusetts. But more than 4 million people live in the Boston metropolitan area.

Boston Boston, the capital of Massachusetts, has more people than any other city in the New England region. The city is a center of industry and **commerce**, or the buying and selling of goods. Many high-tech businesses design and make computers and different kinds of computer products.

If you were to visit Boston, one of the first things you might notice would be the number of young people. There are about 47 colleges and universities in the metropolitan area. Harvard University, the oldest college in the United States, is in Boston.

Hartford Hartford is not only the capital of Connecticut but it is also the "insurance capital of the world." Insurance is a way of giving people protection against loss in a variety of

Exhibits at The Children's Museum in South Boston, Massachusetts, help youngsters learn about science.
▶ What is this boy doing?

situations. Automobile inusrance helps to cover the cost of damages resulting from a car accident. Fire insurance and health insurance are other kinds of insurance. Today more than 30 insurance companies have their headquarters in Hartford.

Montpelier and Barre Montpelier (mahnt PEEL yur), the capital of Vermont, is in a valley of the Green Mountains. The making of granite monuments is one of the important industries in Montpelier. Many people are also employed in the business of state government.

Barre (BAR ee) is a few miles southeast of Montpelier. Granite was first quarried in Barre over a century ago. The city is known as the granite center of the world because the world's largest granite quarries are in and around Barre. Some of the giant granite quarries are open to visitors, who can watch granite cutters at work.

B. Historic Towns and Activities

A Whaling Community New England is famous for its historic towns and villages. Many families enjoy visiting the museums and old buildings in the region to learn about the history of our country.

One such historic town is Mystic, in Connecticut. In the 1800s this town was one of the world's most important centers for the whaling industry. Whaling is the hunting of whales in the ocean. Whaling was dangerous work that called for brave men.

Some granite quarries are more than 100 feet (30 m) deep.
▶ How can you tell that the quarry in the photograph is very deep?

Different parts of the whale were used for different things. Whale oil was used for fuel in lamps. In those days there was no electricity, and whale oil was burned to provide light. Whalebones were used in making many things, such as umbrellas, shoehorns, and jewelry. A part of the whale was even used in the making of perfume.

The town of Mystic has been restored to show what an important whaling town was like years ago. The buildings and ships look like those of the whaling days. You can hear the sounds and see the sights of an old seaport.

You can see people doing and making things related to whaling. You can even climb aboard the famous *Charles W. Morgan*, the only wooden whaling ship left from the old whaling days. It set out on its first voyage in 1841 and sailed more miles than any other whaling ship. Today the ship is a whaling museum.

In recent years, people have become aware that whales have nearly disappeared from the Atlantic Ocean. The leaders of our government, as well as the leaders of several other countries, have decided to protect the whales. Now there is a law that prohibits whaling in the waters that surround our country.

Reading a Time Line Because time is often hard to measure, we frequently use **time lines** to help us keep track of time. A time line is a line that shows facts about events or happenings. Like a map, a time line has a scale. But the scale on a time line measures time, not distance from place to place.

A time line shows events in the order in which they happened. The time line on this page shows seven important events in the story of whaling. To read the time line, begin by looking at the earliest and latest events. What is the first event shown on the time line? What is the last event? What was the name of the first whaler that was built at Mystic, Connecticut?

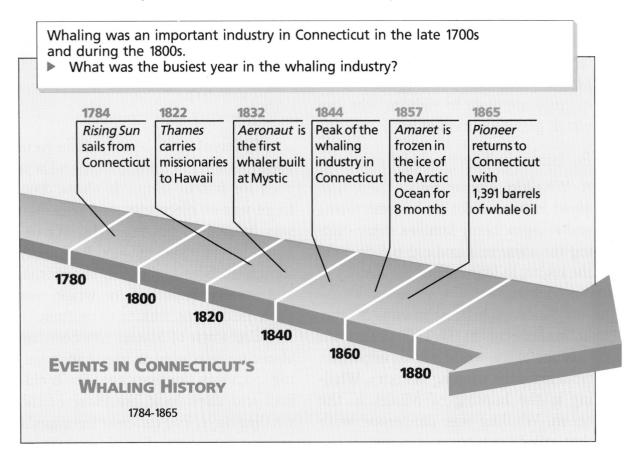

Whaling was an important industry in Connecticut in the late 1700s and during the 1800s.
▶ What was the busiest year in the whaling industry?

1784	1822	1832	1844	1857	1865
Rising Sun sails from Connecticut	*Thames* carries missionaries to Hawaii	*Aeronaut* is the first whaler built at Mystic	Peak of the whaling industry in Connecticut	*Amaret* is frozen in the ice of the Arctic Ocean for 8 months	*Pioneer* returns to Connecticut with 1,391 barrels of whale oil

1780   1800   1820   1840   1860   1880

EVENTS IN CONNECTICUT'S WHALING HISTORY

1784–1865

THINKING CRITICALLY

On a separate sheet of paper, answer the following questions in complete sentences.

1. How did the rocky land and short growing season in New England encourage the growth of industries like shipbuilding?
2. Why were some of the industries that were once important in New England replaced by other industries?
3. Why was New England a good place for high-tech industries to grow?
4. Why is Boston a large metropolitan area although many people in Massachusetts live in villages and towns?
5. Why might it be difficult to make just one poster inviting people to travel in the New England region?

SUMMARIZING THE CHAPTER

Copy this graphic organizer on a separate sheet of paper. Under each heading, write a word or phrase that belongs under the heading.

CHAPTER THEME

New England is a region in the northeastern part of the United States. It is known for its rocky coastline, gently rolling hills, rural villages, and large cities. Manufacturing is an important industry in the region.

Physical Features
1.
2.
3.

Farming
1.
2.
3.

Natural Resources
1.
2.
3.

Important Cities
1.
2.
3.

CHAPTER 4

THE MIDDLE ATLANTIC REGION

More people live in the Middle Atlantic region than in any other region in our country. Farm areas as well as large cities are in the region.

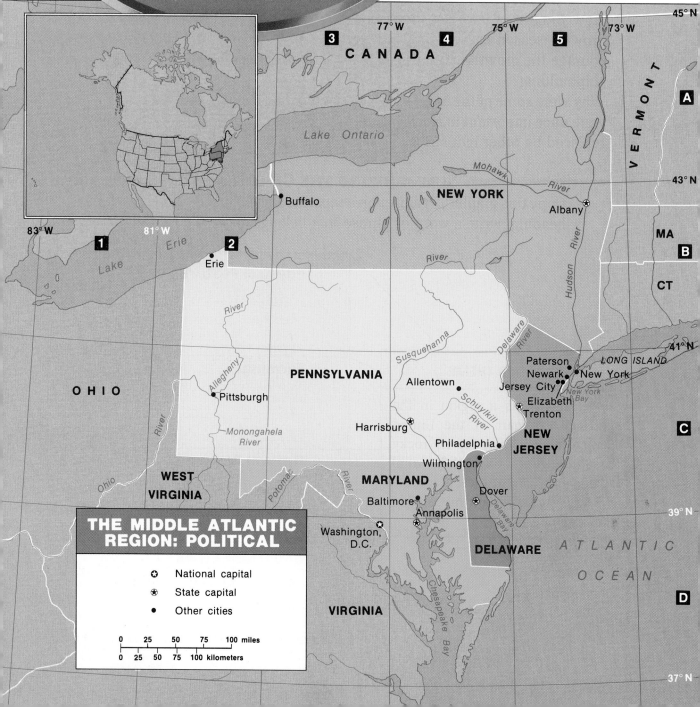

THE MIDDLE ATLANTIC REGION: POLITICAL

✪ National capital
✶ State capital
• Other cities

0   25   50   75   100 miles
0   25   50   75   100 kilometers

The Lands and Waters of the Middle Atlantic Region

THINK ABOUT WHAT YOU KNOW

What are some of the things that are special about your community or state? If you were to write a book about your community or state, what would you include?

STUDY THE VOCABULARY

wilderness   **barge**
canal   **tributary**

FOCUS YOUR READING

What are the main physical features of the Middle Atlantic region?

A. A Place of Great Variety

Imagine yourself swimming in the waters of a beautiful beach on a warm summer day. Think of yourself skiing down the slope of a high mountain on a cold December afternoon. Would you like to go camping where you could fish in a nearby stream and then hike along a winding trail?

Would you like to attend a major league baseball game or a professional football game? Or would you prefer to visit a museum? Perhaps you would like to walk along busy city streets and look up at skyscrapers.

You can do all of these things in the Middle Atlantic region. This part of our country has large cities, small villages, and **wilderness**, or wild area, with no homes or towns.

B. Five States and a District

Location The Middle Atlantic region is between the New England region and the Southeast region. The states in the Middle Atlantic region stretch along the Atlantic Ocean. They are New York, New Jersey, Pennsylvania, Delaware, and Maryland.

In addition to the five states in the Middle Atlantic region, there is a small section that is not a state. The section is called the District of Columbia and it is between the states of Maryland and Virginia. Washington, the capital of the United States, covers the entire District of Columbia.

CITY INDEX

Cities less than 100,000
Albany (NY) B-5
Annapolis (MD) D-4
Dover (DE) C-4
Harrisburg (PA) C-4
Trenton (NJ) C-5
Wilmington (DE) C-4

Cities 100,000 to 499,999
Allentown (PA) C-4
Buffalo (NY) B-3
Elizabeth (NJ) C-5
Erie (PA) B-2
Jersey City (NJ) C-5
Newark (NJ) C-5
Paterson (NJ) C-5

Pittsburgh (PA) C-2

Cities 500,000 to 999,999
Baltimore (MD) C-4
Washington, D.C. D-3

Cities 1,000,000 or more
New York (NY) C-5
Philadelphia (PA) C-4

The Middle Atlantic region has several large cities. Many of its large cities are in the eastern part of the region.
▶ Name the two largest cities in the Middle Atlantic region.

99

When Washington, D.C., was first made our nation's capital, the leaders of our country decided not to make it a part of a state. If they did, that state might have more power in our government than the other states. Read the time line at the bottom of this page to find when Washington, D.C., became the capital of the United States.

Boundaries Most of the boundaries of the Middle Atlantic region are bodies of water. The northwestern part of the region touches two of the Great Lakes. The map on page 9 shows that the Great Lakes are five large bodies of water along the border between the United States and Canada. The western part of the state of New York borders Lake Ontario and Lake Erie. The northwestern part of Pennsylvania borders Lake Erie.

The waters of the Great Lakes empty into the St. Lawrence River. As it flows into the Atlantic, the St. Lawrence forms a part of the northern border of the Middle Atlantic region.

The Middle Atlantic region includes many islands and bays along the Atlantic coast. Long Island, which is part of New York, belongs to the Middle Atlantic region. So does Chesapeake (ches uh PEEK) Bay. Long Island and Chesapeake Bay are easy to find on a map because they make large bulges in the Atlantic coastline.

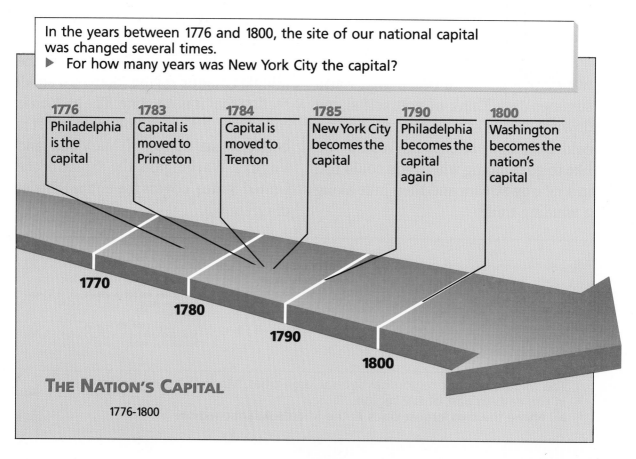

In the years between 1776 and 1800, the site of our national capital was changed several times.
► For how many years was New York City the capital?

1776	1783	1784	1785	1790	1800
Philadelphia is the capital	Capital is moved to Princeton	Capital is moved to Trenton	New York City becomes the capital	Philadelphia becomes the capital again	Washington becomes the nation's capital

1770

1780

1790

1800

THE NATION'S CAPITAL

1776-1800

Hiking is fun in the mountains of the Middle Atlantic region.
► Have you ever gone mountain climbing?

C. Mountains and Their Rivers

Three Mountains The Appalachian Mountains cover a large part of the Middle Atlantic region. In fact, the mountains cover so much of the region that three parts of the mountains have different names. The Allegheny (al uh-GAY nee) Mountains, the Catskill Mountains, and the Adirondack (ad uh-RAHN dak) Mountains are all part of the Appalachian Mountains.

The Allegheny Mountains are in Pennsylvania and western Maryland. The land here was once high and flat. It was divided into many jumbled mountains by rivers and streams that cut down into the earth's surface. Many wilderness areas are found in these mountains.

In New York State, the two main mountain ranges are the Adirondack Mountains and the Catskill Mountains. Find these mountains on the map on page 103.

In the Adironacks there are many tall mountain peaks. The highest of these is Mount Marcy, which is 5,344 feet (1,629 m) above sea level. That is more than 1 mile high.

Long ago, a famous American writer named Washington Irving described the Catskill Mountains in his book *Rip Van Winkle*. As you read his description, try to picture the Catskills in your mind.

Every change of season, every change of weather, indeed, every hour of the day, produces some change in the magical hues and shapes of these mountains. . . . When the weather is fair and settled, they are clothed in blue and purple, and print their bold outlines on the clear evening sky; but sometimes, when the rest of the land scape is cloudless, they will gather a hood of grey vapours about their summits, which, in the last rays of the setting sun, will glow and light up like a crown of glory.

Major Rivers The Hudson River is an important river in the Middle Atlantic region. The Hudson River is wide and deep enough that large ships can travel from the Atlantic Ocean along the river for nearly 150 miles (241 km).

In the 1820s a **canal** was built that connected the Hudson River with the Great Lakes. A canal is a waterway dug across land for ships or boats to go through. The canal was named the Erie Canal. It joined Albany, a city on the Hudson River, with Buffalo, a city on the shore of Lake Erie.

Large flat-bottomed boats called **barges** were used on the canal. Teams of horses or mules trudged along the shore and pulled the barges. Often at the end of a long day, the people who worked the barges would sing the lively song on page 104.

The Mohawk River is the largest **tributary**, or branch, of the Hudson River. Many years ago, people moved along these rivers to get to the western part of New York. The Hudson and the Mohawk rivers still provide a route for barges and boats to haul heavy loads between the two mountainous areas of the state.

The Delaware River begins in the southern part of the Catskill Mountains and winds its way along the eastern border of Pennsylvania. It moves through the Allegheny Mountains and empties into the Atlantic Ocean in Delaware Bay.

D. The Plains of the Middle Atlantic Region

Coastal Plain There are two plains in the Middle Atlantic region. They are the Atlantic Coastal Plain and the Lakes Plain.

In Chapter 3 you learned that the Atlantic Coastal Plain is a broad, flat area that is bordered by a large body of water called the Atlantic Ocean. The coastal plain is widest in the southern part of New Jersey. There it extends all across the state. The entire state of Delaware is in the Atlantic Coastal Plain. Parts of Pennsylvania and New York are on the Atlantic Coastal Plain.

Lakes Plain The Lake Plain is the land around the Great Lakes. The land in the Lake Plain is low and rolling. It has rich soil that is good for farming.

In the Middle Atlantic region, the Lakes Plain stretches along the shores of Lake Erie and Lake Ontario. Niagara Falls, the largest waterfall in North America, is between those two lakes. These falls are shown on page 111.

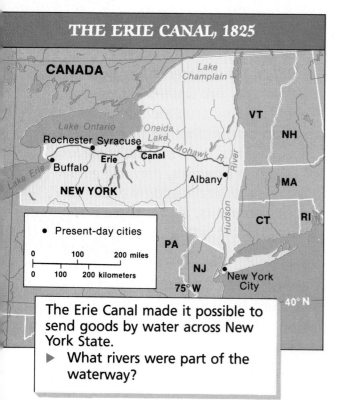

THE ERIE CANAL, 1825

CANADA

Lake Champlain

Lake Ontario

Rochester Syracuse Oneida Lake

Buffalo Erie Canal Mohawk R.

Lake Erie

NEW YORK

VT

NH

Albany

MA

Hudson River

CT RI

• Present-day cities

0   100   200 miles
0 100 200 kilometers

PA

NJ

New York City

75° W

40° N

The Erie Canal made it possible to send goods by water across New York State.
▶ What rivers were part of the waterway?

THE MIDDLE ATLANTIC REGION: PHYSICAL

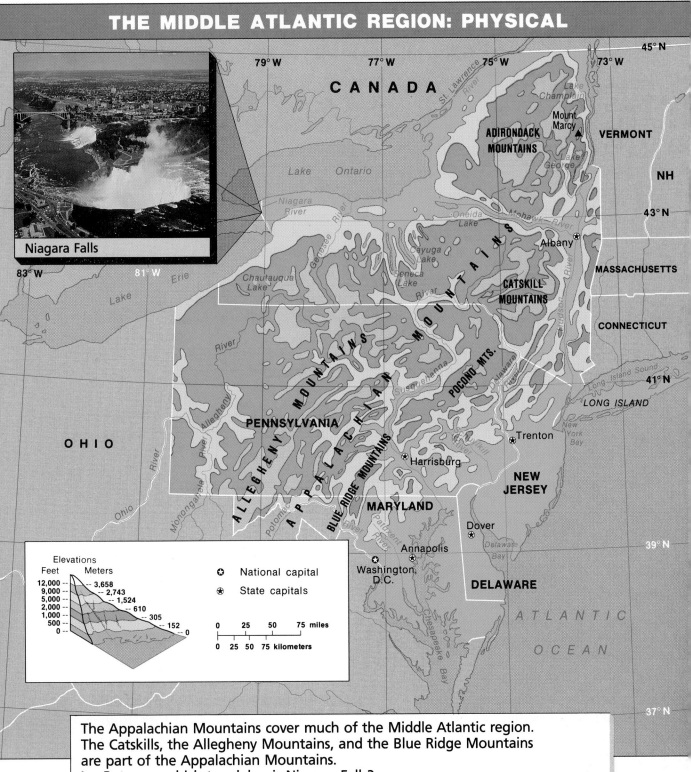

Niagara Falls

The Appalachian Mountains cover much of the Middle Atlantic region.
The Catskills, the Allegheny Mountains, and the Blue Ridge Mountains
are part of the Appalachian Mountains.
▶ Between which two lakes is Niagara Falls?

Erie Canal

American Folk Song

SOLO **Dm** **Gm** **A₇**

I got a ____ mule, her name is ____ Sal,

CHORUS **Dm**

Fif - teen ____ miles on the E - rie Ca - nal! ____

SOLO **Dm** **Gm** **A₇**

She's a good old ____ work - er and a good old ____ pal,

CHORUS **Dm**

Fif - teen ____ miles on the E - rie Ca - nal! ____

SOLO **F** **A₇**

We've hauled some barg - es in our ____ day,

Dm **A₇** **Dm**

Filled with lum - ber, coal, and ____ hay, And we know ev - 'ry

Gm **A₇** **Dm** **C₇**

inch of the way From Al - ba - ny ____ to ____ Buf - fa - lo. ____

Refrain

Low bridge, ev'rybody down,
Low bridge, 'cause we're coming to a town;

And you'll always know your neighbor,
You'll always know your pal,
If you ever navigated on the Erie Canal.

LESSON **1** REVIEW

THINK AND WRITE

A. What makes the Middle Atlantic region a special place?

B. Why is our nation's capital city not in one of the 50 states?

C. Why are the Hudson and Mohawk important rivers?

D. How can you tell that Delaware has flat and not mountainous land?

SKILLS CHECK

MAP SKILL

List the following cities on a separate sheet of paper: New York City, Buffalo, Philadelphia, Baltimore, Washington, D.C. Read the map on page 98 and name the bodies of water closest to each city.

Farming in the Middle Atlantic Region

THINK ABOUT WHAT YOU KNOW
Make a list of your favorite fruits and vegetables. Can you tell which are grown on trees and which are grown in the ground?

STUDY THE VOCABULARY

humidity	**fertile**
produce	**orchard**
truck farm	**vineyard**

FOCUS YOUR READING
How do the climate and location of the Middle Atlantic region encourage farming?

A. The Climate of the Middle Atlantic Region

Location   The Middle Atlantic region stretches more than 480 miles (772 km) from north to south. In the north, there are long, cold winters and short, cool summers. In the south, the winters are mild and the summers are usually hot.

There are other reasons besides northern and southern location for the differences in climate in the Middle Atlantic region. The mountain areas and the shore are usually cooler than other areas. Many city people spend their summer vacations in the mountains of New York and Pennsylvania. They also crowd the sandy beaches along the coast of New York, New Jersey, Delaware, and Maryland.

Humid climate   A fairly warm day can seem uncomfortable if the **humidity** is high. Humidity is the amount of moisture in the air. The air over the Middle Atlantic region, like the air over most of the eastern part of the United States, is often humid. The high humidity makes many people feel hot and sticky even when the temperature is moderate. In summer, people in New York City and other places often complain about the weather. They say, "It's not the heat, it's the humidity."

Winter storms can leave many inches of snow on the ground.
► What are some of the sports and games that can be played in the snow?

B. Farming in the Middle Atlantic Region

Truck Farms There is a special section in the supermarket in which you can find fresh fruits and vegetables, called **produce**. These fruits and vegetables must get from the farm to the store while they are still fresh.

Many fruits and vegetables are grown on farms close to cities where they can be sold. Such farms are called **truck farms** because the produce can be shipped quickly to market by trucks.

The Atlantic Coastal Plain is in a perfect location for truck farms. Millions of people live in the large cities of the Middle Atlantic region. Produce grown in the **fertile**, or rich, soil of the region can be rushed from the farms to the cities every day.

New York, New Jersey, and the Delmarva Peninsula contain hundreds of truck farms. The name *Delmarva* is formed by combining an abbreviated, or short, form of three states—*Del*aware, *Mary*land, and *Vir*ginia.

Truck farms in New York grow huge amounts of strawberries, beans, cauliflower, celery, and peas. In New Jersey, tomatoes, corn, beans, and onions are important crops. The leading vegetable crops grown on truck farms in the Delmarva Peninsula include lima beans, peas, cucumbers, potatoes, and sweet potatoes.

C. Other Kinds of Farms

Poultry Farms The Delmarva Peninsula is famous for its poultry farms. Poultry is the name for chickens, turkeys, and ducks that are raised by farmers. There is a major market for chickens and eggs in the Middle Atlantic region. Chickens are raised by the thousands in long flat buildings called poultry houses or chicken houses.

There are many different kinds of farms in this region.
▶ Which picture shows produce from a truck farm?

Dairy Farms Dairy farming is another kind of farming in the Middle Atlantic region. People in the cities of the Middle Atlantic region use a lot of fresh milk every day. Many of the dairy farms are within an easy drive to the large city markets. This was especially important before there were refrigerated trucks for keeping milk fresh. The Middle Atlantic dairy farms also produce great amounts of butter and cheese.

Fruit-growing Regions Apples, peaches, pears, and cherries are the chief fruits grown in western Pennsylvania and New York. The fruit trees are set out in rows in **orchards**. An orchard is a special field used only for growing fruit trees. When the fruit in a cherry orchard or apple orchard is ripening, the smell of the sweet, ripe fruit fills the air in the surrounding area.

Vineyards In the western part of New York state, there are five narrow lakes that extend like long fingers from north to south. The lakes are called the Finger Lakes. All across the gently sloping hillsides above the lakes are

Fruit is picked from the trees in this orchard in late summer or early fall.
▶ Why is a ladder being used to harvest apples?

hundreds of grape **vineyards** (VIHN-yurdz). A vineyard is a place where grapes are grown.

Every fall fresh grapes from vineyards in the Finger Lakes are shipped to supermarkets. Other grapes are made into jam and jelly, or crushed for grape juice. The area is also famous for the wine that is made from its grapes.

LESSON **2** *REVIEW*

THINK AND WRITE

A. How would you describe the climate of the Middle Atlantic region?
B. Why are truck farms so important in the Middle Atlantic region?
C. What other kinds of farms are in the Middle Atlantic region?

SKILLS CHECK

WRITING SKILL
Imagine that you are a truck farmer in the Middle Atlantic region. You have been asked to write a story about your farm for a farm magazine. In your story describe where your farm is located, what crops you grow, and how your crops are sent to market.

Earning a Living in the Middle Atlantic Region

THINK ABOUT WHAT YOU KNOW

What kind of work would you like to do when you grow up? Could you do that work where you now live?

STUDY THE VOCABULARY

dock	tourism
import	tourist
export	

FOCUS YOUR READING

How do people use the land and natural resources of the Middle Atlantic region to earn a living?

A. Minerals and Mining of the Middle Atlantic Region

Important Minerals A great variety of useful minerals are found in the Middle Atlantic region. Most of these minerals are tucked away in the hills and valleys of mountain ranges.

New York State has several valuable minerals. There are large quantities of zinc, a mineral that is used to help make other metals hard and sturdy. Mining of lead is also important in New York. Lead is used in making products such as paint and batteries.

Large amounts of salt are found near central New York. You probably think of salt as a seasoning for food. Salt is also used to make chemicals in detergents and bleaches like those used in your home. In the parts of the Middle Atlantic region where winters are cold and icy, salt is often spread on snowy streets and highways. The salt melts snow and ice.

Coal Mining Most of the people in the region who make their living in mining work in the coal mines of Pennsylvania. Coal is one of the most common natural resources in the world. It has been found on every continent, including Antarctica.

Mining coal was once very risky work. Miners dug tunnels and climbed down into the earth to find coal. There was always a chance that a tunnel might cave in. Poison gases could seep into a mine.

These miners work below the surface of the earth.
► What means do they use to get to their work?

Steel is important because it is used to make many things.
▶ What things can you name that are made of steel?

Miners used to take canaries into the mines to help check for poison gases. If there was gas, the small birds would become sleepy and fall from their perches. The miners would then get out of that section of the mine quickly. Today, miners use accurate instruments instead of canaries to detect poison gases in a mine.

B. The Iron and Steel Industry

What is Pennsylvania's coal used for? A good deal of it is used as fuel to melt the iron ore that is made into steel. Steel is used to make things such as automobiles, ships, tools, and many household items.

Many older steel mills are located near Pittsburgh, Pennsylvania, and Buffalo, New York. The bigger and newer steel mills are located on rivers near the Atlantic Ocean. Baltimore, Maryland, and Philadelphia, Pennsylvania, are important steel centers. These mills use iron ore that is brought by ships from foreign countries, such as Venezuela and Brazil in South America.

C. Earning a Living from the Sea

Fishing The bays and harbors along the coast of the Middle Atlantic region make good feeding grounds for fish and for shellfish such as oysters and crabs. Chesapeake Bay is famous for crabs. They are cooked in dozens of different ways in restaurants that serve crabs as their special food.

109

Shipping Many people of the Middle Atlantic region make a living in the shipping industry. Some work on the ships or on the **docks** where goods are loaded or unloaded. Others work in the offices of large shipping companies.

Baltimore was once famous for shipbuilding and ship repair. Its location at the northern tip of Chesapeake Bay made it a safe harbor for ships. Today, Baltimore's shipyards are not nearly as busy as they once were.

Huge ships bringing oil and other products from foreign countries often dock at Atlantic coast port cities, such as New York City and Wilmington, Delaware. Oil is unloaded from many of the ships and held in huge tanks.

The ports and harbors of the Atlantic coast are busy as ships and barges of all kinds enter and leave. Some ships carry bulky goods, such as timber and coal, from Atlantic port cities to other cities in the United States. Many other ships arrive with **imports**, which are goods brought into a country from another country. Our country imports many finished products, such as clothing, automobiles, and electronic equipment.

Other vessels leave the Atlantic port cities with **exports**, which are goods sent to another country for sale there. Our country exports many different kinds of goods, such as grain, coal, airplanes, and clothing.

Very large ships bring goods from all over the world.
► What clues can you see that would help you decide that this is a large ship?

D. Service Industries of the Middle Atlantic Region

In Chapter 1 you read about service workers, such as veterinarians, teachers, and police officers. These people work in service industries. A major service industry of the Middle Atlantic region is **tourism**. Tourism is the selling of goods and services to **tourists**, or people who travel especially for pleasure.

The Middle Atlantic region has one of the most famous tourist attractions on the continent of North America. Every year more than 2 million people visit Niagara Falls, which are between Canada and western New York not far from Buffalo. Sightseeing boats and helicopters take tourists on trips around the falls. At night, colored searchlights illuminate the falls.

Delaware is a state that is small in area, but it has many attractions for tourists. Beaches line the shore of the Delaware River and Delaware Bay. The state parks and forests provide still more recreational areas.

Many people come each year to see the mighty Niagara Falls.
► Would you enjoy seeing the Falls from a boat?

New Jersey also has a large number of vacation spots on its coast. Tourists visit the state's wide, sandy beaches during the summer months. Cape May, on the southern tip of New Jersey, is an old beach resort with many large old wooden hotels and cottages.

LESSON **3** *REVIEW*

THINK AND WRITE

A. Why is the Middle Atlantic region an important mineral region?
B. Why are Baltimore, Maryland, and Philadelphia, Pennsylvania, important steel centers today?
C. What makes fishing an important industry in the Middle Atlantic region?

D. Why is tourism important in the Middle Atlantic region?

SKILLS CHECK

MAP SKILL
Use the scale on the map on page 98 to find the distance between the following pairs of cities: Albany, New York, and Baltimore, Maryland; Pittsburgh, Pennsylvania, and Washington, D.C.

People and Cities of the Middle Atlantic Region

THINK ABOUT WHAT YOU KNOW

Where would you prefer to live, in a rural area, a suburb, or a large city?

STUDY THE VOCABULARY

census	legislative
population density	executive
megalopolis	judicial
line graph	monument

FOCUS YOUR READING

How might the cities of the Middle Atlantic region be described?

A. The United States Census

In those days an edict [law] was issued by the Emperor Augustus that a census of the whole world should be taken. It was the first census, taken when Quirinius (kwih RIH nee us) was governor of Syria.

So everyone went to his own town to register. And Joseph went up from Galilee . . . to the city of David called Bethlehem . . . to register with Mary, who was [his wife] and soon to become a mother.

What you have just read is recorded in the Christian Bible. It tells about a Roman emperor, or ruler, who ordered a **census**. A census is a government count of the people living in a certain area. Why do you think a government would want to know the number of people in an area or a country?

The United States government takes a census every decade. A decade is ten years. The last United States census was taken in 1990. That census tells us how many people live in the entire United States and how many live in each of the 50 states. The census also tells how many people live in cities, towns, villages, and other communities.

B. What Population Density Measures

The 1990 census reported that parts of the Middle Atlantic region are very crowded. We can measure how crowded a place is by finding out its **population density**. Population density is the number of people living within a certain area. Cities are usually crowded places. They have a high population density. Rural communities are less crowded. They have a lower population density.

We find the population density of a place by dividing the total number of people who live in an area by the land area of the place. Let's use a simple example. If you asked four people to sit in a floor space of 16 square feet, each person would have 4 square feet of space. If you asked 8 people to sit in that space, how many square feet of space would each person have?

Now let's see how population density works when we think of a city. Trenton, the capital city of New Jersey, is about 7 square miles in area. It has a population density of about 13,000 people per square mile.

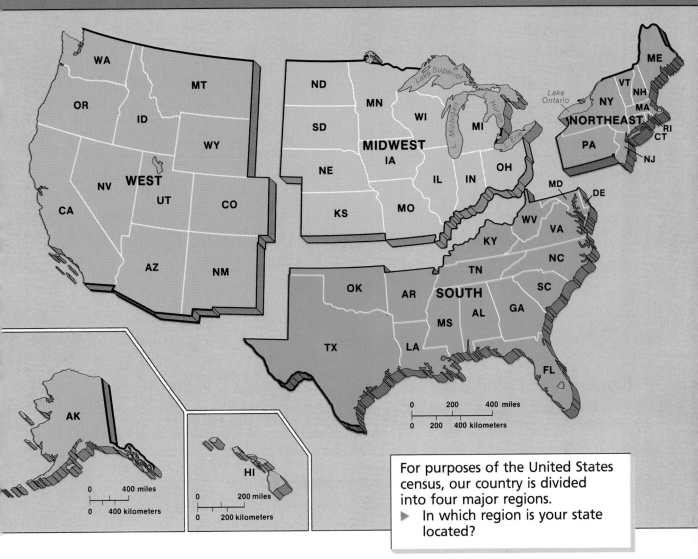

WA
MT
ND
MN
ME
OR
ID
SD
WI
VT
NH
NY
MA
WY
MIDWEST
IA
MI
NORTHEAST
RI
CT
NV
WEST
NE
PA
NJ
CA
UT
CO
IL
IN
OH
MD
DE
KS
MO
WV
VA
AZ
NM
WV
KY
NC
OK
AR
SOUTH
TN
SC
MS
AL
GA
TX
LA
FL

Lake Superior
Lake Michigan
Lake Huron
Lake Erie
Lake Ontario

AK

0   400 miles
0   400 kilometers

HI

0   200 miles
0   200 kilometers

0   200   400 miles
0   200   400 kilometers

For purposes of the United States census, our country is divided into four major regions.
▶ In which region is your state located?

Wilmington, the largest city in Delaware, is also about 7 square miles in area. Its population density is about 7,000 people per square mile. Let's compare the population density of Wilmington with that of Trenton. Seven thousand is almost one half of 13,000, isn't it? That means Trenton, New Jersey, is about twice as crowded a city as Wilmington, Delaware.

C. A Region of Large Cities

There are many large cities and hundreds of smaller cities and towns in the Middle Atlantic region. If you were to go by train from Washington, D.C., to Boston, Massachusetts, you would travel through an almost unbroken line of cities, towns, and suburbs. You would see farmlands from time to time. But most often it would be hard to tell

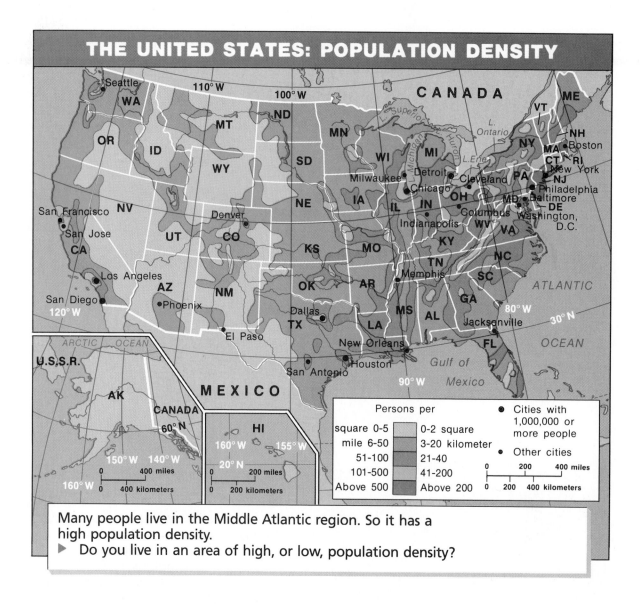

THE UNITED STATES: POPULATION DENSITY

Persons per	
square 0-5	0-2 square
mile 6-50	3-20 kilometer
51-100	21-40
101-500	41-200
Above 500	Above 200

● Cities with 1,000,000 or more people

● Other cities

Many people live in the Middle Atlantic region. So it has a high population density.
▶ Do you live in an area of high, or low, population density?

where one city ends and another begins. The entire area seems to be a single huge city. For this reason, it is called a **megalopolis** (meg uh LAHP uh lihs).

The megalopolis of the Atlantic Coastal Plain is the largest megalopolis in the United States. It extends through both the New England and the Middle Atlantic regions. Boston, New York, Philadelphia, Wilmington, Baltimore, and Washington, D.C., and their surrounding suburbs are part of this megalopolis. Find these cities on the map at the top of this page.

D. Two Well-known Cities in the Middle Atlantic Region

A City of Famous Streets New York is truly a giant of a city. More people live in New York City than in any other city in the United States. It has a population of about 8 million people. Another 9 million people live in the surrounding suburbs. There are many fascinating things to see and do in New York City.

There are thousands of stores in this huge city. Stores along Fifth Avenue are a shopper's dream come true. Large clothing stores, bookshops, video stores, and flower shops are just some of the stores on Fifth Avenue.

Madison Avenue is a street in New York City that is sometimes called the advertising capital of the world. Thousands of people work in offices on Madison Avenue. They make television commercials and write advertisements for newspapers and magazines.

The Thanksgiving Day parade in New York City is a big event.
▶ Have you ever been to or taken part in a parade?

One of the most famous streets in the world is Wall Street. This is a street where many international banks have their offices. More banks have offices in New York City than in any other city in the world.

New York City is also a major cultural center. Broadway is a street that is famous for its theatres where people enjoy plays and musicals. The city has many museums and libraries as well.

A Port City Philadelphia is the most populated city in Pennsylvania and the fifth most populated city in the United States. It is one of the busiest ports and manufacturing centers in the Middle Atlantic region.

Look at the map on page 98. Find Philadelphia where the Delaware River meets the Schuylkill (SKOOL kihl) River. Oceangoing ships travel from the Atlantic Ocean into Delaware Bay. From there they move through deep channels in the Delaware River until they reach the busy docks of Philadelphia.

Philadelphia is well known for its lovely old buildings and tree-shaded streets. On page 116 there is a passage about a house that was built in 1772 in Philadelphia. When the house was built, Philadelphia was the largest city in the American colonies.

Philadelphia is also a modern city with tall buildings and busy streets. And like other important Middle Atlantic cities, its airports, railroad stations, and highways make it a major transportation center as well.

From:

The House on Spruce Street

By: John L. Loeper
Setting: Philadelphia, Pennsylvania

To learn about old houses can be fun. Below are two selections from *The House on Spruce Street*. In the first selection, you can read about a visit to the house on Spruce Street just before the Morton family moved in. The second selection tells you a little more about their home and their life there.

The Morton children, Hannah and Jacob, climbed the wooden stairs to the top floor. The attic rooms would be their bedrooms.

"Look," Jacob shouted to his sister. "My room has a secret staircase!" He opened a narrow door revealing six tiny steps leading to a trapdoor in the roof.

"Don't be silly," Hannah chided. "That's so the chimney sweep can do his work when it's needed."

Then Jacob ran to the dormer window and looked out across the rooftops. "Look," he shouted. "You can see the river and the ships."

The Morton family moved into the house on Spruce Street. A big walnut chest of drawers was placed in the front room. Ladderback chairs were placed around a large pine dining table and pieces of English carpet were laid on the floors. The upstairs bedrooms contained rope beds (a network of ropes strung through the wooden frames supported straw mattresses). And the following spring Mistress Morton and the children planted flowers and herbs in the garden.

The Mortons were . . . happy in their home and lived there for twenty-eight years. While there, they heard the bell in the State House announce the signing of the Declaration of Independence. They watched British troops march up Second Street during the occupation of the city. They lived to hail George Washington as the first President of the United States. These were historic years.

Written and illustrated by John L. Loeper

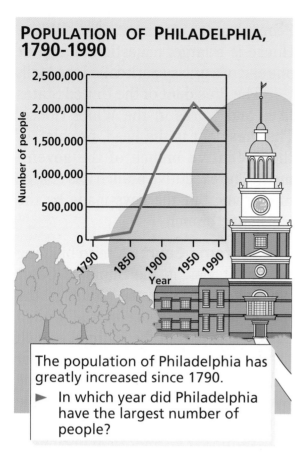

POPULATION OF PHILADELPHIA, 1790-1990

The population of Philadelphia has greatly increased since 1790.

► In which year did Philadelphia have the largest number of people?

Reading a Line Graph A drawing that shows changes over a period of time is called a **line graph**. The line graph on this page shows that fewer people were living in Philadelphia in 1790 than in 1990. The population for each year on the graph is shown by a dot. The change in population is shown by the line that connects the dots.

To get the most information from a graph, study all the parts. The title tells you what the graph is about. At the bottom of the graph, you see the years 1790, 1850, and so on. The numbers along the left side of the graph stand for the number of people in Philadelphia.

Read the graph to find the population of Philadelphia in 1950. To do that, find the year 1950 at the bottom of the graph. Place a finger on that date. Move your finger toward the top of the graph. Stop when you reach a dot. Then move your finger straight across to the left side of the graph. You can see that the population of Philadelphia in 1950 was slightly more than 2 million.

E. A Trip to Washington, D. C.

Congress Let's imagine that we are going to take a tour of Washington, D.C. We could begin our tour of the city at the Capitol building, where Congress meets. The first thing that you might notice inside the Capitol is a huge dome in the central section of the building. The dome separates the Capitol into two wings.

Congress, which meets in this building, is an important part of our government.
► What is this building called?

117

One wing of the Capitol building is where the Senate meets. The other wing is where the House of Representatives meets. The Senate and the House of Representatives are the two houses, or parts, of Congress. Congress is the **legislative** branch, or part, of the government. It makes the laws for all the people in the United States.

The Senate has 100 members who are called senators. There are 2 senators for each of the 50 states. Members of the House of Representatives are called representatives. The number of representatives depends on the state's population. States with small populations have fewer representatives than states with large populations. The census that we have every ten years, determines the number of representative a state has.

The White House   After leaving the Capitol building, we walk along a wide, busy street called Pennsylvania Avenue. The White House is located on Pennsylvania Avenue. The White House is a large, majestic building at one end of a grassy park called the Mall.

The President of the United States lives and works in the White House. The President is the head, or chief, of the **executive** branch of the government. The executive branch has charge of carrying out the laws made by the legislative branch.

The Supreme Court   A third building we might visit is the Supreme Court building. The Supreme Court is the most important court in the United States. It is part of the **judicial** branch of our government. The nine justices, or judges, of the Supreme Court decide whether a law is fair according to the Constitution of the United States. The Constitution is an important document that tells the government what it can and cannot do.

Our nation's President lives and works in the White House.
▶ Which of the people below is our President?

Visitors to the Lincoln Memorial will see this statue.
▶ Are there monuments in your town?

Other Places There are many beautiful **monuments** in Washington, D.C. A monument is a building, tower, or sculpture built in memory of a person or an event. One of the most beautiful monuments is the Washington Monument. The monument is a memorial to George Washington, the first President of the United States. In front of the monument is a long narrow pool.

At the opposite end of the pool is the Lincoln Memorial. It was built to honor Abraham Lincoln, one of our greatest Presidents. Near these two buildings is another beautiful monument—the Jefferson Memorial. This structure contains a huge statue of Thomas Jefferson, the third President of the United States. People from all over the United States and from other countries visit these monuments when they visit our nation's capital.

LESSON 4 REVIEW

THINK AND WRITE
A. Why is it important to take a census?
B. Why do most cities have a high population density?
C. Why is the city area from Boston, Massachusetts, to Washington, D. C., often called a megalopolis?
D. Why is New York City such an important city?

E. In what ways are the three branches of our government different?

SKILLS CHECK

THINKING SKILL
Choose two photographs in this chapter that show different parts of the Middle Atlantic region. Think of two reasons for the difference.

STATES OF THE MIDDLE ATLANTIC REGION

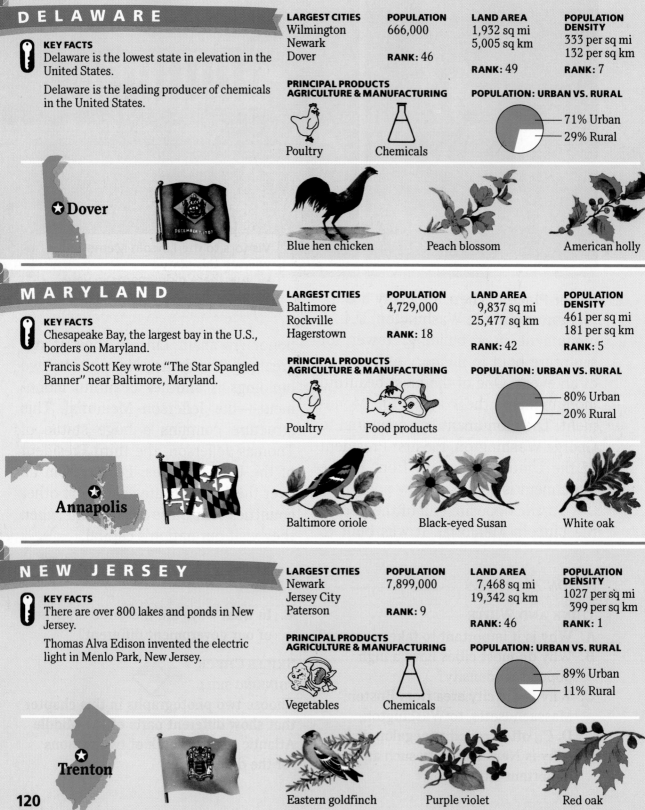

DELAWARE

KEY FACTS

Delaware is the lowest state in elevation in the United States.

Delaware is the leading producer of chemicals in the United States.

LARGEST CITIES
Wilmington
Newark
Dover

POPULATION
666,000

RANK: 46

LAND AREA
1,932 sq mi
5,005 sq km

RANK: 49

POPULATION DENSITY
333 per sq mi
132 per sq km

RANK: 7

PRINCIPAL PRODUCTS AGRICULTURE & MANUFACTURING

Poultry

Chemicals

POPULATION: URBAN VS. RURAL

71% Urban
29% Rural

★ Dover

DECEMBER 7, 1787

Blue hen chicken

Peach blossom

American holly

MARYLAND

KEY FACTS

Chesapeake Bay, the largest bay in the U.S., borders on Maryland.

Francis Scott Key wrote "The Star Spangled Banner" near Baltimore, Maryland.

LARGEST CITIES
Baltimore
Rockville
Hagerstown

POPULATION
4,729,000

RANK: 18

LAND AREA
9,837 sq mi
25,477 sq km

RANK: 42

POPULATION DENSITY
461 per sq mi
181 per sq km

RANK: 5

PRINCIPAL PRODUCTS AGRICULTURE & MANUFACTURING

Poultry

Food products

POPULATION: URBAN VS. RURAL

80% Urban
20% Rural

★ Annapolis

Baltimore oriole

Black-eyed Susan

White oak

NEW JERSEY

KEY FACTS

There are over 800 lakes and ponds in New Jersey.

Thomas Alva Edison invented the electric light in Menlo Park, New Jersey.

LARGEST CITIES
Newark
Jersey City
Paterson

POPULATION
7,899,000

RANK: 9

LAND AREA
7,468 sq mi
19,342 sq km

RANK: 46

POPULATION DENSITY
1027 per sq mi
399 per sq km

RANK: 1

PRINCIPAL PRODUCTS AGRICULTURE & MANUFACTURING

Vegetables

Chemicals

POPULATION: URBAN VS. RURAL

89% Urban
11% Rural

★ Trenton

120

Eastern goldfinch

Purple violet

Red oak

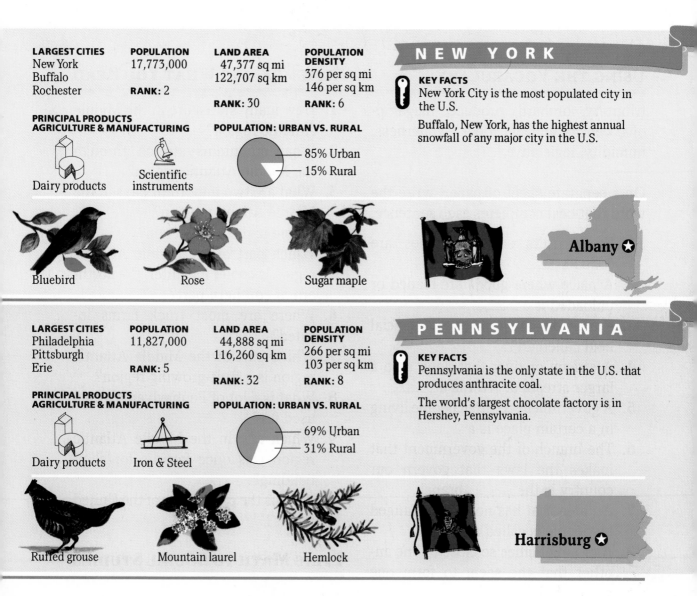

LARGEST CITIES
New York
Buffalo
Rochester

POPULATION
17,773,000

RANK: 2

LAND AREA
47,377 sq mi
122,707 sq km

RANK: 30

POPULATION DENSITY
376 per sq mi
146 per sq km

RANK: 6

KEY FACTS
New York City is the most populated city in the U.S.

Buffalo, New York, has the highest annual snowfall of any major city in the U.S.

PRINCIPAL PRODUCTS
AGRICULTURE & MANUFACTURING

Dairy products

Scientific instruments

POPULATION: URBAN VS. RURAL
85% Urban
15% Rural

Bluebird

Rose

Sugar maple

Albany ⭐

LARGEST CITIES
Philadelphia
Pittsburgh
Erie

POPULATION
11,827,000

RANK: 5

LAND AREA
44,888 sq mi
116,260 sq km

RANK: 32

POPULATION DENSITY
266 per sq mi
103 per sq km

RANK: 8

KEY FACTS
Pennsylvania is the only state in the U.S. that produces anthracite coal.

The world's largest chocolate factory is in Hershey, Pennsylvania.

PRINCIPAL PRODUCTS
AGRICULTURE & MANUFACTURING

Dairy products

Iron & Steel

POPULATION: URBAN VS. RURAL
69% Urban
31% Rural

Ruffed grouse

Mountain laurel

Hemlock

Harrisburg ⭐

121

USING THE VOCABULARY

tributary, orchard, produce, megalopolis, census, judicial, dock, wilderness, humidity, legislative

On a separate sheet of paper, write the word that best completes each sentence.

1. Fresh fruits and vegetables are called _____.
2. A place where goods are loaded or unloaded is a _____.
3. Fruit trees are grown in a special field called an _____.
4. A stream or river that flows into a larger stream or river is a _____.
5. A government count of people living in a certain place is a _____.
6. The branch of the government that makes the laws that govern our country is the _____ branch.
7. An area that has not been changed by people is called a _____.
8. A group of cities so close to one another that the seem to form one giant city is a _____.
9. The branch of the government that decides if a law has been broken is the _____ branch.
10. When the air is very damp, we say there is high _____.

REMEMBERING WHAT YOU READ

1. How many states are in the Middle Atlantic region?
2. What mountains stretch through the Middle Atlantic region?
3. What are two important bays in the Middle Atlantic region?
4. Where is the Lakes Plain?
5. Which part of the Middle Atlantic region is cooler in winter, the northern or southern part?
6. Where are most truck farms located?
7. Which part of the Middle Atlantic region is a fruit-growing region?
8. What is a lot of Pennsylvania's coal used for?
9. Which city in the Middle Atlantic region was once famous for shipbuilding?
10. What is the capital city of the United States?

TYING MATH TO SOCIAL STUDIES

Use the information below to draw a line graph showing the average monthly temperature in Washington, D.C., for the first six months of the year. Remember to give your graph a title.

January	35°F	April	54°F
February	36°F	May	65°F
March	44°F	June	73°F

Old and New in the Southeast

THINK ABOUT WHAT YOU KNOW
Have you ever been in a rainstorm, windstorm or snowstorm? What was it like and how did you feel?

STUDY THE VOCABULARY
hurricane   inland

FOCUS YOUR READING
What are the main physical features of the Southeast?

A. Rebuilding Communities After Hurricane Hugo

The sounds of hammers and saws rang out in the morning air. Trucks carried supplies through the streets. People along the coast of South Carolina were rebuilding their communities.

Only a few days before, the scene had been quite different. At that time a storm was ripping through the area, terrifying people and causing great damage. Now families were trying to save some things from the past.

From June to November, but most often in September, the Southeast region is often hit by heavy winds and rains. Some of these storms are called **hurricanes**. A hurricane has winds of over 75 miles (117 km) per hour and very heavy rainfall. Such a storm can cause serious damage to communities along the coast. Seldom do hurricanes remain strong as they move **inland**, or over land away from an ocean. But floods from their heavy rains can cause damage far from the sea.

This storm, which was called Hurricane Hugo, struck in 1989. One of the strongest hurricanes to hit the Southeast in many years, it pulled huge trees out of the ground. It picked up cars and houses and carried them half a block or more. It swept boats onto the land.

As people hurried to repair their communities after Hurricane Hugo passed, they were thankful that there were few injuries and few deaths. People living along the coast had been

CITY INDEX

Cities less than 100,000		Cities			
Biloxi (MS)	C-2	Baton Rouge (LA)	C-2	Raleigh (NC)	B-5
Charleston (SC)	C-5	Birmingham (AL)	C-3	Richmond (VA)	B-5
Charleston (WV)	A-4	Charlotte (NC)	B-4	Tallahassee (FL)	C-3
Columbia (SC)	C-4	Columbus (GA)	C-3		
Fort Smith (AK)	B-1	Jackson (MS)	C-2	Cities 500,000 to 999,999	
Frankfort (KY)	A-3	Little Rock (AK)	B-1	Jacksonville (FL)	C-4
High Point (NC)	B-4	Louisville (KY)	A-3	Memphis (TN)	B-2
Huntington (WV)	A-4	Miami (FL)	E-4	New Orleans (LA)	C-2
		Mobile (AL)	C-2		
Cities 100,000 to 499,999		Montgomery (AL)	C-3	Cities 1,000,000 or more	
Atlanta (GA)	C-3	Nashville (TN)	B-3	None	
		Norfolk (VA)	B-5		

Virginia, North Carolina, and Florida are three states in the Southeast region that have several large cities.
▶ In which states are the three largest cities in the Southeast region?

warned that Hugo was approaching. They had packed up some of their belongings and taken shelter inland until the storm passed.

People were also thankful that some of the old buildings were still standing. In the coastal city of Charleston, South Carolina, many of the beautiful old mansions are historic homes built in the 1700s and 1800s. They are strong and sturdy, and so they have survived many hurricanes. They retell the proud history of the Southeast.

B. States of the Southeast

Coastal States South Carolina and seven other states of the Southeast have ocean coastlines. The states of Virginia, North Carolina, Georgia, and Florida all border the Atlantic Ocean.

From the map on page 124, you can see that the west coast of Florida borders the Gulf of Mexico. Alabama, Mississippi, and Louisiana also have a coast on the Gulf of Mexico.

Inland States Four states of the Southeast do not have coastlines. They are inland states, but they have important rivers that link them to the Atlantic Ocean. The states are West Virginia, Kentucky, Tennessee, and Arkansas. Find them on the map on page 124.

A Long Coastline Florida is the easiest southeastern state to find on a map. It stretches far out into the Atlantic

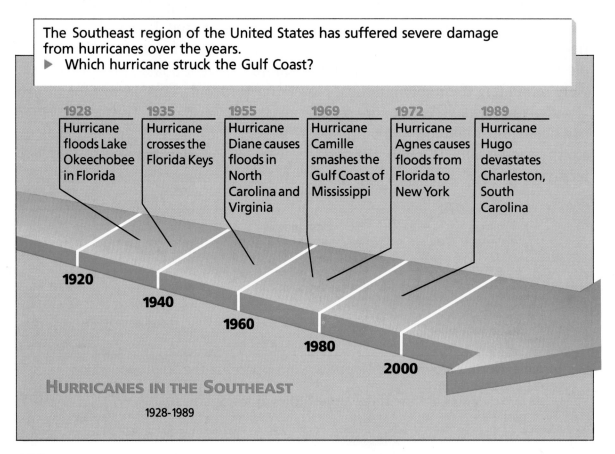

The Southeast region of the United States has suffered severe damage from hurricanes over the years.
▶ Which hurricane struck the Gulf Coast?

1928	1935	1955	1969	1972	1989
Hurricane floods Lake Okeechobee in Florida	Hurricane crosses the Florida Keys	Hurricane Diane causes floods in North Carolina and Virginia	Hurricane Camille smashes the Gulf Coast of Mississippi	Hurricane Agnes causes floods from Florida to New York	Hurricane Hugo devastates Charleston, South Carolina

1920
1940
1960
1980
2000

HURRICANES IN THE SOUTHEAST
1928-1989

The Florida Keys stretch like long fingers from the tip of Florida.
▶ Why, do you think, do many people like to visit the Florida Keys?

Ocean. It has the longest coastline of any state in the Southeast. A string of islands extends from the tip of Florida into the Gulf of Mexico. Bridges connect the islands. This group of islands is called the Florida Keys.

C. Mountains and Plains of the Southeast Region

The Coastal Plain   The Southeast has three main landforms. They are the Atlantic Coastal Plain, the Appalachian Mountains, and the Piedmont (PEED-mahnt) Plateau.

The Atlantic Coastal Plain extends all along the Atlantic coast. New England, the Middle Atlantic region, and the Southeast all share the Atlantic Coastal Plain. This flat, low plain stretches south to Florida and then turns westward along the coasts of Alabama, Mississippi, and Louisiana. In these three states, the plain is called the Gulf Coastal Plain because it borders the Gulf of Mexico.

The Appalachian Mountains   The second major landform of the Southeast is the Appalachian Mountains. This mountain range extends into the Southeast from the Middle Atlantic and New England regions. Do you remember the names of some sections of the Appalachians in the New England and the Middle Atlantic regions?

The Southeast has a part of the Appalachians called the Blue Ridge Mountains. Another section is called the Great Smoky Mountains. The highest peak in the Appalachian Mountains is in North Carolina's Blue Ridge Mountains. Mount Mitchell is 6,684 feet (2,037 m) high.

The Piedmont   The third major landform of the Southeast region is the Piedmont. *Piedmont* is a French word that means "foot of the mountain." The Piedmont lies between the Atlantic Coastal Plain and the Appalachian Mountains. If you stood in this belt of rolling hills, you might be able to look down on the coastal plain and up to the Appalachian Mountains.

127

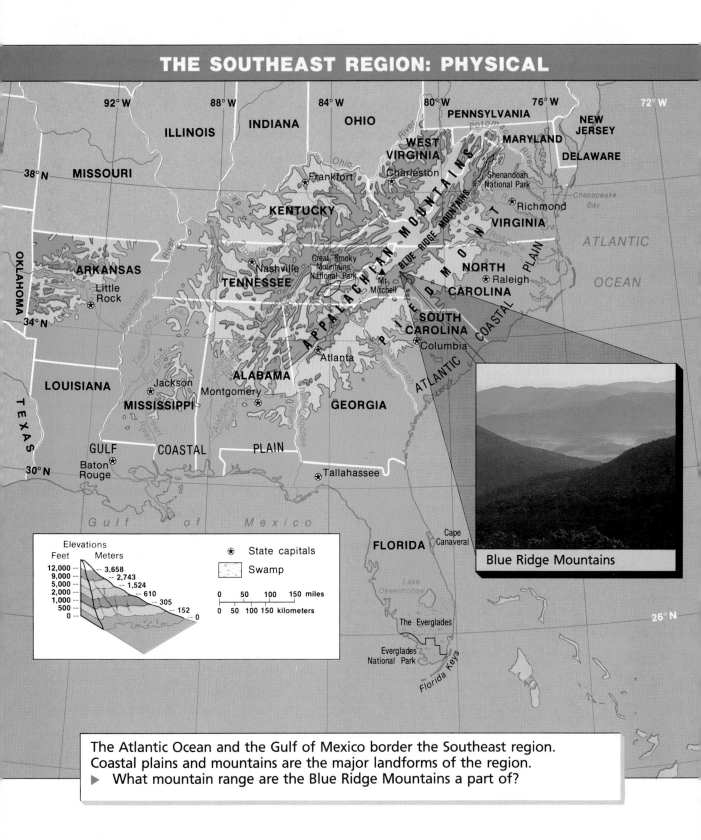

THE SOUTHEAST REGION: PHYSICAL

92° W · 88° W · 84° W · 80° W · 76° W · 72° W

ILLINOIS · INDIANA · OHIO · PENNSYLVANIA · NEW JERSEY

MISSOURI · WEST VIRGINIA · MARYLAND · DELAWARE

38° N

Charleston

Frankfort

Shenandoah National Park

Chesapeake Bay

KENTUCKY · Richmond · VIRGINIA

ATLANTIC OCEAN

ARKANSAS

Nashville

Great Smoky Mountains National Park

PIEDMONT

34° N · Little Rock

TENNESSEE · Mt. Mitchell · NORTH CAROLINA · Raleigh

OKLAHOMA

SOUTH CAROLINA · Columbia

ATLANTIC COASTAL PLAIN

Atlanta

LOUISIANA

Jackson

ALABAMA · GEORGIA

MISSISSIPPI · Montgomery

TEXAS

GULF COASTAL PLAIN

30° N · Baton Rouge · Tallahassee

Gulf of Mexico

FLORIDA · Cape Canaveral

Blue Ridge Mountains

Elevations

Feet	Meters
12,000	3,658
9,000	2,743
5,000	1,524
2,000	610
1,000	305
500	152
0	0

✪ State capitals

Swamp

0   50   100   150 miles
0 50 100 150 kilometers

Lake Okeechobee

26° N

The Everglades

Everglades National Park

Florida Keys

The Atlantic Ocean and the Gulf of Mexico border the Southeast region. Coastal plains and mountains are the major landforms of the region.
▶ What mountain range are the Blue Ridge Mountains a part of?

A towboat pushing several barges is a common sight along the Mississippi River.
▶ What might the barges carry?

D. Rivers of the Southeast

The Mississippi River The Southeast has many rivers. The three most important rivers are the Mississippi, the Ohio, and the Tennessee.

The Mississippi River begins in the state of Minnesota, almost in Canada. It flows south and empties into the Gulf of Mexico. The Mississippi provides the main route for shipping goods into and out of the interior, or central part, of the continent of North America.

The Ohio River The Ohio River forms the northern borders of Kentucky and part of the border of West Virginia. The Ohio River gives towns and farms far from the Atlantic Ocean a river connection to the Gulf of Mexico. Goods can move by boat on the Ohio River, travel downriver to the Mississippi River and then continue to the Gulf of Mexico.

The Tennessee River The Tennessee River begins high in the Appalachians and flows toward the southwest. The Tennessee River bends west, then north, forming a shape like a giant *U*. Finally it crosses the state of Tennessee and empties into the Ohio River.

LESSON 1 REVIEW

THINK AND WRITE

A. Why are hurricanes such dangerous storms?
B. What bodies of water form borders of the Southeast?
C. How are the three landforms of the Southeast different?
D. What are the important uses of the major rivers of the Southeast?

SKILLS CHECK

WRITING SKILL

Imagine that a hurricane will strike your community in one hour. You are preparing to move to a safe place until the hurricane passes. Make a list of five things that you would want to take with you. Write a paragraph explaining why you would take those items.

129

Climate and Agriculture in the Southeast Region

THINK ABOUT WHAT YOU KNOW

What kind of climate do you like best? Give two reasons for your choice.

STUDY THE VOCABULARY

citrus fruit   plantation
orange grove   cash crop

FOCUS YOUR READING

What kinds of crops grow best in the warm, rainy climate of the Southeast?

A. The Southeast's Warm and Moist Climate

Summer Temperatures The Southeast is the only region of the United States, except Hawaii, where the climate is both warm and rainy. In the summer, many parts of the Southeast get hot and steamy. This is especially true of the Atlantic Coastal Plain and the Gulf Coastal Plain. In Miami, near the southern tip of Florida, the temperature often reaches 90°F (32°C) in July. Farther north, summer days are nearly as warm. In Memphis, Tennessee, many July days are 82°F (28°C).

Winter Temperatures Winters are also quite warm in the Southeast. In Atlanta, Georgia, January days often warm up to 50°F (10°C). In West Virginia and Kentucky, winters are a little colder than in Georgia. January days in

these more northern states reach only 41°F (5°C). Alabama and Mississippi, states on the coast of the Gulf of Mexico, have warm winter days of 60°F (16°C) or more.

A Long Growing Season Warm temperatures are important for agriculture because they give farmers a long growing season. Along the coast of the Southeast, farmers have over 240 days each year to grow crops. In southern Florida, crops can be grown 365 days a year because there is hardly ever any frost to kill the plants.

Even the northern states of this region have long growing seasons. Farmers in North Carolina, Tennessee,

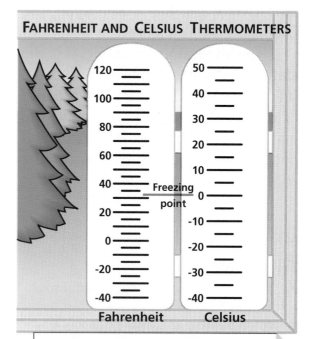

FAHRENHEIT AND CELSIUS THERMOMETERS

A Fahrenheit thermometer is at the left. The Celsius thermometer at the right is part of the metric system.
► What is the freezing point on the Celsius thermometer?

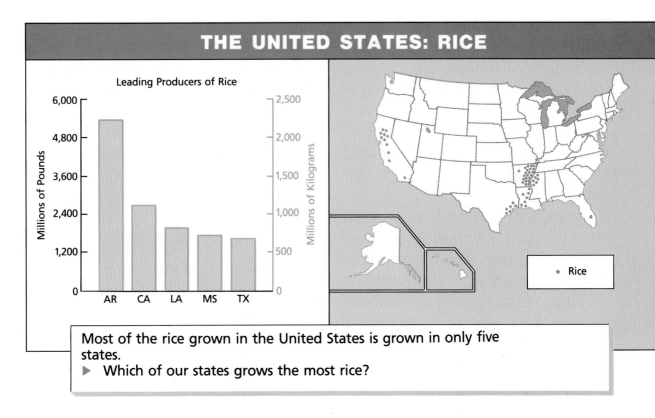

THE UNITED STATES: RICE

Leading Producers of Rice

Most of the rice grown in the United States is grown in only five states.
▶ Which of our states grows the most rice?

and Virginia can begin working in their fields in early April. Farmers in the New England and Middle Atlantic regions have to wait until late April or even into May.

In the Southeast, the first winter frost usually arrives in early November. In New England, the first frost usually arrives in mid-October.

Rainfall Just having a warm climate is not enough to grow crops. Plants need water, too, and the Southeast has a great deal of rain. Over 60 inches (152 cm) of rain usually falls during the year along the coast. Areas away from the coast receive between 40 and 60 inches (102 and 152 cm) of rain a year. This is plenty of moisture for growing most crops.

B. Crops of the Coastal Plains

Two Important Crops Some crops, such as rice, need a lot of water in order to grow well. The plains along the Atlantic coast and the Gulf coast are rainy enough for growing rice. More rice is grown in Arkansas, Louisiana, and Mississippi than in any other states.

The coastal plains are also important for growing vegetables, especially during the winter months, when northern farms are covered with snow. Southern Florida is sometimes called the Winter Gardening District because it is so famous for its winter crops of vegetables. Farmers in Florida specialize in raising celery, lettuce, potatoes, and tomatoes. On a winter's day, people in the northern states can enjoy vegetables from Florida for dinner.

131

Citrus Crops Did you ever bite into a fresh orange and feel the juice spray all over your face? Oranges are a type of **citrus fruit**, along with lemons, grapefruit, and tangerines. Florida is a major producer of citrus fruits. The good soil, climate, and rainfall of central and southern Florida are just right for growing citrus fruits.

Orange groves cover the central part of the state. An orange grove is an orchard of orange trees. Every year millions of fresh oranges and grapefruit are shipped from Florida, and millions more are made into fresh, frozen, or canned juice.

C. Cotton and Peanuts

Cotton For almost 100 years, cotton was the chief crop of the Southeast. This region was once called the Land of Cotton because of the many cotton **plantations** spread across the region. A plantation is a large farm where one main crop is grown.

During the 1800s, cotton was planted in the same fields year after year. Gradually the soils became worn out. There were no minerals, or plant foods, left. Insects like the boll weevil destroyed many cotton fields.

Peanuts At first the cotton farmers were very upset about losing their crops. Many farmers continued to try to grow cotton, but they also started to experiment with other crops. One of these crops was peanuts.

Peanuts were once used mainly as food for hogs. Only very poor people ate peanuts. Then in the late 1800s, a

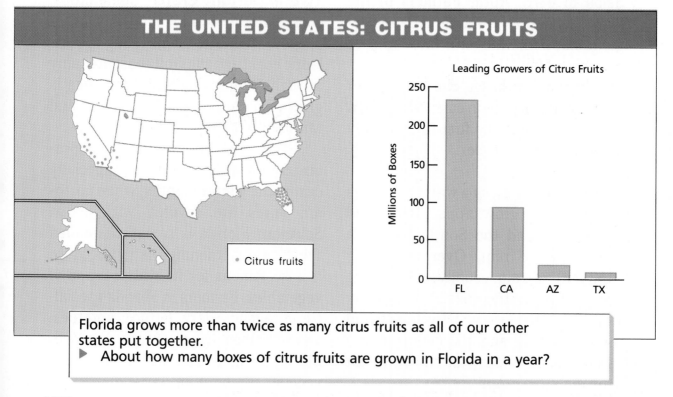

THE UNITED STATES: CITRUS FRUITS

Citrus fruits

Leading Growers of Citrus Fruits

Millions of Boxes

FL   CA   AZ   TX

Florida grows more than twice as many citrus fruits as all of our other states put together.

▶ About how many boxes of citrus fruits are grown in Florida in a year?

PEANUTS: FROM PLANTING TO SHIPPING

1. Peanuts grow underground.

2. The plants are dug up by machine.

3. Peanuts are placed in bins to dry.

5. Workers inspect the peanuts by hand.

4. Peanuts are shelled by machine.

6. The peanuts are bagged and held in a storage area before they are shipped to customers.

Peanuts are an important crop in the Southeast region and in warm regions throughout the world.
► What happens to the peanuts after they have been shelled?

This photograph shows George Washington Carver (second from right) in a chemistry laboratory at Tuskegee Institute in 1906.

▶ How can you tell that this photograph was taken many years ago?

black scientist named George Washington Carver changed the way people felt about the peanut plant. For many years he taught at Tuskegee (tus KEE-gee) Institute in Alabama. Carver set up a laboratory where he worked to find ways to help southern farmers make the best use of their land.

George Washington Carver discovered over 300 uses for the peanut plant. Roasted peanuts and peanut butter are just two foods we get from the peanut plant. The drawing on page 133 shows how peanuts are planted, harvested, and made ready to be shipped to manufacturers of various peanut products.

When Southeastern farmers discovered that peanut plants were almost as valuable as cotton, many of them began raising peanuts. Today, peanuts are an important **cash crop** in Georgia, Alabama, North Carolina, and Virginia. A cash crop is a main crop that a farmer grows to be sold.

D. Farming in the Piedmont and the Mountains

A Hilly Land Farming is more difficult in the Piedmont than it is on the coastal plains. It is difficult to use machinery on the hilly land, but peach trees grow well in its soils. Georgia is known as the

Peach State because there are so many peach orchards scattered throughout the state.

Many Piedmont farmers raise poultry. It does not matter that the soil is sticky red clay or full of rocks, since the poultry is kept and fed in poultry houses. Even a small Piedmont farm can manage several poultry houses. Arkansas, North Carolina, and Virginia are important poultry producers.

Raising Tobacco Tobacco is one of the Piedmont's biggest cash crops. Raising tobacco is difficult work, because tobacco plants are quite fragile, or easily broken. When the plants are mature, or ripe, the leaves must be cured, or dried. Then they have to be sorted, bundled, and tied together. Tobacco is grown throughout the Southeast, with North Carolina, Kentucky, and South Carolina producing the largest amounts.

Mixed Farming High in the Appalachian Mountains, the land is rough, and the soils are thin and rocky. Nearly

Peach trees are in bloom in this orchard in Georgia.
▶ Why, do you think, is Georgia called the Peach State?

every farm grows a combination of products. Vegetables such as corn, potatoes, and cabbage are raised by many farmers. Some farmers raise apples to sell as fresh fruit or for making cider.

LESSON 2

THINK AND WRITE

A. Why is warm weather important to farmers in the Southeast region?
B. Why is Florida important as a farming state?
C. How did George Washington Carver help the farmers of the Southeast?
D. How do the lands and soils of the Piedmont and Appalachian Mountains make farming difficult?

SKILLS CHECK

THINKING SKILL

Why, do you think, do farming areas have a lower population density than suburban areas?

GEORGE WASHINGTON CARVER: WHY DO WE REMEMBER HIM?

In Lesson 2 you learned how George Washington Carver, a famous African-American scientist, helped the cotton farmers of the Southeast. Today we remember Carver because he discovered many uses for peanuts and sweet potatoes. But Americans also remember Carver for the way he lived his life.

George Washington Carver was born into slavery in 1861. People in slavery were considered the property of their owners. While Carver was still a baby, his father died in an accident, and his mother was kidnapped. When Carver was a small child, slavery was outlawed, but he continued to live with his former owners, in the only home he had.

Like most other African Americans of his time, Carver was not allowed to attend school. Instead, he was taught to cook, clean, sew, and wash clothes. However, he learned to read from a spelling book. At a young age, Carver became interested in plants, and he tried to learn everything he could about them.

Carver became determined to go to school to learn more about plants. When he was about 10 or 12 years old, he left home to find a school that would teach black children. From that time on, he was on his own. To support himself, he did the jobs he had been trained to do.

Carver finished high school in Kansas. He became the first black person to graduate from Iowa State College, where he was at the top of his class. Carver studied for advanced degrees and began to write papers and give talks about plants.

In 1896, Carver began to teach at Tuskegee Institute, in Alabama. Booker T. Washington had started this school to teach poor black students. There was little pay and even less scientific equipment at first. But Carver went to Tuskegee because he wanted to help his people.

Carver taught many young students at Tuskegee. He began a "school on wheels," riding in a horse and buggy to teach the farmers of the area. The results of Carver's work became known throughout the world. Many people offered him work at high pay, but he would not leave Tuskegee.

Carver died in 1943. Some years later Congress authorized the establishment of the George Washington Carver Monument near the place where Carver was born in Missouri. It was the first national monument to an African American.

Thinking for Yourself

1. What kind of young person was George Washington Carver?
2. Why, do you think, was a national monument dedicated to Carver?
3. Why, do you think, is George Washington Carver remembered as a great American?

Industries of the Southeast

THINK ABOUT WHAT YOU KNOW

Why, do you think, are certain businesses located where they are?

STUDY THE VOCABULARY

synthetic	petrochemical
tree farm	industry
fall line	reservoir
rapids	hydroelectricity

FOCUS YOUR READING

What industries use the resources of the Southeast?

A. The Riches of the Sea

In a famous story about the Chesapeake Bay, an imaginary Native American named Pentaquod went exploring. It was autumn in the early 1600s. Pentaquod quietly padded his canoe along the marshes at the edge of the bay. He was surprised to find that the bay was rich with wildlife, birds, and fish. This is a description of what he saw.

> *At the sound of his paddle hundreds of birds arose, and he judged that fish must be plentiful, too. As he moved along the marsh he saw . . . little green herons and brilliant cardinals and kingfishers [rise] from their muddy nests, and hundreds of quail making the autumn afternoons ring with their whistling cries.*

Pentaquod was amazed at the many natural resources of the Chesapeake Bay. In the language of the Native Americans who lived there, *Chesapeake* meant "the great river in which shellfish abound." Birds, fish, and shellfish are still abundant in the Chesapeake and other bays along the Atlantic and Gulf coasts. Many rivers empty into the bays along the Atlantic coast. They carry soils and tiny plants that are food for fish and shellfish.

(Left) Oysters in the Chesapeake Bay are harvested by ships that use a machine called a dredge to bring oysters up from the ocean floor.
► What are the workers in the picture on the right doing?

Bays often have waters that are quieter than ocean waters. Birds, fish, and other wildlife use the protected bays for nesting and feeding. There are more kinds of fish and shellfish along the coasts of the Southeast than anywhere else in the United States.

Fish and shellfish are major products of the Southeast's coastal areas. Oysters and clams are found in the bays along the Atlantic coast. Shrimp are especially plentiful along the Gulf coast. On page 140 there is a song about shrimp boats.

Some of the fish caught off the coast of the Southeast is sold fresh or frozen in fish markets and supermarkets. A large amount of fish is ground up and fed to hogs and poultry. Oil from fish is used to make paints, soaps, and certain chemicals.

B. Natural Resources from the Land

Cotton The Southeast gets many products from the land that are used as raw materials in its industries. For example, cotton is an important crop that is used by textile mills to make fabrics. You have already read that the first textile mills in the United States were built in New England. These textile mills depended on a steady supply of cotton that was shipped from the Southeast.

Later, people in the Southeast began to build their own textile mills. The land was cheap and workers could be paid less money than workers in the

Many colored threads are needed to make the cloth shown here.
▶ What is the textile worker holding in her hands?

LEADING TEXTILE-PRODUCING STATES

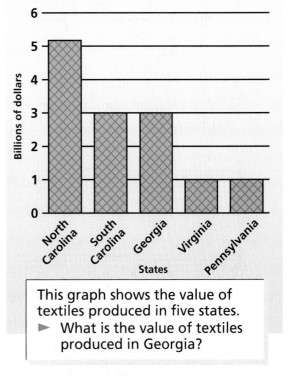

This graph shows the value of textiles produced in five states.
▶ What is the value of textiles produced in Georgia?

139

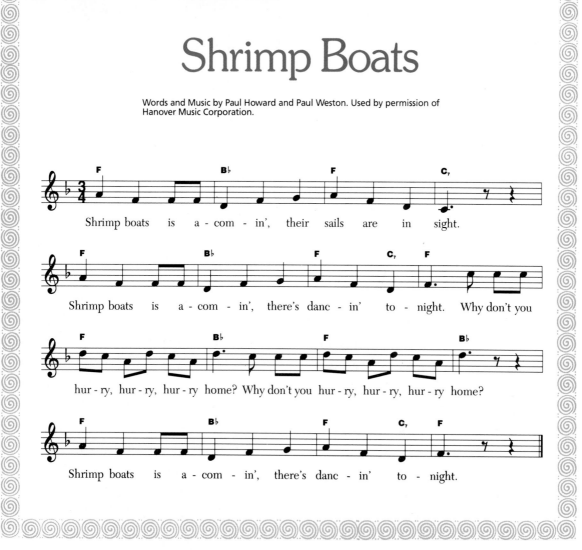

Shrimp Boats

Words and Music by Paul Howard and Paul Weston. Used by permission of Hanover Music Corporation.

Shrimp boats is a - com - in', their sails are in sight.

Shrimp boats is a - com - in', there's danc - in' to - night. Why don't you

hur - ry, hur - ry, hur - ry home? Why don't you hur - ry, hur - ry, hur - ry home?

Shrimp boats is a - com - in', there's danc - in' to - night.

Northeast. Today there are more textile mills in the Southeast than in any other region of the United States. North Carolina and South Carolina lead the nation in producing textiles.

Many of these mills weave cotton threads into textiles. But most of them now weave **synthetic** (sihn THET ihk) fibers, such as nylon and polyester (pahl ee ES tur). Synthetic fibers are made from chemicals rather than from natural fibers. Cotton, which comes from plants, and wool, which comes from animals, are natural fibers.

Forest Products The land also provides southeastern industries with timber. If you flew over the Southeast, you would see cities, towns, farms, and lots of forests. Many of the forests are made up of pine trees. Many of these pine forests are **tree farms** that are owned by paper companies.

On tree farms the pine trees are planted in long, straight rows just as crops are. The biggest difference between farm crops and trees is the length of the time between planting and harvesting. Most farm crops are grown and harvested in less than one year. Trees on a tree farm must grow 20 years before they can be harvested.

Lumber Products An important product that comes from pine trees is wood pulp. You know that wood pulp is wood that has been washed, cut into chips, and boiled. Wood pulp is the raw material that is used to make paper. All across the Southeast there are pulp mills and paper mills.

Another important product that uses lumber is furniture. The city of High Point, North Carolina, is sometimes called the Furniture Capital of the World. Twice each year North Carolina furniture makers show their latest products in a huge exhibit. Thousands of buyers from furniture stores all over the United States come to select furniture for sale in their stores.

141

C. Manufacturing in the Southeast

Rivers Along the Fall Line Textiles, paper, and furniture are just three of the important manufactured goods of the Southeast. Motor vehicles, computer parts, and machinery are also produced in the Southeast. Manufacturing is often found in towns and cities along the rivers of the Southeast.

Many short rivers begin high in the Appalachian Mountains and flow down across the Piedmont to the Atlantic Coastal Plain. These rivers drop quite sharply from the Piedmont to the coastal plain. At this point you find the **fall line**. The rivers fall right off the edge of the Piedmont onto the plain, forming waterfalls and **rapids**. Rapids are places in rivers where the water flows quickly and roughly over rocks.

Where Cities Grew In the past, the falling water was used to turn water wheels to run machinery. Many mills for grinding grain or weaving textiles were built along the fall line because small ships carrying goods could travel from the Atlantic Ocean up the rivers to the fall line rapids.

Communities grew up around the mills and became busy manufacturing cities. Two such cities are Raleigh (RAWL ee), the capital city of North Carolina, and Columbia, the capital city of South Carolina.

D. Mining in the Southeast

Coal Mining Mining is big business in the Southeast. Coal is plentiful in the Appalachians. More coal is mined in the state of Kentucky than in any other state in the United States.

Some of the coal is carried by railroad to the seaports along the Atlantic coast. From there it is shipped to Japan and other countries for use in their industries. Other shipments of coal are sent to Birmingham, Alabama, to be used in making steel.

Reading a Pictograph One of the simplest graphs is called a **pictograph**. A pictograph uses symbols or pictures to stand for information. Look at the pictograph on page 143. What is its title? What symbol is used for coal?.

There are many swift-flowing streams on the eastern edge of the Piedmont.
▶ How can you tell that this stream is along the fall line?

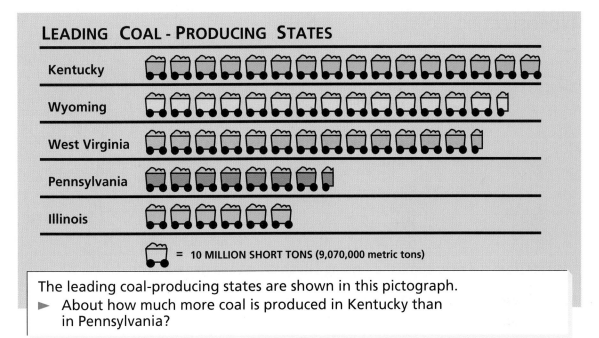

LEADING COAL-PRODUCING STATES

Kentucky

Wyoming

West Virginia

Pennsylvania

Illinois

= 10 MILLION SHORT TONS (9,070,000 metric tons)

The leading coal-producing states are shown in this pictograph.
► About how much more coal is produced in Kentucky than in Pennsylvania?

Look at the row marked "Kentucky." It shows 16 coal cars. Look at the coal car at the bottom of the graph. You can see that each car stands for 10 million short tons. If you multiply 10 million short tons by 16, the answer is 160 million short tons. That is the amount of coal produced in Kentucky.

A Steel Center Birmingham Alabama, is the center in the Southeast for producing steel. There are three main mineral resources needed to make steel. They are coal, iron ore, and a kind of rock called limestone. These resources are all found near Birmingham.

Other minerals are found in the Southeast. Tennessee is our country's top producer of zinc. Gemstones such as emeralds and rubies are found in Tennessee and North Carolina.

E. Energy and Fuels in the Southeast

Petroleum Large deposits of petroleum and natural gas are found in Louisiana along the Gulf of Mexico. Thousands of people in Louisiana work in exploring and drilling for oil and for natural gas.

Petroleum is very important to the **petrochemical industry**. This industry produces many everyday things from the chemicals found in petroleum. Louisiana's petrochemical industry makes plastic goods, fertilizer, paint, antifreeze, insect sprays, and medicines. Many petrochemical plants are found near Baton Rouge (BAT unroozh), the capital of Louisiana.

Water Power An important source of energy in the Southeast is the water in its rivers. In 1933 the United States

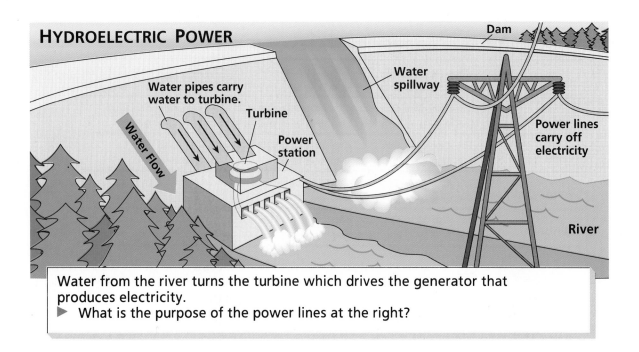

HYDROELECTRIC POWER

Dam

Water pipes carry water to turbine.

Turbine

Water Flow

Power station

Water spillway

Power lines carry off electricity

River

Water from the river turns the turbine which drives the generator that produces electricity.
▶ What is the purpose of the power lines at the right?

government began a project along the Tennessee River. It was called the Tennessee Valley Authority, or TVA.

The TVA project built dozens of dams along the Tennessee River. A dam holds back a river, creating a large lake called a **reservoir** (REZ ur vwahr). Water is released from behind the dam, and as the water flows over the dam, it turns large machines, called turbines,

that create electricity. The electricity that is created with the force of water is called **hydroelectricity**.

The hydroelectricity of the Tennessee River lights up homes, schools, and businesses all over Tennessee. It also provides the energy for manufacturing aluminum, a light metal that is used in making cans, parts of automobiles, and many household appliances.

LESSON 3 REVIEW

THINK AND WRITE

A. Why are the Atlantic coast and the Gulf coast so rich in fish and animal life?

B. What manufactured goods use the Southeast's agricultural and forestry products?

C. Why did manufacturing towns grow up along the fall line?

D. Why is Birmingham, Alabama, a major steel producing city?

E. Why are petroleum and hydroelectricity important to the Southeast?

SKILLS CHECK

MAP SKILL

Write the names of these capital cities on a separate sheet of paper—Little Rock, Tallahassee, Charleston, Richmond. Find the cities on the map on page 124. Next to each city on your list, write the name of the state in which it is located.

LESSON 4

Cities and Vacationlands of the Southeast

THINK ABOUT WHAT YOU KNOW

Where, do you think, is a good place to build a railroad station or an airport?

STUDY THE VOCABULARY

causeway **extraterrestrial**
swamp

FOCUS YOUR READING

What are the most famous cities and natural places of the Southeast?

A. Two Transportation Centers

Atlanta, Georgia In 1836 a man named Stephen H. Long had a stake driven into the ground at a place that later became the city of Atlanta, Georgia. He announced that that point would be the southern end of a railroad that would connect Georgia and Tennessee. Long predicted that Atlanta would become an important transportation center in the United States.

Atlanta, Georgia, did become an important railroad center. How did that happen? The answer has to do with the location of Atlanta. Atlanta is on the Piedmont near the southern end of the Appalachian Mountains. Find Atlanta on the map on page 124.

In the 1800s it cost too much money to build railroads through the Appalachian Mountains. Many tunnels would have had to be blasted through the mountains. Bridges would have had to be constructed. So the first railroads were built around the southern end of the mountains. The city of Atlanta, Georgia, was located where some of these rail lines met.

Through the years, Atlanta grew into the second largest city in the Southeast. Railroads and highways crisscross and encircle the city. Raw materials can easily be carried to its factories from many different places.

Atlanta's airport is one of the busiest airports in our country.
▶ How can you tell that this is a busy airport?

A jazz musician performs in New Orleans during Mardi Gras.
▶ What musical instrument is he playing?

In the center of Atlanta is the famous Peachtree Center, with shops, restaurants, and office buildings. It also has a hotel that is 73 stories high. A large zoo, botanical gardens, and historic homes help make Atlanta one of the most beautiful cities in the country.

New Orleans, Louisiana New Orleans is one of the oldest cities in the United States. It was established in 1718 along a curve in the Mississippi River. Right from the beginning, large ships and small boats docked at New Orleans. There traders bought and sold fish, farm products, furs, manufactured goods, and machinery. Cargo from all along the Mississippi River, all the way up to Minnesota, could be transported down to New Orleans.

Today, New Orleans is still a major port. It is the second busiest port in the United States. Only New York City is a busier port. About 5,000 ships from many foreign countries enter and leave New Orleans every year. Many ships carry goods to and from countries in Latin America. Find New Orleans on the map on page 124.

But New Orleans is known for much more than shipping. In the 1800s it was called The Paris of America because it looked so much like the city of Paris in France. The oldest part of the city is called the French Quarter. If you strolled through the French Quarter, you would see buildings with balconies beautifully shaped from iron bars. You might have dinner in one of the many restaurants that serves French-style foods.

New Orleans is also known for its Mardi Gras (MAHR dee GRAH) celebrations which take place each year near the end of February. Parades and street festivals add noise and excitement to the city until the early morning hours. Jazz, a particular style of American music, was born in New Orleans.

B. Florida, a Vacationland

Southern Florida Have you ever heard someone say, "I'd like to get away from it all"? Most people like to get away from work or school occasionally just to relax. Florida is a popular vacation place for people from all around the United States. Miami, which is near the southeastern tip of

(Center) Marsh grasses cover much of Everglades National Park. Alligators (left) and spoonbills (right) are among the many animals and birds that make their homes in these grasses.
▶ What information might the park ranger be writing about the bird?

Florida, is popular with tourists from all over the world. Miami has parks, beaches, playgrounds, and nearby islands for visitors to enjoy.

Miami began in the 1500s as a small Spanish settlement and fort. Farmers grew fruit and other foods but few people lived in the area. In the late 1800s, a railroad was built along the Atlantic coast to Miami. Miami suddenly began to grow because vacationers could reach that city by railroad. Many people who came to Miami for a vacation decided to stay. They bought land and set up businesses. Today, Miami is a modern, busy city with art galleries, science museums, and shopping centers.

Across the bay from Miami on a long, narrow slice of land is Miami Beach. Visitors can reach Miami Beach by crossing one of the **causeways**, or raised roads, built across the shallow water of the bay.

Near the city of Miami is a large **swamp** called the Everglades. A swamp is wet spongy land. The Everglades is almost 50 miles (80 km) wide and about 6 inches (15 cm) deep. Much of the Everglades is covered with tall marsh grasses. These grasses are pictured at the top of this page.

Everglades National Park is a small part of the Everglades. If you visit this park, you can walk along wooden walkways above the water. An amazing number of animals and tropical birds live in this watery wonderland. If you are lucky, you may spot some bobcats, raccoons, and possibly some alligators. The park has hundreds of birds such as egrets, herons, pelicans, and cranes.

The space shuttle *Columbia* lifts off at the Kennedy Space Center at Cape Canaveral, Florida.
► Have you ever watched a space shuttle launch?

Central Florida In central Florida are two well-known places to visit — Walt Disney World and Cape Canaveral (kayp kuh NAV urul). Walt Disney World is one of the most popular tourist attractions in the United States. Each year more than 10 million people visit Walt Disney World, including the Magic Kingdom, which has many amusements, rides, and restaurants.

Cape Canaveral is a piece of land jutting out into the ocean. Cape Canaveral is a reminder that much of the transportation in the next century may

be **extraterrestrial** (eks truh tuh RES-tree ul). *Extraterrestrial* means "anything that is away from or beyond the earth." Transportation in outer space is extraterrestrial.

Cape Canaveral is the home of the John F. Kennedy Space Center. In 1958, the first United States satellite was launched from Cape Canaveral. In 1962, John H. Glenn, Jr., the first American to orbit the earth, was launched from Cape Canaveral.

The Kennedy Space Center is becoming a transportation terminal of the future. In a few years you may read about regularly scheduled flights from the Kennedy Space Center to space stations, to the moon, or even to Mars.

C. Natural Wonders in the Southeast Region

Scenic Mountains The Great Smoky Mountains form the boundary between the states of Tennessee and North Carolina. The Great Smoky Mountains are among the highest and most rugged mountains in the southeastern part of the Appalachians. On most days of the year, a blue haze that looks like smoke hangs over the Great Smokies. That is how the mountains got their name.

A National Park The Great Smoky Mountains National Park is in the Great Smoky Mountains. Many of its trees are over 100 years old. Some of the trunks measure 25 feet (8 m) around. Over 1,400 different kinds of flowering plants grow in the park.

The Great Smoky Mountains were named for the smoky haze that often covers the mountain peaks.
▶ What can you enjoy in the park?

The trees in the park are protected by the government of the United States. Before the park was established in 1930, timber companies had harvested most of the big trees. The only really old trees left are those on the highest and steepest slopes of the mountains.

A Mountain Road One of the prettiest mountain roads in the Southeast region is the Blue Ridge Parkway. This road extends for 469 miles (755 km) from Shenandoah National Park in Virginia to the Great Smoky Mountain National Park. It mostly follows the high ridges of the Blue Ridge Mountains. Some people say it is one of the most beautiful drives in the world. The beauty of the land in this area has been left as natural as possible.

LESSON 4 REVIEW

THINK AND WRITE

A. Why did Atlanta and New Orleans become important cities?
B. In what ways would a visit to southern Florida be different from a visit to central Florida?
C. Why, do you think, is the Southeast region a good place for national parks?

SKILLS CHECK

MAP SKILL
Find Memphis, Tennessee, and Miami, Florida, on the map on page 124. Use the scale of miles on the map to find the distance in miles between these two cities.

SOUTHEAST REGION

ALABAMA

KEY FACTS
Mobile, Alabama, is one of the busiest ports in the U.S.

George Washington Carver did his famous research on the peanut at Tuskegee Institute.

LARGEST CITIES
Birmingham
Mobile
Montgomery

POPULATION
4,181,000

RANK: 22

LAND AREA
50,767 sq mi
131,487 sq km

RANK: 28

POPULATION DENSITY
80 per sq mi
31 per sq km

RANK: 25

**PRINCIPAL PRODUCTS
AGRICULTURE & MANUFACTURING**

Poultry

Paper

POPULATION: URBAN VS. RURAL

— 60% Urban
— 40% Rural

★ **Montgomery**

Yellowhammer

Camellia

Southern pine
(longleaf)

ARKANSAS

KEY FACTS
One of the world's largest springs is in the northern part of the state.

The only public diamond mine in North America is in Arkansas.

LARGEST CITIES
Little Rock
Fort Smith
North Little Rock

POPULATION
2,427,000

RANK: 33

LAND AREA
52,078 sq mi
134,883 sq km

RANK: 27

POPULATION DENSITY
46 per sq mi
18 per sq km

RANK: 35

**PRINCIPAL PRODUCTS
AGRICULTURE & MANUFACTURING**

Soybeans

Machinery

POPULATION: URBAN VS. RURAL

— 52% Urban
— 48% Rural

★ **Little Rock**

Mockingbird

Apple blossom

Pine

FLORIDA

KEY FACTS
Three-fourths of the nation's oranges and grapefruit are produced in Florida.

There are more thunderstorms in Florida than in any other state.

LARGEST CITIES
Jacksonville
Miami
Tampa

POPULATION
12,818,000

RANK: 4

LAND AREA
54,153 sq mi
140,256 sq km

RANK: 26

POPULATION DENSITY
222 per sq mi
88 per sq km

RANK: 10

**PRINCIPAL PRODUCTS
AGRICULTURE & MANUFACTURING**

Oranges

Food products

POPULATION: URBAN VS. RURAL

— 85% Urban
— 15% Rural

★ **Tallahassee**

Mockingbird

Orange blossom

Sabal palm

150

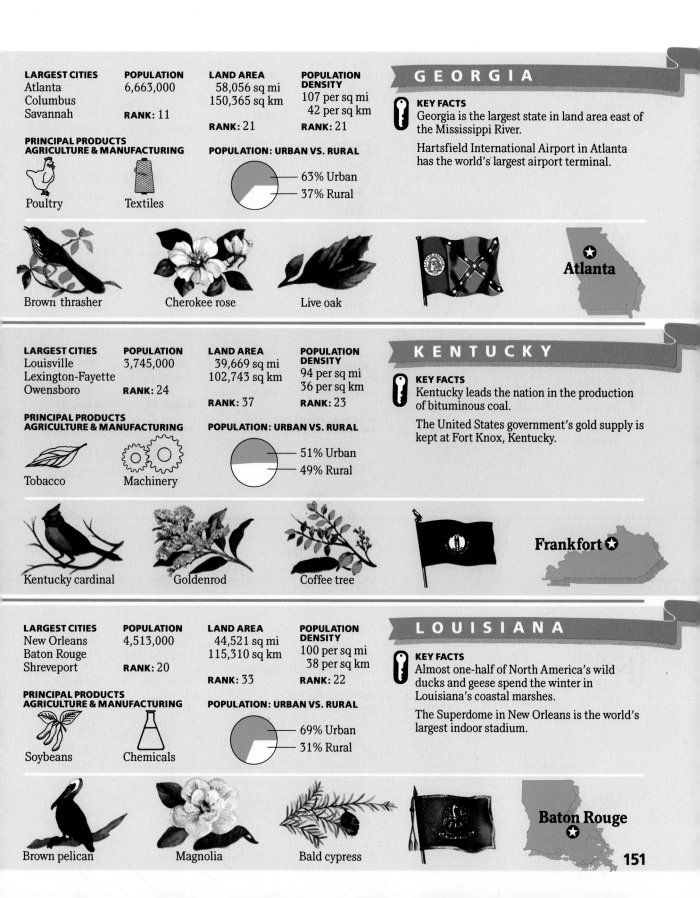

GEORGIA

LARGEST CITIES
Atlanta
Columbus
Savannah

POPULATION
6,663,000

RANK: 11

LAND AREA
58,056 sq mi
150,365 sq km

RANK: 21

POPULATION DENSITY
107 per sq mi
42 per sq km

RANK: 21

KEY FACTS
Georgia is the largest state in land area east of the Mississippi River.

Hartsfield International Airport in Atlanta has the world's largest airport terminal.

PRINCIPAL PRODUCTS AGRICULTURE & MANUFACTURING

Poultry

Textiles

POPULATION: URBAN VS. RURAL
63% Urban
37% Rural

Brown thrasher

Cherokee rose

Live oak

Atlanta

KENTUCKY

LARGEST CITIES
Louisville
Lexington-Fayette
Owensboro

POPULATION
3,745,000

RANK: 24

LAND AREA
39,669 sq mi
102,743 sq km

RANK: 37

POPULATION DENSITY
94 per sq mi
36 per sq km

RANK: 23

KEY FACTS
Kentucky leads the nation in the production of bituminous coal.

The United States government's gold supply is kept at Fort Knox, Kentucky.

PRINCIPAL PRODUCTS AGRICULTURE & MANUFACTURING

Tobacco

Machinery

POPULATION: URBAN VS. RURAL
51% Urban
49% Rural

Kentucky cardinal

Goldenrod

Coffee tree

Frankfort

LOUISIANA

LARGEST CITIES
New Orleans
Baton Rouge
Shreveport

POPULATION
4,513,000

RANK: 20

LAND AREA
44,521 sq mi
115,310 sq km

RANK: 33

POPULATION DENSITY
100 per sq mi
38 per sq km

RANK: 22

KEY FACTS
Almost one-half of North America's wild ducks and geese spend the winter in Louisiana's coastal marshes.

The Superdome in New Orleans is the world's largest indoor stadium.

PRINCIPAL PRODUCTS AGRICULTURE & MANUFACTURING

Soybeans

Chemicals

POPULATION: URBAN VS. RURAL
69% Urban
31% Rural

Brown pelican

Magnolia

Bald cypress

Baton Rouge

151

MISSISSIPPI

KEY FACTS
Mississippi borders four states and the Gulf of Mexico.

There are more tree farms in Mississippi than in any other state.

LARGEST CITIES	POPULATION	LAND AREA	POPULATION DENSITY
Jackson	2,699,000	47,233 sq mi	56 per sq mi
Biloxi		122,333 sq km	21 per sq km
Meridian	RANK: 31	RANK: 31	RANK: 31

**PRINCIPAL PRODUCTS
AGRICULTURE & MANUFACTURING**

Cotton

Transportation equipment

POPULATION: URBAN VS. RURAL
47% Urban
53% Rural

★ Jackson

Mockingbird

Magnolia

Magnolia

NORTH CAROLINA

KEY FACTS
Mount Mitchell in western North Carolina is the highest point east of the Mississippi River.

North Carolina is the leading state in the manufacture of furniture.

LARGEST CITIES	POPULATION	LAND AREA	POPULATION DENSITY
Charlotte	6,690,000	48,843 sq mi	131 per sq mi
Raleigh		126,504 sq km	51 per sq km
Greensboro	RANK: 10	RANK: 29	RANK: 17

**PRINCIPAL PRODUCTS
AGRICULTURE & MANUFACTURING**

Tobacco

Textiles

POPULATION: URBAN VS. RURAL
43% Urban
57% Rural

★ Raleigh

Cardinal

American dogwood

Pine

SOUTH CAROLINA

KEY FACTS
Charleston, South Carolina, has been an important port city since 1670.

The first science museum in the United States was founded in Charleston in 1773.

LARGEST CITIES	POPULATION	LAND AREA	POPULATION DENSITY
Columbia	3,549,000	30,203 sq mi	113 per sq mi
Charleston		78,227 sq km	44 per sq km
North Charleston	RANK: 25	RANK: 40	RANK: 20

**PRINCIPAL PRODUCTS
AGRICULTURE & MANUFACTURING**

Tobacco

Textiles

POPULATION: URBAN VS. RURAL
54% Urban
46% Rural

★ Columbia

Carolina wren

Carolina yellow jessamine

Palmetto

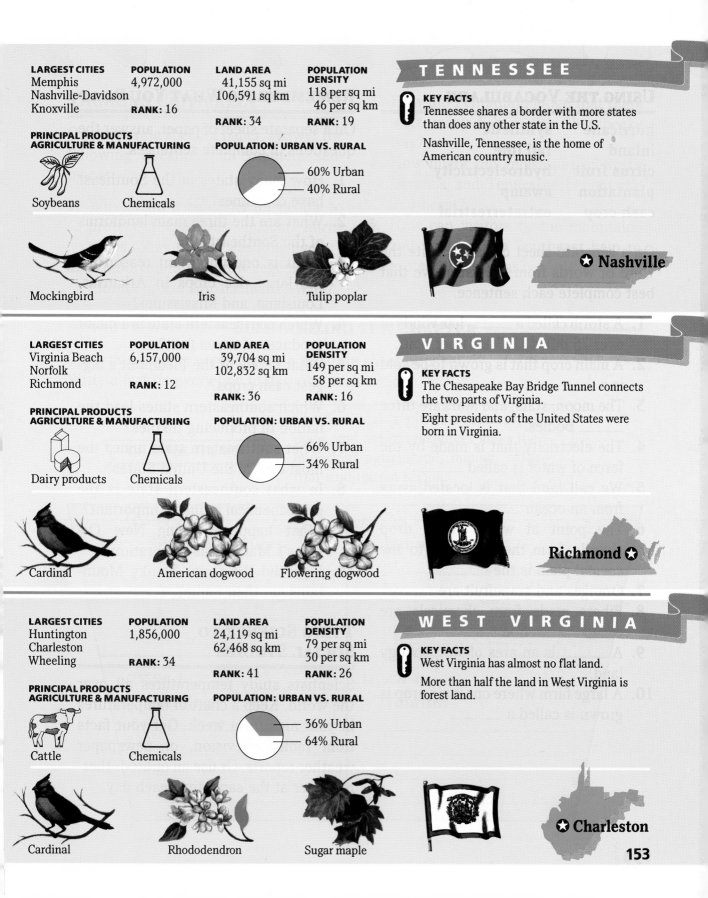

TENNESSEE

LARGEST CITIES	POPULATION	LAND AREA	POPULATION DENSITY
Memphis	4,972,000	41,155 sq mi	118 per sq mi
Nashville-Davidson		106,591 sq km	46 per sq km
Knoxville	RANK: 16		
		RANK: 34	RANK: 19

**PRINCIPAL PRODUCTS
AGRICULTURE & MANUFACTURING**

Soybeans   Chemicals

POPULATION: URBAN VS. RURAL

60% Urban
40% Rural

KEY FACTS
Tennessee shares a border with more states than does any other state in the U.S.

Nashville, Tennessee, is the home of American country music.

Mockingbird   Iris   Tulip poplar

★ Nashville

VIRGINIA

LARGEST CITIES	POPULATION	LAND AREA	POPULATION DENSITY
Virginia Beach	6,157,000	39,704 sq mi	149 per sq mi
Norfolk		102,832 sq km	58 per sq km
Richmond	RANK: 12		
		RANK: 36	RANK: 16

**PRINCIPAL PRODUCTS
AGRICULTURE & MANUFACTURING**

Dairy products   Chemicals

POPULATION: URBAN VS. RURAL

66% Urban
34% Rural

KEY FACTS
The Chesapeake Bay Bridge Tunnel connects the two parts of Virginia.

Eight presidents of the United States were born in Virginia.

Cardinal   American dogwood   Flowering dogwood

Richmond ★

WEST VIRGINIA

LARGEST CITIES	POPULATION	LAND AREA	POPULATION DENSITY
Huntington	1,856,000	24,119 sq mi	79 per sq mi
Charleston		62,468 sq km	30 per sq km
Wheeling	RANK: 34		
		RANK: 41	RANK: 26

**PRINCIPAL PRODUCTS
AGRICULTURE & MANUFACTURING**

Cattle   Chemicals

POPULATION: URBAN VS. RURAL

36% Urban
64% Rural

KEY FACTS
West Virginia has almost no flat land.

More than half the land in West Virginia is forest land.

Cardinal   Rhododendron   Sugar maple

★ Charleston

153

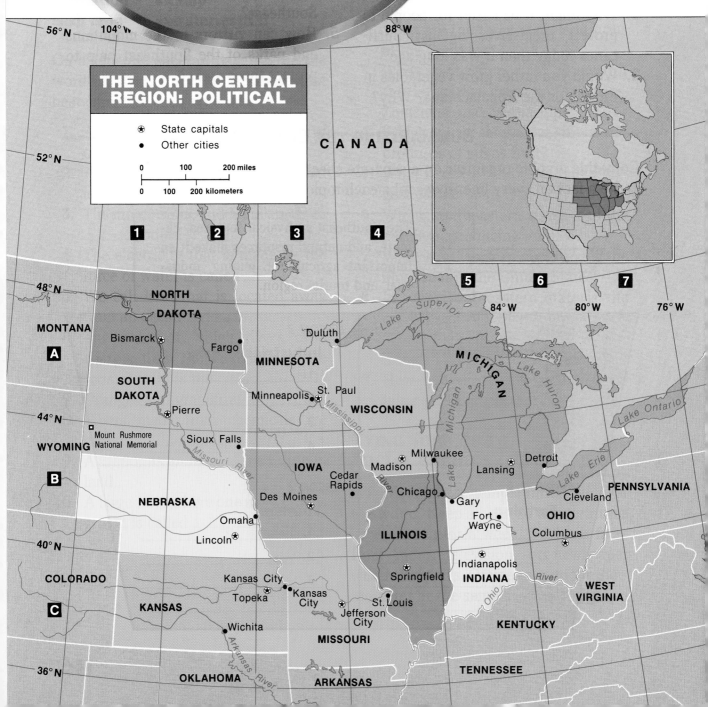

THE NORTH CENTRAL REGION

$\mathcal{M}$uch of the food that we eat is grown on the plains of the North Central region. Several large cities are also located in the region.

THE NORTH CENTRAL REGION: POLITICAL

⊛ State capitals
● Other cities

0   100   200 miles
0   100   200 kilometers

1 **2** **3** **4** **5** **6** **7**

56°N   104°W   88°W

52°N

48°N

44°N

40°N

36°N

84°W   80°W   76°W

CANADA

MONTANA

A

NORTH DAKOTA
Bismarck ⊛
Fargo ●
Duluth ●
MINNESOTA
MICHIGAN
Lake Superior
Lake Huron

SOUTH DAKOTA
Pierre ⊛
Minneapolis ● St. Paul ⊛
WISCONSIN
Lake Michigan
Lake Ontario

WYOMING
□ Mount Rushmore National Memorial
Sioux Falls ●
Missouri River
IOWA
Cedar Rapids ●
Madison ⊛
Milwaukee ●
Lansing ⊛
Detroit ●
Lake Erie

B

NEBRASKA
Des Moines ⊛
Chicago ●
Gary ●
Cleveland ●
PENNSYLVANIA

Omaha ●
Lincoln ⊛
ILLINOIS
Fort Wayne ●
OHIO
Columbus ⊛

A

B

COLORADO
Kansas City ●
Topeka ⊛
Springfield ⊛
Indianapolis ⊛
INDIANA
River
WEST VIRGINIA

C

KANSAS
Kansas City ●
St. Louis ●
Jefferson City ⊛
KENTUCKY
Ohio River

Wichita ●
MISSOURI
Arkansas River

OKLAHOMA
ARKANSAS
TENNESSEE

The Heartland of the United States

Think about why your heart is important to your body. The North Central region is called our nation's heartland. Why might a region be called a heartland?

STUDY THE VOCABULARY

pioneer   economy
prairie

FOCUS YOUR READING

What are the important physical features of the North Central region?

A. Pioneers Traveling West

In St. Louis, Missouri, a shiny steel arch stands tall and proud next to the Mississippi River. The top of the arch's curve reaches 630 feet (192 m) above the ground. The arch is called the Gateway Arch. It is a memorial to the Americans who crossed the Mississippi River in the 1800s.

Who were these Americans? They were **pioneers**, people who moved to an unsettled part of the United States and prepared the way for others to follow them. They worked hard to make their new land a rich farming area.

Laura Ingalls and her family were among those pioneers. When she became an adult, she married Almanzo Wilder. She became a writer and wrote stories about her childhood. Perhaps you have read a book by Laura Ingalls Wilder. Or you may have seen the television series *Little House on the Prairie*, which was based on her books.

One of Laura Ingalls Wilder's books is called *By the Shores of Silver Lake*. In that book she described the **prairie** her family crossed as they traveled west. A prairie is a large area of level or gently rolling land covered with thick grass. Sometimes the grass on a prairie grows 6 feet (2 m) high.

On the following page there is a passage from *By the Shores of Silver Lake*. As you read the passage, imagine that you are with the Ingalls family.

CITY INDEX

Cities less than 100,000
Bismarck (ND) A-1
Duluth (MI) A-3
Fargo (ND) A-2
Jefferson City (MO) C-3
Pierre (SD) A-1
Sioux Falls (SD) B-2

Cities 100,000 to 499,999
Cedar Rapids (IA).............. B-4
Des Moines (IA) B-3
Fort Wayne (IN) B-5

Gary (IN) B-5
Kansas City (KS) C-3
Kansas City (MO) C-3
Lansing (MI) B-5
Lincoln (NE) B-2
Madison (WI) B-4
Minneapolis (MN) A-3
Omaha (NE) B-2
St. Louis (MO) C-4
St. Paul (MN) A-3
Springfield (IL)................ C-4
Topeka (KS) C-3

Wichita (KS) C-2

Cities 500,000 to 999,999
Cleveland (OH) B-6
Columbus (OH) C-6
Indianapolis (IN) C-5
Milwaukee (WI) B-5

Cities 1,000,000 or more
Chicago (IL) B-5
Detroit (MI) B-6

Many cities in the North Central region grew up near bodies of water.
▶ Which North Central cities with populations of more than 500,000 are located near bodies of water?

157

When pioneer families traveled west in wagon trains, they met around a campfire in the evening.

▶ How did these families cook their food?

The road's going down a low bank to the river, but there aren't any trees. There's just a big sky and grassy land, and the little, low creek. It's a big river sometimes, but now it's dried up. . . .

"Drink hearty," Pa said to the horses. "There's no more water for thirty miles."

Laura said to Mary [her blind sister], "This prairie is like an enormous meadow, stretching far away in every direction, to the very edge of the world."

The endless waves of flowery grasses under the cloudless sky gave her a [strange] feeling. She could not say how she felt. All of them . . . and the wagon and team, and even Pa, seemed small.

B. Locating the North Central Region

Twelve Neighboring States The region that Laura Ingalls and her family traveled to is now called the North Central region. There are 12 states in the North Central region.

Minnesota is the largest state in the region. The state of Michigan has two sections. The larger section is shaped like a mitten. The smaller section to the north is separated from the rest of the state by Lake Michigan.

The Interior Lowlands The most important landform of the North Central region is the Central Plains. The eastern part of the Central Plains is called the Interior Lowlands. The states of

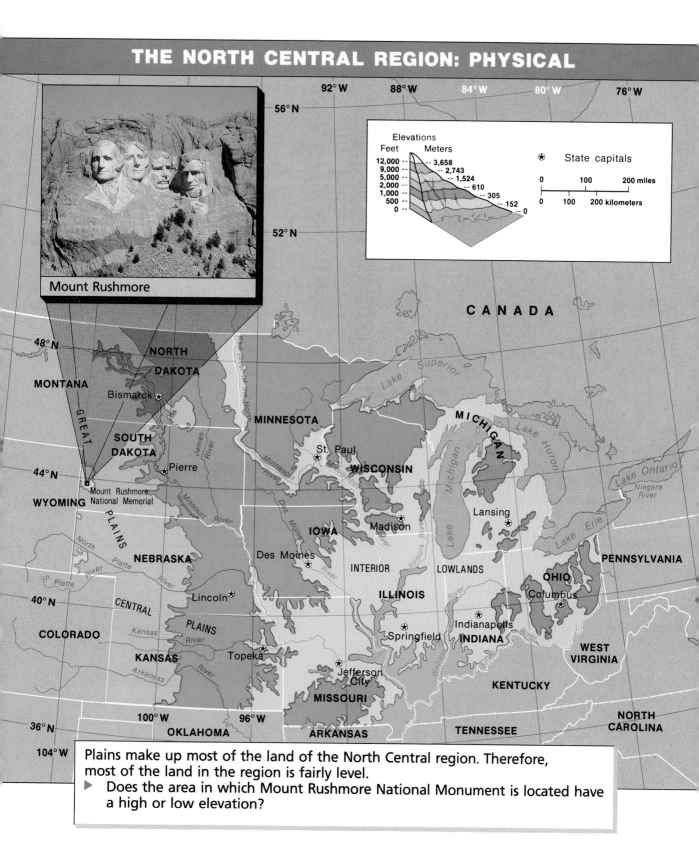

THE NORTH CENTRAL REGION: PHYSICAL

Mount Rushmore

Elevations

Feet	Meters
12,000	3,658
9,000	2,743
5,000	1,524
2,000	610
1,000	305
500	152
0	0

State capitals

0   100   200 miles

0   100   200 kilometers

CANADA

MONTANA

NORTH DAKOTA
Bismarck ⊛

SOUTH DAKOTA
Pierre ⊛

Mount Rushmore National Memorial

WYOMING

GREAT

PLAINS

NORTH Platte River

CENTRAL

PLAINS

Kansas River

NEBRASKA
Lincoln ⊛

COLORADO

KANSAS
Topeka ⊛

Arkansas River

OKLAHOMA

MINNESOTA

James River

Minnesota River

St. Paul ⊛

WISCONSIN
Madison ⊛

Des Moines River

IOWA

Des Moines ⊛

Missouri River

INTERIOR

ILLINOIS

Springfield ⊛

MISSOURI
Jefferson City ⊛

ARKANSAS

Lake Superior

Mississippi River

Lake Michigan

MICHIGAN

Lansing ⊛

Lake Huron

LOWLANDS

Illinois River

INDIANA
Indianapolis ⊛

Wabash River

Ohio River

KENTUCKY

TENNESSEE

Lake Ontario
Niagara River

Lake Erie

PENNSYLVANIA

OHIO
Columbus ⊛

WEST VIRGINIA

NORTH CAROLINA

56°N
52°N
48°N
44°N
40°N
36°N

104°W   100°W   96°W   92°W   88°W   84°W   80°W   76°W

Plains make up most of the land of the North Central region. Therefore, most of the land in the region is fairly level.

▶ Does the area in which Mount Rushmore National Monument is located have a high or low elevation?

159

Ohio, Indiana, Illinois, Michigan, Wisconsin, Iowa, and Missouri are in the Interior Lowlands.

The Great Plains The western part of the Central Plains is called the Great Plains. The states of Minnesota, North Dakota, South Dakota, Nebraska, and Kansas are all part of the Great Plains. If you were crossing the Great Plains by car, you would see flat, almost treeless land that stretches to the horizon.

C. Lakes and Rivers

The Great Lakes Three of the five Great Lakes separate Canada from the states of Wisconsin, Michigan, and Ohio. The Great Lakes are especially important to the North Central region.

They supply the eastern part of the region with water for drinking and for growing crops.

The Great Lakes are a part of an important transportation route. Goods are shipped from the North Central region by means of the St. Lawrence Waterway. The waterway connects the Great Lakes to the Atlantic Ocean.

Rivers The Ohio River is an important river of the Interior Lowlands. It flows along the southern border of Ohio and Indiana and the southeastern edge of Illinois. There the Ohio River reaches the Mississippi River.

You already know that the Mississippi River begins in Minnesota. On its journey south, the Mississippi forms

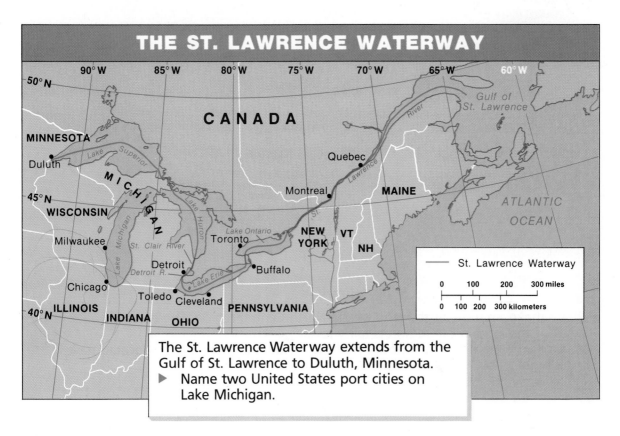

The St. Lawrence Waterway extends from the Gulf of St. Lawrence to Duluth, Minnesota.
▶ Name two United States port cities on Lake Michigan.

Farms stretch for miles across the North Central region.
► What landform do you see in the photograph?

part of the borders of Wisconsin, Iowa, Illinois, and Missouri.

The Missouri River starts in Montana and flows through six of the 12 states in the North Central region. It flows into the Mississippi near St. Louis, Missouri.

D. Why the North Central Region Is Special

Location The North Central region is often called the heartland of our country because of its location. It is west of the Appalachian Mountains and near the middle of our country, just as your heart is near the middle of your body.

Our Nation's Farming Area The North Central region is the most important farming area in the United States. Farmers in the region grow food for people all over the United States. The foods grown in this region help to keep Americans healthy.

A Manufacturing Area Farm products are not the only products of the North Central region. Its manufactured goods are important to the **economy** of the United States, too. The way a country provides and uses goods and services is its economy. You will read more about the economy of the North Central region in this chapter.

LESSON 1 REVIEW

THINK AND WRITE

A. How would you describe a prairie?

B. What physical features make up the North Central region?

C. How do the Great Lakes help the North Central region?

D. What are the two major kinds of products of the North Central region?

SKILLS CHECK

MAP SKILL

Read the map on page 156 to find Lake Superior, Lake Michigan, Lake Huron, and Lake Erie. List the states in the North Central region that border one or more of the Great Lakes.

161

Climate and Crops of the North Central Region

THINK ABOUT WHAT YOU KNOW
Name the kinds of things that plants need to grow. What kind of place would you choose if you were to plant a garden?

STUDY THE VOCABULARY

irrigation	crop rotation
drought	feedlot
erosion	meat-packing
strip cropping	industry

FOCUS YOUR READING
What crops are raised in the North Central region?

A. The Climate in the North Central Region

Hot Summers You have already learned that farmers grow many crops in the North Central region. Some of their products even reach the tables of families in other countries. Why are the farmers in this region able to grow so much food?

The climate in the North Central region helps farmers produce food. Summers are hot, and daytime temperatures are often over 85°F (29°C). Why does the North Central region have such warm summers?

The North Central region is located near the center of North America. The Atlantic and Pacific oceans are quite far away. If a place is near an ocean, the place is often cooled by sea breezes in summer. A place located in the middle of a continent quickly heats up during summer days.

Rainfall Warmth helps the crops of the North Central region, but water is important, too. The eastern part of the North Central region receives more rainfall than the western part. In states such as Ohio, Indiana, and Illinois, the average rainfall for a year is 38 inches (97 cm).

As you travel westward, the amount of rainfall becomes less. In most years the western part of the region receives only about 15 inches (38 cm) of rain. This is barely enough rain to grow hardy, or strong, crops like wheat. Some years even less rain falls in the western part of the region.

President George Bush inspects a drought area in Illinois.
► What crop is growing in this field?

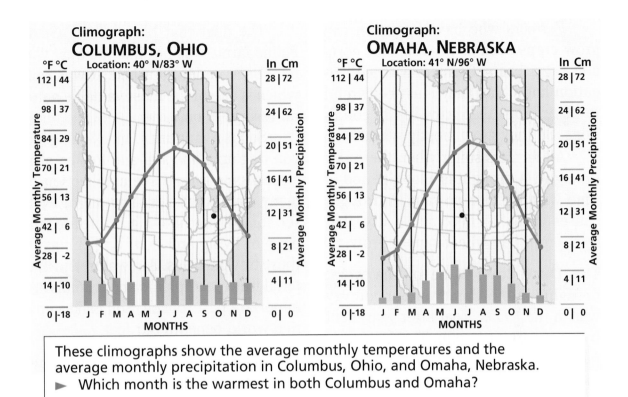

Climograph:
COLUMBUS, OHIO
Location: 40° N/83° W

Climograph:
OMAHA, NEBRASKA
Location: 41° N/96° W

These climographs show the average monthly temperatures and the average monthly precipitation in Columbus, Ohio, and Omaha, Nebraska.
► Which month is the warmest in both Columbus and Omaha?

Reading a Climograph On this page there are two special kinds of graphs. They are called climographs because they show temperatures and precipitation. You already know that temperature and precipitation are two important parts of climate.

Each climograph has temperature scales on the left side. The scale on the outside is for Fahrenheit temperatures. The scale on the inside is for Celsius temperatures. The months of the year are given along the bottom of the graph. The average temperature for each month is shown by a line.

On the right side of each graph are the scales for precipitation. Centimeters are given on the inside. Inches are given on the outside. The bars show the average monthly precipitation.

B. Living with a Dry Climate

Watching for Rain All over the Great Plains, farmers watch the sky each day for signs of rain. They are especially anxious in the spring when the seeds they have planted in their fields need plenty of water to start growing.

Farmers have a good reason to worry. Some years are especially dry and have almost no rainfall. Many farmers who own land along rivers bring water to their fields by means of **irrigation**. Irrigation is a way of watering crops to make sure they will grow. Most of the water used for irrigation in the Great Plains comes from ponds and streams near farms or from rivers that are miles away. In addition, some water comes from wells that are drilled deep into the ground.

Farmers who have irrigation can grow crops such as peas, beans, corn, and sugar beets. Farmers without irrigation know that they must be careful to plant crops that grow in dry conditions. So they grow mostly wheat.

All farmers suffer when there is a **drought**. A drought is a long period of time with little or no rain. A drought causes fields to become so dry that even crops like wheat cannot grow.

The Dust Bowl One of the worst droughts in the history of our country was in the 1930s. Year after year went by with very little rain. The fields and pastures in the Great Plains turned to dust. The Great Plains became known as the Dust Bowl.

Wind carried the dust from the farms of the Great Plains eastward across the United States. Some of the dust blew under the doors of the White House in Washington, D.C., where a group of people were working to help the farmers in the Great Plains.

The dust that blew off the Great Plains farms was not like the dust you might see under your bed. It was soil, which is one of the most valuable natural resources on earth.

Soil is a mixture of many things. If you dug up some soil and looked at it closely, you would see a collection of many small particles. You might even see some things moving. There are millions of living and nonliving things in these tiny particles. Air, water, and material from dead plants and animals are important parts of soil. Soil makes up a rich world beneath our feet.

Soil Erosion When water or wind wears something down or carries it away, we say that **erosion** is occurring. When a farmer's field loses soil through erosion, the field becomes less fertile. Eroded land is no longer good for growing crops.

Preventing Soil Erosion What can farmers do to prevent erosion? Farmers in the Great Plains know that nature's prairie grasses protect the soil. So many farmers practice **strip cropping**.

Wheat is growing in these fields between rows of grass and clover.
▶ How can you tell that wheat is not growing in each row?

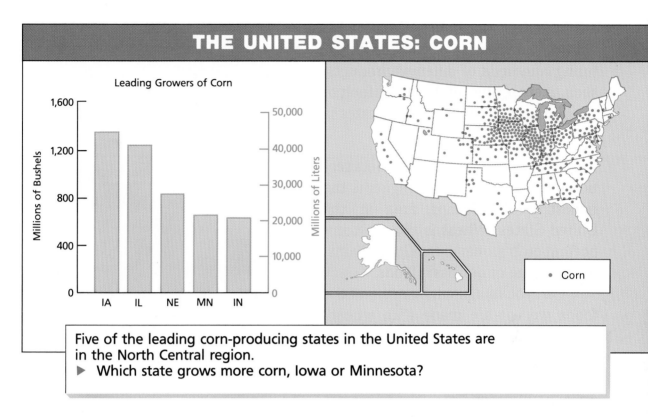

THE UNITED STATES: CORN

Leading Growers of Corn

Five of the leading corn-producing states in the United States are in the North Central region.
▶ Which state grows more corn, Iowa or Minnesota?

They plant one crop, like wheat, in long, narrow rows between bands of thick grass. The grass covers the soil and protects it from wind and rain.

Rotating Crops Other farmers practice **crop rotation**. That means they do not grow the same crops in the same fields year after year. One year they may grow corn in their fields. The next year they may grow clover in those same fields.

Farmers do this so that they will not weaken the soil. A single crop will use up important minerals in the soil if it is grown in the same field year after year. But different kinds of crops planted in the field from year to year will help keep the soil fertile. For example, corn takes nitrogen out of the soil. Clover enriches the soil with nitrogen.

C. Main Farming Areas of the North Central Region

The Corn Belt The North Central region is world-famous for the amount of corn it grows. Corn is so important a crop that part of the region is called the corn belt.

Look at the map above to see where the corn belt is located. It reaches from western Ohio all the way across the states of Indiana, Illinois, and Iowa. It even spills over into Missouri, Minnesota, and Nebraska.

What happens to all the corn that is grown in the United States? You have probably eaten corn on the cob or corn that has been canned or frozen. But corn is used to make many other foods. For example, the oil inside a kernel of corn is used in the making of ice

165

cream and peanut butter. Corn is also an important raw material for manufacturing hundreds of different products, such as soap, glue, and paper. Much of the corn grown in the United States is fed to farm animals.

The Wheat Belt The Great Plains section of the North Central region is the richest wheat-growing area in the United States. Wheat is the most important crop grown in the Great Plains, and it is one of our basic foods.

Can you imagine how many of the foods we eat are made with wheat? Most breads, cakes, and other baked goods contain flour that is made by grinding wheat. Many breakfast cereals, noodles, and pancake mixes are made of wheat. Most of the wheat in our foods comes from the Great Plains.

A big machine called a combine moves through a field of ripe wheat on the Great Plains.
▶ What is the combine doing?

THE UNITED STATES: WHEAT

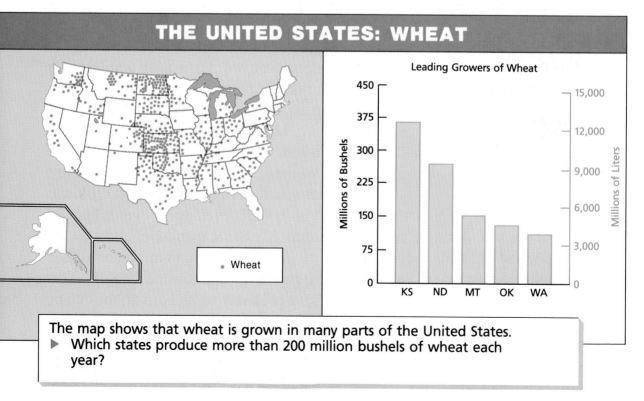

Leading Growers of Wheat

The map shows that wheat is grown in many parts of the United States.
▶ Which states produce more than 200 million bushels of wheat each year?

166

The Dairy Belt The two main dairy states in the North Central region are Wisconsin and Minnesota. Can you find those states on the map at the right? Wisconsin produces so much milk, cheese, and butter that it is often called America's Dairyland.

Why aren't Iowa, Indiana, and Illinois important dairy states, too? Summers in Wisconsin and Minnesota are shorter than those of Iowa, Indiana, and Illinois. In places with a short growing season, corn does not grow as well as grass. When the grass is full-grown, it is cut and dried for hay. Farmers feed the hay to the cattle that produce milk and other dairy products.

THE DAIRY BELT

The dairy belt

Milk, butter, and cheese come from the dairy belt.
▶ Is any part of your state in the dairy belt?

Dairy cattle graze near the barn on a North Central farm.
▶ Do you think the dairy farmer raises crops?

D. Other Farm Products of the Region

Soybeans Many farmers in the North Central region grow a variety of crops. One such crop is soybeans, a type of bean that can be crushed into flakes or boiled to produce oil. Soybeans are added to processed meats, such as patties and sausage. They are used in making mayonnaise, salad dressings, pet food, adhesive tape, and paint.

Beef Cattle Kansas and Nebraska are leading states in the production of beef. The beef comes from cattle that graze on natural prairie grasses during the summer. Farmers often let young beef cattle graze on the land when their land is too dry or not fertile enough for crops to grow.

In the winter, farmers must provide feed for their cattle in addition to the grasses. Some of the feed comes from grains or grasses that the farmers grew on their land during the summer. Some cattle feed is bought at special stores that sell supplies to farmers.

When the beef cattle are a few years old, they are sold and moved to **feedlots**. A feedlot is a large fenced-in pen in which cattle are kept for about four months. There they are fattened up with a special mixture of feed to make their meat more tasty.

PRODUCTS THAT COME FROM BEEF CATTLE

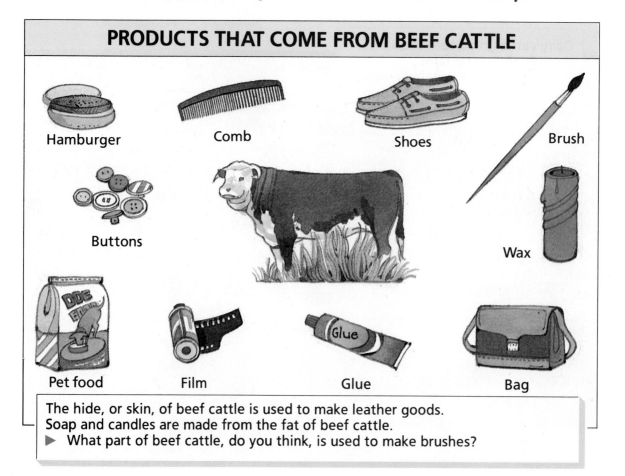

Hamburger   Comb   Shoes   Brush

Buttons   Wax

Pet food   Film   Glue   Bag

The hide, or skin, of beef cattle is used to make leather goods.
Soap and candles are made from the fat of beef cattle.
▶ What part of beef cattle, do you think, is used to make brushes?

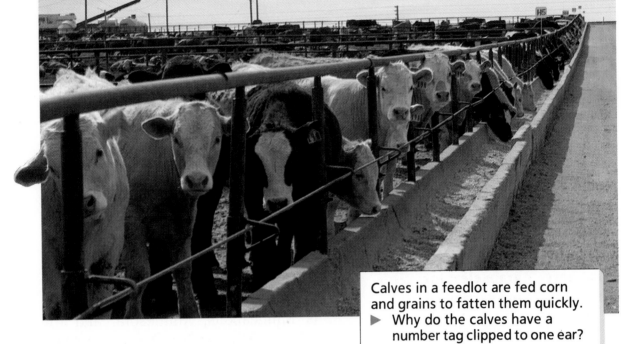

Calves in a feedlot are fed corn and grains to fatten them quickly.
► Why do the calves have a number tag clipped to one ear?

If you think about what happens to people when they exercise, you will better understand how a feedlot works. A person who gets a lot of exercise in sports or at work gets hard muscles and little fat. A person who doesn't get any exercise has soft muscles and a lot of flabby fat.

It is the same with cattle. When cattle graze on the prairie grasses, they get a lot of exercise. They don't gain much weight and they have strong muscles. Their meat becomes tough, not tender and juicy as most people like. In the feedlots, the cattle don't get much exercise, so they get fat and their meat becomes tender.

When the cattle have been fattened at the feedlots, they are ready to be slaughtered, and their meat is sent to a meat-packing plant. The industry that prepared the meat for us to eat is called the **meat-packing industry**.

Omaha, Nebraska, is the most important feedlot and meat-packing city in the United States. Cattle from the entire North Central region are brought to Omaha. Corn to feed the cattle is brought to Omaha from the corn belt.

LESSON 2 REVIEW

THINK AND WRITE

A. Why are summers in the North Central region hot?

B. How do irrigation and strip cropping help farmers?

C. Why are corn, wheat, and dairy products important to the economy of the North Central region?

D. Why are feedlots important to the cattle industry?

SKILLS CHECK

THINKING SKILL

Compare the climate in the area where corn is grown with the climate in the area where beef cattle are raised.

Natural Resources and Industries

THINK ABOUT WHAT YOU KNOW
Think back to what you have learned about industries in other regions of the United States. List three natural resources that industries depend on.

STUDY THE VOCABULARY
cannery   **grain elevator**
milling   **ore carrier**

FOCUS YOUR READING
What kinds of products are made from the natural resources of the North Central region?

A. Farms, Food, and Factories

Canning Foods   You have already learned in Lesson 2 that farms cover miles and miles of land in the North Central region. Corn, wheat, and vegetables are important crops.

Probably you've seen cans of peas, carrots, and other vegetables in your local supermarket. Factories that prepare these vegetables and put them into cans for sale in stores are called **canneries**. Many canneries in the North Central region prepare the foods grown by the farmers in the region.

Farmers in Ohio, Indiana, and Illinois grow fields of tomatoes. Many of the tomatoes are sold in supermarkets, but most are canned in factories. Then the tomatoes are sent to stores around the country. In Indianapolis, Indiana, there are many factories for canning tomatoes. A lot of canned vegetables come from canneries in Des Moines (dih MOYN), Iowa.

Flour Mills   Another way that crops are prepared for our tables is by **milling**. Milling is grinding a crop such as wheat or rice into flour for cooking or baking. The flour is made into breakfast cereals, bread, and other baked goods.

Two cities of the North Central region are important milling centers. One is Minneapolis, Minnesota, and the other is Kansas City, Missouri. These two cities are alike in an interesting way. Each is part of a pair of twin cities.

Minneapolis is located on the west bank of the Mississippi River, and its twin city across the river is St. Paul. Kansas City, Missouri, is separated from its twin, Kansas City, Kansas, by the Kansas River.

Canneries in the North Central region process food grown by the farmers in this area.
▶ What fruit is being canned?

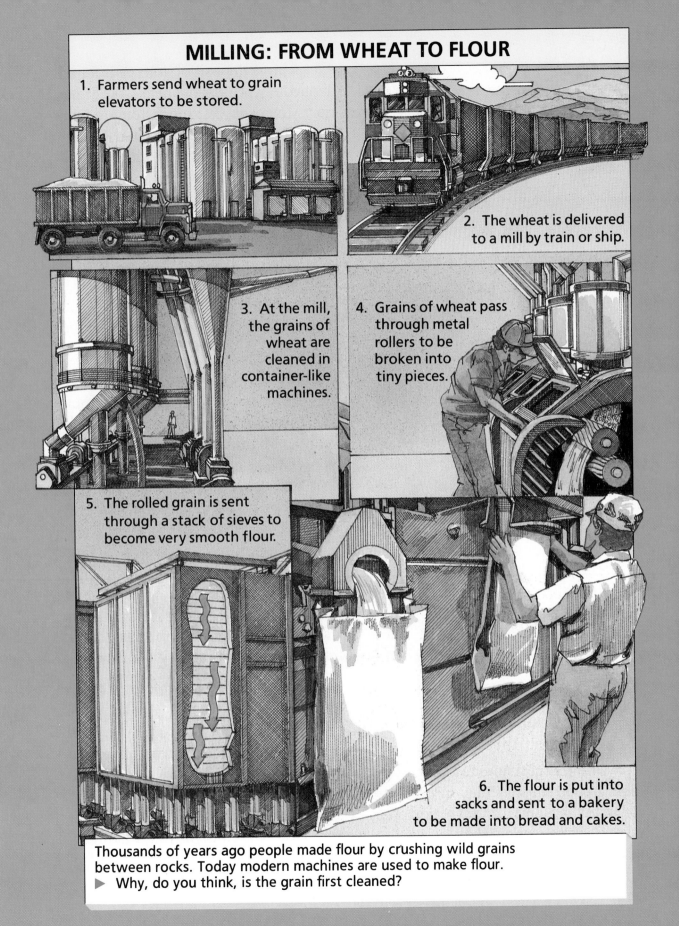

MILLING: FROM WHEAT TO FLOUR

1. Farmers send wheat to grain elevators to be stored.

2. The wheat is delivered to a mill by train or ship.

3. At the mill, the grains of wheat are cleaned in container-like machines.

4. Grains of wheat pass through metal rollers to be broken into tiny pieces.

5. The rolled grain is sent through a stack of sieves to become very smooth flour.

6. The flour is put into sacks and sent to a bakery to be made into bread and cakes.

Thousands of years ago people made flour by crushing wild grains between rocks. Today modern machines are used to make flour.
► Why, do you think, is the grain first cleaned?

Huge grain elevators store wheat grown on the Great Plains until it is shipped to flour mills.

▶ How, do you think, is the flour shipped to the mills?

Storing Grains No farmer alone could supply all the wheat a flour mill needs. Wheat farmers sell their wheat to the owner of a nearby **grain elevator**. This is a tall building where wheat is stored. The wheat is kept in the grain elevator until it is sent by train to a flour-milling center. Grain elevators stand tall and proud across the flat landscape of the Great Plains.

B. Mining and Manufacturing in the North Central Region

Iron Ore Large amounts of one of the most important minerals on earth are found in the North Central region. That mineral is iron ore, which is used to make steel. Steel is needed for many kinds of products.

A large deposit of iron ore is found in northern Minnesota near Lake Superior. Minnesota has more iron ore than any other state in the United States. There is so much iron ore in northern Minnesota that several small towns have the word *iron* in their name. Ironwood, Iron River, and Iron Mountain are just some of the towns.

When iron ore is mined, or dug, from the earth, it is in the form of huge lumps of rock. Only a small part of the rock contains iron. The ore must be processed to become useful.

Moving Iron Ore Let's follow some iron ore after it is mined in Minnesota. The iron ore is taken by truck or train to Duluth, Minnesota. Duluth is located along Lake Superior and is the busiest port on the Great Lakes. Most ships that leave Duluth carry iron ore.

In Duluth the iron ore is loaded onto a large ship called an **ore carrier**. The ship travels across Lake Superior, through a part of Lake Huron, and down Lake Michigan. Its destination is Gary, Indiana. On the map on page 156, follow the route taken by the carrier.

Using Iron Ore Steel mills in Gary, Indiana, produce many tons of steel each year. The steel is usually formed into bars or long sheets, which are used to make steel products.

The steel that we are following leaves Gary by railroad. It travels to our next stop, which is Detroit, Michigan. Detroit is one of our leading manufacturing centers.

Mount Rushmore in the Black Hills is a memorial to four great American Presidents.
▶ Which Presidents do you recognize?

In Detroit the steel shipped from Duluth is used in making automobiles. Among the many parts of an automobile that are made of steel are the body and engine. The finished automobiles are sent by truck or by train to many cities of the United States to be sold.

C. Other Minerals in the North Central Region

Two Valuable Minerals The North Central region has large supplies of two valuable minerals — lead and zinc. Missouri produces most of our nation's lead. Do you remember some of the ways that lead and zinc are used?

Gold and the Black Hills Another valuable mineral of the North Central region is the gold of South Dakota. A large gold deposit is mined in the southwestern corner of the state. This part of South Dakota forms the hilliest area of the Great Plains, called the Black Hills.

LESSON 3 REVIEW

THINK AND WRITE

A. Why are there many canneries in the North Central region?
B. Why are many automobile factories located in the North Central region?
C. Why is mining an important industry in the North Central region?

SKILLS CHECK

MAP SKILL
Locate these cities on the map on page 156: Chicago, Cleveland, Detroit, Duluth, Gary. Then use the Gazetteer to find the latitude and longitude of each city.

Living in the North Central Region

List three things you like to do in your free time. Do these things depend on where you live?

STUDY THE VOCABULARY

livestock   harvest
pasture   stockyard

FOCUS YOUR READING

What kinds of communities make up the North Central region?

A. Life on a Dairy Farm

Jason and Jennifer Bennett live on a modern dairy farm in Wisconsin. Their family owns a herd of dairy cows. They own other **livestock** as well. Livestock are farm animals such as cows, horses, and sheep.

Families who raise livestock must plan their work carefully. The Bennetts must be sure to have enough food for all the animals. In the summer, dairy cows graze in the **pasture**, or grassy field, where animals can feed.

Winter is a different story. Pasture for animals cannot grow in Wisconsin during the long, cold winter months. So the livestock must eat hay and other foods. These foods are raised on the farm during summer months.

The Bennett farm has a large hayfield and a field for corn. Some of the corn is fed to the livestock during the winter. Mrs. Bennett has a large vegetable garden. She also takes care of an orchard so that the family can enjoy fresh fruits.

With pastures, cornfields, and orchards, the Bennetts and their neighbors need a lot of land. So families in the region are usually spread far apart. Jason and Jennifer must take a long bus ride to and from school.

In the morning before leaving for school, Jason and Jennifer get up early

A recent snowfall blankets this land in Wisconsin.
▶ How do you think people in this area make a living?

174

FROM:

Farmer Boy

By: Laura Ingalls Wilder
Setting: The United States in the late 1890s

In *Farmer Boy*, Laura Ingalls Wilder described a school long ago. As you read the passage that follows, think how the school is different from your school.

. . . **M**r. Corse rapped on his desk with his ruler; it was time for school to begin. All the boys and girls went to their seats. The girls sat on the left side of the room and the boys sat on the right side, with the log stove and wood-box in the middle between them. The big ones sat in the back seats, the middle-sized ones in the middle seats, and the little ones in the front seats. All the seats were the same size. The big boys could hardly get their knees under their desks, and the little boys couldn't rest their feet on the floor. . . .

No whispering was permitted in school, and no fidgeting. Everyone must be perfectly still and keep his eyes fixed on his lesson. Almanzo and Miles held up their primers and tried not to swing their legs. Their legs grew so tired that they ached, dangling from the edge of the seat. . . .

At recess the girls were let out first. They put on their hoods and cloaks and quietly went outdoors.

After fifteen minutes, Mr. Corse rapped on the window and they came in, hung their wraps in the entry, and took their books again. Then the boys would go out for fifteen minutes.

They rushed out shouting into the cold. The first out began snowballing the others. All that had sleds scrambled up Hardscrabble Hill; they flung themselves, stomach-down, on the sleds and swooped down the long, steep slope. They upset in the snow; they ran and wrestled and threw snowballs and washed one another's faces with snow, and all the time they yelled as loud as they could.

Written by Laura Ingalls Wilder. Illustrated by Garth Williams.

Children who live on a farm often have daily chores.
▶ How is the girl taking good care of her pet calf?

enough to help with farm chores. Jason feeds the pigs and chickens. He also cares for his rabbits. Fluffy, his favorite rabbit, won a blue ribbon at a county fair last year. Jennifer helps to feed the young animals and the dog and cats.

Jason and Jennifer also have chores to do after school. Jason helps his father milk the cows. Sometimes he works in the fields with his father or helps him clean out the barn and stable. Jason is too young to drive the tractor or pickup truck, but someday soon he will help with that, too.

After school, Jennifer helps her mother with many chores. Often she helps with the cooking. Then Mrs. Bennett has more time to pay bills and

Some inventions that improved farming in the United States and other countries are shown on this time line.
▶ Which was invented first — the reaper or the steel plow?

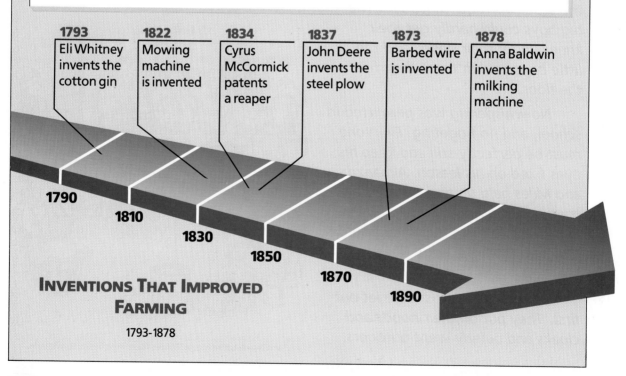

1793 Eli Whitney invents the cotton gin

1822 Mowing machine is invented

1834 Cyrus McCormick patents a reaper

1837 John Deere invents the steel plow

1873 Barbed wire is invented

1878 Anna Baldwin invents the milking machine

1790 1810 1830 1850 1870 1890

INVENTIONS THAT IMPROVED FARMING
1793-1878

A machine called a baler is used to harvest hay. The baler presses the cut hay in rectangular bales.
► How are the two men in the field getting the work done?

order supplies for the farm. Mrs. Bennett has a computer in the farm office, where she takes care of the farm's business. Last years thousands and thousands of dollars were spent on feed for the animals and farm equipment.

Summertime is the busiest season for the Bennetts. When the corn and hay are ripe, the whole family must work together. Sometimes Mr. Bennett hires workers to help. The hay must be cut and bundled together in bales, or large square piles pulled together with wire or strong cord.

In the summer Mrs. Bennett's fruits and vegetables are ready to be **harvested,** or picked. She and Jennifer spend a lot of time preserving these foods. She stores the jars of tomatoes, beans, carrots, and peaches in the basement of her home. In the cold winter months, the family enjoys eating the vegetables and fruits that they grew on the farm.

The Bennetts try to take a vacation once a year. But they cannot just lock up their home and leave on a trip, as many other families do. Their livestock depend on them for food and protection. Dairy cows have to be milked every day and the other animals must be fed. Mr. Bennett must hire someone to care for the livestock while the family is away. After all, the Bennetts depend on their animals.

B. The Largest City of the North Central Region

Chicago, Illinois Not everyone in the North Central region lives on a farm. About two thirds of the people in the North Central region live in cities. Chicago, Illinois, is the largest city in population in the North Central region. It is also the third largest city in population in the United States.

The Windy City Chicago is called the Windy City because it has more windy days than most places in the United States. If you look at the map on page 156, you can see that Chicago is at the southern end of Lake Michigan.

Winds often blow across Lake Michigan. These winds usually start out as mild breezes from the north or northwest. But as they cross the flat lake waters, they become stronger and stronger. By the time they reach Chicago, they are very strong.

A Transportation Center Chicago, which is a port city, is the largest city near the center of the United States. This means that many trains, trucks, and automobiles pass through Chicago. Many people who travel across the United States must pass through this central city.

Many airplanes also pass through Chicago. Chicago's O'Hare Airport is the busiest in the United States. More than 2,000 planes arrive and take off each day. That is more than one flight every minute.

Chicago, Illinois, is located on Lake Michigan.
► By looking at the photograph, what kind of recreation do you think is popular in Chicago?

The Civic Center (left) and the Old Cowtown Museum (right) are both located in Wichita.
► What does the museum tell you about Wichita's past?

C. A Modern City That Was Once a Cow Town

Some cities of the Great Plains were once small towns known as cow towns. Cowboys from far and wide drove their herds along cattle trails into these towns. There they sold the cattle to a **stockyard**. A stockyard is a large yard in which livestock are kept for a short time before they are slaughtered or shipped to market.

Wichita (WICH uh taw), Kansas, was once known as a cow town. It started to grow when a railroad was built nearby in 1872. The town became an important shipping point for cattle. Soon many people arrived to buy and sell cattle. A hotel, a post office, and a bank were built. Gradually, other buildings were added. Today, Wichita is the most populated city in Kansas.

Wichita and other cities of the Great Plains are still important for their stockyards. In Wichita you can visit a museum park called Historic Wichita Cow Town. There you can relive the life of Wichita's people in the late 1800s.

LESSON **4** REVIEW

THINK AND WRITE

A. Why do dairy farmers in Wisconsin plant corn during the summer?

B. Why can Chicago be called a major transportation center?

C. What helped Wichita, Kansas, to grow from a small town to a large city?

SKILLS CHECK

MAP SKILL
Find Chicago, Illinois, and Wichita, Kansas, on the map on page 156. Use the scale bar to find the distance in miles between the two cities.

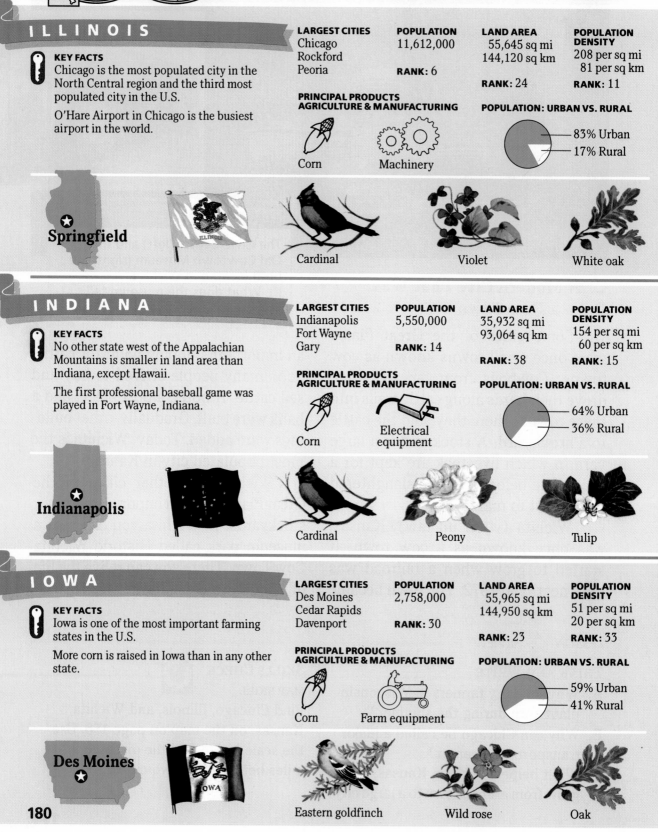

ILLINOIS

KEY FACTS
Chicago is the most populated city in the North Central region and the third most populated city in the U.S.

O'Hare Airport in Chicago is the busiest airport in the world.

LARGEST CITIES
Chicago
Rockford
Peoria

POPULATION
11,612,000

RANK: 6

LAND AREA
55,645 sq mi
144,120 sq km

RANK: 24

POPULATION DENSITY
208 per sq mi
81 per sq km

RANK: 11

PRINCIPAL PRODUCTS AGRICULTURE & MANUFACTURING

Corn

Machinery

POPULATION: URBAN VS. RURAL
83% Urban
17% Rural

Springfield

Cardinal

Violet

White oak

INDIANA

KEY FACTS
No other state west of the Appalachian Mountains is smaller in land area than Indiana, except Hawaii.

The first professional baseball game was played in Fort Wayne, Indiana.

LARGEST CITIES
Indianapolis
Fort Wayne
Gary

POPULATION
5,550,000

RANK: 14

LAND AREA
35,932 sq mi
93,064 sq km

RANK: 38

POPULATION DENSITY
154 per sq mi
60 per sq km

RANK: 15

PRINCIPAL PRODUCTS AGRICULTURE & MANUFACTURING

Corn

Electrical equipment

POPULATION: URBAN VS. RURAL
64% Urban
36% Rural

Indianapolis

Cardinal

Peony

Tulip

IOWA

KEY FACTS
Iowa is one of the most important farming states in the U.S.

More corn is raised in Iowa than in any other state.

LARGEST CITIES
Des Moines
Cedar Rapids
Davenport

POPULATION
2,758,000

RANK: 30

LAND AREA
55,965 sq mi
144,950 sq km

RANK: 23

POPULATION DENSITY
51 per sq mi
20 per sq km

RANK: 33

PRINCIPAL PRODUCTS AGRICULTURE & MANUFACTURING

Corn

Farm equipment

POPULATION: URBAN VS. RURAL
59% Urban
41% Rural

Des Moines

Eastern goldfinch

Wild rose

Oak

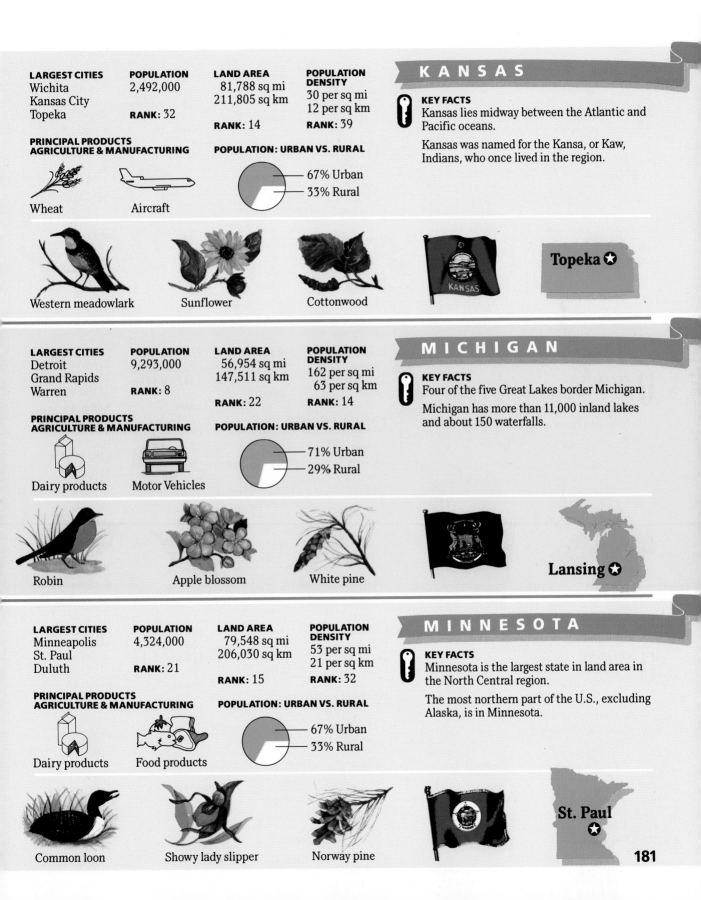

KANSAS

KEY FACTS

Kansas lies midway between the Atlantic and Pacific oceans.

Kansas was named for the Kansa, or Kaw, Indians, who once lived in the region.

LARGEST CITIES	POPULATION	LAND AREA	POPULATION DENSITY
Wichita	2,492,000	81,788 sq mi	30 per sq mi
Kansas City		211,805 sq km	12 per sq km
Topeka	RANK: 32	RANK: 14	RANK: 39

PRINCIPAL PRODUCTS
AGRICULTURE & MANUFACTURING

Wheat   Aircraft

POPULATION: URBAN VS. RURAL

67% Urban
33% Rural

Western meadowlark   Sunflower   Cottonwood

Topeka ★

MICHIGAN

KEY FACTS

Four of the five Great Lakes border Michigan.

Michigan has more than 11,000 inland lakes and about 150 waterfalls.

LARGEST CITIES	POPULATION	LAND AREA	POPULATION DENSITY
Detroit	9,293,000	56,954 sq mi	162 per sq mi
Grand Rapids		147,511 sq km	63 per sq km
Warren	RANK: 8	RANK: 22	RANK: 14

PRINCIPAL PRODUCTS
AGRICULTURE & MANUFACTURING

Dairy products   Motor Vehicles

POPULATION: URBAN VS. RURAL

71% Urban
29% Rural

Robin   Apple blossom   White pine

Lansing ★

MINNESOTA

KEY FACTS

Minnesota is the largest state in land area in the North Central region.

The most northern part of the U.S., excluding Alaska, is in Minnesota.

LARGEST CITIES	POPULATION	LAND AREA	POPULATION DENSITY
Minneapolis	4,324,000	79,548 sq mi	53 per sq mi
St. Paul		206,030 sq km	21 per sq km
Duluth	RANK: 21	RANK: 15	RANK: 32

PRINCIPAL PRODUCTS
AGRICULTURE & MANUFACTURING

Dairy products   Food products

POPULATION: URBAN VS. RURAL

67% Urban
33% Rural

Common loon   Showy lady slipper   Norway pine

St. Paul ★

MISSOURI

KEY FACTS

The Mississippi and Missouri rivers have made Missouri an important transportation center.

Mark Twain, a well-known writer, was born in Missouri.

LARGEST CITIES
Kansas City
St. Louis
Springfield

POPULATION
5,192,000

RANK: 15

LAND AREA
68,945 sq mi
178,568 sq km

RANK: 18

POPULATION DENSITY
74 per sq mi
29 per sq km

RANK: 27

PRINCIPAL PRODUCTS AGRICULTURE & MANUFACTURING

Soybeans

Transportation equipment

POPULATION: URBAN VS. RURAL

68% Urban
32% Rural

Jefferson City

Bluebird

Hawthorn

Flowering dogwood

NEBRASKA

KEY FACTS

Tall prairie grasses grow in parts of eastern Nebraska.

Nebraska has more than 2,000 lakes.

LARGEST CITIES
Omaha
Lincoln
Grand Island

POPULATION
1,588,000

RANK: 37

LAND AREA
76,644 sq mi
198,508 sq km

RANK: 10

POPULATION DENSITY
21 per sq mi
8 per sq km

RANK: 41

PRINCIPAL PRODUCTS AGRICULTURE & MANUFACTURING

Cattle

Food products

POPULATION: URBAN VS. RURAL

63% Urban
37% Rural

Lincoln

Western meadowlark

Goldenrod

Cottonwood

NORTH DAKOTA

KEY FACTS

North Dakota lies in the center of the North American continent.

North Dakota was named for the Sioux Indians, who called themselves Dakota, meaning "friends."

LARGEST CITIES
Fargo
Bismarck
Grand Forks

POPULATION
660,000

RANK: 47

LAND AREA
69,300 sq mi
179,486 sq km

RANK: 17

POPULATION DENSITY
10 per sq mi
4 per sq km

RANK: 45

PRINCIPAL PRODUCTS AGRICULTURE & MANUFACTURING

Wheat

Farm equipment

POPULATION: URBAN VS. RURAL

49% Urban
51% Rural

Bismarck

Western meadowlark

Wild prairie rose

American elm

182

O H I O

LARGEST CITIES
Columbus
Cleveland
Cincinnati

POPULATION
10,791,000

RANK: 7

LAND AREA
41,004 sq mi
106,201 sq km

RANK: 35

POPULATION DENSITY
263 per sq mi
102 per sq km

RANK: 9

KEY FACTS
Eight Ohio cities on Lake Erie are ports of the St. Lawrence Seaway.

Ohio is the birthplace of seven presidents of the U.S.

PRINCIPAL PRODUCTS AGRICULTURE & MANUFACTURING

Soybeans

Transportaion equipment

POPULATION: URBAN VS. RURAL
73% Urban
27% Rural

Cardinal

Scarlet carnation

Buckeye

Columbus

S O U T H   D A K O T A

LARGEST CITIES
Sioux Falls
Rapid City
Aberdeen

POPULATION
708,000

RANK: 45

LAND AREA
75,952 sq mi
196,715 sq km

RANK: 16

POPULATION DENSITY
9 per sq mi
4 per sq km

RANK: 47

KEY FACTS
Carvings of the heads of George Washington, Thomas Jefferson, Theodore Roosevelt, and Abraham Lincoln were made on Mount Rushmore.

South Dakota has the smallest number of foreign-born residents in the U.S.

PRINCIPAL PRODUCTS AGRICULTURE & MANUFACTURING

Cattle

Meat products

POPULATION: URBAN VS. RURAL
46% Urban
54% Rural

Ring-necked pheasant

American pasqueflower

Black Hills spruce

Pierre

W I S C O N S I N

LARGEST CITIES
Milwaukee
Madison
Green Bay

POPULATION
4,808,000

RANK: 17

LAND AREA
54,426 sq mi
140,964 sq km

RANK: 25

POPULATION DENSITY
88 per sq mi
34 per sq km

RANK: 24

KEY FACTS
There are more dairy cows in Wisconsin than in any other state in the U.S.

Wisconsin was the first state to adopt the number system for marking highways.

PRINCIPAL PRODUCTS AGRICULTURE & MANUFACTURING

Dairy Products

Machinery

POPULATION: URBAN VS. RURAL
64% Urban
36% Rural

Robin

Wood violet

Sugar maple

WISCONSIN
1848

Madison

183

USING THE VOCABULARY

prairie	feedlot
economy	grain elevator
irrigation	milling
erosion	pasture
crop rotation	harvest

On a separate sheet of paper, write the word or words from the list above that best complete each sentence.

1. A way of watering crops is called _____.
2. Grinding a crop such as wheat or rice into flour is called _____.
3. Farmers who grow a different crop in the same field each year practice _____.
4. When crops are ready to be picked, they are ready for the _____.
5. A _____ is level or rolling land covered with grass.
6. Wheat is stored in a _____ before it is sent to a flour mill.
7. Beef cattle are fattened in a large fenced-in pen called a _____.
8. Water or wind can cause a farmer's field to lose soil through a process called _____.
9. The grassy field where cows graze is a _____.
10. The way a country provides and uses goods and services is its _____.

REMEMBERING WHAT YOU READ

On a separate sheet of paper, answer the questions in complete sentences.

1. Why were the pioneers who crossed the Mississippi River important?
2. Why is "the heartland of our country" a good name for the North Central region?
3. Why does a place located in the middle of a continent heat up quickly in the summer?
4. Why are soybeans an important crop of the North Central region?
5. What is the name of the most important feedlot and meat-packing city in the United States?
6. What happens to the tomatoes grown in Ohio, Indiana, and Illinois?
7. What are the Black Hills of South Dakota known for?
8. Why are Wisconsin's dairy cows fed differently in summer?
9. Why is Chicago called the Windy City?
10. What is the busiest airport in the United States?

TYING LANGUAGE ARTS TO SOCIAL STUDIES

Pretend you are a farm child in the Great Plains Dust Bowl. Write to a friend, explaining why your family has decided to leave the farm. Tell how you feel about leaving your home.

THINKING CRITICALLY

On a separate sheet of paper, answer the following questions in complete sentences.

1. If you were a blind pioneer like Laura Ingall's sister Mary, how would you know what the land and climate on your journey west were like?
2. Why do farmers all over the Great Plains watch the sky every day?
3. Why is Wisconsin called America's Dairyland?
4. Name some products made from steel.
5. If you lived on a farm as Jason and Jennifer Bennett do, which would be your favorite chore? Which would you enjoy least?

SUMMARIZING THE CHAPTER

Copy this graphic organizer on a separate sheet of paper. Under the main idea for each lesson, write three items that support that idea.

CHAPTER THEME The North Central region is a leading agricultural and industrial region of the United States.

LESSON 1

The North Central region has several important geographic features.

1. _____
2. _____
3. _____

LESSON 3

The North Central region has several major industries.

1. _____
2. _____
3. _____

LESSON 2

The climate and technology of the North Central region support different types of agriculture.

1. _____
2. _____
3. _____

LESSON 4

While farming is very important in the North Central region, most of the people live and work in cities.

1. _____
2. _____
3. _____

CHAPTER 7

THE SOUTHWEST REGION

*L*arge cattle and sheep ranches are an important part of the Southwest region. And its oil fields have brought much industry to the region.

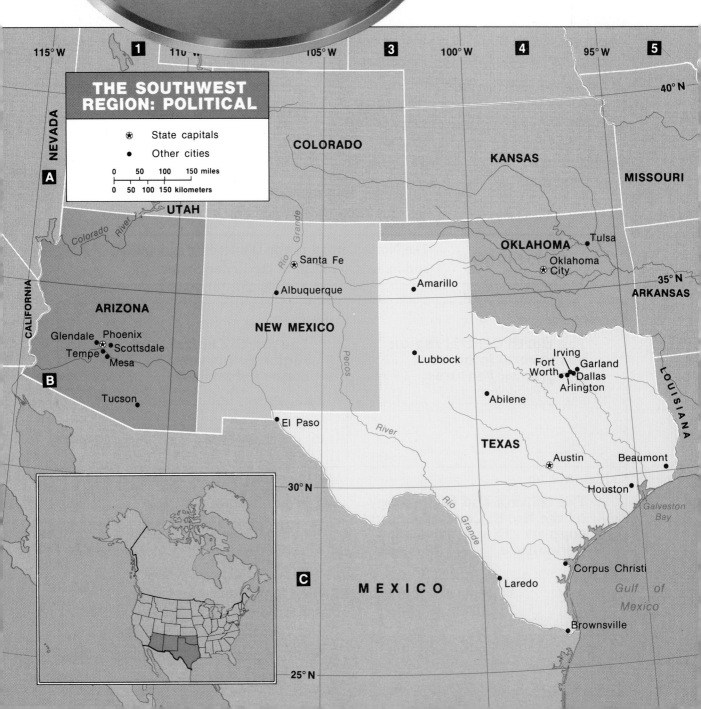

THE SOUTHWEST REGION: POLITICAL

⊛ State capitals

• Other cities

0   50   100   150 miles

0   50   100   150 kilometers

NEVADA

COLORADO

KANSAS

MISSOURI

UTAH

OKLAHOMA

Tulsa

Santa Fe

Oklahoma City

ARKANSAS

Albuquerque

Amarillo

ARIZONA

NEW MEXICO

CALIFORNIA

Glendale Phoenix
Tempe Scottsdale
Mesa

Lubbock

Irving
Fort Garland
Worth Dallas
Arlington

LOUISIANA

Tucson

Abilene

El Paso

TEXAS

Austin

Beaumont

Houston

Galveston Bay

Corpus Christi

MEXICO

Laredo

Gulf of Mexico

Brownsville

Colorado River

Rio Grande

Pecos River

Rio Grande

The Land in the Southwest

THINK ABOUT WHAT YOU KNOW

Think about a trip that you have taken. What sights did you see?

STUDY THE VOCABULARY

mesa   panhandle
butte   reservation

FOCUS YOUR READING

What kinds of land are found in the Southwest?

A. A Spectacular Place

The Grand Canyon "Fantastic," gasped Tommy as he stared off into the distance. Tommy and his parents were driving to the Grand Canyon for a vacation. They had come a long way and had seen miles of desert, desert plants, and long straight roads all day.

Suddenly Tommy saw an enormous steel bridge looming ahead on the road. He pressed his nose against the car window as they crossed the bridge. He couldn't believe his eyes. Far below them, like a tiny silver ribbon, was a river. Tommy asked, "Is that the river that goes through the Grand Canyon?"

"Yes," said Tommy's mother, "that's the Colorado River. It doesn't look like much from up here, but it carved out the walls of the Grand Canyon over millions of years."

The Grand Canyon of the Colorado River is located in northwestern Arizona. Some people believe it is the most spectacular place on earth. A famous traveler named Richard Halliburton once visited the Grand Canyon. This is how he described what he saw.

When you see the thing with your own eyes, the sight strikes you speechless — that mile drop to the river — that ten-mile [empty space] across to the other brink — those color-splashed temples and towers and pyramids of rock that swell up from terraced walls — that yawning sea of painted splendor falling away into bottomless mysteries.

CITY INDEX

Cities less than 100,000		
Santa Fe (NM) A-2		

Cities of 100,000 to 499,999	Corpus Christi (TX) C-4	Tempe (AZ) B-1
Abilene (TX) B-4	El Paso (TX) B-2	Tucson (AZ) B-1
Albuquerque (NM) A-2	Fort Worth (TX) B-4	Tulsa (OK) A-4
Amarillo (TX) A-3	Garland (TX) B-4	
Arlington (TX) B-4	Glendale (AZ) B-1	Cities of 500,000 to 999,999
Austin (TX) B-4	Irving (TX) B-4	Phoenix (AZ) B-1
Beaumont (TX) B-5	Laredo (TX) C-4	
Brownsville (TX) C-4	Lubbock (TX) B-3	Cities of 1,000,000 or more
	Mesa (AZ) B-1	Dallas (TX) B-4
	Oklahoma City (OK) A-4	Houston (TX) C-4
	Scottsdale (AZ) B-1	

The Southwest region has one city of more than 500,000 people and two cities of more than 1 million people.
▶ Which of the three most populated cities in the region is near the Gulf of Mexico?

Rock Formations Many other interesting landforms are found near the Grand Canyon. Steep rock walls lead up to **mesas** (MAY suz). The word *mesa* means "table" in Spanish. It was the word used by Spanish explorers to describe a high broad and level area that is smaller than a plateau.

In other places a **butte** (byoot), or single flat-topped hill, juts up from the level land around it. A butte usually has the same kind of steep rock walls a mesa has. These, and many other unusual features, make the Southwest a very interesting region.

B. Sizes, Shapes, and Borders

Sizes The Southwest region is made up of the states of Oklahoma, Texas, New Mexico, and Arizona. It is not difficult to find these states on a map if you first look for Texas. Texas is easy to find because it is so large. It is the second largest state in our country, after Alaska. New Mexico, the next largest state in the Southwest, is less than half the size of Texas.

Texas has the most people of any state in the Southwest. It has a population of over 16 million. The population of Oklahoma, New Mexico, and Arizona adds up to only about half of the number of people in Texas.

Shapes You may have noticed on the map on page 186 that Texas and Oklahoma each have straight sections of land that reach out past the main parts of the states. These sections are called **panhandles** because they look like the handle of a pan. Oklahoma's panhandle stretches to the west, just north of the Texas panhandle.

Borders The Rio Grande (REE oh-grand) is a long river that forms part of the border between the United States and Mexico. The name *Rio Grande* means "large river" in Spanish, a good name for this long, wide river.

You might have noticed that the border between Arizona and New Mexico is a straight line. This straight line continues north, also separating the states of Utah and Colorado, which are not part of the Southwest region.

This butte is located near the Grand Canyon, in Arizona.
► How is a butte different from other hills?

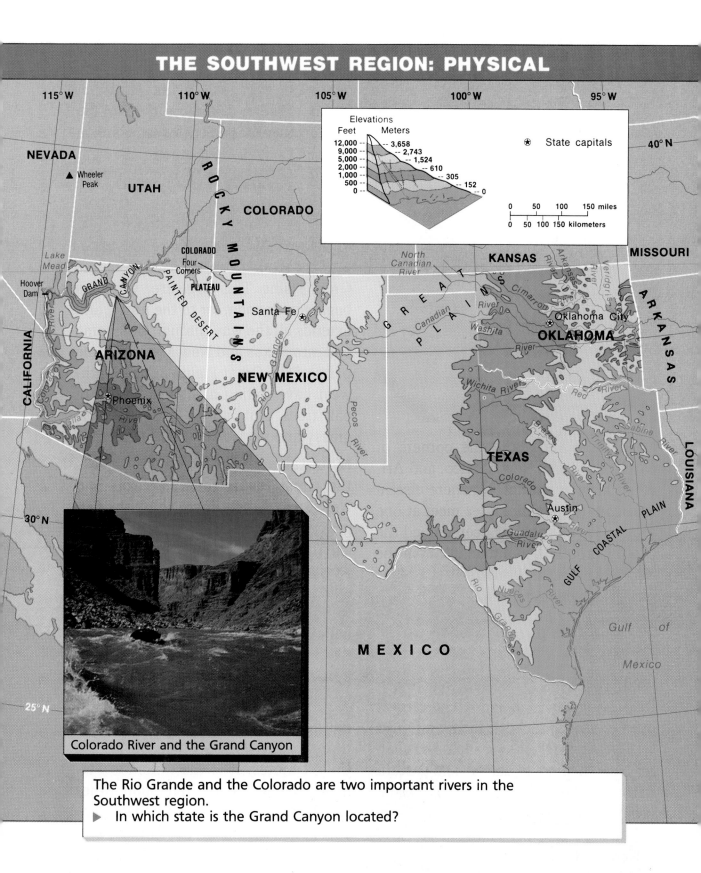

THE SOUTHWEST REGION: PHYSICAL

Elevations

Feet	Meters
12,000	3,658
9,000	2,743
5,000	1,524
2,000	610
1,000	305
500	152
0	0

⊛ State capitals

0   50   100   150 miles

0   50 100 150 kilometers

NEVADA

▲ Wheeler Peak

UTAH

COLORADO

R O C K Y   M O U N T A I N S

Lake Mead

Hoover Dam

GRAND CANYON

PAINTED DESERT

COLORADO PLATEAU

Four Corners

CALIFORNIA

ARIZONA

Gila River

Phoenix

Rio Grande

NEW MEXICO

Santa Fe ⊛

Pecos River

North Canadian River

G R E A T   P L A I N S

Canadian River

Washita River

KANSAS

Arkansas River

Cimarron River

Verdigris River

Oklahoma City

OKLAHOMA

Wichita River

Red River

Salt Fork

MISSOURI

ARKANSAS

LOUISIANA

TEXAS

Brazos River

Colorado River

Trinity River

Sabine River

Austin ⊛

Guadalupe River

GULF COASTAL PLAIN

Nueces River

Rio Grande

MEXICO

Gulf of Mexico

40° N

30° N

25° N

115° W   110° W   105° W   100° W   95° W

Colorado River and the Grand Canyon

The Rio Grande and the Colorado are two important rivers in the Southwest region.

▶ In which state is the Grand Canyon located?

The Four Corners monument marks the place where Utah, Colorado, New Mexico, and Arizona meet.
▶ What landform can you see in the background?

The place where the corners of Utah, Colorado, New Mexico, and Arizona meet is special. Nowhere else in our country do four states meet at one point. So the spot has been named the Four Corners. A monument marks the place where the borders of the four states come together.

C. Physical Features of the Southwest

Plains and Hills The Southwest region has many kinds of land. The largest part of the Southwest, including most of Texas and Oklahoma and nearly half of New Mexico, is plains. The eastern part of Texas is part of the Gulf Coastal Plain. This large area stretches from Florida all the way along the Gulf of Mexico into the country of Mexico.

Texas is the only state in the Southwest with a seacoast and the only one with a coastal plain. Houston, Dallas, and San Antonio — three of the largest cities of the Southwest — are on the Gulf Coastal Plain. Austin, the capital city of Texas, is also on the Gulf Coastal Plain.

The Great Plains A hilly area lies just to the west of Austin. These hills separate the Gulf Coastal Plain from the Great Plains. This large area of plains begins in Canada, far to the north, and extends all the way through Oklahoma and into Texas and New Mexico. Some parts of the Great Plains in the Southwest have rolling hills with forests of oak trees. But most of the plains is grassy and flat.

Mountains If you drove west across the Great Plains through Texas and New Mexico, you might think the flat, grassy plains would never end, but eventually you would come to the Rocky Mountains. These mountains extend across New Mexico from north to south, nearly cutting the state in half. Wheeler Peak, the highest peak in the Southwest, is in the Rocky Mountains. Wheeler Peak is 13,065 feet (3,982 m) high.

Plateaus The Colorado River cuts through the largest plateau in the United States. It is the Colorado Plateau. The Colorado River and other smaller rivers have cut many deep canyons, such as the Grand Canyon, into the surface of the Colorado Plateau.

(left) This Navajo woman teaches the art of rug weaving.
▶ What is the job of the Navajo men at the right?

Many Indian **reservations** are located on the Colorado Plateau. An Indian reservation is an area that is set aside by the United States government for Native American people to live in. The Navajo (NAV uh hoh) Reservation, which covers parts of Arizona, New Mexico, and Utah is the largest in the United States. About 95,000 Navajo live on the reservation.

Ranges and Basins The area of southern Arizona and New Mexico and southwestern Texas includes many mountain ranges. The mountain ranges are separated by broad, flat valleys called basins. This is a desert land and so it gets very little rain. Find this area on the map on page 189.

LESSON *1* REVIEW

THINK AND WRITE

A. Why is the Grand Canyon called "spectacular"?
B. Name a special fact about the Southwest for each word: (1) size, (2) shape, (3) borders.
C. Explain this statement: The Southwest region has several different land features.

SKILLS CHECK

MAP SKILL

Find the following rivers on the map on page 189: Red River, Rio Grande, Colorado River. Write the names on a sheet of paper. Next to the name of each river write the name of the southwestern state or states in which that river forms a border.

Farms and Ranches of the Southwest

THINK ABOUT WHAT YOU KNOW
Make a list of some of your favorite foods. Do any of them come from a special region in the United States? Think of the farm products from the other regions you have studied.

STUDY THE VOCABULARY
cactus   ranch
pesticide

FOCUS YOUR READING
How do people use the land and climate of the Southwest to produce food?

A. A Land of Sunshine

Sunny Skies Can you imagine living in a place where the sun shines almost every day? Parts of the Southwest region have more sunny days during the year than any other region of the United States.

All that sunshine keeps temperatures high in the summer. South Texas and southern Arizona have warm winters, too. Many January days in southern Arizona warm up to 70°F (21°C) or more. But winter temperatures can get very low in the areas of the Southwest that are part of the Great Plains, the Rocky Mountains, and the Colorado Plateau.

Precipitation Sunny weather may be nice, but it means that many parts of the Southwest region get very little precipitation. The deserts of southern Arizona and New Mexico and western Texas get less than 10 inches (25 cm) of rain a year.

The plains get more rain than that, but even so, many of those areas have problems getting enough water for farming. Only in eastern Texas and Oklahoma is there usually enough precipitation for farming.

High up in the Rocky Mountains there are frequent winter snows. The snow melts in the spring and summer, feeding the Colorado River, the Rio Grande, and other important rivers of the Southwest.

Natural Vegetation You already know that most of the plains of the

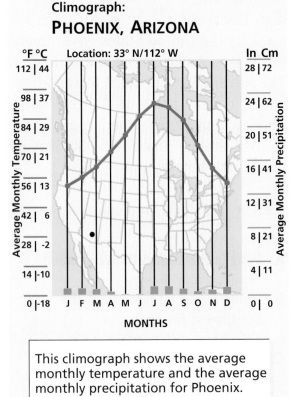

Climograph:
PHOENIX, ARIZONA

Location: 33° N/112° W

This climograph shows the average monthly temperature and the average monthly precipitation for Phoenix.
► Which month is warmer, July or August?

192

Giant cactuses thrive in Saguaro National Monument, in Arizona.
► Why do cactuses grow well in desert areas?

but they don't have leaves. Cactuses come in many shapes and sizes, from small barrel shapes with thorny spikes to large treelike varieties.

B. Farming and Irrigation

Watering the Land Because so much of the Southwest region lacks rain, many farmers use irrigation to grow crops. Without irrigation of the land, farming would hardly be possible in western Oklahoma and Texas or anywhere in New Mexico and Arizona. But with irrigation, the Southwest region has become a leader in the production of certain crops.

Cotton grows in this irrigated field in Texas.
► Where do you think the water comes from?

Southwest are grassy. Many of the mountain areas are covered with forests of pine trees that grow well in those cool areas.

In the deserts, plants must adjust to being without water for a long time in hot weather. One of the plants that can go for a long time without water is the **cactus**.

Cactuses are native to North America and South America. There are over 2,000 varieties of cactuses. Most cactuses have thick stems and thorns,

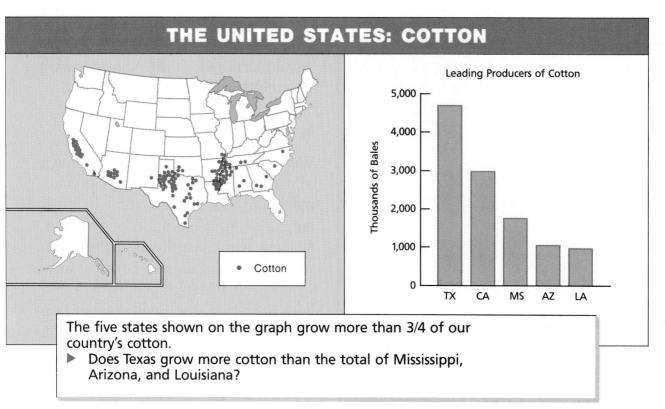

THE UNITED STATES: COTTON

Leading Producers of Cotton

The five states shown on the graph grow more than 3/4 of our country's cotton.
▶ Does Texas grow more cotton than the total of Mississippi, Arizona, and Louisiana?

Cotton   Cotton is a major crop of the Southwest region. Texas is the largest cotton producer in the United States.

You learned in Chapter 5 that the Southeast region once grew the most cotton. It has a warm climate and lots of rain, which cotton needs. The Southwest has the warm climate, but it did not have enough water to grow cotton as a cash crop until irrigation systems were built. Now, water is taken from wells and from rivers, such as the Colorado River, which is a major source. The water is carried to the cotton fields by pipes or in ditches. The Southwest has become the New Cotton Belt because of irrigation.

Other Crops   Rice is an important crop that is grown on the Gulf Coastal Plain in eastern Texas. Rice is a plant that needs to spend part of its growing time in water. Even though eastern Texas gets lots of rain, irrigation is still used to flood the rice fields to help the rice grow.

Citrus fruits, such as oranges and lemons, are grown in great quantities in the Southwest. Vegetables are important agricultural crops, too. Many of these products are shipped to other states in the winter so that people can buy fresh produce.

C. Problems Caused by Irrigation

Using Chemicals   Modern farmers use many different kinds of chemicals to help them get better crops. Fertilizers help crops grow, but they contain many chemicals that are harmful to animals and human beings. **Pesticides** are

194

chemicals used to prevent insects and diseases from destroying crops.

Dangers of Chemicals We usually think that anything like fertilizers or pesticides that helps farmers grow more or better food is good. But many things that help farmers grow large and healthy crops have a bad effect on the soil and water.

When water is taken from a river or well to irrigate crops, it is usually free of the chemicals that are in fertilizers and pesticides. When the irrigation water is put on the farmers' fields, it absorbs many chemicals that the farmers use to protect and improve their crops. All these chemicals pollute, or harm, the irrigation water as it flows across the land.

This might not matter much if the water just disappeared after irrigation. But it doesn't disappear. Instead, the water seeps into the ground. Once in the ground, the water may get into wells, or some of it may flow into nearby rivers, lakes, and ponds. Then animals or even people may drink the polluted water. Many of the chemicals kill the fish and plants that live in the rivers, lakes, and ponds.

D. Cattle in the Southwest

Arrival of Cattle Texas raises more beef cattle than any other state. Texas is also our leading sheep-raising state. Cattle, horses, sheep, and goats were all brought to the Southwest by Spanish explorers who had traveled north from Mexico. Perhaps the most famous explorer was Francisco Coronado, who was searching for seven cities of gold in the 1540s. This was long before the Pilgrims arrived at Plymouth Rock in Massachusetts.

Coronado and his men did not find the seven cities of gold, but they explored the Southwest and claimed it for Spain. The horses and cattle Coronado's army had brought roamed freely over the land.

Ranches Coronado and the explorers who followed him established towns in the area that is now the Southwest region. They traded with the Native Americans who lived there. Some of

Francisco Coronado explored much of the Southwest.
► Which person do you think is Coronado?

Good grazing land spurred the growth of cattle ranches in the Southwest region.

▶ What is the cowhand in the photograph doing?

the new Spanish settlers used livestock from Mexico to start **ranches**. A ranch is a large farm with grazing land for raising cattle, sheep, or horses.

By the early 1800s many people from the eastern United States had begun moving into the Southwest. They learned to raise cattle on the land. They, too, started ranches as the Spanish settlers had done. Today, there are large cattle ranches in many parts of the Southwest.

LESSON 2 REVIEW

THINK AND WRITE

A. Why might people who enjoy summer and winter sports move to the Southwest region?

B. Why is farming difficult in many parts of the Southwest?

C. Why do farmers have to be careful about using chemicals in their fields?

D. How did Spanish explorers help the Southwest to grow?

SKILLS CHECK

WRITING SKILL

Review what you have learned about irrigation in the Southwest. Write a report comparing the benefits and problems of irrigation.

Natural Resources of the Southwest Region

THINK ABOUT WHAT YOU KNOW

What natural resources have you learned about that can be used to produce the power we need to run machines?

STUDY THE VOCABULARY

petroleum   oil rig
oil refinery   oil tanker
offshore field

FOCUS YOUR READING

What are the main natural resources of the Southwest?

A. Oil, the Black Gold of the Southwest

Discovery In 1859, **petroleum**, or oil, was discovered in the United States near Titusville, Pennsylvania. Soon oil was discovered in many other parts of Pennsylvania. But at that time no one knew of the many uses for this thick, smelly liquid. Nor did anyone realize that the oil industry would become one of the world's biggest and most important industries.

By the time oil was discovered near Houston, Texas, in 1901, however, people understood that it was a valuable resource. It was so valuable that they soon called it black gold.

Products Petroleum is usually taken from the oil well to an **oil refinery**. An oil refinery is a big industrial plant, or factory, where machines separate the petroleum into many different liquids. Some of these liquids are used to make certain chemicals and plastics.

Oil Sites Today, Texas is our leading producer of petroleum. Oklahoma, another state in this region, is the fourth leading producer of petroleum in our country. Some of the oil comes from wells that are drilled deep into the earth. In certain places oil is found in cracks and spaces between rocks many feet below the surface of the earth.

A great deal of the Texas oil comes from **offshore fields**, which are petroleum fields found off the coast, in the Gulf of Mexico. The oil-bearing rock is under the ocean floor.

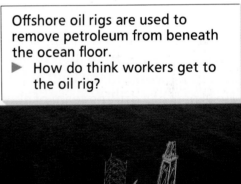

Offshore oil rigs are used to remove petroleum from beneath the ocean floor.
▶ How do think workers get to the oil rig?

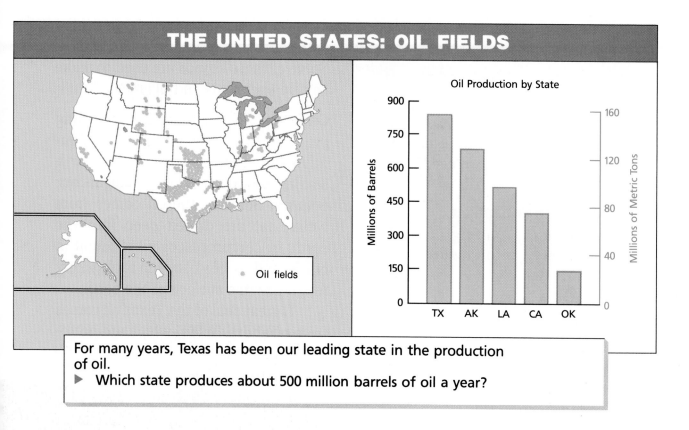

THE UNITED STATES: OIL FIELDS

Oil Production by State

- Oil fields

For many years, Texas has been our leading state in the production of oil.
▶ Which state produces about 500 million barrels of oil a year?

Working on a Oil Rig Carlos Vega is an oil driller who lives in Houston, Texas, but he works in the Gulf of Mexico. He is part of a drilling team of about 70 people. These people work for 2 weeks at a time on an **oil rig**. An oil rig is a platform that is held up by "legs" fastened to the sea floor. Workers are taken to and from the oil rig by boat or helicopter.

An offshore rig is built to drill for oil, but it is a home as well as a workplace. There is space for the workers to sleep and eat. There is a game room and sometimes a library. Movies are shown regularly.

But the workers don't have much time for recreation. The drilling goes on every day, 24 hours a day.

B. The Petroleum Industry in the Southwest

Oil Towns You read earlier that oil was discovered near Houston, Texas. Eventually petroleum fields were discovered up and down the Gulf Coastal Plain. Experts who explored and drilled for oil rushed to the oil fields in eastern Texas. Workers who pumped and shipped the oil to the refineries also came.

Hundreds of people moved to eastern Texas. Many of them brought their families. When they arrived, they needed homes, schools for their children, hospitals, and other things important for living. And so, many small towns quickly grew larger, almost overnight, in that part of Texas.

Houston, Texas Of all the towns that grew with the oil industry, Houston has the greatest success story. Today, Houston is the fourth most populated city in the United States.

Houston not only has oil fields nearby. It also has an excellent location for shipping the oil out and bringing equipment and supplies in. It is located quite close to a large harbor called Galveston Bay, on the Gulf of Mexico. A wide channel was dug from Houston to a nearby river that empties into Galveston Bay. Now large ships can enter and leave Houston through this channel which is called the Houston Ship Channel. Many of these ships are **oil tankers**, which are huge ships with big tanks used for shipping oil.

C. Minerals and Metals of the Southwest

Turquoise Oil may be the most valuable product of the Southwest, but the most beautiful products are probably the jewelry made in this region. Many Native Americans living here are talented and skilled craftspersons who make beautiful rings, bracelets, and other items from silver and turquoise (TUR kwoiz). Turquoise is a greenish-blue mineral.

Silver Arizona and New Mexico are important producers of silver in the United States. This metal is used not only for jewelry but also in the making of photographic supplies, batteries, and other products.

Copper In addition to silver, Arizona and New Mexico have valuable deposits of copper. About two-thirds of the copper mined in the United States comes from Arizona. In Chapter 8 you will read more about copper mining.

Uranium Another kind of material found in the Southwest is uranium. New Mexico has the largest deposit of uranium in the United States. Uranium is mined and then is used in nuclear (NOO klee ur) power plants as a source of energy for producing electricity.

This silversmith, a Zuni Indian, makes beautiful silver and turquoise jewelry.
▶ What is he making?

D. Water, a Valuable Resource

Using Water In Lesson 2 you read about the importance of water for farming in the Southwest. Without irrigation, farming would be impossible in many parts of the region.

The Colorado River supplies great amounts of water that is used for irrigation and other purposes. In fact, the homes, factories, and farms in Arizona, Colorado, Utah, Nevada, and California use up almost all of the river's water for their daily needs. The mighty Colorado River is just a trickle by the time it crosses a small section of Mexico and reaches the Gulf of California.

Saving Water In some places along its course, the Colorado River is blocked by dams. The water in the reservoirs behind the dams can be used for making electricity, for irrigation or for drinking. One of our country's largest dams, Hoover Dam, is located on the Colorado River. The lake behind Hoover Dam is Lake Mead, and it forms part of the border between the states of Arizona and Nevada. Hydroelectricity from Hoover Dam is used in industries, farms, and homes of Arizona, Nevada, and California.

Hoover Dam supplies electric power to Arizona, Nevada, and California.
► What is used to help to produce that electric power?

AVERAGE WATER USE

Function	Amount
Shower	25 to 50 gallons (at 5 gallons per minute)
Bath	25 gallons
Washing Machine	24 to 44 gallons
Washing Dishes (by hand)	20 gallons
Dishwasher	10 gallons
Outdoor Watering	5 to 10 gallons per minute
Flushing Toilet	5 to 7 gallons
Washing Hands	2 gallons
Brushing Teeth	2 gallons
Drinking	2 to 3 quarts

Average Amount Used Per Person Each Day: About 70 gallons

Each person in the United States uses about 70 gallons of water every day.
► How much water does a washing machine use?

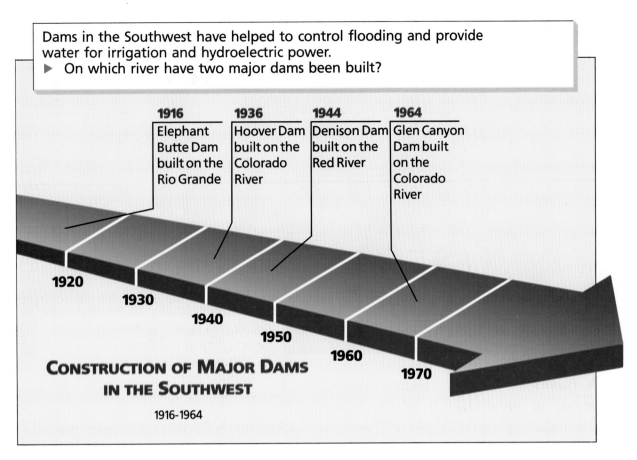

Dams in the Southwest have helped to control flooding and provide water for irrigation and hydroelectric power.
▶ On which river have two major dams been built?

1916 Elephant Butte Dam built on the Rio Grande

1936 Hoover Dam built on the Colorado River

1944 Denison Dam built on the Red River

1964 Glen Canyon Dam built on the Colorado River

1920 1930 1940 1950 1960 1970

CONSTRUCTION OF MAJOR DAMS IN THE SOUTHWEST
1916-1964

E. Industrial Cities of the Southwest

Modern Industries For many years, Houston was known as a center for the shipping and petroleum industries. In the 1950s, the city added a modern industry to its list. It has become world-famous as the location of the Lyndon B. Johnson Space Center. From here, space flights are guided and controlled.

An Electronic Center Phoenix (FEE-nihks), the capital city of Arizona, has many industries producing electronic equipment and aircraft. Phoenix has become a city of tall glass and concrete buildings. Many small businesses as well as huge companies have their home offices in Phoenix. Thousands of people have found work in aircraft, chemical, and other industries. These industries have helped Phoenix become the tenth most populated city in the United States.

A Manufacturing Center Oklahoma City expanded quickly after petroleum was found in Oklahoma in the 1920s. The oil industry is still important there, but today, Oklahoma City is far more than just an oil center.

Oklahoma City is the capital of the state of Oklahoma. It has many factories that make automobile parts, construction equipment, and electronic equipment. Many companies that produce machines and tools for the oil industry started in Oklahoma City.

201

Dallas, Texas, is the second largest city in the Southwest.
► What is the land around Dallas like?

A Business Center Dallas, Texas, began to grow in the 1870s, when the railroads came. The city became an important cotton-marketing center. Dallas is now a business center. It has more insurance companies than any other city in the United States. Many banks are located in Dallas, which is now the second most populated city in the Southwest.

A Research Center Albuquerque (AL-buh kur kee) is the largest city in New Mexico. It is an important center for research on nuclear energy. Can you guess why Albuquerque is a center for this kind of research? New Mexico has large deposits of uranium, the mineral that is used to make nuclear energy.

LESSON 3 REVIEW

THINK AND WRITE

A. Why is oil often called black gold?
B. How did the oil industry help Houston grow?
C. What are some of the uses of the minerals from the Southwest?
D. What purposes do dams serve on the Colorado River?
E. In what ways are the chief cities in the Southwest alike?

SKILLS CHECK
MAP SKILL
Use the map on page 186 to find the latitude and longitude of Oklahoma City, Oklahoma, and Austin, Texas. Which of these two cities is farther north? Now find the latitude and longitude of Phoenix, Arizona, and Dallas, Texas. Which of these two cities is farther west?

202

The Three Cultures of the Southwest

THINK ABOUT WHAT YOU KNOW

Can you think of some words, songs, foods, and customs that have come to us from other countries?

STUDY THE VOCABULARY

**pueblo   adobe
mission**

FOCUS YOUR READING

What is special about each of the three cultures of the Southwest?

A. Chili, a Southwestern Specialty

Have you ever tasted New England clam chowder, Boston baked beans, or Southern fried chicken? Each region of the United States has its own special foods. They come from the background of the people and the region's agricultural products. The United States is a land rich in foods from different cultures.

Chili is a food that originated in the Southwest. It is a spicy food, usually made with meat, tomatoes, onions, and peppers. The peppers are hot red, green, or yellow peppers. They can be cut into small pieces and added to chili, or they can be dried, ground up, and added as a powder.

Chili peppers were first popular among the Native Americans, who raised them for centuries. Today, New Mexico leads the United States in the production of chili peppers.

You have already read that the Spanish brought cattle with them into the Southwest. In Texas, where cattle became so important, the Spanish added beef to chili. In New Mexico and Arizona, where sheep were common, chili was often made with lamb, or mutton, which is the meat of sheep.

Later, settlers from the eastern United States changed the recipe for chili a little more. Some added beans, and others added their own favorite spices or seasonings. This popular food of the Southwest can be found in all parts of the United States.

Chili cookoffs are popular in many parts of the United States.
► What, do you think, is the purpose of a cookoff?

B. Native Americans of the Southwest

The story of southwestern food is also the story of the three cultures of the Southwest. These three cultures are the Native American, or American Indian culture, the Spanish culture, and what is often called the Anglo culture. The Anglo culture has its roots in England. It originally was found mostly in the eastern part of the United States.

Native Americans were the first to inhabit, or live in, the Southwest, probably more than 23,000 years ago. Corn, beans, and squash were the crops the American Indians learned to plant and harvest. These three foods became important parts of their diet.

Native American children are enjoying a festival in New Mexico.
▶ What do you think the children are doing?

Some Native Americans made permanent homes by digging round pits in the ground and covering them with logs, branches, and soil. Later, many lived in large communities in multi-story apartment houses called **pueblos** (PWEB lohz). Ruins of these old pueblos can still be seen in northern Arizona and New Mexico.

Today some descendants of the early Indians live like most modern Americans, but many still keep traditions that date back thousands of years. Many Native Americans live in cities in the Southwest, and quite a few live on reservations.

C. The Spanish and Anglo Cultures

Spanish Settlements You have already read that Francisco Coronado began exploring what is now the southwestern region of the United States in the 1500s. That opened the way for other explorers and settlers from Spain. At that time the southwestern area had few European settlers. The Spanish built cities all over Mexico and the Southwest. One of the first cities was Santa Fe (SAN tuh FAY), which was built in 1610.

Tucson (TOO sahn), Arizona, San Antonio, Texas, and Santa Fe, New Mexico, are southwestern cities that began near Spanish **missions**. A mission was a church and settlement built by Roman Catholic priests from Spain. The priests came to teach the Native Americans about the Christian religion.

This pueblo in Taos, New Mexico, was built over 1,000 years ago.
▶ What building material was used in this pueblo?

Spanish Contributions What are the Spanish contributions to the Southwest? The first Spanish and Mexican settlers spoke Spanish and gave Spanish names to many places in the Southwest. The *Colorado River*, for example, is *Rio Colorado* in Spanish. It means "reddish-brown river," and indeed the river sometimes carries muddy red soil.

Spanish architecture became very popular in the Southwest. In such a dry climate, there is not much wood for construction, and a better building material is **adobe** (uh DOH bee). Adobe is a clay that is shaped into blocks and baked in the sun into hard bricks.

Spanish settlers learned from the Native Americans that adobe bricks keep a house cooler than wood timbers do.

Anglo Contributions The Anglos from the eastern United States began arriving in the Southwest in great numbers in the 1800s. What did the Anglos add to the Native American and the Spanish cultures of the Southwest? They added ranches and farms. They built forts to protect themselves. They built roads and businesses. They also made cattle ranching a big business in the Southwest.

LESSON 4 REVIEW

THINK AND WRITE

A. What does the history of chili tell us about the culture of the Southwest?
B. What important contributions have Native Americans made to life in the Southwest?
C. How is Spanish culture evident in the Southwest today?

SKILLS CHECK

THINKING SKILL

Three different cultures are important in the southwestern part of the United States. How might you help to preserve the culture of your community?

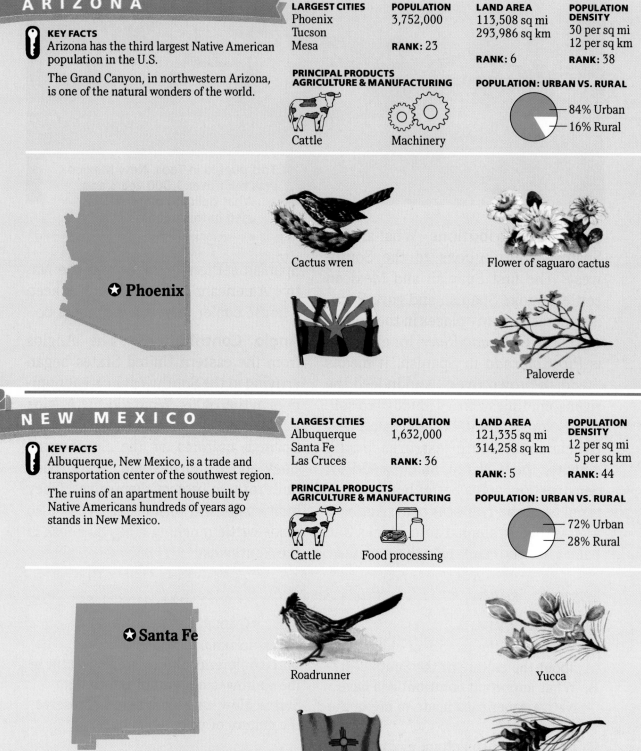

ARIZONA

KEY FACTS
Arizona has the third largest Native American population in the U.S.

The Grand Canyon, in northwestern Arizona, is one of the natural wonders of the world.

LARGEST CITIES
Phoenix
Tucson
Mesa

POPULATION
3,752,000

RANK: 23

LAND AREA
113,508 sq mi
293,986 sq km

RANK: 6

POPULATION DENSITY
30 per sq mi
12 per sq km

RANK: 38

PRINCIPAL PRODUCTS AGRICULTURE & MANUFACTURING

Cattle

Machinery

POPULATION: URBAN VS. RURAL
84% Urban
16% Rural

★ Phoenix

Cactus wren

Flower of saguaro cactus

Paloverde

NEW MEXICO

KEY FACTS
Albuquerque, New Mexico, is a trade and transportation center of the southwest region.

The ruins of an apartment house built by Native Americans hundreds of years ago stands in New Mexico.

LARGEST CITIES
Albuquerque
Santa Fe
Las Cruces

POPULATION
1,632,000

RANK: 36

LAND AREA
121,335 sq mi
314,258 sq km

RANK: 5

POPULATION DENSITY
12 per sq mi
5 per sq km

RANK: 44

PRINCIPAL PRODUCTS AGRICULTURE & MANUFACTURING

Cattle

Food processing

POPULATION: URBAN VS. RURAL
72% Urban
28% Rural

★ Santa Fe

Roadrunner

Yucca

Piñon

LARGEST CITIES
Oklahoma City
Tulsa
Lawton

POPULATION
3,285,000

RANK: 27

LAND AREA
68,655 sq mi
117,817 sq km

RANK: 19

POPULATION DENSITY
48 per sq mi
28 per sq km

RANK: 34

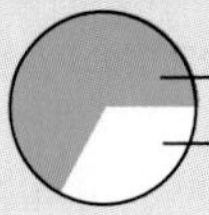

KEY FACTS
Most of the people who live in Oklahoma were born in the state.

The first school for Native Americans was started in Oklahoma.

PRINCIPAL PRODUCTS AGRICULTURE & MANUFACTURING

Cattle

Machinery

POPULATION: URBAN VS. RURAL
67% Urban
33% Rural

Scissortailed flycatcher

Mistletoe

Oklahoma City

OKLAHOMA

Redbud

LARGEST CITIES
Houston
Dallas
San Antonio

POPULATION
17,712,000

RANK: 3

LAND AREA
262,017 sq mi
678,623 sq km

RANK: 2

POPULATION DENSITY
64 per sq mi
25 per sq km

RANK: 29

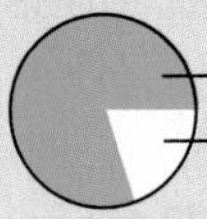

KEY FACTS
The Rio Grande separates Texas from Mexico.

Houston, the most populated city in the Southwest region, is the fourth most populated city in the U.S.

PRINCIPAL PRODUCTS AGRICULTURE & MANUFACTURING

Cattle

Oil Refining

POPULATION: URBAN VS. RURAL
80% Urban
20% Rural

Mockingbird

Bluebonnet

Austin

Pecan

207

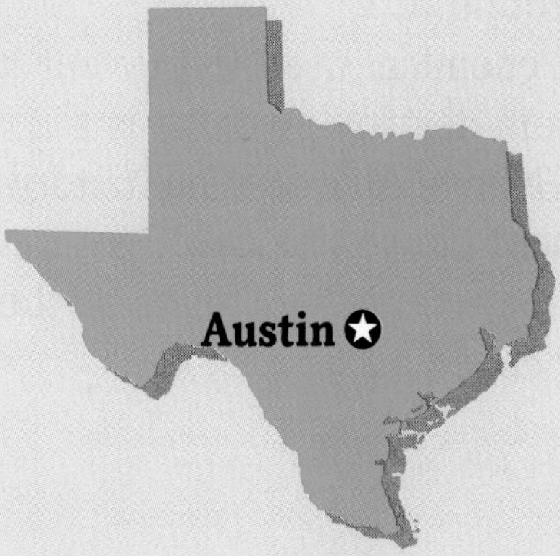

USING THE VOCABULARY

mesa	petroleum
butte	offshore field
reservation	oil tanker
pesticide	pueblo
ranch	mission

On a separate sheet of paper, write the word or words from the list above that best complete each sentence.

1. A high, broad, and level area that is smaller than a plateau is a _____.
2. Another word for oil is _____.
3. A _____ is a large farm with grazing land for cattle, sheep, or horses.
4. An Indian _____ is an area set aside by the United States government for Native Americans to live in.
5. A _____ was a church and settlement built by Roman Catholic priests from Spain.
6. A ship with big tanks used for shipping oil is called an _____.
7. A _____ is a single flat-topped hill that juts up from the level land around it.
8. A chemical used to prevent insects from destroying crops is a _____.
9. A Native American multistory apartment house was called a _____.
10. A petroleum field found off the coast is called an _____.

REMEMBERING WHAT YOU READ

On a separate sheet of paper, answer the questions in complete sentences.

1. What states make up the Southwest region?
2. What is the name of the highest peak in the Southwest?
3. Name a desert plant that can live a long time without water.
4. What is our nation's leading sheep-raising state?
5. What was Francisco Coronado searching for in the 1540s?
6. In what state in the United States was oil first discovered?
7. How are oil rig workers taken to and from the rig?
8. What is the capital city of Oklahoma?
9. In what country did the Anglo culture have its roots?
10. What does *Rio Colorado* mean in Spanish?

TYING READING TO SOCIAL STUDIES

Sometimes the same words in English can have different meanings. In this chapter you learned why a section of Texas and one in Oklahoma are called *panhandles*. In the dictionary, find another meaning for the word *panhandle*.

THINKING CRITICALLY

On a separate sheet of paper, answer the following questions in complete sentences.

1. Many people believe that the Grand Canyon is the most spectacular place on earth. What place do you think is very special? Explain why.

2. Why is snow important to farming in the Southwest?

3. What takes place in an oil refinery?

4. Is it a good idea that many cities of the Southwest have businesses and industries not related to oil? Why or why not?

5. What food from a special culture do you enjoy?

SUMMARIZING THE CHAPTER

Copy this graphic organizer on a separate sheet of paper.
Write at least three facts to describe each main topic.

CHAPTER THEME

The Southwest region is an area of diverse landforms, spectacular scenery, and important mineral resources. With the help of irrigation, this region is also an important agricultural area.

LESSON 1

Land Features

1. _____
2. _____
3. _____

LESSON 2

Farms and Ranches

1. _____
2. _____
3. _____

LESSON 3

Natural Resources

1. _____
2. _____
3. _____

LESSON 4

Cultures

1. _____
2. _____
3. _____

CHAPTER 8

THE MOUNTAIN WEST REGION

*T*he discovery of silver first attracted people to the Mountain West. Cities gradually grew here. Today many tourists visit the Mountain West.

CANADA   50° N

2   **3**   **4**   **5**

WA   **A**

MONTANA   NORTH DAKOTA

⊛ Helena   46° N

• Billings

IDAHO   SOUTH DAKOTA

OREGON   **B**

⊛ Boise   WYOMING

Casper •   NEBRASKA

Pocatello   42° N

PACIFIC   Cheyenne

OCEAN   Ogden   ⊛

Great Salt Lake   ⊛ Salt Lake City   Denver   **C**

Reno   Provo •   Lakewood ⊛ • Aurora   KS

Carson City   UTAH   Colorado Springs •

38° N   NEVADA   Pueblo •

CALIFORNIA   COLORADO

OK

Las Vegas   **D**

THE MOUNTAIN WEST REGION: POLITICAL

NEW MEXICO

⊛   State capitals

•   Other cities

ARIZONA   34° N

| 0 | 100 | 200 miles |
| 0 | 100 | 200 kilometers |

124° W   120° W   116° W   112° W   108° W   104° W

Getting to Know the Mountain West

THINK ABOUT WHAT YOU KNOW

How might places in a mountain region be different from places on a plain?

STUDY THE VOCABULARY

basin   semidesert
Continental Divide

FOCUS YOUR READING

What kinds of physical features are found in the Mountain West?

A. A Region Full of Treasures

A Special Place   Some of the wildest and most rugged land in the United States is found in the Mountain West. The six states that make up the Mountain West region are Montana, Wyoming, Colorado, Utah, Nevada, and Idaho. Locate each of these states on the map on the opposite page. Parts of some of these states have towering mountain peaks and deep canyons. Other parts of these states have forests, plains, and desert areas.

To someone from the eastern part of our country, the Mountain West might seem to be a place of wide-open space. Busy city streets, traffic jams, and buildings crowded together are not as common in the Mountain West as they are in some eastern states. To many people who live in the Mountain West, the towns and cities are just right—not too quiet and not too crowded.

A Large Region   The Mountain West region occupies one fourth of all the land area of the United States, excluding the state of Alaska. The fourth largest state in the country is in the Mountain West. By looking at the map on page 210, can you tell which state that is? If you answer Montana, you are correct. Only Alaska, Texas, and California are larger in area than Montana.

A Small Population   Although the Mountain West is a large region, it has fewer people than other regions of our country. Only 3 percent of the people of the United States live there. More people live in Michigan than in all the Mountain West states combined.

CITY INDEX

Cities with less than 100,000	Cities with 100,000 to 499,999	Cities with 500,000 to 999,999
Aurora (CO) C-4	Boise (ID) B-1	Denver (CO) C-4
Billings (MT) B-3	Colorado Springs (CO)........ C-4	
Carson City (NE) C-1	Lakewood (CO) C-4	**Cities with 1,000,000 or more**
Casper (WY) B-4	Las Vegas (NE) D-2	None ....
Cheyenne (WY) C-4	Pueblo (CO) C-4	
Helena (MT) A-2	Reno (NE) C-1	
Ogden (UT).................. C-3	Salt Lake City (UT) C-3	
Provo (UT)................... C-3		
Pocatello (ID) B-2		

The Mountain West region is large, but throughout the region there are vast areas with few people.
▶ Which states in the region have no cities with more than 500,000 people?

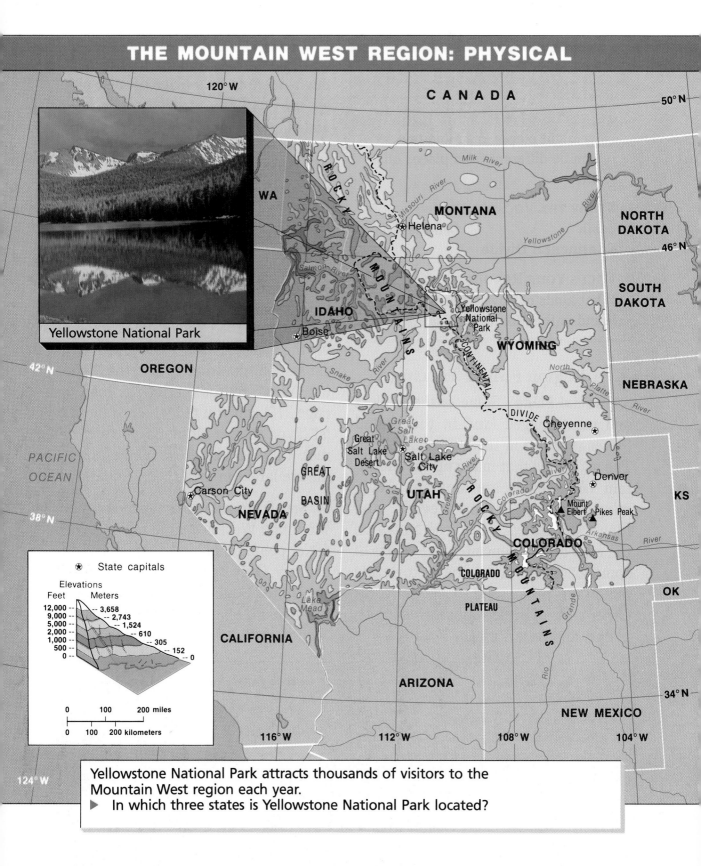

THE MOUNTAIN WEST REGION: PHYSICAL

Yellowstone National Park

State capitals

Elevations

Feet	Meters
12,000	3,658
9,000	2,743
5,000	1,524
2,000	610
1,000	305
500	152
0	0

0   100   200 miles

0   100   200 kilometers

Yellowstone National Park attracts thousands of visitors to the Mountain West region each year.
▶ In which three states is Yellowstone National Park located?

Colorado has the largest population of the Mountain West states. More than 3 million people live in Colorado, and many of them are residents of Denver, Colorado's capital city. Denver is an important city for the entire western part of the United States. It is much like other big cities with busy streets, crowded neighborhoods, tall office buildings, hotels, museums, and other city features.

B. Physical Features of the Mountain West Region

Two Common Features The Mountain West states have two things in common. They all have mountain ranges with high elevations, and they all have somewhat dry climates.

The Rocky Mountains The Mountain West gets its name from the Rocky Mountains, a mountain range that extends from the northern edges of Canada and Alaska to Mexico in the south. The Rocky Mountains make up the largest mountain range in the United States. The Rockies are much higher than the Appalachians, which are found in the eastern part of our country. The highest peak in the Mountain West is Mount Elbert in Colorado, which reaches 14,433 feet (4,399 m) in elevation.

Not all of the Mountain West is rugged land. There are some areas of flat land in the region. The eastern parts of Montana and Colorado are fairly level because they include part of the Great Plains. You read about the Great Plains in Chapter 6.

The Great Basin Another important physical feature of the Mountain West covers most of Nevada and Utah. This area is called the Great Basin. A **basin** is an area almost entirely surrounded by higher land. The Rocky Mountains are on the east side of the Great Basin and the Sierra Nevada (see ER uh nuh-VAD uh) Mountains lie to the west.

Rivers of the Region In Chapter 7 you read about the Colorado River. This river is the most important river in the Mountain West. The Colorado

Skiing is a popular activity at Beaver Creek, Colorado.
▶ What other winter sports might be popular here?

River begins in the Rocky Mountains in northern Colorado. It flows mostly to the south and west as it journeys through the Mountain West region and the Southwest region until it reaches the Gulf of California.

The Snake River begins in northwestern Wyoming. It curls like a snake through southern Idaho and then continues into Washington. The Snake River is like many rivers of the Mountain West because it begins high in the Rockies.

The Continental Divide A line of ridges runs north to south through the Rocky Mountains. This line, called the **Continental Divide**, divides the continent of North America into two sections. Rivers that begin to the west of the Continental Divide generally flow to the west. The Snake River is one such river.

The rivers that begin to the east of the Continental Divide flow toward the Atlantic Ocean or the Gulf of Mexico. These rivers include the Missouri River and the Arkansas River.

C. Desert Areas in the Mountain West

Parts of Utah and Nevada are largely desert and **semidesert**. You have already learned that a desert is dry land in which there is little plant growth. A semidesert is not as dry and bare as a desert.

One famous desert in the Mountain West region is the Great Salt Lake Desert. That desert is easy to locate on a map if you first look for the Great Salt Lake in Utah. The desert is southwest of the Great Salt Lake.

Some important cities of the Mountain West region are located in desert or semidesert areas. Three of those cities are Las Vegas, Reno, and Salt Lake City. Find these cities on the map on page 210.

(Left) The Mountain West has some deserts and semideserts. (Right) Many kinds of cactus grow in these areas.
▶ What other plants grow here?

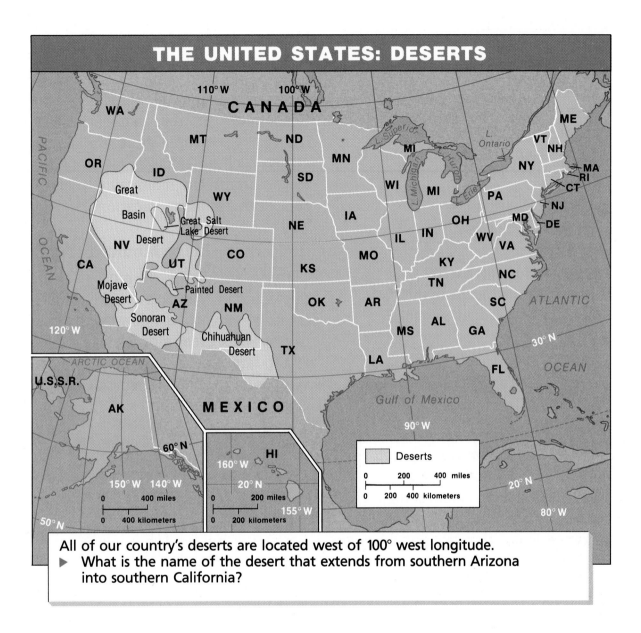

THE UNITED STATES: DESERTS

All of our country's deserts are located west of 100° west longitude.
► What is the name of the desert that extends from southern Arizona into southern California?

LESSON 1 REVIEW

THINK AND WRITE

A. What are some of the things that make the Mountain West region a special place?

B. What are the main physical features of the Mountain West?

C. Why can't the deserts and semideserts of the Mountain West be described as empty land?

SKILLS CHECK

MAP SKILL

Read the map on page 212 to find three rivers in the Mountain West region that flow toward the east and three rivers that flow toward the west.

Earning a Living in the Mountain West

If you were going to take a vacation in a mountain region, what kinds of clothes would you take with you?

STUDY THE VOCABULARY
blizzard   **brand**
roundup

FOCUS YOUR READING
How does the climate in the Mountain West affect farming?

A. Cool Climates at High Elevations

Location and Climate The story of climate in the Mountain West is a tale told by mountains. Places at higher elevations have cooler climates than places at lower elevations at the same latitude. In fact, temperatures drop about $3\frac{1}{2}°$F for every 1,000 feet of elevation (2°C per 300 m).

Snowy Winters Snow remains on the ground in some parts of the Mountain West region for many months of the year. The snow that falls in the Rocky Mountains is usually very fine and powdery. That kind of snow is excellent for skiing. Skiing is possible from Thanksgiving until early June in the areas of higher elevation. Rocky Mountain ski resorts attract vacationers from all over the world.

216

Summer Attractions The mountain lakes, beautiful forests, and cool summer temperatures make the Mountain West region popular for summer vacations, too. In the summer, "flatlanders," or people from the flatter states, such as Texas and Oklahoma, travel up into the mountains to enjoy cool, scenic summer vacations.

B. Farming in the Mountain West

Climate and Land In most parts of the Mountain West region, the climate is too dry and cool to allow many crops to grow well. Steep slopes make it difficult to farm the land. So the Mountain West is not a leading agricultural region of the United States.

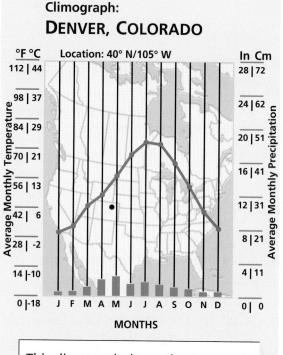

Climograph:
DENVER, COLORADO

This climograph shows the average monthly temperature and the average monthly precipitation for Denver.
► Which month is the coldest and driest?

This does not mean that very little farming takes place in the region. Several states in the Mountain West are among the leading growers in the United States of certain crops.

Chief Crops Most crops in the Mountain West are grown on the level lands of eastern Colorado and Montana. Montana is the most important producer of wheat in the region. It is the third leading producer of wheat in the United States.

Colorado farmers grow large amounts of potatoes, onions, lettuce, cabbage, and sweet corn. On the level lands of Idaho, potatoes are grown in great quantities. More potatoes are grown in Idaho than in any other state in the country.

Another important crop grown on Mountain West farms is sugar beets. These beets are similar to red beets, but they are a creamy-white color. The root of the sugar beet contains sugar, which can be separated from the rest of the plant. Sugar beets need cool temperatures at night. They grow well in places where sugarcane cannot survive.

Each state of the Mountain West has at least a few farms where many different crops are grown. Corn, apples, barley, and oats are grown in small amounts throughout the region.

After the sugar beets are inspected (left), they are harvested and stored (center), and then sent to a plant to be processed.
▶ Why, do you think, are the farmers inspecting the crop?

C. Sheep and Cattle Ranching in the Mountain West

Good Pastures The land of the Mountain West produces excellent grasses that provide food for sheep and cattle. For many months of the year, sheep and cattle ranchers in this region turn the animals loose on large pastures to eat the grass that grows naturally there.

Ranching Areas Large sheep and cattle ranches are scattered throughout the Rocky Mountains and the Great Basin. These ranches are much larger than those in the North Central region because the mountainous landscape provides less grazing land.

Montana and Wyoming are among the five leading sheep ranching states in our country. Beef cattle are also raised in this region, but the Mountain West states do not produce nearly as much beef as Texas.

Life on a Ranch Bob and Joan Smith own a ranch in the central part of Wyoming. They have over 25,000 sheep and 5,000 head of cattle that graze on 475 square miles (1,230 sq km) of pasture on their ranch.

"Ranching is a tough job," Bob says. "Each day I am up before the sun to tend to the cattle."

Joan agrees. "We have worked in **blizzards**, or blinding snowstorms when the winds were very strong and temperatures were as low as -25°F (-33°C). We have hauled water to cattle when the sun was blazing down and the temperature topped 100°F (38°C)."

In spite of the hard work and long hours, Bob and Joan like ranching and love the mountains. They especially enjoy **roundup** time, when they hire extra ranch hands, or workers, to help gather all the animals together.

At a roundup, new calves that were born during the spring or summer are branded. A **brand** is an identification mark that is burned into the animal's hide. The brand for the Smith ranch, called The Lazy S Ranch, shows a letter *S* lying on its side.

During roundup, the animals are also counted and checked for diseases. The animals that are ready to be shipped to stockyards are separated from the rest of the herd and loaded into trucks.

During the winter ranchers in Wyoming often bring out hay to feed their cattle.
▶ Why is this necessary?

D. Life as a Sheep Herder Working in the Rockies

Hector Mendiburu (ek TOHR mihn DEE boo roo) is a sheep herder. Every year from April through September, Mendiburu works alone in the high pastures and peaks of Colorado.

Mendiburu is almost 40 years old now, but he was only 18 when he arrived in the United States from Spain. At that time he signed a 3-year contract, or written agreement, to work as a sheep herder in Wyoming. Later he moved to Colorado.

A Lonely Job "I like herding sheep, but it is a lonely job," Mendiburu says. "I take the sheep up to the high pastures and graze them to fatten them up. I protect them from bears and other wild animals."

Early in the spring, Mendiburu sets up camp near a small stream high in the Rocky Mountains. Every morning he gets up before dawn and with the help of his dog moves the sheep to a new pasture. He watches the sheep

A ranch hand feeds a lamb on this ranch in Idaho.
▶ What kind of ranch do you think this is?

carefully all day and then takes them to water before dark. After about ten days, Mendiburu moves his camp to a different location.

"I like my job and I like sheep," he says. "These sheep are friendly companions, because they are good listeners and they never argue with me."

LESSON **2** REVIEW

THINK AND WRITE

A. What kinds of places in the Mountain West region have cool climates?

B. Why are most crops of the Mountain West region grown in Colorado and Montana?

C. Why are there roundups on cattle ranches?

D. What are some of the daily responsibilities of a sheep herder?

SKILLS CHECK

THINKING SKILL

Compare the life of the sheep herder with that of the ranchers that you read about in the lesson. Decide which you would rather be. List three reasons for your choice.

219

Mining and Manufacturing in the Mountain West

THINK ABOUT WHAT YOU KNOW

Look around your classroom. Name the items that are made of metal.

STUDY THE VOCABULARY

prospector	oil shale
ghost town	smelter
open-pit mining	

FOCUS YOUR READING

What minerals are found in the Mountain West region?

A. Prospecting in the Mountain West

The Search for Silver The year was 1878 and the place was Leadville, Colorado, high in the Rocky Mountains. The city was filled with hungry, tired miners looking for new deposits of silver. These miners, called **prospectors**, searched the countryside for new sites to mine precious metals.

Thousands of holes dug by hand dotted the hillsides where men searched for the metals they hoped would make them rich. Large tents had been put up to provide sleeping places for the miners. Some miners slept in stables and on any other available floor space in town. Shootings over mining claims occurred every day, and laws against cheating, shooting, and theft were almost never honored.

Leadville's Story Leadville soon became a city of almost 30,000 people. Silver was the reason it grew so rapidly. Leadville was like many other Mountain West towns and mining camps that suddenly appeared in the region.

After all the silver in Leadville had been mined, the prospectors left the mining camps to look for metals in other places. Towns that were once large and prosperous but now have few or no residents are called **ghost towns**. One of these ghost towns is shown below. Today, Leadville, Colorado, has only about one-tenth the number of people that it had in the 1870s.

This ghost town was once a bustling mining camp.
▶ At what time of year was this photograph taken?

Mining Today Minerals and metals are still valuable natural resources in the Mountain West. Nevada is our country's largest supplier of gold, and Montana ranks third. Gold is one of the most valuable and beautiful of all the minerals on earth.

Gold is important everywhere in the world, and it is recognized by all countries as a form of money. Every country has its own type of coins and paper money. The United States uses dollars, France uses francs, and Japan uses yen. But when banks want to know what a dollar or franc is really worth, they figure out how much it is worth in gold.

Over the years, millions of dollars worth of silver have been taken from the earth in the Mountain West states. Nevada, Montana, and Colorado all have large silver deposits. By looking at the graph on page 222, you can see that Nevada produces more than three times as much silver as Montana and Colorado combined.

B. Another Important Metal

Copper For centuries, gold and silver have been valued by people all over the world. But one metal in the Mountain West was unused until it was discovered that wires made of copper would carry electricity. Today, millions of miles of copper wire carry electricity in electric and telephone cable wires throughout the world.

Bingham Canyon One of the world's largest copper mines is in Bingham Canyon near Salt Lake City, the capital city of Utah. Miners use huge cranes

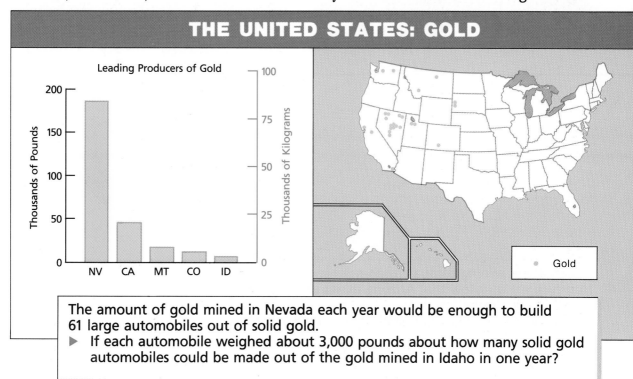

THE UNITED STATES: GOLD

Leading Producers of Gold

The amount of gold mined in Nevada each year would be enough to build 61 large automobiles out of solid gold.
▶ If each automobile weighed about 3,000 pounds about how many solid gold automobiles could be made out of the gold mined in Idaho in one year?

THE UNITED STATES: SILVER

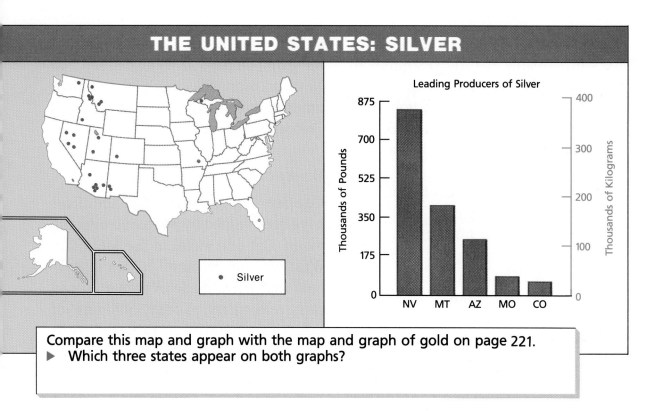

Leading Producers of Silver

Compare this map and graph with the map and graph of gold on page 221.
▶ Which three states appear on both graphs?

THE UNITED STATES: COPPER

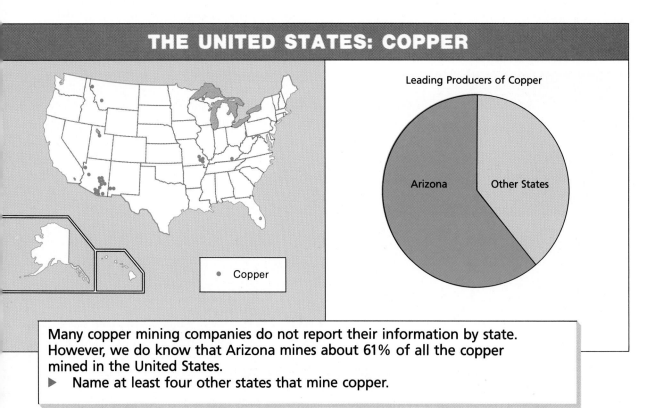

Leading Producers of Copper

Many copper mining companies do not report their information by state. However, we do know that Arizona mines about 61% of all the copper mined in the United States.
▶ Name at least four other states that mine copper.

and power shovels to scoop out the copper ore in the mine. This kind of mining, done on top of the ground, is called **open-pit mining**.

The picture on this page shows part of the Bingham Canyon mine. The mine is so big that an astronaut standing on the moon could possibly see it with a little help from a telescope.

Railroad trains circle their way around layers, or steps, of the open-pit mine. The copper ore is loaded onto the trains and hauled up and out of the pit. As more and more ore is mined, the pit is made wider. The town of Bingham was actually moved back to make room for the mine.

C. A Storehouse of Petroleum

A Valuable Resource Another natural resource in the Mountain West is **oil shale**, a kind of rock that has a tar-like substance in it. Within the substance are millions of tiny drops of oil. But they are not able to flow through the rock and form pools of oil that miners can reach. When the rock is crushed and heated to a temperature of over 900°F (480°C), the tarlike substance is changed to liquid oil.

Over 2 trillion barrels of oil are locked in the rock of this region, especially in Wyoming, Utah, and Colorado. That is enough oil to supply the United States for 100 years.

This copper mine in Utah is the largest open-pit mine in the world. The copper ore is removed in horizontal layers called benches.
▶ What do you think the power shovel is used for?

Mining Problems Shale oil is not used much because the process of releasing the oil from the rock is expensive. Also, removing the rock that contains shale oil causes great damage to the environment. Large chunks of mountains must be blasted away, leaving deep scars on the earth's surface. If shale oil is removed, the rock that is left over ends up in huge, ugly waste piles. In addition, the air becomes unhealthy when fuel is burned to heat the rock and remove the oil.

Scientists are looking for ways to overcome the problems of mining oil shale. Oil shale may someday become an important source of oil as the supply of petroleum, which is easier to find and mine, grows less and less.

D. Major Industries in the Mountain West

Using Local Minerals Near many of the mines in the Mountain West are industries that make minerals and metals into useful products. For example, **smelters** are close to the copper mines near Salt Lake City. A smelter is a huge plant where ores are heated in order to get the metal out of them. The metal is then used in making products. Some products made from copper are plumbing pipes, copper wires, and many kinds of kitchen equipment.

New Industries Many new industries, such as the manufacturing of electronic equipment, aerospace products, and computers, are located in the

Brass foundries process ores mined in the Mountain West.
▶ Why are these workers' jobs dangerous?

Mountain West region. These industries use many of the region's minerals. The cost of transporting the minerals is low because the factories that process them are located nearby.

Petroleum refining and the making of petroleum products are becoming important businesses in the Mountain West region. The production of gasoline and plastic goods is growing especially in Wyoming.

Research Centers There are many government research centers in the region. At these centers, many people test missiles, aircraft, and military weapons. An open space such as the

Weapons are tested at a research center in New Mexico.
▶ What kind of weapon is shown in the photograph?

Great Basin of the Mountain West is ideal for experimenting with missiles and weapons. Research and testing sites are found mostly in the southern three states of the region. They employ many people.

Forests High in the Rocky Mountains, forests of pine and spruce trees are cut for many purposes. Some logs are used for lumber in construction, while others are used for making wood pulp, paper, and newsprint. The lumber industry and the manufacturing of wood products are especially important in the three northern states of the Mountain West—Wyoming, Idaho, and Montana.

LESSON 3 REVIEW

THINK AND WRITE

A. Why did many people rush to the Mountain West in the 1800s?
B. Why was copper not considered valuable at first?
C. Why is oil shale valuable?
D. What industries use the natural resources of the Mountain West region?

SKILLS CHECK

WRITING SKILL
Imagine that you are a storekeeper in a mining town in the Mountain West in the 1800s. Write a story describing what it was like to run a store in the town.

Cities of the Mountain West

THINK ABOUT WHAT YOU KNOW

Think about a city you have studied. How did location help the city grow?

STUDY THE VOCABULARY

**transcontinental railroad   mint
interstate highway**

FOCUS YOUR READING

Why have Denver and Salt Lake City become important cities?

A. Transportation Lines Across the Mountain West

A Giant Barrier Before airplanes were invented, the Rocky Mountains were a giant barrier to transportation. Mules and horses provided the only means of transportation, so crossing the Rocky Mountains was very slow and difficult. It took weeks to guide the animals and wagons carrying goods and people through the valleys of the mountains.

Early Railroads In the 1800s many railroads began to be built in the eastern part of the United States. The first **transcontinental railroad** was built by two railroad companies.

On May 10, 1869, the two lines of track met at a place called Promontory Point near Ogden, Utah. A golden spike was driven into the last rail to show that the first transcontinental railroad had been completed. People could now travel from California to New York City on the railroad.

Traveling or shipping goods by rail was much faster than by horse or mule. Every year more settlers moved to the West to start new farms and businesses. More products from the Mountain West could be sent east to be sold in big cities.

The two lines of the first transcontinental railroad have just been joined.
▶ What are these people doing?

I've Been Working on the Railroad

Old American Work Song

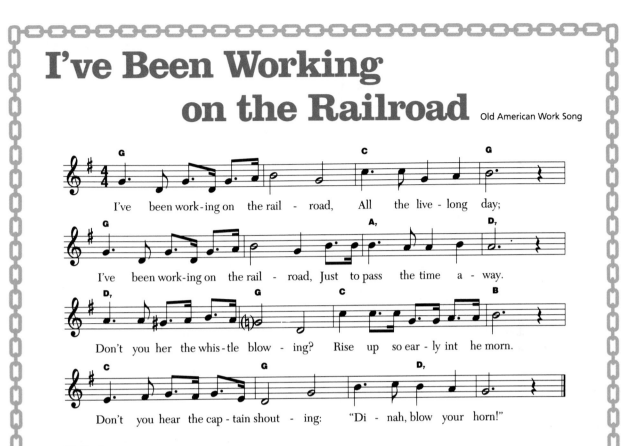

I've been work-ing on the rail - road, All the live - long day;

I've been work-ing on the rail - road, Just to pass the time a - way.

Don't you her the whis-tle blow - ing? Rise up so ear - ly int he morn.

Don't you hear the cap - tain shout - ing: "Di - nah, blow your horn!"

Refrain

Dinah, won't you blow, Dinah, won't you blow,
Dinah, won't you blow your horn?

Dinah, won't you blow, Dinah, won't you blow,
Dinah, won't you blow your horn?

The Granger Collection

A Highway Network In 1954 the United States Congress passed a law requiring that a network of highways be built to connect all the major cities and industrial centers in the country. The highways were to be at least four lanes wide and paved so that they could be used all year round. The highways were to be called **interstate highways** because they were to connect one state with another. This interstate system is shown on the map below.

Today, interstate highways are the lifelines of the Mountain West. Cars and trucks now zip in and out of places that were once reached only by narrow winding roads. Factories, stores, and businesses can be built in mountain areas and still have customers and get supplies without problems. Even when other roads in the highest mountains are closed in wintertime because of snowdrifts, the interstate highways usually remain open.

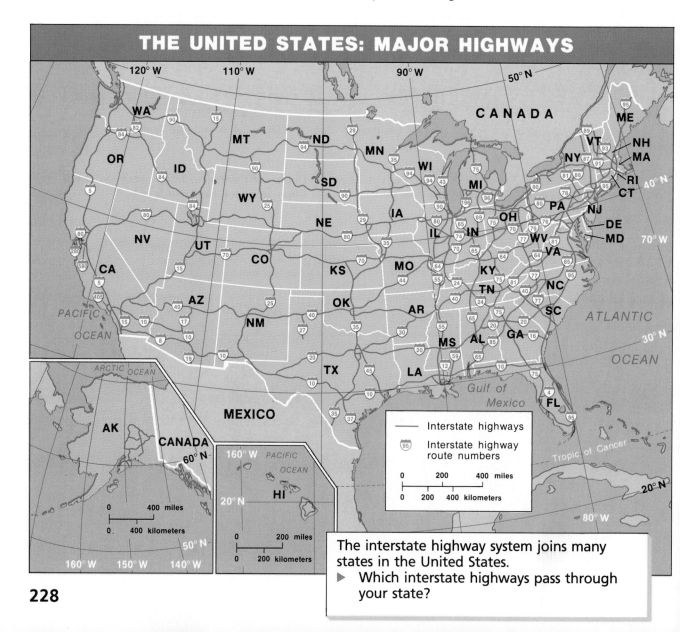

THE UNITED STATES: MAJOR HIGHWAYS

The interstate highway system joins many states in the United States.
▶ Which interstate highways pass through your state?

Salt Lake City, Utah, has grown into a busy city since it was founded by the Mormons in 1847.
▶ Which building, do you think, is owned by the Mormon Church?

B. Salt Lake City, the Largest City in Utah

The First Settlers In 1847 a brave group of men, women, and children left their homes in Illinois and began a westward journey. They were members of the Church of Jesus Christ of Latter-Day Saints, more commonly known as the Mormons. They followed their leader, Brigham Young, in search of a new home in the West.

After many months of travel across the Great Plains, the Mormons reached the edge of the Great Basin. They decided to build a community near the Great Salt Lake. This community became Salt Lake City.

Salt Lake City Today At first, most of the people who lived around Salt Lake City were farmers. Over the years, many people who had skills in industry also came to Utah. Factories were built in Salt Lake City and other places throughout Utah.

Today, Salt Lake City is a center for the production of metal products, foods, and electronic equipment. The city also remains an important religious center for the Mormons.

C. Denver, the Mile-High City

A Large City Denver is Colorado's capital city and the largest city of the Mountain West region. On a map, Denver and cities such as Colorado Springs and Pueblo look as though they are stretched out along a line that runs from north to south through the middle of Colorado. These cities are at the edge of the Rocky Mountains.

Location of Cities Why were cities built at the edge of the Rocky Mountains, where the plains meet the mountains? When many of these cities were started in the 1800s, horses and wagons were used to carry goods into the mountains. Supplies that arrived by railroad or on large wagons from the East were unloaded and repacked so that they could be carried on horseback or on smaller wagons along the trails into the mountains.

Denver is one of the places where the repacking of supplies was done. Warehouses were built for the trade

229

(Left) In the mint in Denver, Colorado, rolls of copper are moved to stamping machines where pennies will be cut out (center). At the right, a worker counts and bags the finished coins.
▶ What kind of machine is the worker on the left using?

and transportation companies. People started factories called smelters to process the ore that was mined in the mountains.

A Modern City Denver is still the center of much business activity. Many oil, gas, and mining companies have their main offices in Denver. Flour mills and canneries process the agricultural products, and stockyards process the livestock of the eastern plains.

One of the United States **mints**, or factories that produce coins, is located in Denver. If you look closely at a quarter, dime, nickel, or penny, you might see the letter *D* engraved on it. That means the coin was made in the United States mint in Denver.

A Nearby Information Center The United States government has its National Earthquake Information Center (NEIC) in Golden, a city just 10 miles (16 km) west of Denver. Thanks to special measuring equipment, workers at the center can monitor, or watch, earthquake activity all over the world.

At NEIC there is an alarm system that rings when an earthquake is being recorded in the United States. Scientists at NEIC immediately locate the earthquake. Then they get the information as quickly as possible to emergency officials in the affected area.

Problems for the City Denver is often called the Mile-High City because it is located 1 mile (1,609 km) above sea level. Its location at the base of the Rocky Mountains is beautiful, but that location also creates problems.

Gases from automobile exhaust, factory smokestacks, and home fireplaces often get trapped under air that

The discovery of gold and other minerals helped the Mountain West region to grow.
▶ What were two minerals that were discovered in Colorado?

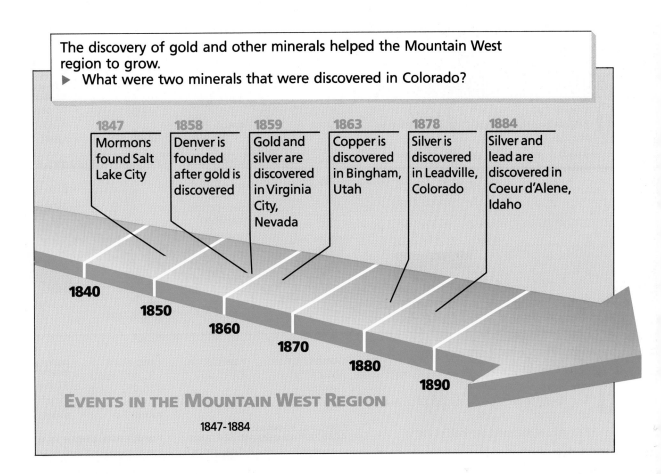

1847	1858	1859	1863	1878	1884
Mormons found Salt Lake City	Denver is founded after gold is discovered	Gold and silver are discovered in Virginia City, Nevada	Copper is discovered in Bingham, Utah	Silver is discovered in Leadville, Colorado	Silver and lead are discovered in Coeur d'Alene, Idaho

1840　1850　1860　1870　1880　1890

EVENTS IN THE MOUNTAIN WEST REGION
1847-1884

flows down from high mountain peaks. These gases, or pollutants, sometimes get so thick and heavy that people up in the mountains cannot see the city below them. The pollutants form a yellow-brown haze that is dangerous for people with health problems.

Looking for Solutions Denver's leaders and citizens are proud of the natural beauty of their region. They have decided to try to clean up the air. They encourage owners of factories to find ways to produce less smoke and pollution.

LESSON **4** REVIEW

THINK AND WRITE

A. How have railroads and interstate highways helped the Mountain West region grow?
B. How did Salt Lake City begin?
C. How is Denver trying to solve problems of being a mile-high city?

SKILLS CHECK

MAP SKILL

Look at the map on page 228. On a separate piece of paper, make a list of the six states in the Mountain West region. Next to each state write the numbers of the interstate highways that pass through that state.

COLORADO

KEY FACTS
Colorado is the highest state in elevation in the U.S.

The U.S. Air Force Academy is close to Colorado Springs.

LARGEST CITIES
Denver
Colorado Springs
Aurora

POPULATION
3,434,000

RANK: 26

LAND AREA
103,595 sq mi
268,311 sq km

RANK: 8

POPULATION DENSITY
32 per sq mi
12 per sq km

RANK: 37

PRINCIPAL PRODUCTS AGRICULTURE & MANUFACTURING

Cattle

Construction equipment

POPULATION: URBAN VS. RURAL
81% Urban
19% Rural

Denver

Lark bunting

Rocky Mountain columbine

Colorado blue spruce

IDAHO

KEY FACTS
The Rocky Mountains form Idaho's largest land region.

Forest covers almost one half of Idaho.

LARGEST CITIES
Boise City
Pocatello
Idaho Falls

POPULATION
1,017,000

RANK: 42

LAND AREA
82,412 sq mi
216,432 sq km

RANK: 12

POPULATION DENSITY
12 per sq mi
5 per sq km

RANK: 43

PRINCIPAL PRODUCTS AGRICULTURE & MANUFACTURING

Potatoes

Food products

POPULATION: URBAN VS. RURAL
54% Urban
46% Rural

Boise

Mountain bluebird

Syringa

White pine

MONTANA

KEY FACTS
Montana is the largest state in land area in the Mountain West region.

The Continental Divide winds through Montana.

LARGEST CITIES
Billings
Great Falls
Butte-Silver Bow

POPULATION
805,000

RANK: 44

LAND AREA
145,388 sq mi
376,555 sq km

RANK: 4

POPULATION DENSITY
6 per sq mi
2 per sq km

RANK: 48

PRINCIPAL PRODUCTS AGRICULTURE & MANUFACTURING

Cattle

Lumber

POPULATION: URBAN VS. RURAL
53% Urban
47% Rural

Helena

MONTANA

Western meadowlark

Bitterroot

Ponderosa pine

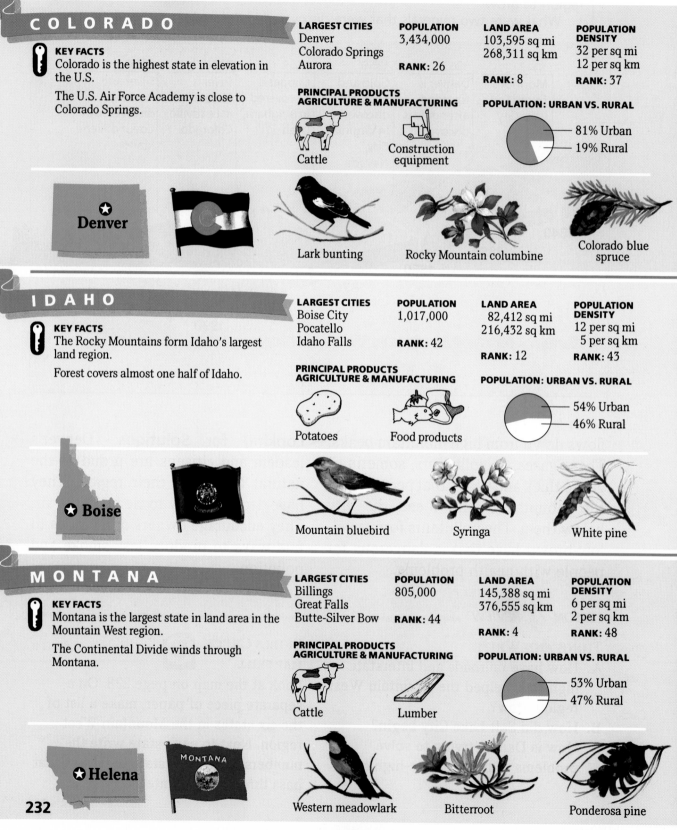

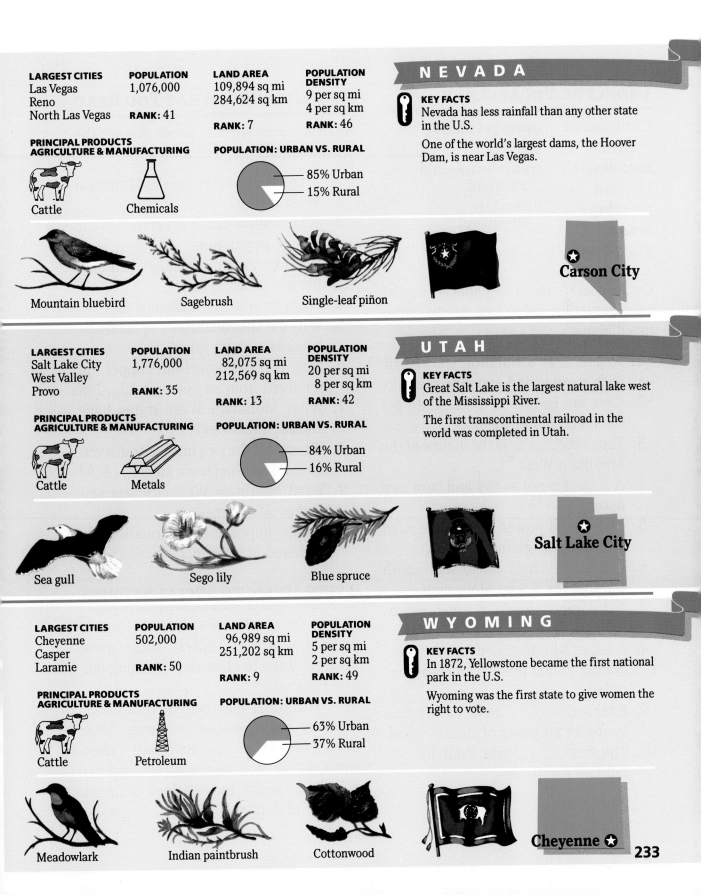

NEVADA

LARGEST CITIES	POPULATION	LAND AREA	POPULATION DENSITY
Las Vegas	1,076,000	109,894 sq mi	9 per sq mi
Reno		284,624 sq km	4 per sq km
North Las Vegas	RANK: 41	RANK: 7	RANK: 46

KEY FACTS
Nevada has less rainfall than any other state in the U.S.

One of the world's largest dams, the Hoover Dam, is near Las Vegas.

PRINCIPAL PRODUCTS
AGRICULTURE & MANUFACTURING

Cattle

Chemicals

POPULATION: URBAN VS. RURAL
85% Urban
15% Rural

Mountain bluebird

Sagebrush

Single-leaf piñon

Carson City

UTAH

LARGEST CITIES	POPULATION	LAND AREA	POPULATION DENSITY
Salt Lake City	1,776,000	82,075 sq mi	20 per sq mi
West Valley		212,569 sq km	8 per sq km
Provo	RANK: 35	RANK: 13	RANK: 42

KEY FACTS
Great Salt Lake is the largest natural lake west of the Mississippi River.

The first transcontinental railroad in the world was completed in Utah.

PRINCIPAL PRODUCTS
AGRICULTURE & MANUFACTURING

Cattle

Metals

POPULATION: URBAN VS. RURAL
84% Urban
16% Rural

Sea gull

Sego lily

Blue spruce

Salt Lake City

WYOMING

LARGEST CITIES	POPULATION	LAND AREA	POPULATION DENSITY
Cheyenne	502,000	96,989 sq mi	5 per sq mi
Casper		251,202 sq km	2 per sq km
Laramie	RANK: 50	RANK: 9	RANK: 49

KEY FACTS
In 1872, Yellowstone became the first national park in the U.S.

Wyoming was the first state to give women the right to vote.

PRINCIPAL PRODUCTS
AGRICULTURE & MANUFACTURING

Cattle

Petroleum

POPULATION: URBAN VS. RURAL
63% Urban
37% Rural

Meadowlark

Indian paintbrush

Cottonwood

Cheyenne

233

USING THE VOCABULARY

Continental Divide
semidesert
blizzard
roundup
brand
prospector
open-pit mining
smelter
transcontinental railroad
interstate highway

On a separate sheet of paper, complete each sentence, using one of the terms listed above.

1. A _____ is a blinding snowstorm with strong wind and extreme cold.
2. Ores are heated in a _____ to get the metal out of them.
3. Today the _____ is the lifeline of the Mountain West.
4. A _____ is not as dry and bare as a desert.
5. Cranes and power shovels are used on top of the ground in _____.
6. The _____ runs north and south through the Rocky Mountains.
7. Extra ranch workers are hired to help at _____ time.
8. A miner who searched for new sites, hoping to find precious metals, was called a _____.
9. Ranchers _____ new calves and lambs for purposes of identification.
10. The first _____ was built by two railroad companies.

REMEMBERING WHAT YOU READ

On a separate sheet of paper, answer the questions in complete sentences.

1. What states make up the Mountain West region?
2. Which Mountain West state has the largest population?
3. What sport attracts many visitors to the Mountain West?
4. What crop is Idaho famous for?
5. Why did the community of Leadville become a ghost town?
6. How is the scooped-out copper ore removed from an open-pit mine?
7. What Mountain West states have lumber industries?
8. Where did the two lines of transcontinental railroad track meet in 1869?
9. What Mountain West city was settled by Mormons?
10. What important information is gathered at Golden, Colorado?

TYING MUSIC TO SOCIAL STUDIES

People have always enjoyed singing while they worked. Special songs grew up around the hard work of building our first railroads.

With other members of your class, learn the old American work song "I've Been Working on the Railroad." Then write one or two sentences telling how this song might have helped railroad builders of long ago.

THINKING CRITICALLY

On a separate sheet of paper, answer the following questions in complete sentences.

1. Lesson 1 calls the Mountain West "a region full of treasures." What kinds of treasures are meant?
2. What is a major difference between the life of the Smiths and that of Hector Mendiburu? What kind of person would prefer Mendiburu's life?
3. What kind of business might you like to start in a ghost town?
4. Which of the Mountain West industries do you think might still be in existence 200 years from now?
5. In which of the Mountain West cities would you prefer to live? Tell why.

SUMMARIZING THE CHAPTER

Copy this graphic organizer on a separate sheet of paper. Under the main idea for each lesson, write four facts that support the main idea.

CHAPTER THEME	The beauty of its landscape and the richness of its mineral resources are the best-known features of the Mountain West. However, industry and cities are growing in this area.		
LESSON 1	The huge Mountain West region has some of the most rugged and beautiful land in the United States.	1. ___ 2. ___	3. ___ 4. ___
LESSON 2	There is some agriculture in the Mountain West region.	1. ___ 2. ___	3. ___ 4. ___
LESSON 3	Mineral and metal resources are important to the economy of the Mountain West.	1. ___ 2. ___	3. ___ 4. ___
LESSON 4	Transportation helped Mountain West cities grow.	1. ___ 2. ___	3. ___ 4. ___

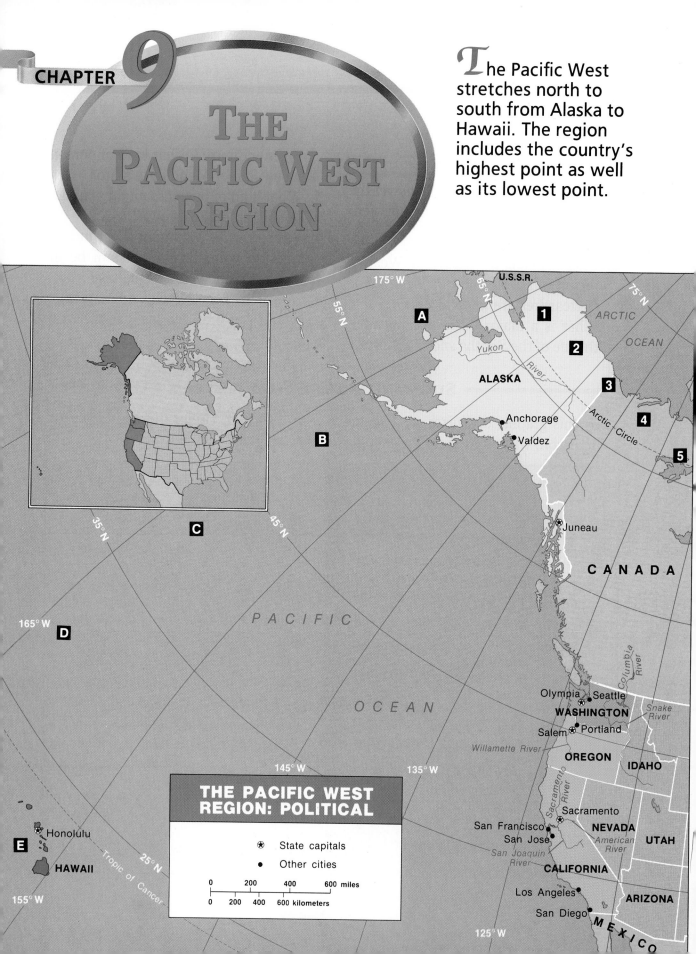

CHAPTER **9**

THE PACIFIC WEST REGION

*T*he Pacific West stretches north to south from Alaska to Hawaii. The region includes the country's highest point as well as its lowest point.

THE PACIFIC WEST REGION: POLITICAL

⊛ State capitals

• Other cities

| 0 | 200 | 400 | 600 miles |
| 0 | 200 | 400 | 600 kilometers |

A Land of Great Variety

THINK ABOUT WHAT YOU KNOW
What three questions would you ask to learn about the Pacific West region?

STUDY THE VOCABULARY
volcano   lava

FOCUS YOUR READING
What is the land like in the Pacific West?

A. A Hidden Treasure in the Mountains

In 1851 an army officer named Major James Savage led a scouting party through the mountains of California. They were in the area that is now Yosemite (yoh SEM ut ee) National Park. Suddenly the party came to the edge of a precipice, or cliff. Major Savage was astounded by the beauty of the view he saw ahead of him.

Richard Halliburton has told the story of Major Savage's discovery in a book called *Complete Book of Marvels.*

The paragraphs below describe what Major Savage saw so many years ago.

Their path, winding through dense forests, suddenly brought the party to the edge of a precipice. Major Savage, at the head of his column, looked over the brink. What he saw made him forget [everything else].

For he beheld a great gorge in the mountains, floored with forests and meadows, and surrounded by cliffs and rocktowers that rose thousands of feet—rose so sheer and smooth that not even the smallest tree could find a crack in which to grow.

Plunging down into the valley from the tops of these giant cliffs were waterfalls the like of which no white man in all the history of the world had ever before seen. . . .

Quickly the Major led his men down the steep trail to the river at the bottom of the canyon. Opposite, they beheld a gray granite precipice three thousand feet high, smooth and clean, and shining in the sun.

CITY INDEX

Cities less than 100,000
Juneau (AK) A-4
Olympia (WA).................. B-5
Salem (OR) C-5
Valdez (AK) A-2

Cities 100,000 to 499,999
Anchorage (AK)............... A-2

Honolulu (HI) E-1
Portland (OR)................. B-5
Sacramento (CA).............. C-5
Seattle (WA) B-5

Cities 500,000 to 999,999
San Francisco (CA) C-5
San Jose (CA) C-5

Cities 1,000,000 or more
Los Angeles (CA) D-5
San Diego (CA)............... D-5

The Pacific West is the only region in the United States in which the states are not located in the same part of our country.
▶ About how far is the northern tip of Alaska from the southern tip of California?

B. Locating the Pacific West

Coastal States On the map on page 239, you can see that five states in the United States border the Pacific Ocean. These states are California, Oregon, Washington, Alaska, and Hawaii. In Chapter 2 you read that Alaska and Hawaii are the only two states that do not touch any other state.

Hawaii is the most unusual state in the United States because it is a group of many islands in the Pacific Ocean. Honolulu (hahn uh LOO loo), the capital and the largest city of Hawaii, is on the island of Oahu (oh AH hoo).

Mountain Ranges All five of the Pacific West states have mountainous parts. The highest mountain in all of North America is in Alaska. It is Mount McKinley, with a height of 20,320 feet (6,194 m). Mount McKinley is more than three times as high as Mount Washington in the White Mountains of the New England region.

If you were to fly over the states on the Pacific coast, you would see two chains of mountains, with long, narrow valleys in between. One chain, called the Coastal Ranges, stretches along the Pacific coast. In many places the Coastal Ranges drop straight into the Pacific Ocean and form spectacular cliffs along the water's edge.

Inland there is another chain of mountains. These mountains, called the Cascades, almost divide the states of Washington and Oregon in half, north to south. They extend into the northern part of California.

Through most of California this mountain range is called the *Sierra Nevada* (see ER uh nuh VAD uh). The name means "snowy range" in Spanish. Mount Whitney is located in this range. It is the highest peak in the United States outside of Alaska.

Many people enjoy backpacking in the Sierra Nevada Mountains.
► Why, do you think, do people like to go backpacking?

THE PACIFIC WEST REGION: PHYSICAL

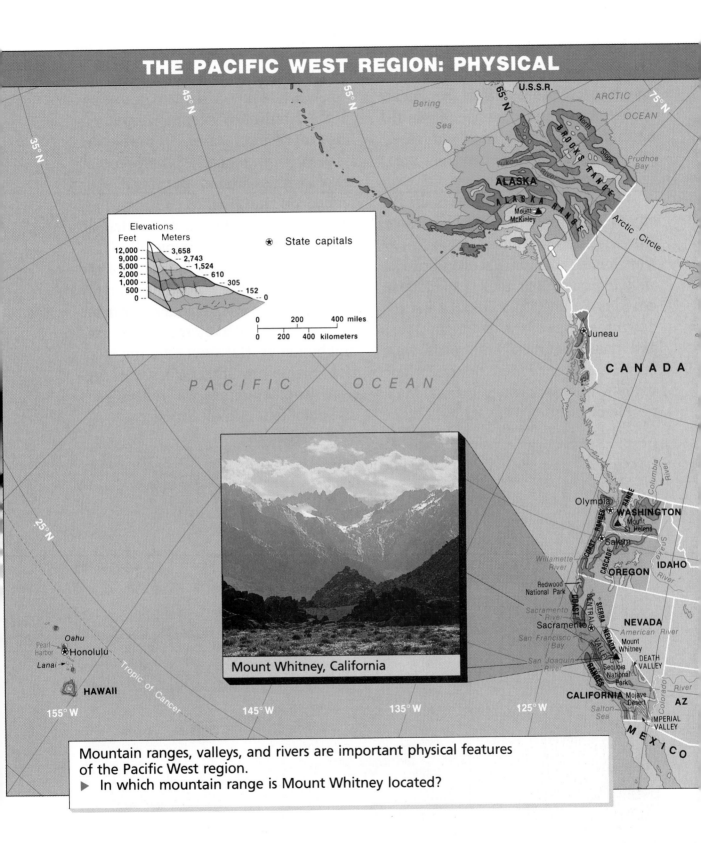

Elevations

Feet	Meters
12,000	3,658
9,000	2,743
5,000	1,524
2,000	610
1,000	305
500	152
0	0

⊛ State capitals

0   200   400 miles
0   200   400 kilometers

U.S.S.R.

Bering Sea

ARCTIC OCEAN

Prudhoe Bay

North Slope

BROOKS RANGE

ALASKA

Yukon River

ALASKA RANGE

Mount McKinley

Arctic Circle

CANADA

PACIFIC OCEAN

Juneau

Columbia River

Olympia

⊛ WASHINGTON

Mount St. Helens

COAST RANGES

CASCADE RANGE

Salem ⊛

Snake River

OREGON

IDAHO

Willamette River

Redwood National Park

Sacramento River

COAST RANGES

SIERRA NEVADA

CENTRAL VALLEY

NEVADA

American River

Mount Whitney

Sacramento ⊛

San Francisco Bay

San Joaquin River

DEATH VALLEY

Sequoia National Park

CALIFORNIA

Mojave Desert

Salton Sea

Colorado River

AZ

IMPERIAL VALLEY

MEXICO

Oahu

Pearl Harbor

⊛ Honolulu

Lanai

HAWAII

Tropic of Cancer

25° N

155° W   145° W   135° W   125° W

35° N   45° N   55° N   65° N   75° N

Mount Whitney, California

Mountain ranges, valleys, and rivers are important physical features
of the Pacific West region.
▶ In which mountain range is Mount Whitney located?

Volcanic Mountains The islands of Hawaii were formed millions of years ago by **volcanoes** under the Pacific Ocean. A volcano is an opening in the earth from which steam and gases, stones, ashes, and melted rock burst forth from time to time.

Recently, two volcanoes in the Pacific West erupted in different ways. One of these volcanoes was Kilauea (kee lou AY uh), on the island of Hawaii. Fiery melted rock, called **lava**, oozed out of the top of Kilauea and ran down the sides of the mountain. Trees and houses burned, and roads were buried under many feet of lava, which hardens into rock when it cools. Most people in the area were able to escape when Kilauea erupted, but they lost their homes and possessions.

When Mount St. Helens, a volcano in the state of Washington, erupted, huge rocks and tons of ash shot out of its peak with a roar. The blast uprooted trees for miles around. Burning cinders landed on the ground, causing forest fires. Ash many feet deep settled on everything like a dirty snowfall.

Ice and snow on the sides of the mountain melted, flooding nearby land and causing landslides down the mountain. Flooded rivers buried cars and buildings. But soon after the eruption, plants and insects began to appear. In time, nature will return trees and wildlife to Mount St. Helens.

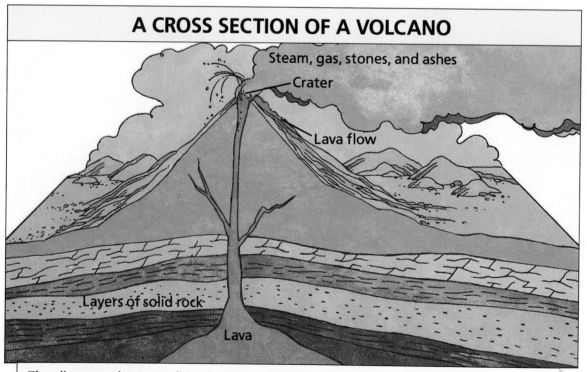

A CROSS SECTION OF A VOLCANO

Steam, gas, stones, and ashes

Crater

Lava flow

Layers of solid rock

Lava

The diagram above explains how a volcano erupts. Lava, or melted rock, is forced through a vent at the top of the volcano.
► What else, besides lava, is forced out of the volcano?

THE ERUPTION OF MOUNT ST. HELENS

About 8:30 A.M. on May 18, 1980, a loud boom was heard all over southwestern Washington. A cloud of smoke and ash rose high in the air over Mount St. Helens. The day became as dark as night.

A few days later a scientist visited Mount St. Helens. He later described in his journal what he had seen. Here is a part of what he wrote.

The piece of 35-millimeter film in my hands was unlike any I had ever seen. It had no image on it and the emulsion had been burned so that only small patches of what was originally there still remained. I could see the sprocket holes and the shape of the film, but it was now curled and warped. The photographer using it had been seven miles away from Mount St. Helens when the volcano erupted.

The day after the blast a young helicopter pilot named Chris Lane flew a colleague and myself up to where Blackburn [the photographer] had been.

We could see the top of a Volvo sedan sitting above the ash. The ash deposits around it on the road were about even with the trunk lid and the engine hood. As we flew by we could see no sign at all of disturbance of the ash. We circled again to come closer to make sure that there was no one in the car.

Understanding Source Material

1. What was the film like when the scientist found it?
2. How deep were the ash deposits?
3. How can a scientist's journal help other scientists?

The House I Live In

by Lewis Allan and Earl Robinson

Very freely

What _____ is A - me - ri - ca to me? A
name, a map, the flag I see. _____ A cer-tain word, _____ De -
mo - cra - cy. What is A - me - ri - ca _____ to me?

A tempo–Slow

The House I Live In, A dream that must come true _____ A
land of food and shel - ter, and there's work for all to do, The
right to earn a liv' - ing To make us real - ly free, Where
ev - 'ry - one is work - ing, That's A - me - ri - ca to me.

Portland, Oregon, is a major city in the Pacific West region.
► How can you tell that people in Portland enjoy boating?

C. Valleys of the Pacific West

The Central Valley Between the mountain ranges of the Pacific West states are a number of valleys. The Central Valley of California is the largest valley of the Pacific West.

The Central Valley is about 400 miles (644 km) long, but it is only about 60 miles (97 km) wide. Sacramento, the capital city of California, is in this important valley. Find the Central Valley on the map on page 239.

Willamette Valley The Willamette (wih LAM iht) Valley is the second largest valley of the Pacific West. It is in the northwest corner of Oregon. The Willamette Valley follows the Willamette River as far north as the Columbia River.

Portland, the most populated city in Oregon, is in the Willamette Valley. Salem, the capital city of Oregon, is also in that valley.

A Song About Our Country You can now identify the physical regions of the United States. On the opposite page there is a song about our country —"the house" we live in. What does the song tell you about our country?

LESSON 1 REVIEW

THINK AND WRITE

A. What is one of the main natural features of the Pacific West region?
B. In what ways are Alaska and Hawaii different from all the other states of the United States?
C. Where is the Central Valley located?

SKILLS CHECK

MAP SKILL

Find Mount St. Helens on the map on page 239. Use the scale bar to find whether Salem or Olympia is closer to Mount St. Helens.

LESSON 2

Climates and Farms of the Pacific West

THINK ABOUT WHAT YOU KNOW
How do plants and trees that grow in a rainy climate differ from plants and trees that grow in a dry climate?

STUDY THE VOCABULARY
aqueduct   **sugarcane**

FOCUS YOUR READING
What is the climate like in the Pacific West?

A. A Region of Many Climates

A Hot and Dry Climate Let's imagine that you have just won a contest, and the prize is a trip to a place of your choice in the Pacific West. How would you decide where to go?

You might make your decision based on the climate. The Pacific West has a greater variety of climates than any other region of the United States. Extremely hot, cold, dry, and rainy climates are all found in this region.

If you were to go to southern California, you might find yourself in a large area of barren land called the Mojave (moh HAH vee) Desert. Barren land cannot be used to grow crops or, for that matter, plants of almost any kind. The temperature can be as high as 120°F (49°C).

Death Valley is north of the Mojave Desert. It is one of the hottest and driest places in the United States. And

Death Valley is the lowest place in North America. It is 282 feet (86 m) below sea level.

Irrigated Farmlands Can farming be done in the dry areas of the Pacific West region? The answer is yes. The Central Valley and the eastern parts of Washington and Oregon receive up to 20 inches (51 cm) of precipitation each

Irrigation canals near Bakersfield, California, provide water for crops.
▶ Which part of the photograph shows land that has been irrigated for crops?

244

LEADING PRODUCERS OF CERTAIN FRUITS

Apricots	Grapefruit	Oranges	Peaches	Strawberries
California	Florida	Florida	California	California
Washington	California	California	South Carolina	Florida
Utah	Texas	Arizona	Pennsylvania	Oregon

Of the states shown on the chart, only one is among the leading producers of all the produce listed.
► What is the state?

year. That is moisture enough to grow wheat, but it is not enough to grow vegetables or fruits.

To grow vegetables and fruits in this area, farmers irrigate their fields with water from nearby rivers. The Sierra Nevada usually receives a lot of snow, and some of the rivers that begin in the mountains flow across dry areas on their way to the Pacific Ocean.

Large dams have been built across some of these rivers that flow from the mountains to make reservoirs. Long **aqueducts** (AK wuh dukts), or waterways, have been dug from these reservoirs to carry water to the fields and orchards of the region.

California is the leading agricultural state in the United States. It leads the nation in growing grapes and ranks second in the production of cotton, sugar beets, and tomatoes. The table on this page shows where California ranks in growing certain fruit.

B. Moist, Cool Climates

A Coastal Climate Instead of a hot, dry desert, you might prefer to visit a cooler place. Along the coasts of northern California, Oregon, and Washington, temperatures are much lower than they are in southern California. Summer temperatures often stay below 70°F (21°C).

This part of the Pacific West receives a great deal of precipitation. Some places receive 50 inches (127 cm) per year, and other places receive as much as 200 inches (508 cm).

A Cool Valley In the Willamette Valley the climate is good for farming. Barley, oats, and hay for dairy cattle grow on many farms. Vegetables such as potatoes, green beans, onions, cauliflower, and broccoli add to the abundance of foods grown in this area. Orchards of plums, cherries, pears, and peaches stretch across the land.

245

Fertile soil and a period of mild temperatures make it possible to grow some crops in the Mantanuska Valley, in Alaska. What crop is shown here?

C. The Climate of Alaska

Northern Alaska If you would like to visit a state with a great variety of climates, you might choose Alaska. In the far northern part of Alaska, along the Arctic Ocean, lakes and rivers are frozen most of the year. The winter temperature often drops as low as $-80°F$ $(-62°C)$. Fierce winds make the temperature seem even colder.

Southern Alaska Juneau (JOO noh) is the capital of Alaska. Find Juneau on the map on page 236. Notice that Juneau is far to the south of the main landmass of Alaska. Summer temperatures are pleasant in Juneau. They often reach as high as 70°F (21°C).

The soils are good for farming in the small area of Alaska near Anchorage. Crops such as potatoes, hay, and barley grow well there. Some vegetables and fruits, such as carrots, cabbages, and strawberries, grow to tremendous sizes.

D. Hawaii — A Tropical Land

Climate and Rainfall Perhaps you really don't like cold weather. Hawaii might be just the place for your trip. It is warm in this state the year round. There is no noticeable change of seasons. The temperature stays about the same all the time.

Parts of the Hawaiian Islands receive great amounts of rainfall, as much as 400 inches (1,016 cm) per year. Palm trees and other kinds of tropical plants and flowers grow well on the islands. With the warm climate, plentiful rainfall, and rich volcanic soil, there are many farms in Hawaii.

Growing Pineapples You have probably eaten pineapple, a fruit that grows very well in a wet tropical climate. One of the Hawaiian Islands, named Lanai (lah NAH ee), is called the pineapple island. The whole island is owned by one company that grows pineapples.

Growing Sugarcane Hawaii's most important crop is **sugarcane**. It is the plant from which we get sugar. Sugarcane is grown on plantations.

To plant a cane field, the workers cut small pieces of sugarcane and put them in the ground. The pieces soon take root. In a year or two, the plants are 15 feet (4½ m) high and are ready for harvest.

The first step in harvesting is to set the cane fields on fire! The fire burns the leaves from the stems of the cane. Workers then cut the cane and load it on trucks bound for the sugar mill.

At the mill the sugarcane is washed, cut into pieces, and crushed. The juice that is squeezed out is heated to remove the water. Finally, sugar is produced. At this point it is a yellowish-brown color. It has to be treated further before it becomes the white grains that we use to sweeten foods.

Other crops from Hawaii are bananas, rice, coffee, vegetables, macadamia (mak uh DAY mee uh) nuts, and

Sugarcane is burned before it is harvested. The fire cooks juices and seals them in the stalks.
▶ What part of the field has not been burned yet?

beef cattle. Yes, even beef cattle! On the largest island in the chain — the Big Island, Hawaii — several large cattle ranches are located.

LESSON *2* REVIEW

THINK AND WRITE

A. How do farmers grow crops in dry areas of the Pacific West?
B. Why are there farms along the coast of northern California, Oregon, and Washington?
C. How is it possible for a part of Alaska to have some farming?
D. Why is Hawaii an excellent place for farming?

SKILLS CHECK

WRITING SKILL
Write a letter to a friend, describing how it feels to be in a California desert, in a cold part of Alaska, or in Hawaii.

SHARING THE HARVEST
IN THE PACIFIC WEST

In communities all over the United States, people work together to help others. This is the story of how people in Seattle, a city in the Pacific West, helped their neighbors. To provide this help, people shared their harvests.

Mr. Hillis belonged to the Rotary Club in Seattle, Washington. Each year his club raised money to help people in need. One year a great number of people in Seattle were out of work. Many of them did not have enough food to eat. But the members of the Rotary Club could not raise enough money to buy food for so many people.

Then Mr. Hillis had an idea. At the next club meeting he stood at the microphone and said: "Fellow Rotarians, as you know, there are a lot of people in our community who do not have enough to eat. Have you stopped by a neighborhood food bank lately? At the food banks, the lines of hungry people are getting longer every day, and not enough food comes in to feed them.

"Summer is coming, and I know many of you are getting ready to plant a garden in your backyard. Would you please raise one extra plant of whatever you grow this year? When the first harvest comes along, keep what you need, but bring whatever is left for the poor. I will find some way to take it to the food banks."

What an idea! The members of the Rotary Club were excited. When harvest came, they had raised lots of extra food that could be taken to the food banks. Soon people from all over Washington State found out about the Rotary Club project. They wanted to give the extra food they had raised too. Many trucks were needed to take all the food to the food banks.

The Rotary Club's food project was shown on national television. The President of the United States said that this project showed what people can do to help their neighbors. But Mr. Hillis remained very humble about his idea. He was just happy to be working on a project that helped so many people.

Thinking for Yourself

1. Mr. Hillis's idea helped people who needed food. What other help might these people need?
2. Rotary is one community organization that helps people. Can you think of other helpful service organizations and what they do?
3. Why, do you think, was the Rotary food project so successful?

Natural Resources of the Pacific West

THINK ABOUT WHAT YOU KNOW

Name three natural resources in the region in which you live. How do people use these natural resources?

STUDY THE VOCABULARY

boom town   **tundra**

FOCUS YOUR READING

What are the most important natural resources of the Pacific West?

A. Gold and the Pacific West

One January day in 1848, James Marshall was working at a new sawmill along the American River, in northern California. Suddenly he noticed a small, shiny rock in the bed of the river. He picked it up and studied it.

Marshall tested his rock and discovered that it was gold. He found several more nuggets and showed them to John Sutter, the owner of the mill. They wanted to keep their valuable discovery a secret, but that was hard to do. Soon the word was out.

By 1849, thousands of people had journeyed to California, hoping to find gold and make their fortunes. They came from all over the United States. Some even came from other countries. This was the beginning of a gold rush.

> After the discovery of gold in 1849, mining camps sprang up all over California.
> ▶ What were some of the tools that the gold miners used?

The Granger Collection

Communities sprang up wherever gold mines were started. These communities were called **boom towns** because they grew so fast. After all the gold had been mined from the earth, many of these communities slowly died away and became ghost towns.

Fifty years later, there was a second big gold rush much farther north. People went north by the thousands. Settlers moved into the Yukon (YOO-kahn) River valley of Alaska to seek their fortunes in gold. Today most of the gold in Alaska is mined by mining companies. Not many individual miners still search for gold in Alaska.

B. Alaska and the Oil Boom

Discovering Oil In the northern part of Alaska, the land slopes gradually down to the Arctic Ocean. This region is called the North Slope. The ground in this area is flat, and there are many lakes and marshes. But there are no trees. This type of cold, treeless area is called a **tundra**.

In the 1960s, large underground pools of petroleum were discovered under the North Slope at a place called Prudhoe (PROOD oh) Bay. The North Slope oil fields provide about one fifth of all the oil produced in the United States. Alaska now produces more oil than any other state except Texas.

Mining the Oil A long pipeline called the Trans-Alaska Pipeline carries the oil from the North Slope to the southern Alaskan port of Valdez (val DEEZ),

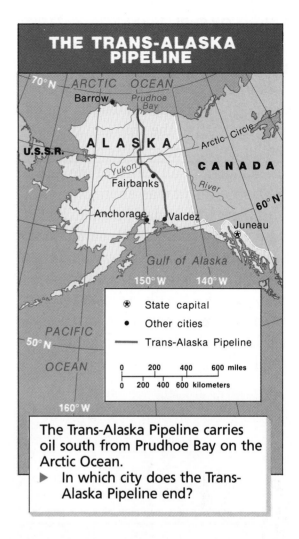

The Trans-Alaska Pipeline carries oil south from Prudhoe Bay on the Arctic Ocean.
▶ In which city does the Trans-Alaska Pipeline end?

on Prince William Sound. There, huge tankers, or supertankers, carry the oil south to other parts of the world.

The Trans-Alaska Pipeline is unusual because in places it is built above the ground instead of underneath the surface. This was done where the ground is frozen for much of the year.

Some of Alaska's oil is shipped to cities on the Pacific Coast—for example, San Francisco—where refineries make the oil into useful fuel for homes, cars, and factories. A lot of the oil is shipped to Japan.

251

A Huge Oil Spill In the spring of 1989, the fully loaded supertanker *Exxon Valdez* ran aground in Prince William Sound. Eleven million gallons of thick, black, gooey crude oil began spilling over the gash in the ship and soon was spoiling hundreds of miles of shoreline. The damage to all forms of life and to the environment was enormous.

Many hundreds of people, including volunteers from all parts of the United States, tried to clean up the area. But it was a major disaster. It will take years for the shoreline to become clean and safe again and for the fish, wildlife, and birds to return to their natural habitats.

C. Timber in the Pacific West

Giant Trees California is well known for two special kinds of evergreen trees. The redwoods are among the tallest of living trees, and the giant sequoias (sih-KWOI uhz) are some of the oldest and largest living things on earth.

Many redwoods reach 200 to 275 feet (61 to 84 m) in height. That's almost the length of a football field! They get their name from the color of their bark and wood.

These tall trees grow in forests along the Pacific Coast of Califonia and Oregon. The branches of these close-growing trees prevent much sunlight from reaching the floor of a redwood

The large photograph shows workers trying to clean up part of the shoreline that was damaged after the oil spill at Valdez, Alaska.
▶ What are the women in the smaller photograph doing?

forest. The lack of sunlight keeps other plants to a minimum.

Redwood logs are long and straight, and the wood resists decay. Telephone poles and outdoor furniture are some of the products made from redwood. But many of the redwood trees are hundreds of years old. Our government protects those trees by not allowing them to be cut for timber.

Giant sequoias are relatives of the redwoods. The sequoias, however, are much older, some as much as several thousand years old. And the sequoias grow mostly in the Sierra Nevada mountains.

The General Sherman Tree is a giant sequoia and is probably the largest tree on earth. Scientists estimate that it weighs over 6,000 tons (5,442 t). It was named for a famous general in American history. This tree and many of the rare giant sequoias are growing in Sequoia National Park, where they are protected.

Lumbering One tree that is important for timber is the Douglas fir, which grows in Washington and Oregon. Douglas fir trees grow to over 150 feet (46 m) tall. They are the major source of lumber for boards, doors, and flooring.

Logs that are cut in the mountains are floated down rivers to sawmills. Sawmills are found all along the coasts of Oregon, Washington, and Alaska. Production of paper and other wood products is a major industry in these three states.

D. Fishing Along the Pacific Coast

Pacific Salmon For hundreds of years the Native American people have fished for salmon (SAM un) along the coasts of Washington and Alaska. Today catching and canning salmon is a big industry in Washington and Alaska. Most of the salmon is canned in fish canneries on the Pacific Coast. Then it is shipped to stores throughout the United States.

Migration of Salmon Salmon hatch from eggs laid by female salmon in freshwater streams. The young salmon develop and live in the streams for up to

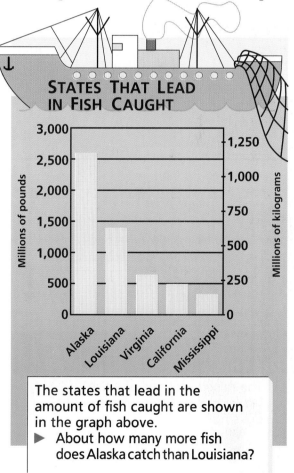

STATES THAT LEAD IN FISH CAUGHT

The states that lead in the amount of fish caught are shown in the graph above.
▶ About how many more fish does Alaska catch than Louisiana?

three years after they hatch. Then they swim out into the Pacific Ocean. They may live in the ocean for as long as 10 years before returning to lay their eggs in the stream where they were born.

Fish Ladders In some places, large dams kept these fish from swimming to their destinations. So fish ladders were built to let the salmon get past the dams on their streams.

A fish ladder is made up of a series of pools separated by walls. Count the walls in the diagram of the fish ladder

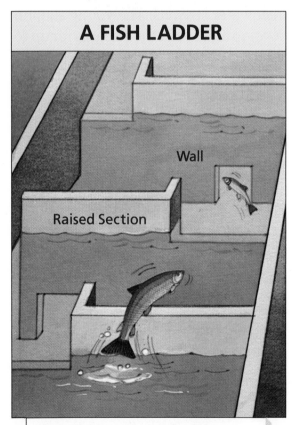

A FISH LADDER

Wall

Raised Section

The raised sections of a fish ladder make places where water does not flow.
▶ Why, do you think, might fish rest in these places?

on this page. Each pool is a little higher than the one below it. Water flows from pool to pool over many small waterfalls that look like a flight of steps. Fish either jump the walls or swim through holes at the bottom of the walls.

E. Manufacturing in the Pacific West

A Manufacturing State California leads the nation in manufacturing. More goods are made or processed in the state of California than in many countries of the world. If California were a country, it would be the seventh leading manufacturing country in the world.

Seattle, Washington, and southern California are important centers of the aircraft industry. This industry has many engineers and scientists who design and test military aircraft and equipment for the United States government. They also design aircraft for airline companies throughout the world. The warm dry climate of southern California permits aircraft companies to fly and test their airplanes the whole year around.

There are also other important manufacturing industries in the Pacific West region. Battleships, tankers, and fishing boats are made and repaired in such cities as Seattle, Washington, and Honolulu, Hawaii.

Food Processing Another important industry in the Pacific West is food processing. The processed foods include

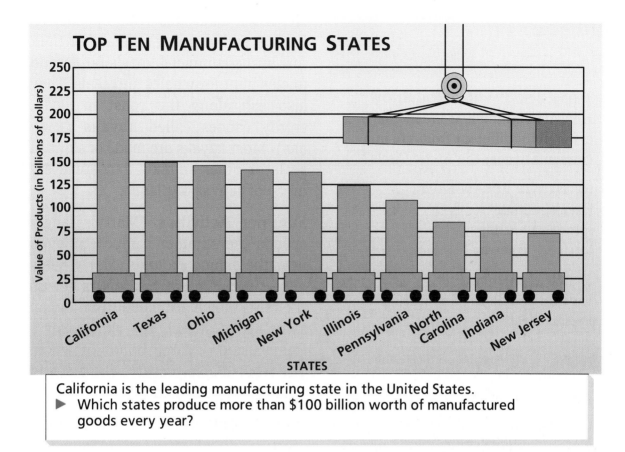

TOP TEN MANUFACTURING STATES

Value of Products (in billions of dollars) vs **STATES**

States: California, Texas, Ohio, Michigan, New York, Illinois, Pennsylvania, North Carolina, Indiana, New Jersey

California is the leading manufacturing state in the United States.
► Which states produce more than $100 billion worth of manufactured goods every year?

crabs and salmon from Alaska, Washington, and Oregon. Portland, Oregon, and Salem, Oregon, have many canneries and freezing plants. Many of the fruits and vegetables grown in the rich soils of the Willamette Valley are processed in these canneries and plants.

Silicon Valley Near San Francisco there is an area that is called Silicon (SIHL ih kaln) Valley. The valley gets its name from silicon chips, the tiny electrical parts that store information in computers. Huge quantities of these chips are manufactured in the valley.

LESSON  REVIEW

THINK AND WRITE

A. Why did many mining towns become ghost towns after being boom towns?

B. How did the oil industry change Alaska?

C. Why is lumbering an important industry in the Pacific West?

D. How do fish ladders help to preserve the natural life cycle of salmon?

E. What are some ways that people in the Pacific West might make a living?

SKILLS CHECK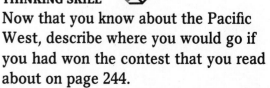

THINKING SKILL

Now that you know about the Pacific West, describe where you would go if you had won the contest that you read about on page 244.

255

Ways of Life in the Pacific West

THINK ABOUT WHAT YOU KNOW

How, do you think, is life in your community different from life in a community near the Arctic Circle?

STUDY THE VOCABULARY

kayak	luau
igloo	heritage
lei	freeway

FOCUS YOUR READING

How do people live and work in the Pacific West?

A. Eskimos of the Pacific West

Inuit The people of northern Alaska are often called Eskimos, but they call themselves *Inuit* (IHN oo wiht), which means "people" in the Inuit language. Let's find out how an Inuit family lives.

Marty, a young Inuit girl, has a busy life that changes with the seasons. Her father makes his living by hunting, fishing, and trapping animals for their fur. In the summer Marty's father and uncles hunt for whales and seals. They also fish along the coast in small, sturdy canoes called **kayaks** (KYE-aks). Most kayaks are made of skins of seals or other animals, but some are made of canvas or plastic.

Summer Activities Marty's family spends the summer camped in tents near the fishing grounds. Marty helps her mother, sisters, and aunts set up the tents which are made from animal skins. They stretch the skins over a frame made of large bones or wood. The women also preserve the fish and animals that the men catch.

Winter Activities In the winter, Marty's father hunts seals, rabbits, and foxes. The waters are frozen. So a hunter can travel a long distance across the ice and snow, using a sled and a team of dogs. Some Inuit hunters use snowmobiles for winter hunting.

Inuit children in Point Barrow, Alaska, enjoy a blanket toss.
▶ Was the weather warm or cold when this picture was taken?

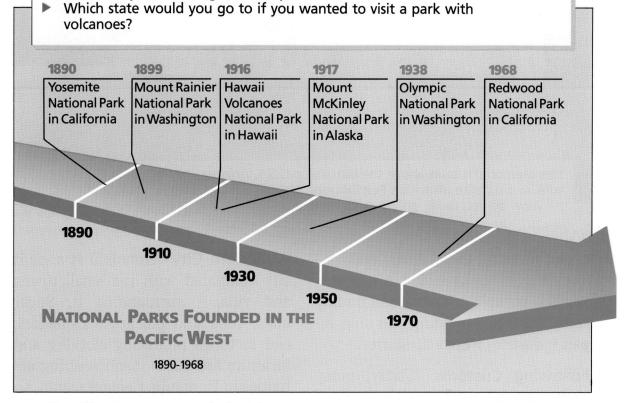

The United States government has preserved much of the beauty of the Pacific West by establishing national parks.
▶ Which state would you go to if you wanted to visit a park with volcanoes?

1890	1899	1916	1917	1938	1968
Yosemite National Park in California	Mount Rainier National Park in Washington	Hawaii Volcanoes National Park in Hawaii	Mount McKinley National Park in Alaska	Olympic National Park in Washington	Redwood National Park in California

1890   1910   1930   1950   1970

NATIONAL PARKS FOUNDED IN THE PACIFIC WEST

1890-1968

Families may set up their winter camps in **igloos** (IHG looz), or homes built of ice. Marty's family also has a home in a town. That home has electricity, running water, and a television. Marty goes to school during the winter.

Old and New Ways In the past, Inuit families spent many hours telling their children Inuit legends. They also taught the children such crafts as carving bones into tools or figures of animals. Today many Inuit children prefer to go to a movie or listen to the radio. Inuit parents want to preserve some of their culture. So they are organizing festivals and classes to teach the children traditional legends and crafts.

B. The Polynesian Culture of Hawaii

Early Days Thousands of years ago, people lived on a group of small islands scattered across the central Pacific Ocean. We call these islands Polynesia (pahl uh NEE zhuh). *Polynesia* means "many islands."

The people of Polynesia knew how to build strong canoes and navigate, or find their way, through the ocean. Some of the Polynesians landed on the islands we call Hawaii and settled there. They fished, grew crops, and built strong kingdoms.

In the late 1700s, Europeans discovered the Hawaiian Islands and also

This memorial is built above the battleship U.S.S. *Arizona,* which was sunk in a surprise attack on Pearl Harbor, Hawaii, on December 7, 1941.

▶ Why, do you think, do we build memorials like this?

began to settle there. Many missionaries arrived, along with businesspeople who set up plantations and trading companies. Shipbuilding and ship repair industries were also started.

Following Customs Today, many Hawaiians follow some of the ways of their grandparents and great-grandparents. And they enjoy sharing their customs with other people. For example, visitors to Hawaii may be greeted with the word *aloha* (ah LOW huh). One meaning of the word is "hello." Then they might be given **leis** (layz), or garlands of flowers that are worn around the neck.

Hawaiian music is quite unusual and often uses the ukulele (yoo kuh-LAY lee), a stringed instrument that is played much as a guitar is played. Tourists enjoy learning about Hawaii's culture by attending a **luau** (LOO ou), a Hawaiian-style dinner with performances by singers and dancers.

A Modern City Honolulu is a giant city compared with the small towns and villages surrounding it. Sugar mills, tuna and pineapple canneries, and factories producing clothing and furniture are major manufacturing activities in Honolulu. Cement plants, an oil refinery, and a steel mill are also found in Honolulu.

Tourism Every year thousands of tourists visit Hawaii, so many Hawaiians work for airline companies, travel agencies, restaurants, car-rental agencies, and gift shops. Honolulu is a popular tourist center, and its famous beach, Waikiki (wye kee KEE), attracts many people who like to swim and surf.

Some tourists climb Diamond Head, a spectacular inactive volcano. Still others visit Pearl Harbor, where United States Navy ships were bombed during World War II, many decades ago. Today, the United States Navy still has a large, important base in Hawaii.

C. Major Cities of the Pacific West Region

San Diego The first European settlement in California was a mission. It was founded in 1769, at the place where the city of San Diego (san dee AY goh) is now located. Many other missions, such as those at Los Angeles and San Francisco, were soon after established along California's coast.

San Diego is now a large city. Museums, the old missions, and Spanish-style buildings show the **heritage**, or history, of this city. But the new face of the city is growing, too.

Thousands of residents of San Diego work for the United States Navy. The city is located on an excellent harbor, which even the largest ships can enter and leave safely. Shipbuilding and ship repair are also important in San Diego's economy.

Companies that build missiles and aircraft depend on good weather year-round to test their products outdoors. San Diego's favorable weather has attracted many such companies.

Los Angeles Los Angeles has the second largest population of any city in the United States. The city began to grow quickly after the invention of the automobile. Los Angeles was the first city in the country to build **freeways**. A freeway is a superhighway on which there are no tolls, or charges for use.

Los Angeles was founded by Spanish explorers and missionaries when California and Mexico were part of Spain's empire. Today Los Angeles has more immigrants from Mexico than any other city in the United States. Many Mexican Americans speak both Spanish and English.

Freeways have helped the city of Los Angeles to grow rapidly.
▶ What are two problems that you think Los Angeles might have because of all these automobiles?

San Francisco, which was founded by Spanish settlers in 1776, is built on and around 40 hills.

▶ How can you tell from the photograph that the city is hilly?

San Francisco When the gold rush began in 1849, San Francisco became a busy place overnight. Thousands of people came to build homes and businesses in this hilly location.

Many immigrants have come to live in San Francisco. Almost half of them are from countries in Asia, especially China.

For many generations, Chinese immigrants have settled in a neighborhood of San Francisco called Chinatown. In Chinatown you can buy Chinese books and magazines, admire the Chinese-style street lights, and enjoy Chinese foods in restaurants.

San Francisco has a busy harbor. Ships enter San Francisco Bay loaded with oil, iron ore, fish, and lumber. San Francisco's factories turn these raw materials into products such as paper, chemicals, and machinery. Ships leaving San Francisco Bay carry canned foods and fish, gasoline, textiles, and electronic equipment to sell in many places throughout the world.

LESSON 4 REVIEW

THINK AND WRITE

A. Why do the Inuit make their living differently in summer than they do in winter?

B. What are some things that make Hawaii's culture different from that of the rest of the United States?

C. What do San Diego, Los Angeles, and San Francisco have in common?

SKILLS CHECK

MAP SKILL

Use the map on page 236 to plan a trip in the Pacific West region. Choose five cities that you would visit. Estimate the latitude and longitude of each city. Then look in the Gazetteer, on pages 400–409, to find the exact latitude and longitude of the cities.

PACIFIC WEST REGION

ALASKA

LARGEST CITIES	POPULATION	LAND AREA	POPULATION DENSITY
Anchorage	576,000	570,833 sq mi	1 per sq mi
Fairbanks		1,478,458 sq km	.4 per sq km
Juneau	RANK: 48	RANK: 1	RANK: 50

KEY FACTS

Alaska has the longest coastline of any state in the U.S.

Almost one-third of Alaska is north of the Arctic Circle.

PRINCIPAL PRODUCTS AGRICULTURE & MANUFACTURING

Potatoes   Seafood processing

POPULATION: URBAN VS. RURAL

64% Urban
36% Rural

Yellowhammer   Forget-me-not   Sitka spruce

Juneau

CALIFORNIA

LARGEST CITIES	POPULATION	LAND AREA	POPULATION DENSITY
Los Angeles	29,126,000	156,299 sq mi	177 per sq mi
San Diego		404,814 sq km	70 per sq km
San Jose	RANK: 1	RANK: 3	RANK: 12

KEY FACTS

The lowest point below sea level in the U.S. is in Death Valley.

The redwood trees of California are the tallest living things in the world.

PRINCIPAL PRODUCTS AGRICULTURE & MANUFACTURING

Cattle   Aircraft

POPULATION: URBAN VS. RURAL

92% Urban
8% Rural

California valley quail   Golden poppy   California redwood

Sacramento

HAWAII

LARGEST CITIES	POPULATION	LAND AREA	POPULATION DENSITY
Honolulu	1,141,000	6,425 sq mi	168 per sq mi
Pearl City		16,641 sq km	66 per sq km
Kallua	RANK: 40	RANK: 47	RANK: 13

KEY FACTS

Hawaii is the only state that is not on the continent of North America.

Hawaii is the only state that is made up entirely of islands.

PRINCIPAL PRODUCTS AGRICULTURE & MANUFACTURING

Sugar cane   Food processing

POPULATION: URBAN VS. RURAL

87% Urban
13% Rural

Nene
(Hawaiian goose)   Hibiscus   Kukui

Honolulu

261

OREGON

KEY FACTS

The Willamette Valley is Oregon's center for trade and industry.

Crater Lake in Oregon is the deepest natural lake in the U.S.

LARGEST CITIES	POPULATION	LAND AREA	POPULATION DENSITY
Portland	2,766,000	96,184 sq mi	28 per sq mi
Eugene		249,117 sq km	11 per sq km
Salem	RANK: 29		
		RANK: 11	RANK: 8

PRINCIPAL PRODUCTS
AGRICULTURE & MANUFACTURING

Wheat

Lumber

POPULATION: URBAN VS. RURAL

68% Urban
32% Rural

★ Salem

STATE OF OREGON

Western meadowlark

Oregon grape

Douglas fir

WASHINGTON

KEY FACTS

Washington is the only state of the U.S. named for one of the nation's Presidents.

Washington has important shipping centers on the Pacific Ocean.

LARGEST CITIES	POPULATION	LAND AREA	POPULATION DENSITY
Seattle	4,657,000	66,511 sq mi	68 per sq mi
Spokane		172,264 sq km	27 per sq km
Tacoma	RANK: 19		
		RANK: 20	RANK: 28

PRINCIPAL PRODUCTS
AGRICULTURE & MANUFACTURING

Wheat

Transportation equipment

POPULATION: URBAN VS. RURAL

74% Urban
36% Rural

★ Olympia

Willow goldfinch

Rhododendron

Western hemlock

262

USING THE VOCABULARY

volcano	boom	lei
lava	town	luau
aqueduct	tundra	heritage
sugarcane	kayak	

On a separate sheet of paper, write the word or words from the list above that best complete each sentence.

1. A _____ is an opening in the earth from which steam, gases, stones, ashes, and melted rock burst from time to time.
2. In Hawaii, a garland of flowers is called a _____.
3. A plant from which we get sugar is _____.
4. The history of a city can also be called its _____.
5. A waterway that has been built to carry water from a reservoir to fields and orchards is called a _____.
6. A community that sprang up near an area where a gold mine was started was called a _____.
7. A _____ is a Hawaiian-style dinner at which singers and dancers perform for the guests.
8. A certain type of cold, treeless area is called _____.
9. A fiery, melted volcanic rock is called a _____.
10. A small, sturdy canoe used by Inuits is called a _____.

REMEMBERING WHAT YOU READ

On a separate sheet of paper, answer the questions in complete sentences.

1. Why can Hawaii be called the most unusual state in the nation?
2. What and where is the highest mountain in all of North America?
3. What and where is the lowest place in North America?
4. What are four kinds of climates found in the Pacific West?
5. What is the capital of Alaska?
6. What is the first step in harvesting sugarcane?
7. Why is the Trans-Alaska Pipeline built above the ground in places?
8. What Pacific West state leads the nation in manufacturing?
9. Why has the city of San Diego attracted many companies that build missiles and aircraft?
10. What Pacific West city was first in the nation to build freeways?

TYING ART TO SOCIAL STUDIES

In this chapter you were asked to choose a place in the Pacific West region that you would like to visit. Make a poster to help persuade other people that they, too, would enjoy visiting the place. Find ways to make the poster as attractive as possible.

On a separate sheet of paper, answer the following questions in complete sentences.

1. You read that a Hawaiian volcano erupted and destroyed homes. If you had lived in one of those homes, would you rebuild your home or move away? Explain your choice.

2. Would you rather live where there is, or is not, a change of seasons? Explain your choice.

3. Was the discovery of oil in Alaska good for our country? Why or why not?

4. Will Inuits continue building ice houses and using dog sleds much longer? Explain your answer.

5. Why did San Francisco become a busy place overnight in 1849?

SUMMARIZING THE CHAPTER

This graphic organizer shows the main ideas for Chapter 9. Copy the graphic organizer on a separate sheet of paper. Fill in as many facts as you can.

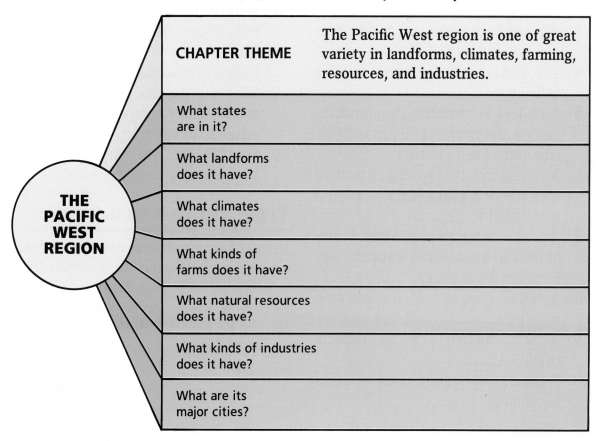

THE PACIFIC WEST REGION

CHAPTER THEME — The Pacific West region is one of great variety in landforms, climates, farming, resources, and industries.

What states are in it?

What landforms does it have?

What climates does it have?

What kinds of farms does it have?

What natural resources does it have?

What kinds of industries does it have?

What are its major cities?

COOPERATIVE LEARNING

In Unit 2 you learned about the regions of the United States. You learned about the natural features and natural resources of each region. You also learned about the people and some of the major cities in the region.

PROJECT

Your group is to make a board game about the region that your teacher assigns to you. To help you plan the board game, talk about different kinds of board games. Be sure that everyone in your group has a chance to share his or her ideas. Listen carefully as each person speaks.

Use the ideas you have discussed to design a new board game. Have each member of the group complete a part of the board game.

• One member of the group should design the board, using cardboard or strong construction paper.

• One member should design the cards for the game.

• Two members should write the cards. Each card is to have a question on one side and the answer on the other side.

• One member should write a list of rules for the game.

• Play the game as a group to make sure that it works. Correct anything that does not work well.

PRESENTATION AND REVIEW

• Trade the game with another group.

• After the members of that group have played the game, ask how they liked the game. Ask how they think the game might be improved.

• Meet with your group again to talk about how well you worked together as a group. Ask whether everyone had a chance to share his or her ideas. Did everyone take part in making the game?

REMEMBER TO:
• Give your ideas.
• Listen to others' ideas.
• Plan your work with the group.
• Present your project.
• Discuss how your group worked.

265

A. WHY DO I NEED THIS SKILL?

In Unit 2 you read about some of the major cities in the United States. Imagine that you could visit some of the cities that you have read about. One of the first things you might want to know is how far the cities are from your home.

A map scale is one way to find out how far one place is from another. A second way is to use a mileage chart. A mileage chart is usually found on a road map. It shows the distance between cities.

B. LEARNING THE SKILL

The mileage chart on page 267 shows the distances between some of the major cities in the United States. Notice that there are cities listed at the left side of the chart. Those cities are also listed at the bottom of the chart.

Suppose you want to find the distance between Charleston, South Carolina, and Washington, D.C. Place a finger on Charleston on the left side of the chart. Place a finger of your other hand on Washington, D.C., at the bottom of the chart. Now move both fingers, one across and the other up, until they meet. They should meet at the block that is numbered 532. That means that the distance between Charleston and Washington is 532 miles (856 km).

To find the two cities that are closest together, look for the smallest number on the mileage chart. Move a finger of one hand from that number to the name of the city at the left. Then move a finger of the other hand from the number to the name of the city at the bottom of the column. The two cities on the mileage chart that are closest together are New York City and Boston.

C. PRACTICING THE SKILL

Practice reading the mileage chart by answering the following questions.

1. What is the distance in miles between Chicago and San Francisco?
2. What is the distance in miles between Denver and Houston?
3. Which city is closest to New Orleans?
4. Which city is farther from Wichita, Chicago or Houston?
5. Which two cities on the mileage chart are farthest apart?

D. APPLYING THE SKILL

Most road maps have a mileage chart. Look in your school library or at home for a road map of your state. Or find a mileage chart in a road atlas. Read the mileage chart to find the distance between the capital city in your state and five other cities in your state.

MILEAGE CHART

	Boston, MA	Charleston, SC	Chicago, IL	Denver, CO	Houston, TX	Los Angeles, CA	New Orleans, LA	New York, NY	San Francisco, CA	Washington, DC	Wichita, KS
Boston, MA		936	994	1998	1830	3017	1507	208	3128	448	1634
Charleston, SC	936		906	1721	1047	2485	726	768	2821	532	1236
Chicago, IL	994	906		1021	1091	2048	919	809	2173	709	728
Denver, CO	1998	1721	1021		1034	1031	1277	1794	1255	1616	520
Houston, TX	1830	1047	1091	1034		1541	352	1610	1911	1365	618
Los Angeles, CA	3017	2485	2048	1031	1541		1858	2794	387	2646	1391
New Orleans, LA	1507	726	919	1277	352	1858		1335	2278	1099	848
New York, NY	208	768	809	1794	1610	2794	1335		2930	237	1424
San Francisco, CA	3128	2821	2173	1255	1911	387	2278	2930		2843	1698
Washington, DC	448	532	709	1616	1365	2646	1099	237	2843		1284
Wichita, KS	1634	1236	728	520	618	1391	848	1424	1698	1284	

Writing
SKILLBUILDER
a Report

A. WHY DO I NEED THIS SKILL?

Has your teacher ever asked you to find more information about something you have studied in class and then to write a report? Knowing how to write a report will help you to organize information. It will help you to make good use of the information you gather.

B. LEARNING THE SKILL

Before you begin to write a report, you should plan the report carefully. Here are six steps that you might follow when you write a report.

1. Select a topic The topic is what the report is about. Sometimes your teacher will give you the topic. Other times you will be asked to choose the topic that you would like to report on.

2. Gather information A good place to start looking for information for a report is the library. You could look in the school library or in a public library if there is one near your home.

Start with books such as encyclopedias, atlases, and almanacs. These books have information about many topics. Then look in the card catalog to see if there are any books on your topic in the library. Choose the most helpful books.

Next, take notes on the information you find. To do this, write down the important and interesting facts that you might want to include in your report.

3. Organize the information Before you begin to write, you need to organize the information you have gathered. One way to organize the information is to separate the ideas into groups. Write a heading for each group of ideas. Then decide on a way of presenting the information in a clear and interesting way.

Another way to organize information is to make a writing map like the one on page 269. The writing map is for a report on Oregon. Notice that the writing map is divided into sections. Each section has a heading to help you fill in important information about Oregon.

4. Write the first draft The first draft of a report is a rough copy from which the final copy is written. As you write the first draft, make sure that you keep together all the ideas that belong under one heading. Organize your ideas.

5. Revise and edit After you have written your report, you will need to revise your writing. To revise means "to read over to correct or improve." You edit your report when you check the spelling and punctuation and make sure that all your sentences are clear.

6. Write the final draft In this last step, write the version of your report that you will hand in. Your report should be in your neatest handwriting. If you use a computer, make sure that the report looks neat and has no typing errors.

C. PRACTICING THE SKILL

Write a report on a state in the United States. First, select a state. Then gather information about the state you have chosen. You might like to make a writing map to help you organize your report. Be sure to revise and edit the first draft of your report.

D. APPLYING THE SKILL

Use the six steps that you have just read about the next time you are asked to write a report. Remember that much of the work you do will come before you begin to write the report. If you gather the information carefully, the writing of the report will be much easier.

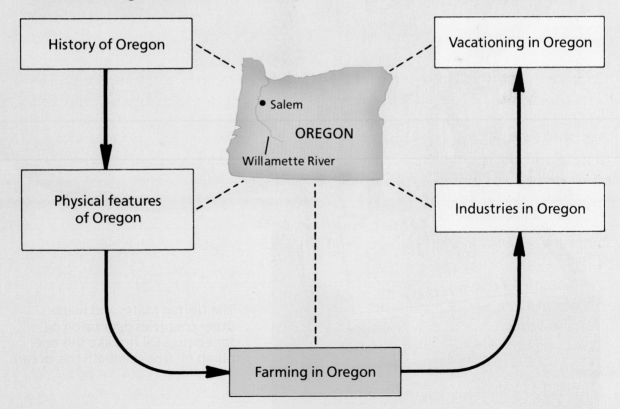

Land is a precious resource. Where farmland is scarce, farmers have learned to use their land wisely. ▶

The United States and many other countries depend on oil for energy. Oil rigs like this one pump oil from beneath the ocean.

UNIT 3 CONNECTIONS: THE UNITED STATES AND THE WORLD

To meet their needs and wants, people throughout the world use resources in many different ways.

▲

Many people throughout the world use computers. A computer was used to make this map of the world.

10

CONNECTIONS WITH DISTANT LANDS

*A*ll people depend on one another in many different ways. That is true of countries as well as people.

ALCALDIA

American Citizens in Faraway Lands

THINK ABOUT WHAT YOU KNOW

Which state of the United States is completely surrounded by the Pacific Ocean? Which continent is surrounded by the Pacific and Indian oceans? Do you know of any places that are as far away as these two places?

STUDY THE VOCABULARY

embassy   **ambassador**

FOCUS YOUR READING

What ties do some United States citizens have with faraway places?

A. United States Citizens in Other Countries

Many United States citizens live outside our country. Some live in other countries and work for our government. Some work at military bases that are operated by our country in other parts of the world. Then there are people who move to other parts of the world to work for American or foreign companies that have offices outside the United States.

Some United States citizens work in foreign countries in the **embassies** of the United States. An embassy is a building in a foreign country where an official of another country works. The official is called an **ambassador**.

In addition to the ambassador, other United States citizens work in each of our embassies. Some people are assistants to the ambassador, and others are experts in the laws and language of the country.

The embassy workers, the people in the military service, and the people working for American companies will return to the United States someday. They will have learned many things about the people and countries where they lived and worked.

American volunteers and village officials work together to help improve the life of the people in a village in Kenya.
▶ Why, do you think, do people volunteer to work in other countries?

B. Attending School in a Faraway Land

For the past three years, Peter has lived in Frankfurt, West Germany. Peter's father is a sergeant in the United States Army. Peter lives with his parents and two sisters on an army base in Frankfurt. Peter and his sisters attend Department of Defense Dependents Schools in Frankfurt.

The Department of Defense Dependents School (DoDDS) system was established to educate the children of members of the armed forces stationed overseas. There are DoD schools, as they are often called, in 19 foreign countries. Japan, Italy, Norway, Iceland, and South Korea are just some of the countries where there are DoD schools. Over 150,000 American children attend these schools.

In their schools Peter and his sisters study the same subjects that children in the United States study. They also play soccer and volleyball, tug of war, and many games played by children in the United States.

This school year Peter's class acted out a play to celebrate Columbus Day. They wrote a musical to celebrate Thanksgiving Day. The children from a local German school were invited to

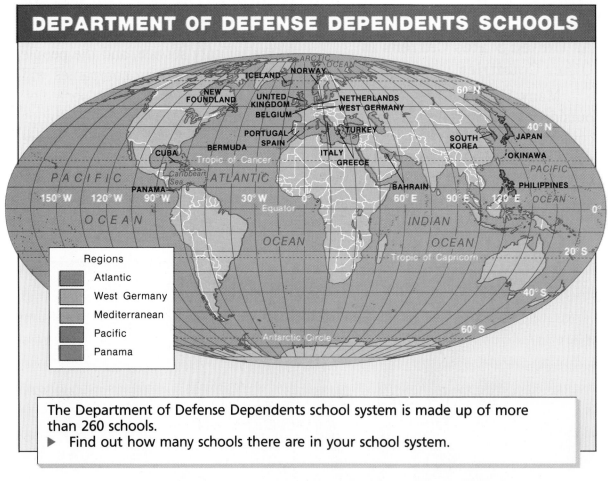

DEPARTMENT OF DEFENSE DEPENDENTS SCHOOLS

Regions
- Atlantic
- West Germany
- Mediterranean
- Pacific
- Panama

The Department of Defense Dependents school system is made up of more than 260 schools.
▶ Find out how many schools there are in your school system.

Two different views of Frankfurt, West Germany, are shown above.
► Which photograph shows the newer part of the city?

the musical. They brought cookies and some pies and homemade bread to share with their American friends.

Later in the year Peter's class was given a tour of the German children's beautiful new school building. After the tour, there were refreshments for everyone. Peter and his classmates hope to go skiing with their new German friends next winter.

Peter likes his school very much because he meets children from many different parts of the United States and from foreign countries. He learns a lot about the history and geography of the United States. He also learns about West Germany, his host country. Although he enjoys learning, sharing, and having fun in the DoD school, Peter says he will be happy to return to the United States. After all, the United States is his home country.

LESSON *1* REVIEW

THINK AND WRITE

A. What are some of the reasons that American citizens live and work in faraway countries?

B. How are DoD Schools and your school alike?

SKILLS CHECK

THINKING SKILL

Why, do you think, is it important for children in DoD schools to learn about the United States?

Some Islands of the Caribbean Sea

THINK ABOUT WHAT YOU KNOW

Imagine that you have just won a trip to an island in the Caribbean Sea. What do you already know about the Caribbean Sea?

STUDY THE VOCABULARY

plantain	emigrate
trade wind	desalination
bilingual	

FOCUS YOUR READING

How are Puerto Rico and the Virgin Islands alike?

A. A Letter from Maria

"*Hola, me llamo Maria.* (OH lah-may YAH moh muh REE uh). In English that means, 'Hi, my name is Maria.' I would like to tell you about myself and about Puerto Rico.

"I live on a beautiful island in the Caribbean Sea. I am in the fourth grade and I like school. At home we speak Spanish, but in school we speak both Spanish and English. I work very hard on my English, because someday I want to visit my relatives who live in the United States.

"I do homework as soon as I come home from school. But after that is finished, I go swimming with my friends, or I play with them on the beach near my home.

"My mother's name is Dolores, and she is a very good cook. She often uses an old family recipe to make a dish called *mofongo. Mofongo* is made from green **plantains** that are cooked and then mashed. Do you have plantains at your grocery store? They look like bananas, but they must be cooked. They are delicious!

"My father's name is Luis (loo-EES), and he works for a large pharmaceutical (fahr muh SOOT ih kul) company. His company makes many helpful drugs and medicines. These drugs are used in hospitals and clinics in the United States. His company also makes cold remedies, soaps, shampoos, and skin lotions.

> Puerto Rico is famous for its sandy beaches.
> ▶ What is special about the trees near the beach?

This fort stands in San Juan, the capital of Puerto Rico.
▶ Why, do you think, is an American flag flown at the fort?

"My two brothers, Carlos and Ricardo, go to school also. Their favorite sport is football, which I think you call soccer. Carlos and Ricardo practice almost every afternoon. My whole family likes football.

"We Puerto Ricans are citizens of the United States just as you are, but Puerto Rico is not a state of the United States. It is a commonwealth or, as we say, a Free Associated State. This means that Puerto Rico agrees to be a part of the United States.

"In 1898 the United States fought a war with Spain, a country in Europe. The United States won the war, and Puerto Rico, which had been a colony of Spain, became a colony of the United States five months later.

"Puerto Ricans elect a governor who runs the government of the island just as the governor of a state does. But Puerto Ricans do not vote for the President of the United States, and there are no senators or representatives from Puerto Rico in the United States Congress. To have representation, Puerto Rico would have to be a state.

"I wish you could visit me in Puerto Rico some day. There are many pretty beaches here, and we would have a lot of fun swimming in the ocean. The water is always warm. And we could go hiking in the mountains with my family."

B. The Land and Climate of Puerto Rico

A Caribbean Island The island of Puerto Rico is located about 2,000 miles (3,218 km) southeast of Florida. It is one of the largest islands in the Caribbean Sea. The island is smaller than any state in the United States, except Rhode Island and Delaware.

The island has many different kinds of landscapes. If you spent a day driving around the island, you could see thick forests, sandy beaches, and rugged mountain cliffs.

A line of mountains runs through the center of Puerto Rico. These mountains almost fill up the island, so there is very little flat land.

A Warm, Rainy Climate The most important winds that reach Puerto Rico are called the **trade winds**. In tropical areas, trade winds blow across the ocean toward the Equator. The trade winds helped Columbus sail from Europe to America on his famous voyage in 1492. The trade winds moved trading ships until steamships were invented.

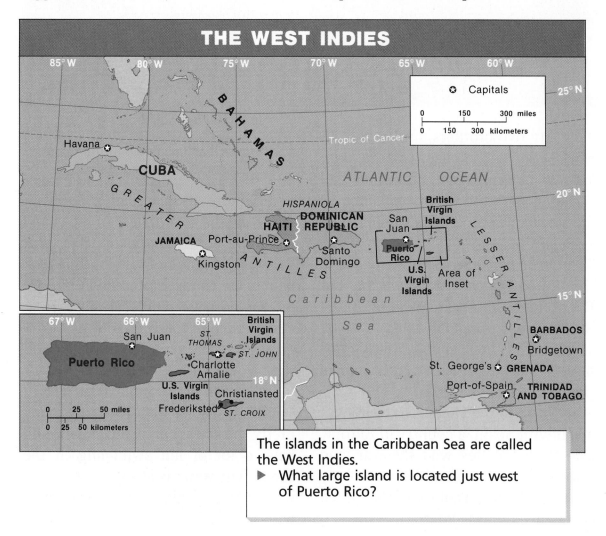

THE WEST INDIES

The islands in the Caribbean Sea are called the West Indies.
▶ What large island is located just west of Puerto Rico?

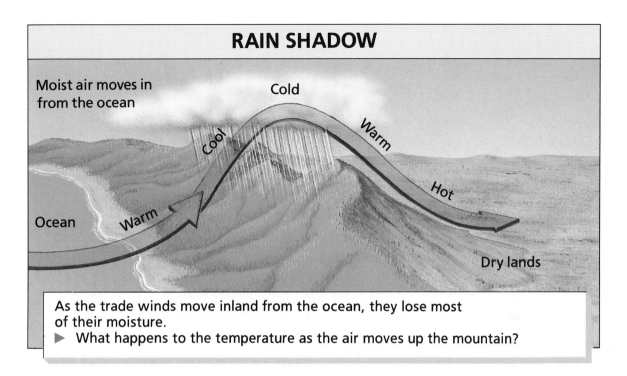

RAIN SHADOW

Moist air moves in from the ocean

Cold

Cool

Warm

Hot

Warm

Ocean

Warm

Dry lands

As the trade winds move inland from the ocean, they lose most of their moisture.
► What happens to the temperature as the air moves up the mountain?

As the trade winds blow across the ocean, they pick up lots of moisture. When the trade winds reach the land, they are pushed up over the mountains. The air cools as it goes over the mountains, and that causes rain. By the time the air has crossed the mountains, it has lost most of its moisture, so the other side of the mountains is dry. This is known as the rain shadow effect.

The trade winds that blow across Puerto Rico come from the northeast. That is why the northern coast of Puerto Rico has heavy rainfalls and the southern coast has a drier climate.

It is warm in Puerto Rico year-round. In the summer the average temperature is about 85°F (29°C), and in the winter the average temperature is about 73°F (23°C). These temperatures make it possible to grow crops all year long.

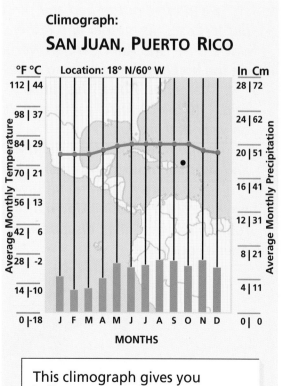

Climograph:

SAN JUAN, PUERTO RICO

Location: 18° N/60° W

This climograph gives you information about the climate in San Juan, Puerto Rico.
► Which month has the least precipitation?

Yagua Days

By: Cruz Martel
Setting: Ponce, Puerto Rico

When Adan Riera and his parents went to visit relatives in Puerto Rico, he learned what his parents meant when they spoke about yagua (JAH qwah) days.

In the morning Adan, waking up cozy under his mosquito net, heard rain banging on the metal roof and coquies beeping like tiny car horns.

He jumped out of bed and got a big surprise. His mother and father, Uncle Ulise, and Aunt Carmen were on the porch wearing bathing suits.

"Vamonos, Adan," his father said. "It's a wonderful yagua day. Put on your bathing suit!"

In the forest he heard shouts and swishing noises in the rain.

Racing into a clearing, he saw boys and girls shooting down a runway of grass, then disappearing over a rock ledge.

Uncle Ulise picked up a canoelike object from the grass. "This is a yagua, Adan. It fell from this palm tree."

"And this is what we do with it," said his father. He ran, then belly-flopped on the yagua. He skimmed down the grass, sailed up into the air, and vanished over the ledge. His mother found another yagua and did the same.

"Papi! Mami!"

Uncle Ulise laughed. "Don't worry, Adan. They won't hurt themselves. The river is down there. It pools beneath the ledge. The rain turns the grass butter-slick so you can zip into the water. That's what makes it a yagua day! Come and join us!"

Written by Cruz Martel. Picture by Jerry Pinkney.

C. Puerto Rico's People and Industries

People Nearly everyone in Puerto Rico speaks Spanish, because people from Spain settled this island nearly 500 years ago. Many people on the island are **bilingual**, or able to speak two languages.

Over half the people in Puerto Rico live along the coast, where most of Puerto Rico's cities are. San Juan (san-WAHN), the most populated city, has over 1 million inhabitants.

Over the years, many people from Puerto Rico have **emigrated**, or moved from their country, to the United States. Most Puerto Ricans in the United States live in large cities, where there are opportunities for work.

Farming Until about 1950, most people in Puerto Rico earned their living by farming. Many farmers worked hard to grow crops on the mountain slopes. Others worked on large farms and plantations along the coasts.

Industries Some of the oldest industries in Puerto Rico are tied to agricultural products, especially fruits. The canning of pineapples is a large industry on the island and so is the preparation of molasses from sugarcane. Coconuts, oranges, and avocados are also a part of the food industry.

Besides the pharmaceutical industry, in which Maria's father works, the petrochemical industry is important in Puerto Rico. This industry imports petroleum and separates useful

At the edge of this field, there is a truck with what looks like a long arm that extends into the field.
▶ What fruit are the workers gathering?

chemicals from it. The chemicals are then used to manufacture plastic goods, metal products, and fertilizers.

Tourism The warm winter temperatures are inviting to tourists looking for a vacation spot in the winter months. Over 2 million tourists visit Puerto Rico each year. The largest number come from the United States. Many visitors arrive in Puerto Rico on cruise ships.

Scuba diving, deep-sea fishing, and swimming are popular with people who like water sports. Sightseeing in Puerto Rico's beautiful old cities, visiting museums and parks, and shopping are other popular activities.

281

D. The U.S. Virgin Islands

Other Caribbean Islands The Virgin Islands are a group of islands about 60 miles (97 km) east of Puerto Rico. Some of the Virgin Islands belong to Great Britain and some belong to the United States. There are dozens of islands in the U.S. Virgin Islands, but three of them are much larger than the others. They are St. Croix (saynt kroi), St. Thomas, and St. John.

The total area of the U.S. Virgin Islands is only 133 square miles (344 sq km). Even though the islands are small, they are well-known to Americans who like to vacation there.

Charlotte Amalie (SHAHR lut uh-MAHL yuh), the capital city of the U.S. Virgin Islands, is on the island of St. Thomas. Over 100,000 people live in this city. It has an excellent harbor and is important for importing and exporting goods. Charlotte Amalie is also a busy tourist center.

Like Jewels in the Sea One reason the U.S. Virgin Islands are so beautiful is that most of them were originally volcanos. Their steep slopes rise dramatically from the sea. The three United States islands have peaks between 1,000 and 1,500 feet (305 and 457 m) high. Strips of sandy beaches separate these peaks from the sea.

Tourists find this scenery irresistible. Over 1 million people visit the islands each year, and they spend millions of dollars. The tourist industry provides most of the jobs in the U.S. Virgin Islands.

Other Industries Like people in Puerto Rico, the people of the U.S. Virgin Islands are building new industries. Importing crude petroleum, refining it, and exporting the refined oil has become a big business in the U.S. Virgin Islands.

Many petrochemical plants are in this region. Other new factories produce watches and textiles. Many of the industries are starting up on St. Croix.

The harbor at Charlotte Amalie is surrounded by tree-covered hills.
▶ What might you do as a tourist in Charlotte Amalie?

The towers of this petroleum-refining plant stand tall on the island of St. Croix.

▶ How can you tell that many people are needed to work here?

A Water Shortage The one big problem facing the U.S. Virgin Islands seems strange when you first think of it. The islands, which are surrounded by the Caribbean Sea, have a shortage of water. There are no rivers or lakes on these islands to provide fresh water for drinking, cooking, cleaning and other uses. The few small streams that do exist are simply not large enough to supply all the water that is needed for the islands. As a result, fresh water has to be imported from other places.

The fact that the U.S. Virgin Islands are in the Caribbean Sea does not lessen the problem. Sea water, or ocean water, is salt water. The amount of salt it contains makes it harmful for humans to drink. The salt also makes the water difficult to use for washing and other purposes.

Collecting Fresh Rainwater Rainwater must be collected in cisterns (SIHS turnz), or underground tanks. Some water is also gathered from water wells on the islands of St. Croix and St. John.

A third way that fresh water is collected is through the **desalination** of sea water. *Desalination* means "the removal of salt from sea water to make it fresh."

In desalination, sea water is warmed, either by the sun or some other heat source. The sea water evaporates, or changes from a liquid to steam, leaving the salt from the sea water behind. When the steam cools, it changes back into a liquid, but now it is fresh water. This fresh water is collected for future use. Look at the diagram on page 284. It shows one of the ways to desalinate sea water.

283

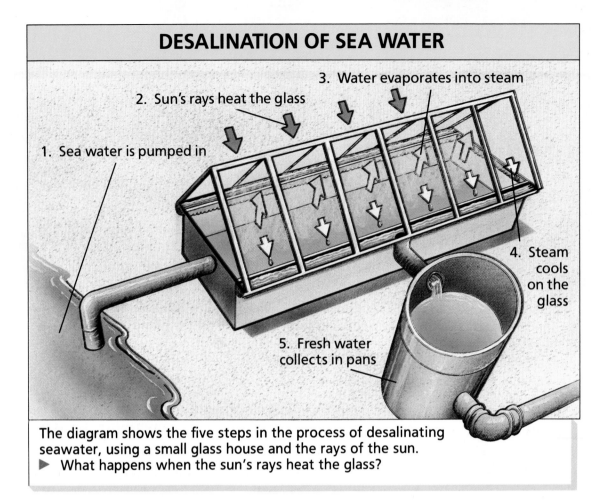

DESALINATION OF SEA WATER

2. Sun's rays heat the glass

3. Water evaporates into steam

1. Sea water is pumped in

4. Steam cools on the glass

5. Fresh water collects in pans

The diagram shows the five steps in the process of desalinating seawater, using a small glass house and the rays of the sun.
▶ What happens when the sun's rays heat the glass?

A Recent Problem With such a shortage of water, it is hard to imagine that the Virgin Islands could have too much water. But in September 1989, a fierce tropical storm called Hurricane Hugo struck the Virgin Islands and Puerto Rico. It brought winds of 150 miles (241 km) per hour and drenching rains to the islands. The winds and rain did millions of dollars worth of damage to the Virgin Islands and even more damage to Puerto Rico.

LESSON **2** REVIEW

THINK AND WRITE

A. How is Puerto Rico like your state, and how is it different?

B. How do mountains and trade winds keep Puerto Rico's southern coast drier than the northern coast?

C. How has the way that most people in Puerto Rico earn their living changed?

D. How do the Virgin Islands obtain their fresh water?

SKILLS CHECK

WRITING SKILL

Write a letter to Maria, telling her about your community and the kinds of things you do in your everyday life.

Some Islands in the Pacific Ocean

THINK ABOUT WHAT YOU KNOW

Most of the Pacific Islands are near the Equator. What kind of climate do you think they have?

STUDY THE VOCABULARY

typhoon	coral
volcanic island	atoll

FOCUS YOUR READING

What are the two main kinds of islands in the Pacific Ocean?

A. Living on a Pacific Island

The wind roared in David's ears and bent the palm tree outside his hut almost in half. Rain fell in sheets, pounding everything in sight. David thought about the new school he and his neighbors had just finished building. He hoped that the school would still be standing when the storm passed.

The storm passing by David's village was a **typhoon**. A typhoon is a violent wind storm, like a hurricane, that usually occurs in the Pacific Ocean. It brings heavy rains and strong winds that quickly uproot trees, ruin roads, and flood homes and fields. David's village was lucky this time. The typhoon did not hit the island directly.

Many Pacific Islands The island that David lives on is in the Pacific Ocean. As you know, the Hawaiian Islands form a state of the United States in the Pacific Ocean. There are thousands of other islands in the Pacific Ocean also, and a number of them have close connections with the United States. Each island or group of islands has its own government.

Many of the islands depend on the United States for military protection. They also depend on economic aid from the United States. In return, they may allow the United States to operate military bases in their territories.

The People of the Pacific The cultures and languages of most people of the small islands in the Pacific Ocean are alike in many ways. Even thousands of years ago, people traveled back and forth between the islands in strong canoes and other vessels. They shared ideas and beliefs. Today we find similar words, music, and legends in different Pacific islands.

Agana is the capital city of the island of Guam.
► Would you like to live in a city like this?

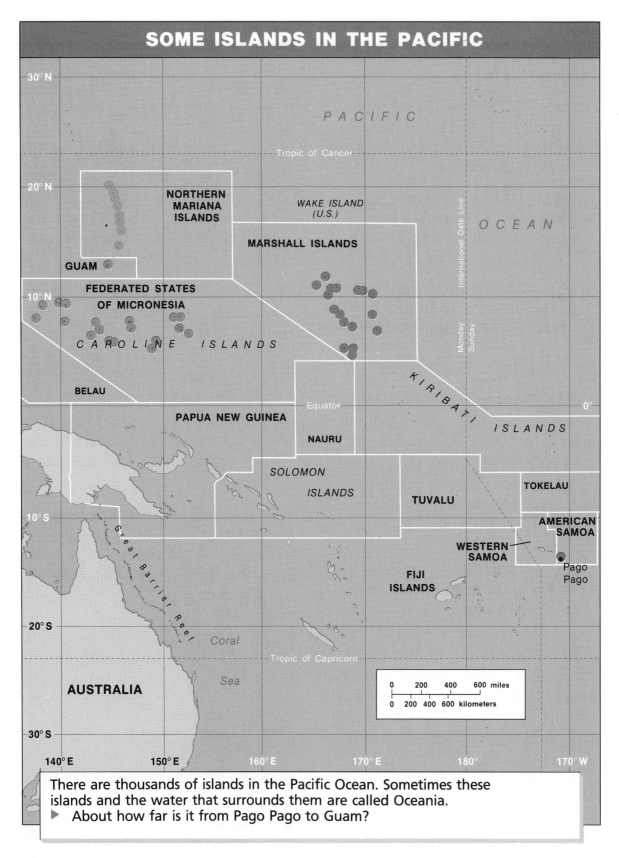

SOME ISLANDS IN THE PACIFIC

30° N

PACIFIC

Tropic of Cancer

20° N

NORTHERN
MARIANA
ISLANDS

WAKE ISLAND
(U.S.)

OCEAN

MARSHALL ISLANDS

GUAM

FEDERATED STATES

10° N

OF MICRONESIA

International Date Line

CAROLINE ISLANDS

Monday
Sunday

BELAU

KIRIBATI

Equator

0°

PAPUA NEW GUINEA

ISLANDS

NAURU

SOLOMON

ISLANDS

TOKELAU

TUVALU

10° S

AMERICAN
SAMOA

Great Barrier Reef

WESTERN
SAMOA

Pago
Pago

FIJI
ISLANDS

20° S

Coral

Tropic of Capricorn

Sea

0   200   400   600 miles

AUSTRALIA

0   200 400 600 kilometers

30° S

140° E   150° E   160° E   170° E   180°   170° W

There are thousands of islands in the Pacific Ocean. Sometimes these
islands and the water that surrounds them are called Oceania.
▶ About how far is it from Pago Pago to Guam?

B. Two Kinds of Islands

Volcanic Islands Two types of islands are found in the Pacific Ocean. One type is the **volcanic island**. A volcanic island is formed over thousands of years. Lava oozes out of a crack in the ocean floor. The lava hardens in the sea water, and in time more layers are deposited on top of it.

Gradually a peak is built up until it reaches the surface of the water. Volcanic peaks can reach several thousand feet or more above sea level.

Coral Islands Some islands in the Pacific Ocean are really beds of **coral**. Coral is a chalky material that is as hard as rock. It is formed, over a long period of time, from the skeletons of thousands of tiny sea animals called coral polyps (PAHL ihps).

The skeletons accumulate on the ocean floor and gradually build up to a height just above the water. Coral islands are usually flat and low.

An Atoll Sometimes the center of the coral island sinks below the surface of the ocean water. Only the outer edges of the coral island remain above water. If you looked down on such an island from an airplane, it would look like a giant ring of coral with a shallow pool in the center.

Such a coral ring is called an **atoll** (A tohl). The largest atoll in the Pacific Ocean is 80 miles (129 km) long and 20 miles (32 km) wide. Can you imagine how many trillions of skeletons of tiny coral polyps make up this large atoll?

A CORAL ATOLL

Lagoon

Channel

The shallow pool in the center of an atoll is called a lagoon.
▶ What is the opening in the coral atoll called?

C. The Island of Guam

Landforms Guam (gwahm) is an island in the western Pacific Ocean about 3,700 miles (5,953 km) west of Honolulu, Hawaii. The island has a flat, low coral plateau in the north on which there are thick forests. The southern part of the island has low volcanic hills covered with tough grasses and scrubby plants. Guam receives a tremendous amount of rain, about 95 inches (241 cm) per year.

History In 1898 our country received Guam from Spain after winning a war against that country. About one third of the island of Guam is owned by the United States Armed Forces. An Air Force base, a submarine base, and a shipyard for repairing ships are located on the island. Guam's residents are citizens of the United States.

Industry and Tourism Farmers on Guam grow corn, sugarcane, bananas, and sweet potatoes. But there is not enough land to produce food for everyone on the island. So other foods have to be imported, along with oil, farm machinery, and transportation equipment.

Many people on Guam work in factories where watches, clothing, beverages, and small machines are produced. Others work on the military bases, and many work in the tourist industry. Tourism is Guam's second most important industry, after the employment provided by the military bases.

D. Micronesia and American Samoa

Three Island Groups Over 2,000 small islands in the Pacific Ocean make up three more groups with ties to the United States. The chains of islands are the Northern Mariana Islands, the Federated States of Micronesia (mye-kruh NEE zhuh), and the Marshall islands. These groups of islands are separate countries, with their own governments, but they are protected by the United States.

American Samoa Far to the southeast of Guam, and south of the Equator, is a group of seven small islands called American Samoa (suh MOH uh). See if you can locate these islands on the map on page 286.

Why would the United States be interested in such distant islands? The main reason is Pago Pago (PAHNG oh-PAHNG oh), the capital city of American Samoa. Pago Pago is located on a deep and protected harbor.

In 1900, the United States Navy began storing coal near Pago Pago. The coal was used to refuel Navy ships that traveled through the Pacific Ocean.

One of the first sights that many tourists in Pago Pago see is the beautiful harbor.
▶ How can you tell that many tourists arrive by ship?

People Use Transportation

Name at least four kinds of transportation that people in your community use.

locomotive   **supertanker**
freight   **navigable**

How have ways of moving people and goods changed through the years?

A. Moving People and Goods

Early Forms of Travel How did you get to school today? If you live close enough to school, you may have walked. If you live too far away to walk, you may have come by car or you may have taken a bus.

For thousands of years, people could travel only by walking. Eventually, people learned to catch horses and tame them for riding. Riding a horse made travel easier and much faster.

Moving Goods Several thousand years ago, people learned to make carts with wheels that could be pulled or drawn by large animals, such as horses and oxen. Traveling by wheeled cart was not as fast as riding a horse. The use of carts, however, made it possible for people to transport heavy loads over long distances.

Until the early 1800s, people traveled on foot, on horseback, and by wheeled cart. These forms of land transportation were so slow that people preferred to travel by boat whenever possible. In 1825, however, that began to change. In that year, trains powered by steam engines were first used to carry passengers.

B. A Race Between a Horse and a Train

The First Trains Trains that were pulled by steam engines were the first kind of land transportation to use mechanical power instead of animals. **Locomotives** are the engines that pull trains. Steam locomotives were an impressive sight as they pulled long lines of railroad cars over the tracks. The engines roared and hissed and sent clouds of smoke into the air.

The first steam locomotive made in the United States was built in 1830 by Peter Cooper of New York. His locomotive called the *Tom Thumb* pulled the first trains on the Baltimore and Ohio Railroad, which at that time was only 13 miles (21 km) long.

A Train Versus a Stagecoach The *Tom Thumb* took business away from the stagecoach company that had carried passengers over this route for many years. The owners of the company decided to have a race to show that stagecoaches could move along the rails faster than trains. There is a description of the race on the next page.

The start being even, away went horse and engine, the snort of the one and the puff of the other keeping time and tune. . . . The horse was perhaps a quarter of a mile ahead when the safety-valve of the engine lifted and the thin blue vapor issuing from it showed an excess of steam. The blower whistled, the pace increased, the passengers shouted, . . . the race was neck and neck, nose to nose —then the engine passed the horse, and a great hurrah hailed the victory.

But just when the [horse's] master was about giving up, the band which drove the pully . . . slipped from the drum, . . . and the engine . . . began to wheeze and pant. . . . the horse gained on the machine, and passed it; [soon] . . . the horse was too far ahead to be overtaken and came in the winner of the race.

Even though the *Tom Thumb* lost the race, people soon saw that trains were usually faster than horse-drawn vehicles. In the 1830s and 1840s, larger and better steam locomotives were built. As a result, railroad transportation grew rapidly.

C. Travel on Land

Growth of Rail Lines At first, railroads in the United States served mainly the northeastern part of the country, where most people lived. Most farms and factories were there, too. People used railroads to transport crops and manufactured goods.

Little by little, the rail lines extended out into areas where fewer people lived. In 1835 the first railroad line reached Chicago, Illinois. In those days, Chicago was not a great city but a frontier town.

In 1869 the transcontinental railroad linked the eastern and western parts of the United States. People could now cross the United States in about one week. Before the transcontinental railroad was built, it took months to cross the country by stagecoach or on horseback.

The Granger Collection

In 1830 the Tom Thumb locomotive owned by the Baltimore and Ohio Railroad raced against a horse-drawn railroad car.
▶ Which one appears to be winning—the locomotive or the horse?

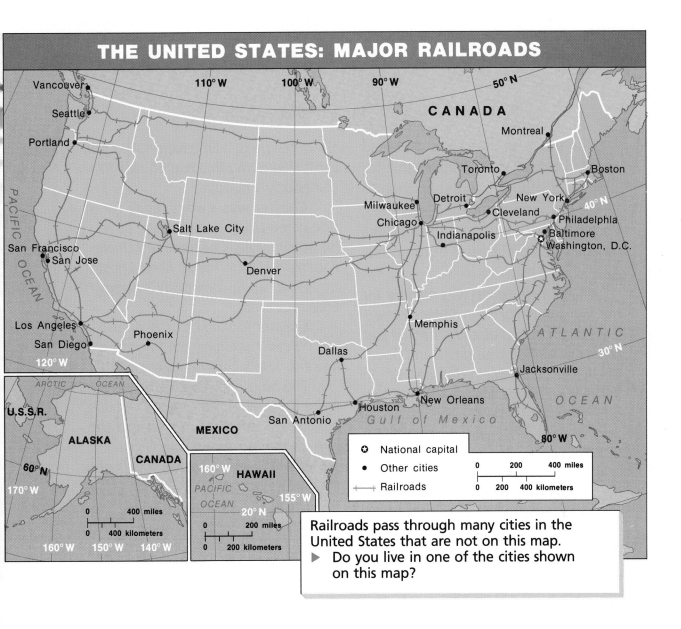

THE UNITED STATES: MAJOR RAILROADS

Legend:
- ✪ National capital
- • Other cities
- ┼┼┼ Railroads

0   200   400 miles
0   200   400 kilometers

Railroads pass through many cities in the United States that are not on this map.
▶ Do you live in one of the cities shown on this map?

Automobiles The first cars built in the United States were powered by electricity. Later, gasoline-powered cars were built, but they were expensive. In 1903, Henry Ford of Detroit, Michigan, decided to build a car that ordinary people could afford.

The first cars made in Ford's factory were the Model T, which people called the Tin Lizzie. Riding in one of those cars could be an adventure. You can read what it was like on page 296.

In the 1950s many people began to travel by airplane. To stay in business, the railroads began to concentrate on hauling **freight**, or goods. Trains are useful for hauling heavy loads over long distances. One locomotive can carry hundreds of times as much freight as a truck.

295

Uncle Fonzo's Ford

By: Miska Miles

Setting: The United States in the early 1900s

In this selection you can read about the day Uncle Fonzo came for Effie after school, driving his brand-new Ford automobile. As you read, try to decide whether you would like to ride in Uncle Fonzo's automobile.

Effie's Uncle Fonzo was coming for her in his new Ford. And Effie wished he wouldn't. And already, he had run out of gasoline three times and once he almost hit a cow in the road. Somehow, things always seemed to go wrong for Uncle Fonzo. . . .

"Is your uncle coming for you?" Chester asked.

"Yes he is," Effie said. "And you can't ride with him. You go ride in somebody's buggy."

Chester was always ready for a ride when Uncle Fonzo drove up in his automobile. Chester liked Uncle Fonzo and Uncle Fonzo liked Chester.

"You go in somebody's buggy," Effie repeated.

Chester looked out the door.

"I can't see him, but I hear him," he said. "He's coming up the hill."

The boys and girls whose parents were there with buggies ran outside, hunching their shoulders against the rain — running — slipping —

"Look," said Chester. "He's got the top down."

Uncle Fonzo drove right up the middle of the street, cut across the school yard and slid over to the schoolhouse steps.

"Hurry up, Effie," he said. "I don't dare stall the motor and we'd better get going before the horses get too scared. Get in, Effie. You, too, Chester."

Effie and Chester climbed in while Uncle Fonzo explained about the top. "I was putting the side curtains up to keep out the rain, and the top fell down. I couldn't get it up again. And I didn't want to keep you waiting." The rain was coming down hard.

Written by Miska Miles. Illustrated by Wendy Watson.

D. Travel by Water

Busy Ocean Routes Imagine that you have 100 automobiles that you need to transport between Japan and the United States. How could you transport them across the Pacific Ocean? Automobiles and most other products that are transported from one continent to another are moved by ship.

For thousands of years, ships have been used to transport cargo and passengers. Some of the first ships used long, heavy oars and hundreds of rowers to move across the sea, but most ships used sails.

Today, many ships crisscross the oceans, carrying goods from one country to another. The busiest ocean-shipping route in the world goes from the Persian Gulf around the southern tip of Africa to Europe. This is the route that **supertankers** take to transport oil from Saudi Arabia and its neighbors, where it is produced, to countries in Europe, such as France, West Germany, and the Netherlands. A supertanker is a huge ship, longer than three football fields and over 150 yards (46 m) wide. Supertankers carry oil to ports all over the world.

Oil is not the only product carried by ships. Bulky and heavy goods, such as grain, minerals, and timber, are also transported by ship. If your family has a foreign-made product, it was probably brought to the United States by ship.

Oil tankers unload their cargo in Rotterdam, in the Netherlands.
▶ What are the circular containers on the right used for?

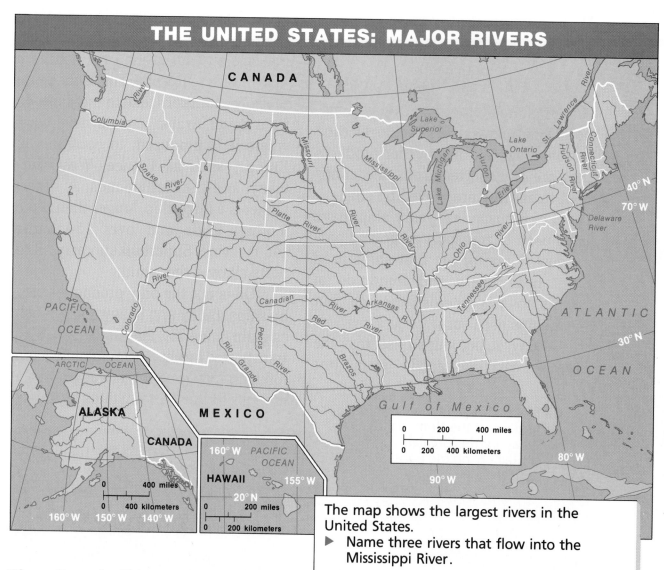

THE UNITED STATES: MAJOR RIVERS

CANADA

Columbia River

Snake River

Platte River

Missouri River

Lake Superior

Lake Michigan

L. Huron

Lake Ontario

St. Lawrence River

Hudson River

Connecticut River

Mississippi River

L. Erie

Delaware River

40° N

70° W

PACIFIC OCEAN

Colorado River

River

Pecos River

Rio Grande

Canadian River

Red River

Arkansas R.

Brazos R.

Ohio River

Tennessee

ATLANTIC

OCEAN

30° N

ARCTIC OCEAN

ALASKA

CANADA

MEXICO

Gulf of Mexico

0   200   400 miles
0   200   400 kilometers

80° W

160° W   PACIFIC OCEAN

HAWAII   155° W

20° N

0   400 miles
0   400 kilometers

160° W 150° W 140° W

0   200 miles
0   200 kilometers

90° W

The map shows the largest rivers in the United States.
▶ Name three rivers that flow into the Mississippi River.

River Travel Ships and barges also travel across parts of the continents, using **navigable** rivers and canals. A navigable river is one big enough for ships or barges. As you can see on the map on this page, there are many rivers in the United States. Of course, not all of them are big enough for large ships to travel on. The most important rivers in the United States are the Mississippi River, the St. Lawrence River, and the Columbia River. Find these three rivers on the map above.

Canals Canals help ships and barges move between oceans, rivers, or lakes. The Panama Canal, in the country of Panama, connects the Caribbean Sea with the Pacific Ocean. The Suez (soo-EZ) Canal in Egypt, a country in Africa, connects the Red Sea with the Mediterranean Sea. The Erie Canal connects Lake Ontario with the Hudson River.

E. Travel by Air

A Marvelous Invention   Have you ever flown in an airplane? If you flew in a large jet plane, you may have flown so high and so smoothly that you hardly knew you were moving. If you flew in a smaller aircraft, you could probably feel the motion of the plane and see the land you were passing over.

The airplane was invented less than 100 years ago. On December 17, 1903, on the windy beach at Kitty Hawk, North Carolina, Orville Wright flew a "heavier-than-air" machine for 12 seconds. Later that day his brother, Wilbur, made a 59-second flight. Many people refused to believe a flight had really happened. It was too amazing to think that people could fly! But they could fly, thanks to these two hard-working brothers.

The Speed of Flight   Today, airplanes carry millions of passengers and thousands of tons of cargo every year. Because of the airplane, no place in the world is more than 24 hours away from any other place.

The fastest passenger airplane today is the Concorde, a supersonic jet. The Concorde travels at 1,200 miles (1,931 km) per hour. It crosses the Atlantic Ocean between London, England, and New York City in less than four hours. In 1492 it took Christopher Columbus 70 days to cross this ocean.

The Granger Collection

The Wright brothers' first flight in 1903 lasted only 12 seconds. Today the Concorde crosses the Atlantic Ocean in less than 4 hours.
▶ Is the Concorde in this photograph taking off or landing?

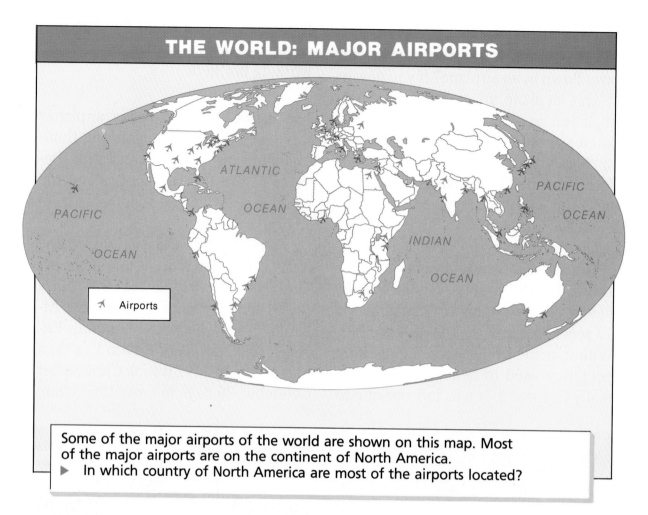

THE WORLD: MAJOR AIRPORTS

Airports

Some of the major airports of the world are shown on this map. Most of the major airports are on the continent of North America.
▶ In which country of North America are most of the airports located?

The modern ways of transportation that you have read about in this lesson allow businesses to have offices and factories in many countries. They also make it possible for people at distant locations to work together.

LESSON 1 REVIEW

THINK AND WRITE

A. Why was the transportation of people and goods once so slow?

B. How did the *Tom Thumb* help to change transportation in the United States?

C. Why are there fewer railroads in the United States today than there were 50 years ago?

D. What kinds of goods are most often carried by ship?

E. How has travel by air improved transportation?

SKILLS CHECK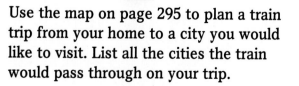

Use the map on page 295 to plan a train trip from your home to a city you would like to visit. List all the cities the train would pass through on your trip.

How Trade BegAN

THINK ABOUT WHAT YOU KNOW

Suppose you want a bicycle that is for sale. Would you rather use money you have saved to buy the bicycle or trade something that you already own to get it?

STUDY THE VOCABULARY

specialize **standard of**
barter **living**

FOCUS YOUR READING

Why do people trade one kind of goods for another kind of goods?

A. A Journey to Punt

Sailing from Egypt As the sun came up one morning long ago, a small fleet of sailing ships put out to sea from Egypt. Men pulled long rows of oars that looked like the legs of giant water bugs and moved the ships slowly away from the land.

Soon the ships were far enough from the shore to catch the wind. The sailors raised the sails and put up the oars. Now the wind could carry these ships to their destination — the ancient land of Punt. There the sailors would get incense for their queen, Hatshepsut (hat SHEP soot).

Incense is a substance that gives off a sweet, spicy smell when it is burned. It comes from trees that grow in parts of Asia and Africa. Incense was important to Hatshepsut and the ancient Egyptians. They believed that if they burned incense when they prayed, the gods would be pleased.

Exchanging Goods At last, the Egyptian sailors arrived at Punt. They put on display all the things they had taken to offer in exchange for the trees. Hatshepsut had sent many beautiful things, such as jewelry, food, perfume, and gold.

The people of Punt carefully examined the goods they had been offered. Then they chose what they wanted and showed the Egyptians how many trees they would offer in return. If the Egyptians did not think they had been offered a fair number of trees in exchange for their goods, they would silently take back their things, sit down, and wait for a better offer.

The Granger Collection

This statue of Queen Hatshepsut of Egypt was carved more than 3,000 years ago.
► What do you think the statue is made of?

Rowers provided most of the power for this Egyptian merchant boat.
▶ What else helped to move the boat through the water?

It took a long time to make the exchange, but eventually each group ended up with what it wanted. When that happened, the Egyptians loaded their boats with the precious trees and sailed for home.

B. Trading Goods Long Ago

People on the Move Long ago, people did not have money. It may be difficult to believe, but at one time there was nothing to buy. People lived by moving from place to place looking for food. They gathered nuts and berries, fished, and hunted animals.

Because they were always on the move, people had few possessions. What they had, they made themselves.

People of ancient times did not depend on others for the things they needed.

Settling in One Place After many centuries, people learned to use seeds to grow their own food. Then they became farmers and settled down in one place to tend their crops. Soon people learned to do other kinds of work, too, like making tools and furniture.

Some people were better at certain tasks than others. Soon the people who were best at each task **specialized** in that kind of work. *Specialize* means "to work at only one kind of task."

Exchanging Goods The people who made the best tools found that they could trade their tools for grain with people who could not make tools. This kind of trade, in which goods are paid for with other goods instead of with money, is called **barter**.

Bartering continued for thousands of years. Even today, people barter to get things they want or need. If you give your tuna sandwich to a friend in exchange for a peanut butter sandwich, you are bartering.

Bartering works well in many situations, but it also can be a problem. First, you have to find someone who wants what you have to trade. That person also must have something that you want in return. Then if you decide to barter something like an apple for some cookies, you must decide how many cookies make a fair trade.

C. Making Trade Easier

Using Forms of Money In time, people decided that it would be easier to trade if, instead of bartering, they could use something that everyone considered valuable. This thing would be a kind of money, although the word *money* was not used yet.

Anything can be used for money as long as everyone agrees on what the item will be. The seeds from which chocolate is made were once used by the Aztecs as money. The Aztecs were Native Americans who lived in Mexico hundreds of years ago.

Nearly 3,000 years ago, people in China began to make small metal disks with a design stamped on them. At about the same time, people who lived on islands in the Mediterranean Sea began to do the same thing. They used these disks as money. These disks were the world's first coins.

Using Paper Money There was one problem with using coins to trade. Coins could be very heavy. Imagine what it would be like to carry just ten dollars worth of pennies in your pocket.

To solve this problem, people began to use paper money. Paper money is easier to carry than coins. The people of China used paper money more than 500 years ago. Today, people all over the world use paper money as well as coins.

Money makes trade easier and faster because money is very easy to

Before the use of money, people often bartered for goods.
▶ Do you ever barter with your friends?

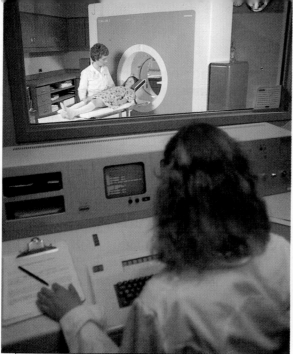

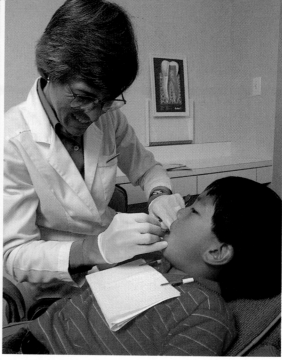

Diagnostic tests (left) and new dental procedures (right) are examples of medical technology.
▶ Do you think these people have a high standard of living?

exchange. Suppose your friend wants the apple in your lunch box and offers to trade you an orange for it. If you take the orange, you have to either eat it or find someone else to trade with. If instead of giving you an orange, your friend gives you a quarter, you can use the quarter for any purpose that you choose.

D. Making More Goods Available

When people began to specialize, they made a greater variety of goods to trade. More people could sell more things and earn more money. Then these people could buy more things with the money they earned.

Specialization and trade allowed people to improve their **standard of living**. Standard of living refers to the way people live. Countries that have an advanced technology have a high standard of living.

LESSON **2** REVIEW

THINK AND WRITE

A. Why did Queen Hatshepsut have her sailors travel from Egypt to Punt?
B. How does barter work?
C. How did money make trade easier?
D. How have specialization and trade helped to make more goods available to people?

SKILLS CHECK

MAP SKILL

Queen Hatshepsut ruled the country of Egypt. Look at the map of Africa on page 393 in the Atlas. Write at least two facts about Egypt's location.

The Importance of International Trade

THINK ABOUT WHAT YOU KNOW

Some of the foods you eat, clothes you wear, and items in your home were grown or manufactured in faraway countries. List at least four countries from which items like those come.

STUDY THE VOCABULARY

domestic trade   **surplus**
international trade

FOCUS YOUR READING

Why has international trade hepled to bring people closer together?

A. Countries Depending on Other Countries

Trade in a Country   The trade that takes place within a country is called **domestic trade**. Through domestic trade, goods that are grown or made in one part of a country can be bought in other parts of the country. For example, grapes are grown in the sunny and mild climate of California. Maine is much too cold for grapes to grow, but because of domestic trade, people in Maine can purchase grapes.

Today the United States buys products from other countries. Many people buy products such as televisions and automobiles that are manufactured in Japan. We can buy dishes that are made in England or Germany.

Most of the bananas that we eat come from Ecuador and Costa Rica. Goods that are brought into one country from another country are imports.

The United States sells many of its products in other countries. Wheat, coal, and machinery are just a few of those products. Products that one country sends to other countries are called exports.

Every day, men and women in all parts of the world work hard to produce the goods we buy and use. Every day these goods are sent to nations near and far. We call trade between countries **international trade**.

Grapes grow well in the mild climate and fertile soil of California's Napa Valley.
► What is holding up the grapevines?

305

Cableways move bananas from a plantation in Ecuador to a station where they are boxed for shipment to other countries.
▶ Can you find the cableways?

B. An International City

Brussels Brussels is the capital city of Belgium, a small country in Europe. Belgium is not much larger than the state of Maryland. On a map, Belgium looks as though it had been sandwiched between four countries—the Netherlands, West Germany, France, and Luxembourg. Belgium has a short coastline. Only a small part of the country touches the North Sea.

Brussels is over 1,000 years old. Almost from the start, Brussels was a busy city, often filled with merchants and traders. It was well known as a center for trade.

Brussels is still an important trade center. In fact, it is one of Europe's most important international trade centers. It ranks second to New York City as a trade center, although Brussels is a much smaller city. More than 7 million people live in New York City. Brussels has less than 1 million people.

Without international trade, Americans would have to do without many items. For example, we could not have bananas or pepper. These products can be grown only in lands that are always hot. In the United States, only Hawaii has the right climate for growing these crops.

It is important for the United States to sell to other countries as well as to buy from them. We often produce more than we can use of items such as wheat and coal. We depend on other countries to buy **surplus**, or extra, goods from us.

Location and Place One reason that Brussels is an important trade center has to do with its location. Brussels is close to several important cities in Europe. Paris, the capital city of France, is less than one hour away by airplane. The distance between Brussels and Cologne (kuh LOHN), a large city in West Germany, is about three hours by car.

Another reason that Brussels is an important trade center has to do with Belgium itself. Railroads crisscross the country like a giant web. Belgium has excellent roads and highways. Rivers

306

THE EUROPEAN COMMUNITY

○ Capital cities

The European Community is also called the Common Market.
▶ How many nations are members of the European Community?

and canals allow large ships to travel to some inland cities. Although Brussels is nearly 100 miles (161 km) from the North Sea, a canal allows huge barges to dock at its port.

C. The European Community

An Important Center One of the largest and most interesting buildings in Brussels stands on a hill. It has so many windows that it seems to be made of glass. It is the headquarters of the European Community, or the *Common Market*, as it is often called.

In 1957 six countries in Europe decided to start the European Community. The countries were France, West Germany, Italy, Belgium, Luxembourg, and the Netherlands. Sixteen years later, Denmark, Ireland, and Great Britain joined the member countrie Greece became a member in 19 Spain and Portugal joined in 1986

Cooperation The countries in the European Community work together to help each other with international trade. There are no trade barriers, or blocks, to trade among the member nations. Members of the community do not charge each other *tariffs*. A tariff is a tax on imports and exports.

Trade among the member nations is as free as trade among states in the United States. Belgium, for example, can import perfume from France without having to pay a tax. Denmark can import shoes made in Italy. Cheese from the Netherlands can be exported to Ireland. Automobiles made in West Germany can be sold in Spain.

The members of the European Community are looking for other ways to work together. One thing they want to do is to make travel easier among the Common Market countries. They want to have a driver's license that is valid, or legal, in all the countries. Each country now has its own laws to obtain a driver's license.

Another thing the members of the European Community hope for is to have the same *currency*, or money, for all the member nations. The countries in the European Community are working hard to make a dream come true. Their dream is to help all the people of Europe grow closer together.

The headquarters of the European Community are located in Brussels.
▶ What countries do you think are represented by the flags in front of the building?

There are no tariffs on products that are traded between members of the European Community.
▶ What product is for sale at this market in the Netherlands?

D. The Growing Importance of International Cooperation

Countries in other parts of the world have seen the success of the European Community, and they are beginning to cooperate, too. The United States and Canada have more trade with each other than they do with any other countries. In 1988, the governments of these two countries agreed to make trade between them even easier.

Many of the countries of the Caribbean, South America, Africa, and Asia have also agreed to work together to improve trade. More and more countries are realizing that cooperation with their neighbors will improve trade and help all people have a better standard of living.

LESSON **3** *REVIEW*

THINK AND WRITE

A. How is international trade different from domestic trade?

B. Why is Brussels an important trade center?

C. Why do people often think of Brussels when they hear the words *European Community*?

D. Why are more and more countries working together to increase international trade?

SKILLS CHECK

MAP SKILL

Locate the 12 countries of the European Community on the map on page 307. Name the countries that are islands and the countries that border the Mediterranean Sea.

USING THE VOCABULARY

locomotive	barter
freight	standard of living
supertanker	domestic trade
navigable	international trade
specialize	surplus

On a separate sheet of paper, write the word or words from the list above that best completes each sentence.

1. A train needs a _____ to pull it along the tracks.
2. Instead of paying money, people sometimes _____ to get the things they want.
3. Sometimes our country has _____ goods, which we depend on other countries to buy from us.
4. People who _____ are usually very good at the one task they do.
5. Hauling _____ over long distances helps the railroads stay in business.
6. People prefer to have a high _____.
7. Without _____ rivers, inland water travel would be very difficult.
8. Trade that takes place between countries is _____.
9. A huge amount of oil can be shipped anywhere in the world in a _____.
10. Because of _____, oranges grown in the warm climate of Florida can be bought in stores in the cooler state of Minnesota.

REMEMBERING WHAT YOU READ

On a separate sheet of paper, answer the questions in complete sentences.

1. Before 1830, why did people prefer to travel by boat if possible?
2. What was Peter Cooper's countribution to transportation in America?
3. Why couldn't most people buy the first gasoline-powered cars?
4. In what way has the airplane made the world seem a smaller place?
5. Why did people who lived in Egypt long ago exchange goods with the people who lived in Punt?
6. Why did people who searched for food have few possessions?
7. What problem was solved when people began using paper money?
8. What do we call products that one country sends to other countries?
9. Why would Americans not have enough bananas or pepper without international trade?
10. What is the great dream of the European Community countries?

TYING MATH TO SOCIAL STUDIES

For a week, keep a record of where the goods you use or buy are produced. Make a list of products made or grown in our country and a list of those from other lands. Find out whether most of the products come from domestic or international trade.

THINKING CRITICALLY

On a separate sheet of paper, answer the following questions in complete sentences.

1. Why were the first railroads in the United States built mainly in the Northeast?
2. You know about the benefits we have gained from modern transportation. What is one problem that modern transportation has caused?
3. What one task would you like to specialize in? Why?
4. Do some Americans have different standards of living than others? Give an example.
5. What might happen if the town nearest yours used a different kind of money?

SUMMARIZING THE CHAPTER

Copy this graphic organizer on a separate sheet of paper. Under the main idea for each lesson, write four facts that support that idea.

CHAPTER THEME	People began to trade thousands of years ago. New forms of transportation increased trade and brought people all over the world closer together.

LESSON 1	Ways of moving people and goods began to improve greatly after about 1830.	1. ___ 2. ___ 3. ___ 4. ___
LESSON 2	Long ago when people settled down and became farmers, they had time for other kinds of work.	1. ___ 2. ___ 3. ___ 4. ___
LESSON 3	Through trade, people can enjoy a great variety of goods from all over the world.	1. ___ 2. ___ 3. ___ 4. ___

12

FARMING AROUND THE WORLD

*W*herever people live they need food. Nearly all the food we eat comes from crops and livestock that are raised on farms or ranches.

Land from the Sea

THINK ABOUT WHAT YOU KNOW
How can the natural environment cause problems for people? How have people tried to solve the problems?

STUDY THE VOCABULARY
dike   polder
reclaim

FOCUS YOUR READING
Why is farmland so valuable to the people of the Netherlands?

A. The Boy Who Saved His Land

Many years ago, according to an old story, a boy named Peter saved his village from being flooded. The boy lived in the Netherlands, a country in Europe. The boy's village, like much of the rest of the country, was always in danger of being flooded because it was below sea level. To hold back the sea, the people of the village had built a strong wall of sand, clay, and stones. Such a wall is called a **dike**. The dike rose high above the flat countryside and kept the lands behind it dry.

One day Peter walked along the grassy banks of the dike near his village, looking for wildflowers. Suddenly he noticed water trickling through the grass. This was very strange, for he knew it had not rained for many days. He tasted the water. It was salty.

He realized that the only place the water could be coming from was the sea on the other side of the dike. His heart almost beat out of his chest with excitement and fear. He knew that a small leak would quickly grow into a large break in the dike, and soon the land would be flooded.

For many years young people have enjoyed the story of the little Dutch boy who saved his village from being flooded.
► How did the Dutch boy save his village?

Peter ran up to the side of the dike and discovered a small hole about the size of his finger. He shouted for help, but no one could hear him. Soon the hole had become as large as his arm.

There was nothing nearby to use to stop the leak. So Peter thrust his arm into the narrow muddy hole to prevent it from getting any bigger. He remained there throughout the night with his arm stuck fast in the dike.

When Peter did not return home after dark, his mother became worried. She asked her neighbors to help her look for him. Early the next morning a neighbor noticed someone standing near the dike. He shouted to the others. As they came closer to the dike, they realized that they had found the missing boy.

When the searchers realized why the boy was there, they quickly brought some tools and materials to repair the hole in the dike. The next day the boy was honored as a hero, for he had truly saved his land. Peter was happy because he had saved his village which he loved very much.

B. Land Won from the Sea

Holding Back the Sea The dike in the story of the brave little Dutch boy is but one of many that have been built in the long struggle between the Dutch people and the sea. For hundreds of years the Dutch have built huge dikes to hold back the waters of the sea.

Dairy cattle graze on reclaimed land in the Netherlands.
▶ What is the purpose of the windmill?

They also built windmills to pump water out of low-lying farmlands. The water pumped by the windmills was channeled into canals that carried it back to the sea. Today many windmills in the Netherlands have been replaced by giant electric pumps.

C. From Zuider Zee to Polderlands

Making More Land If you look at the map on this page, you can see that the Netherlands borders on the North Sea. The North Sea is the part of the Atlantic Ocean that is between the continent of Europe and the British Isles.

A large, shallow bay once extended well into the Netherlands from the North Sea. The bay was called the Zuider Zee (ZYE dur ZEE). In their search for more farmland, the Dutch decided that they would **reclaim** the Zuider Zee. *Reclaim* means "to bring back to a useful condition."

The Dutch first shut off the Zuider Zee from the North Sea by building a huge dam across the entrance to the Zuider Zee. Once the sea was blocked out by the dam, the water in the Zuider Zee gradually became a shallow freshwater lake called IJsselmeer (EYE sul-mer). Find the dam and IJsselmeer on the map.

Other dams were built around sections of the lake, and huge pumps removed the water from within the dikes. The areas of dry land that were reclaimed in this way are called **polders** or polderlands.

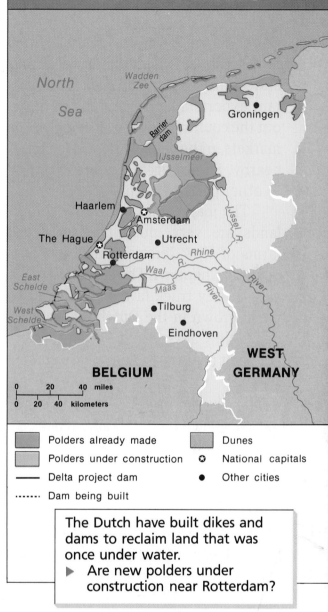

THE NETHERLANDS: BUILDING POLDERS

Legend:
- Polders already made
- Polders under construction
- Delta project dam
- Dam being built
- Dunes
- ✪ National capitals
- ● Other cities

The Dutch have built dikes and dams to reclaim land that was once under water.
▶ Are new polders under construction near Rotterdam?

Farming in the Polders The polders that were reclaimed from the bottom of the Zuider Zee became the richest farmland in the Netherlands. Now this land is used mainly for pastures for dairy cattle, and it has become a good dairying region. Some of the most

315

important farm products that the Netherlands exports are butter, cheese, and evaporated milk.

Other Farm Products Other Dutch farmers in the polderlands raise pigs and poultry. Bacon and eggs are important exports. Market gardens throughout the country grow vegetables for the markets in the densely populated cities nearby. Some vegetables are exported to other parts of Europe.

The market gardens in the polderlands are very much like the truck farms of New Jersey, which you read about in Chapter 4. The crops grown on New Jersey truck farms are similar to those grown in the Dutch market gardens. New Jersey and Dutch farmers sell their produce in large nearby cities.

D. A Colorful Landscape

Fields of Flowers Imagine that you are flying over the polderlands of the Netherlands in the springtime. The flat lands below you would look like a huge striped carpet of many beautiful colors. These are the famous flower fields of the Netherlands. There are fields of white hyacinths (HYE uh sihnths). Other fields are covered with deep purple hyacinths. Many fields of different-colored tulips and golden daffodils are spread below you.

Dutch Bulbs More than 300 years ago, tulip and hyacinth bulbs were brought to the Netherlands from a country in Asia that is now known as Indonesia (ihn DUH nee zhuh). The Dutch traders and merchants

Shoppers in the city of Rotterdam inspect vegetables at a market.
▶ What do you think the black signs say?

(Left) Shoppers browse at a flower market in the city of Haarlem, in the Netherlands.
► What kind of flowers are shown at the right?

discovered that the bulbs could be sold for high prices in Europe. Dutch farmers found that flower bulbs grew well in the soil of their low-lying farms. That is how the flower and bulb business began in the Netherlands. Ever since, the Dutch have been famous for flower farming.

Today, some of the tulips and hyacinths are grown to be cut and sold, but most are grown for their bulbs. Flower bulbs are sold to florists and gardeners around the world. The world's biggest flower market is in the city of Haarlem (HAHR lum), which is near the coast of the Netherlands.

LESSON *1* REVIEW

THINK AND WRITE

A. What is the purpose of a dike?
B. What kinds of machinery have the Dutch used to pump water out of low-lying farmlands?
C. Why have the Dutch worked to reclaim large areas of land from the sea?
D. How did the Dutch become involved in growing flowers?

SKILLS CHECK

THINKING SKILL

The story of the little Dutch boy is a legend, or a story handed down from olden times. Most legends describe a person who has important virtues, such as honesty, kindness, and patience. What virtues did the Dutch boy show in the story in this lesson?

317

Farming in an African Rain Forest

THINK ABOUT WHAT YOU KNOW

Have you and your family ever moved to a new home? How did you feel about moving?

STUDY THE VOCABULARY

shifting
  agriculture

cassava

slash-and-burn
  farming

tropics

rain forest

FOCUS YOUR READING

What is farming like in a rain forest community in Africa?

A. The Time a Village Moved

Apoka listened as his father told him that the people of their village in West Africa were going to move. The soil on their farms was no longer rich enough to grow crops. The villagers had grown crops in the same soil for too many years in a row.

The next day, Apoka's uncle returned from a scouting trip to report on the new village site. He had found a place about 15 miles (24 km) away. The trees were not big, so they would be fairly easy to remove. It looked like a good place to farm and hunt.

B. A Special Kind of Farming

Clearing the Land Soon after the villagers arrived in their new home, all the men went out to begin the hard task of clearing a new field. They cut down the trees, while the women made piles out of the cut branches.

After the villagers had finished clearing the land, they dug a ditch around the whole field. This was hard work and Apoka did not understand why it was necessary to dig a ditch.

SLASH-AND-BURN FARMING

Villagers cut down trees and brush. | The cleared area is burned. | Women plant seeds.

Apoka's father explained that the ditch would act as a kind of fence. When the dry spell came, the villagers would set the piles of brush on fire. The brush would burn for about two days. Because bare earth does not burn, the ditch would stop the fire from spreading out of the area that had been cleared.

Planting Crops   Finally the women went into the newly cleared patch to plant the crops. They planted several kinds of crops. Some had shallow roots, while others had deep roots.

The crops could all be planted in the same field without interfering with one another. In fact, it was useful to plant crops close together. The leaves of all the different plants broke the fall of the raindrops so that the soil would not be washed away. The people of the village looked forward to the harvest, which was always good in the first year after a move.

Shifting Agriculture   The kind of farming that Apoka's family and village do is called **shifting agriculture**. In shifting agriculture the forest is cleared and burned in small patches. Farmers slash, or cut, all the trees and bushes in the small patches of land. Next, they burn the cut trees and bushes that are on the ground. Only the tree stumps are left.

The fires create a lot of wood ash, which helps to make the soil fertile. The farmers then plant their crops of corn, yams, beans, and **cassava** (kuh SAH-vuh) among the stumps. Cassava is a plant with a large root that is made into

The drawing below shows the steps in slash-and-burn farming.
▶ After the cleared area has been burned, how do the women plant the seeds?

Plants grow in the rich soil.

Trees grow tall and strong.

Much of the food that is grown in the farming areas of Africa is shipped to markets in cities such as Kano, Nigeria.

▶ Why, do you think, are some people carrying umbrellas?

flour. Another name for shifting agriculture is **slash-and-burn farming**.

Wet Regions Shifting agriculture is most often carried out in regions around the Equator called the **tropics**. Where Apoka lives is a special kind of region called a **rain forest**.

Rain forests develop in areas that get a lot of rain. There are many tall trees and other plants in rain forests because hot, rainy lands are good places for plants to grow.

You might think that the soils in rain forests are rich, but that is not so. Trees in a rain forest survive by getting food from the leaves and dead trees that fall to the floor of the forest and decay. When forest areas are cut down to plant crops, the soil quickly loses the few nutrients it has. Crops do poorly in this soil, so farmers soon must look for new places to clear in the forest.

Apoka's Future This was Apoka's first move to a new village. He will probably make five or six more moves in his lifetime.

After many years, his villagers may return to the place that they left this year. By then there will be nothing left of the earlier settlement. The trees and bushes will have had time to grow back. When the trees grow back, they enrich the soil so that the land can be farmed again.

LESSON 2 REVIEW

THINK AND WRITE

A. Why did Apoka's village have to move?

B. Describe how slash-and-burn farming works.

SKILLS CHECK

WRITING SKILL

Reread the description of shifting agriculture on pages 319–320. Then close your book and list the steps that the people who practice shifting agriculture follow.

320

Rice Farming in East Asia

THINK ABOUT WHAT YOU KNOW

Many people in Asia eat rice as their chief food. In which countries in Asia might these people live?

STUDY THE VOCABULARY

paddy　　　**kernel**
monsoon

FOCUS YOUR READING

What is it like to live in a rice-growing region of the world?

A. Rice Around the World

An Important Food Did you have rice cereal for breakfast this morning? Sometimes, American families eat rice instead of potatoes or bread with their dinner. Perhaps you have eaten at an Asian restaurant and had rice served as part of your meal.

Rice is one of the world's leading grain crops. Rice is the main food crop for about one half of the world's people. Most of these people live on the continent of Asia. Rice grows well in places that are too warm and too wet for growing wheat.

B. Stair-step Farmlands of East Asia

Some parts of East Asia are low and flat and can easily be flooded. Rice is widely grown in flooded fields called **paddies**. The soils are fertile, and plenty of rainfall comes every year.

Many sections of Vietnam and Japan, two countries in East Asia, are very hilly and mountainous. For thousands of years, people have lived and

Rice paddies are a frequent sight in East Asia.
▶ Do you think this area has a dry or rainy climate?

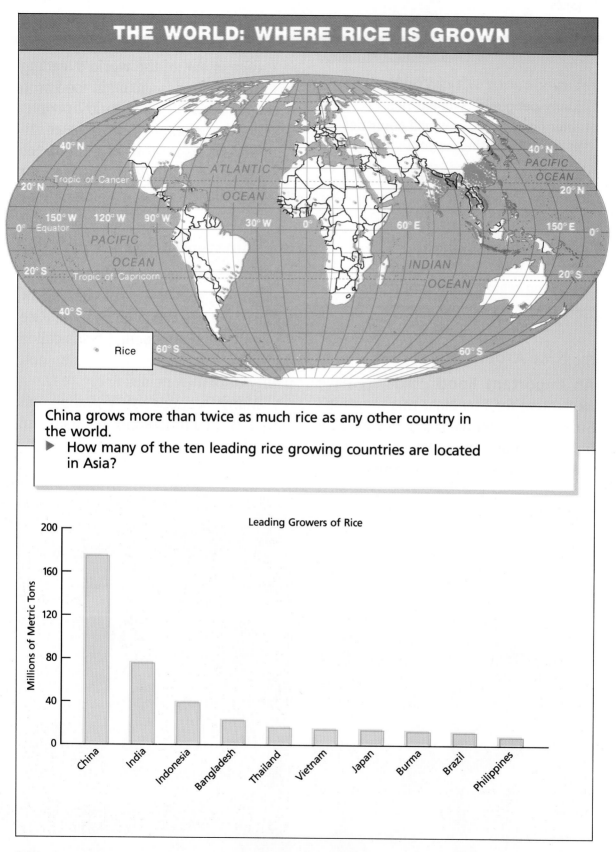

THE WORLD: WHERE RICE IS GROWN

40°N
PACIFIC
OCEAN
20°N
Tropic of Cancer
ATLANTIC
OCEAN
150°W   120°W   90°W
0°
Equator
30°W
0°
60°E
150°E   0°
PACIFIC
OCEAN
INDIAN
20°S
Tropic of Capricorn
OCEAN
20°S
40°S

Rice
60°S
60°S

China grows more than twice as much rice as any other country in the world.

▶ How many of the ten leading rice growing countries are located in Asia?

Leading Growers of Rice

Millions of Metric Tons

200

160

120

80

40

0

China   India   Indonesia   Bangladesh   Thailand   Vietnam   Japan   Burma   Brazil   Philippines

farmed on the steep hillsides. They grow rice in paddies just as the people in the lowlands do.

You are probably wondering how there can be rice paddies on hillsides. You might think that if a farmer tried to flood a field on a hillside, the water would very quickly run right down to the valley below.

So where in these mountainous regions can people possibly raise paddy rice? In our imagination let's follow a path that winds among the houses of a Vietnamese village. Cam, a girl who lives in the village, will be our guide.

Cam meets us near the low wall that surrounds the village. On the other side of the wall, a whole hillside of rice fields descends toward the valley far below. The hillside looks just like a giant stairway because the paddies are stacked up the side, one above the other. Each paddy is located on a terrace, or flat step, formed out of a hillside. Cam says it took hundreds of years to build all these terraces.

As we move closer to the terraced hillside, Cam points out that around each terrace there is a low dike of stone and earth. These low dikes, she explains, hold in the water for each rice paddy. If the water ran over the dike, it would flow down from one terrace to the one below.

Cam explains that the water fills the paddies during the rainy season of the year. Where Cam lives, about half the year is very rainy, while the other half is very dry.

C. The Rice Paddies Throughout the Year

Planting Time   The rains come to Cam's country in the late spring and last until October. The steady wind called the **monsoon** blows in from the ocean in summer, resulting in heavy rains. In the winter, the monsoon is dry because then it blows from the land to the ocean.

When the rains start, the soaked fields of water and mud are plowed. The rice seeds, which were from last year's harvest, have already been planted in special seed beds to begin growing. Soon the plants will be moved to the rice paddies.

Throughout East Asia rice plants are grown in flooded fields called paddies.
▶ What is shown in the smaller photograph?

323

In a few weeks the rice plants have grown large enough to be transplanted into the paddies. The whole family helps with this task. The women remove the plants gently from the beds so as not to damage the small roots. Cam and the other children carry the plants carefully to the paddies. There the plants are set out in straight rows in the soil of the flooded paddies.

Transplanting the rice plants is backbreaking work. Adults stand in the paddies from dawn to dusk in mud and water up to their knees, stepping over the tiny plants.

Tending the Crop Because the paddies are flooded while the rice is growing, the farmers don't often use a hoe. Instead, they use their feet. With their bare toes they pull out weeds and press the soil carefully around the roots of the plants. They are very skillful at this "toeing." An experienced farmer can toe two rows of rice with each foot, or four rows altogether, as he or she walks slowly back and forth across the paddy.

Protecting the Rice A task that is often given to the children is to protect the rice crop from birds. Just as birds in the United States like to eat the grains that farmers grow, so do Vietnamese birds. Vietnamese farmers use scarecrows to scare birds away.

Farmers also string bright bits of metal across the paddies. When the metal moves in the wind and glitters in the sunshine, the birds are frightened away. Sometimes children are assigned to beat drums and make so much noise that the birds stay away.

Harvesting the Rice After the rainy season ends, the long days of sunshine help the rice plants grow tall. Finally, the crop is ready to be cut. The water is

These women are removing rice seedlings from a pool.
▶ Where will these seedlings be transplanted?

After the rice crop is harvested, workers have to separate the rice kernels from the stalks.
▶ Why, do you think, are these workers wearing hats?

drained out of the paddies, and the farmers cut the rice by hand. They use sickles, which are sharp, curved knives. Everyone helps to gather the cut rice stalks into small bundles.

The bundles are carried back to the village, and the heads are broken off the stalks. The heads are spread upon the hard ground, and the people walk back and forth over them, breaking open the husks and leaving the rice **kernels**. The kernels of rice plants are the parts that are eaten. The rice kernels are then stored in large baskets.

When the rice kernels are needed, they may be used whole, as we usually eat them. Or the rice kernels may be spread onto a pounding board and crushed into meal or flour. Rice meal or flour is used in cooking the many different foods such as noodles and cakes.

Cam tells us that the stalks, or straw, from the harvested rice plants are not thrown away. They are stored and can be used later to build or repair a roof or to be burned as fuel.

LESSON 3 REVIEW

THINK AND WRITE
A. Why is rice an important crop?
B. How can paddy rice be grown on hillsides?
C. Why is the monsoon important to rice farmers?

SKILLS CHECK

MAP SKILL
Turn to the political map of Eurasia on pages 396–397 in the Atlas. Find Japan and Vietnam on the map. Use information from the map to describe the location of each country.

Ranching Down Under

THINK ABOUT WHAT YOU KNOW

You have already studied about ranching in the United States. What kinds of land and climate are good for ranching?

STUDY THE VOCABULARY

station	shearing
outback	paddock
jackeroo	dingo

FOCUS YOUR READING

What is life like on a sheep ranch in Australia?

A. A Trip to Australia

Susan Duncan was tired. It had been a long flight from her home, in New York City, across the United States to Los Angeles, California, and then to Sydney, Australia. But Susan was also very excited! She was on her way to spend her winter vacation with her cousin Theresa. Theresa lives on a large sheep ranch in the middle of Australia. In Australia a sheep ranch is called a **station**. The sheep ranch is near the town of Alice Springs. Find Alice Springs on the map on this page.

In Sydney, which is located on the southeastern coast of Australia, Susan boarded a train that would carry her to Adelaide. Another train would then take her to Alice Springs. Find Sydney and Adelaide on the map. About how many miles apart are Sydney and Adelaide?

Upside-down Seasons Shortly after the train had left the terminal in Sydney, Susan began to see rich farmland and golden wheat fields. She found it strange that the weather was so warm. She was used to snow and low temperatures during the winter.

Then Susan remembered. Australia is in the Southern Hemisphere. When it is winter in the Northern Hemisphere, it is summer in the Southern Hemisphere. Do you remember why this is so? If you need help remembering, look at the diagram of the Four Seasons on page 37.

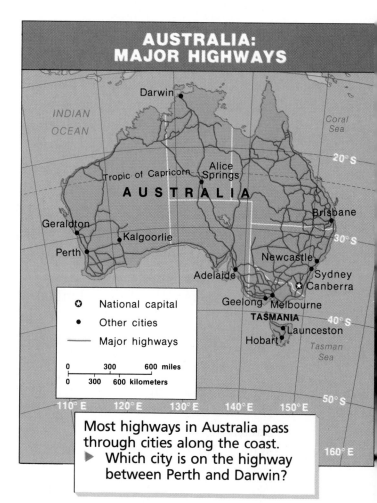

AUSTRALIA: MAJOR HIGHWAYS

- ✪ National capital
- • Other cities
- — Major highways

0   300   600 miles
0   300   600 kilometers

Most highways in Australia pass through cities along the coast.
▶ Which city is on the highway between Perth and Darwin?

B. Regions in Australia

The Great Dividing Range Soon the train climbed steeply, crossing a range of mountains called the Great Dividing Range. On the west side of the mountains, Susan noticed that the land had changed. The area was much drier and flatter than the land she had seen earlier. There were wheat fields as far as the eye could see.

The part of Australia that Susan had just traveled through was the eastern coastal region. Most Australians live in this region, which has fertile soil and a climate that varies from hot to mild. Most of the country's big cities and rich farmland are in this region. Plentiful rainfall allows farmers in the eastern coastal region to grow a wide variety of crops.

The Outback The part of Australia that Susan was now entering is what the Australians call the **outback**. The outback refers to all the land in the middle and western areas of the Australian continent.

The outback is separated from the coastal region by the Great Dividing Range. These mountains act as a barrier to block out the moist air from the Pacific Ocean. The outback side is much drier than the coastal region. In fact, it becomes drier the farther west you go. Most of central and western Australia is desert.

The outback is sparsely populated, which means that it has few people living on large amounts of land. Much of the land in the outback is good for raising sheep, cattle, and wheat.

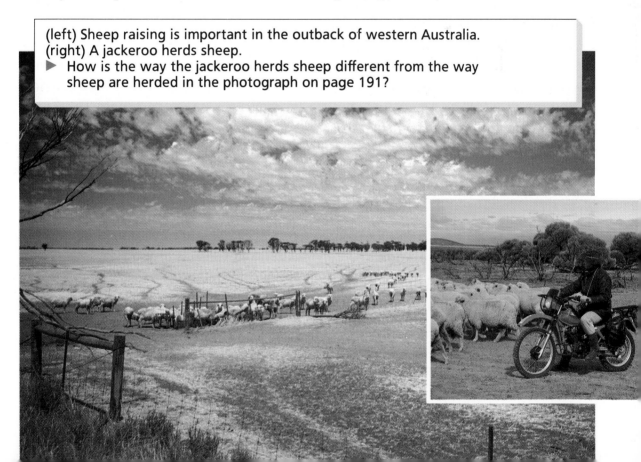

(left) Sheep raising is important in the outback of western Australia.
(right) A jackeroo herds sheep.
▶ How is the way the jackeroo herds sheep different from the way sheep are herded in the photograph on page 191?

In remote areas of Australia students who live too far from a school study at home and talk to their teacher over a radio.

▶ What does this boy have at home that you have in your classroom?

The towns in the outback are small. There is often only one store that carries everything the ranchers need — from cornflakes to jeep parts to medicines. Telephones are uncommon. Instead, ranchers communicate with one another by shortwave radio.

Some children in remote parts of Australia do not attend school. They study at home and talk with their teachers over two-way radios. Other children have to travel many miles to attend school.

C. A Visit in Alice Springs

Carolina Station Taking the train from Adelaide, Susan at last arrived in Alice Springs. She was met by Theresa and her parents, who had driven the 100 miles (160 km) from Carolina Station in their four-wheel-drive jeep. By the time they all arrived at the sheep station, Susan was very tired from her long journey, and all she wanted to do was go to sleep.

The next morning, Theresa showed Susan her family's station. Because it was so big, they had to ride horses from place to place. There are thousands of acres of grassland in each sheep station. Theresa said that raising sheep required few people but much land. In fact, there are about ten times as many sheep as there are people in Australia. There are more sheep in Australia than in any other country in the world.

Buildings on the Station Theresa and her family lived in a large, rambling house that had porches all the way around it. The porches provided shade and helped the family take advantage

328

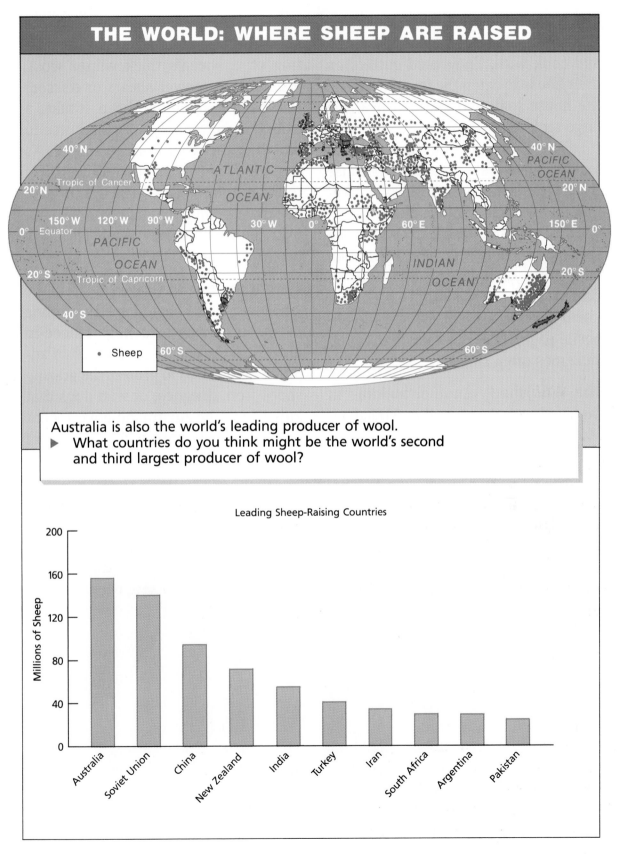

THE WORLD: WHERE SHEEP ARE RAISED

• Sheep

Australia is also the world's leading producer of wool.
▶ What countries do you think might be the world's second and third largest producer of wool?

Leading Sheep-Raising Countries

Millions of Sheep

Australia, Soviet Union, China, New Zealand, India, Turkey, Iran, South Africa, Argentina, Pakistan

of the cool breezes. Theresa explained that her family used rainwater to drink and cook with. They used gutters on their house to catch the rain that fell on the house roof, and emptied it into a large tank on the ground.

The center of Carolina Station looked almost like a village because there were so many buildings. In addition to the main house, there was a guest house, and a barracks where the **jackeroos** lived. A jackeroo is a man who works on a sheep station. In the United States he might be called a ranch hand or a shepherd. On the opposite page, there is a song that young jackeroos often sing.

The Woolshed Another building in the station center is the woolshed. Most of Australia's sheep are raised for their wool. The woolshed is a build-ing where the sheep are brought for **shearing**. Shearing is a term for cutting off a sheep's thick winter wool. Workers use power shears or scissors to cut the wool off the sheep. It takes a skilled jackeroo only a few minutes to cut all of the wool from an animal. As the wool is sheared from the sheep, it is rolled into large bales and tightly tied. Every year, mill owners come from all over the world to buy wool. They will use it to make woolen cloth.

Where the Sheep Graze Beyond the woolshed, Susan could see thousands of sheep grazing in a huge fenced-in area. This is called a **paddock**. Paddocks are needed to protect the grazing sheep from **dingoes**, or wild dogs that kill sheep. The Australian government pays people a bounty, which is a kind of reward, for shooting dingoes.

A prize-winning sheep is shown on the left. At the right, a sheep is being sheared.
▶ Why are sheep sheared?

Waltzing Matilda

Words by A.B. Paterson.
Music by Marie Cowan

Once a jol - ly swag - man sat be - side the bil - la - bong,

Un - der the shade of a coo - li - bah tree, And he

sang as he sat and wait - ed till his bil - ly boiled,

"You'll come a - waltz - ing, Ma - til - da, with me."

Refrain

Waltzing Matilda, waltzing Matilda,
You'll come a-waltzing, Matilda, with me.

And he sang as he sat and waited till his billy boiled
"You'll come a-waltzing, Matilda, with me.

D. Australian Wildlife

The Kangaroo Australia is home to many animals that are not found anywhere else in the world. The most famous, of course, is the kangaroo. There are more than 40 kinds of kangaroos in Australia. The largest kind can weigh up to 200 pounds (91 kg). On their powerful hind legs they can cover more than 25 feet (8 m) in one jump.

When a baby kangaroo is born, it is only about an inch (2 cm) long. It stays in its mother's pouch until it is big enough to hop around on its own. Even then, the baby kangaroo climbs back into the pouch whenever there is danger or when it is tired.

Kangaroos, like dingoes, are a problem for Australian ranchers. Away from the cities, large mobs of kangaroos roam the countryside. It would not be unusual to see thousands of kangaroos in a day's drive. Unfortunately, the kangaroos eat grasses that are needed for cattle and sheep. For this reason, they are often hunted by ranchers. Some people think that all kangaroos should be protected by law.

An Unusual Animal The most unusual animal that lives in Australia is the platypus (PLAT ih pus). The platypus looks something like a muskrat, with a furry body and four short legs. Its mouth is shaped like a duck's bill.

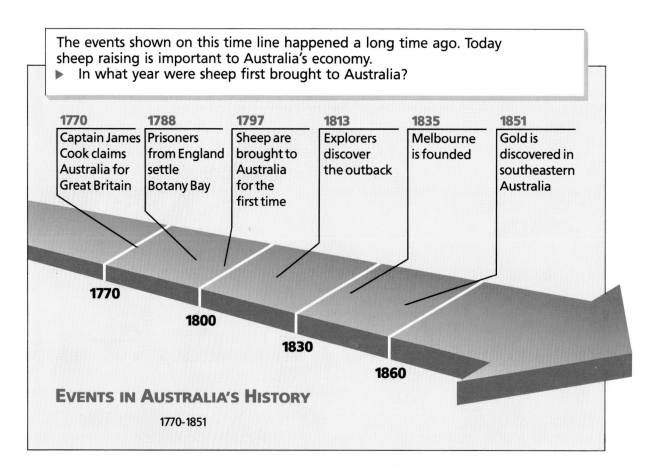

The events shown on this time line happened a long time ago. Today sheep raising is important to Australia's economy.
▶ In what year were sheep first brought to Australia?

1770 Captain James Cook claims Australia for Great Britain

1788 Prisoners from England settle Botany Bay

1797 Sheep are brought to Australia for the first time

1813 Explorers discover the outback

1835 Melbourne is founded

1851 Gold is discovered in southeastern Australia

1770
1800
1830
1860

EVENTS IN AUSTRALIA'S HISTORY
1770–1851

The platypus (left) and the kangaroo (above) are two animals that are found only in Australia.
► What is unusual about the kangaroo's legs?

The platypus has such an unusual combination of features that when it was first brought to Europe from Australia, animal experts who looked at it refused to believe that it was real. They thought that the person who had brought it back was trying to play a joke on them. They thought he had brought them an animal that was sewn together from parts of other animals.

LESSON 4 REVIEW

THINK AND WRITE

A. Why is it summer in Australia when it is winter in the United States?
B. How is the outback different from eastern Australia?
C. Why does a typical station in Australia look almost like a village?
D. Why do Australian ranchers hunt kangaroos?

SKILLS CHECK

WRITING SKILL
Imagine that you have a pen pal in Australia. Write a letter to your friend, describing where you live. Describe the landscape, climate, seasons, and anything that you think would interest someone living in Australia.

USING THE VOCABULARY

dike
polder
shifting
  agriculture
tropics
rain forest

monsoon
kernel
outback
shearing
paddock

On a separate sheet of paper, write terms from the list to correctly complete the sentences.

1. A small field near a house that is used as a pasture is a _____.
2. The walls of the _____ hold back the water.
3. Trees grow tall in the _____.
4. The part of the rice plant that is eaten is the _____.
5. The land of a _____ is fertile and good for farming.
6. Not many people live in the _____ of Australia.
7. It is hot and rainy in the region of the _____.
8. Wool is removed from sheep by _____.
9. Farmers who practice _____ must move from place to place.
10. People know that the summer _____ will bring heavy rains.

REMEMBERING WHAT YOU READ

On a separate sheet of paper, write your answers in complete sentences.

1. Describe the steps taken in reclaiming land after a dike has been built.
2. What farm products are exported from the Netherlands?
3. How does wood ash affect soil?
4. What crops are grown by farmers in the tropics?
5. Why does the soil lose its nutrients so quickly in places where slash-and-burn farming is used?
6. How are farmers in East Asia able to grow rice on steep hillsides?
7. How does the monsoon bring rain to an area?
8. What are the main farming regions in Australia?
9. Why is wool an important product in Australia?
10. What are three kinds of wild animals found in Australia?

TYING ART TO SOCIAL STUDIES

Choose one of the farming regions you have learned about in this chapter. Make a picture that shows something about how people farm in that region. You can draw the picture or you can make a collage or a montage.

THINKING CRITICALLY

On a separate sheet of paper, write your answers in complete sentences.

1. Why are floods such a danger in the Netherlands?
2. Why does rain-forest soil wear out quickly when it is farmed?
3. What might happen to a rice farm if the monsoon did not come one year?
4. In what ways are Australia and the United States alike?
5. Why aren't there any big cities in the outback?

SUMMARIZING THE CHAPTER

Copy this graphic organizer on a separate sheet of paper. Under the main idea for each lesson, write three items that support the main idea.

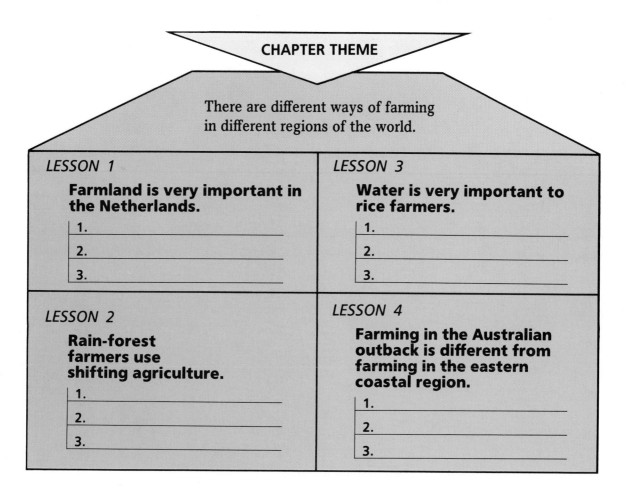

CHAPTER THEME

There are different ways of farming in different regions of the world.

LESSON 1

Farmland is very important in the Netherlands.

1. _____
2. _____
3. _____

LESSON 2

Rain-forest farmers use shifting agriculture.

1. _____
2. _____
3. _____

LESSON 3

Water is very important to rice farmers.

1. _____
2. _____
3. _____

LESSON 4

Farming in the Australian outback is different from farming in the eastern coastal region.

1. _____
2. _____
3. _____

13

ENERGY SOURCES AROUND US

*W*e use some kind of energy every day. Some forms of energy cannot be replaced. So it is important that everyone learns to respect the earth's energy sources and to use them wisely.

Energy That Comes from Wells

THINK ABOUT WHAT YOU KNOW

What kinds of energy are used to run cars, trains, airplanes, and many of the appliances people have?

STUDY THE VOCABULARY

renewable resource	fossil fuel
nonrenewable resource	pollution
conserve	acid rain

FOCUS YOUR READING

Why is petroleum an important natural resource?

A. Using Energy

Have you ever worked or played so hard that afterward you just wanted to do nothing for a while? You might have said you had run out of energy.

Energy makes things work. The kind of energy that you "run out of" when you play is the kind of energy that makes our bodies move and do work. We get the energy that we need from the food we eat.

Of course, the energy that makes our bodies work is just one of many different kinds of energy. Everything that moves uses energy. It takes energy to move the car or bus that you ride in. Energy is also used to heat and cool things. It takes energy to cook the food you eat, to heat the water you bathe in, and to warm or cool your home.

B. Energy and Natural Resources

You learned in Chapter 1 that a natural resource is something that is provided by nature and useful to people. Wood, petroleum, natural gas, and coal are all examples of natural resources that are used to make energy.

Some natural resources are called **renewable resources**. A renewable resource can be replaced by nature or by people. When we build a wood fire to keep us warm, we are using a renewable resource. The logs we use to build the fire come from trees. When trees are cut down, they are destroyed, but people can plant new trees to replace the ones that they have cut down.

There are some natural resources that cannot be replaced once they have been used. Because those resources will run out someday, they are called **nonrenewable resources**. Coal, oil, and other kinds of minerals that are taken from the ground are nonrenewable resources. They have been formed over millions of years. Once coal and oil have been burned, they are gone and cannot be replaced.

C. Conserving Natural Resources

Imagine that you are stranded on a desert island. All you have for food is a loaf of bread. You don't know when you will be rescued. What will you do when you get hungry? If you are wise, you will not eat the entire loaf at once. You will **conserve** your food. *Conserve* means "to avoid wasteful use." So you will eat only what you need each day, to make your food supply last as long as possible. Luckily, we do not have to conserve our food so strictly every day. But we do have to conserve our supply of natural resources. People need natural resources to survive.

There are many ways to conserve natural resources. At home, you conserve natural resources that are used to make electricity when you turn off the lights as you leave a room. Many families turn down the heat in their homes at night before they go to sleep. Some people share rides or take buses or trains to work to conserve gasoline.

Trees are being planted to replace ones that were destroyed in a fire in Idaho.
▶ Are trees a renewable or nonrenewable resource?

D. Important Sources of Energy

Petroleum, natural gas, and coal are important sources of energy. They are burned to make heat, which can be used to run many different kinds of engines. We call the sources of energy that burn, such as petroleum, natural gas, and coal, **fossil fuels**.

Some fossil fuels are found in rocks under the surface of the earth. They are formed from fossils, or the remains of animals and plants that lived on the earth millions of years ago.

E. Getting Oil from the Earth

Drilling for Oil Since petroleum is a liquid, water or air pressure is used to force it to the surface of the land or sea. Then it can be pumped through pipes to a refinery where it is made into gasoline and many other useful products.

Petroleum from Other Countries The United States uses more petroleum than any other nation. We are one of the world's leading producers of petroleum, but we do not produce all the petroleum we need. So we buy petroleum from other countries.

Much of the petroleum we buy comes from Saudi Arabia. Saudi Arabia is a country on a peninsula where Europe, Africa, and Asia meet. Find Saudi Arabia on the map on page 396.

Saudi Arabian oil is pumped from the wells and sent through pipelines to port cities. At the ports the petroleum is placed in large storage tanks. The petroleum is held in these tanks until

PETROLEUM: FROM DRILLING TO CONSUMER

1. A derrick is built over the spot where petroleum is found.

2. Petroleum is pumped from the oil well to the surface.

3. Petroleum travels through pipelines into storage tanks.

4. At a refinery many products are made from petroleum.

OIL

5. Huge tanker trucks deliver some of the products to many parts of the country.

Heavy machines and equipment are used to make petroleum into products that many people use every day.
► What happens to the petroleum after it is pumped from a well?

it is sent through other pipelines to tankers. These huge ships carry millions of gallons of petroleum to the United States every year. The tankers also carry petroleum to other nations in the world.

Look at the bar graph about petroleum production on the facing page. What are the four leading petroleum-producing nations? Where does the United States rank in petroleum production? Which country produces more petroleum, Mexico or Venezuela?

F. Damage to the Environment

Acid Rain When coal and oil are burned, they give off gases that bring **pollution**. That is, they make the air and land and water dirty. Polluted air is unhealthy for people and animals. Chemicals in the air change the precipitation that falls to the earth in the form of rain, snow, sleet, or hail. **Acid rain** is the name given to precipitation that has been polluted.

The Greenhouse Effect Carbon dioxide (KAHR bun dye AHK syd) is a gas that is made every time something burns. Carbon dioxide traps heat near the earth, just as a blanket keeps heat from escaping from your body while you sleep. The warming or heating of the atmosphere near the earth is called the greenhouse effect.

Many fossil fuels are burned in our environment every day. The amount of

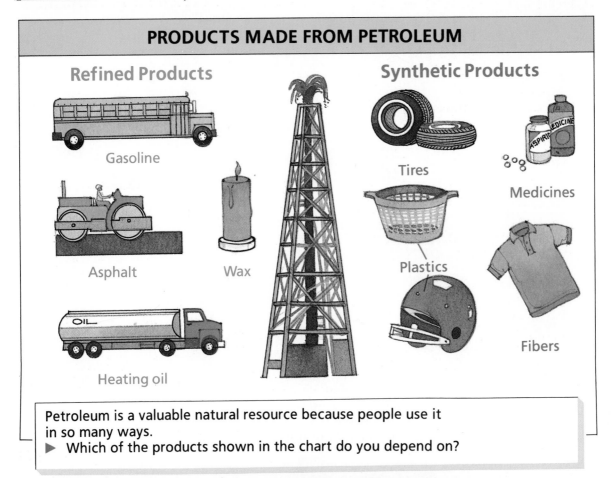

PRODUCTS MADE FROM PETROLEUM

Refined Products

Gasoline

Asphalt

Wax

Heating oil

Synthetic Products

Tires

Medicines

Plastics

Fibers

Petroleum is a valuable natural resource because people use it in so many ways.
► Which of the products shown in the chart do you depend on?

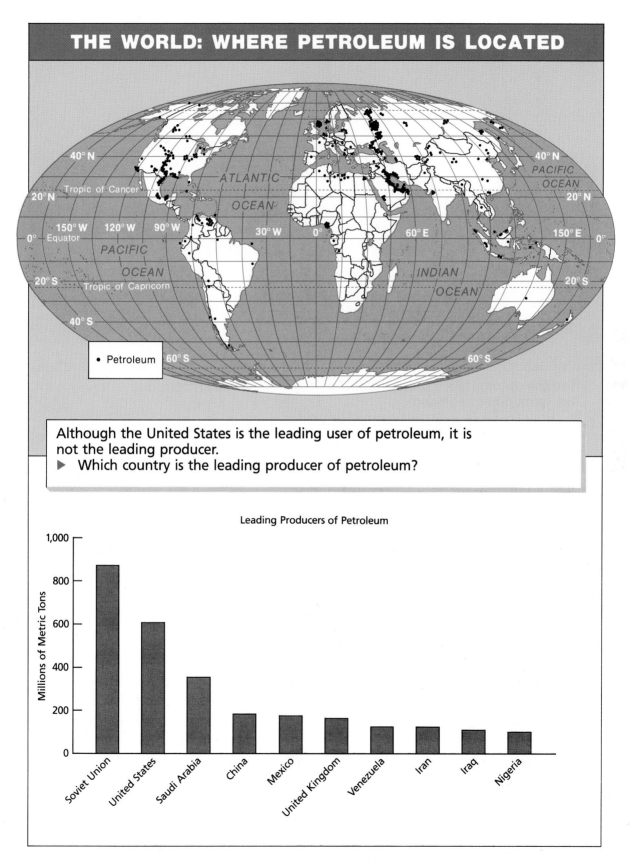

THE WORLD: WHERE PETROLEUM IS LOCATED

40° N

PACIFIC
OCEAN

40° N

Tropic of Cancer

ATLANTIC

20° N

20° N

OCEAN

150° W   120° W   90° W   30° W   0°   60° E   150° E   0°

0° Equator

PACIFIC

60° E

INDIAN

20° S

OCEAN

OCEAN

20° S

Tropic of Capricorn

40° S

• Petroleum   60° S

60° S

Although the United States is the leading user of petroleum, it is
not the leading producer.
▶ Which country is the leading producer of petroleum?

Leading Producers of Petroleum

Millions of Metric Tons

1,000

800

600

400

200

0

Soviet Union · United States · Saudi Arabia · China · Mexico · United Kingdom · Venezuela · Iran · Iraq · Nigeria

ACID RAIN

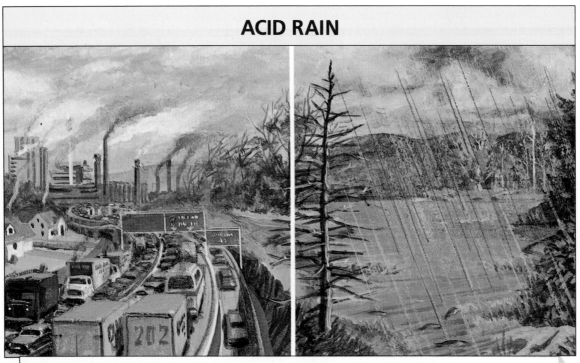

The use of fossil fuels, such as coal and petroleum, is the first step in the formation of acid rain.

▶ How are lakes and rivers harmed by acid rain?

carbon dioxide that is in the air increases from year to year. As a result the greenhouse effect is growing stronger every year.

What might be some results of the greenhouse effect? The entire earth may become warmer. If that happens, deserts might form where there is rich farmland today. Giant icecaps in Antarctica and Greenland might melt and cause the ocean to rise. If this happens, large areas of land might be flooded.

LESSON 1 REVIEW

THINK AND WRITE

A. Why is energy important?

B. Why is coal a nonrenewable resource?

C. What are some of the ways that people can conserve natural resources?

D. How are fossil fuels formed?

E. Why does the United States buy a lot of petroleum from Saudi Arabia?

F. How can people help to prevent pollution in the community?

SKILL CHECK

THINKING SKILL

It is difficult for some people to conserve energy because they have become used to the convenience of all the machines in our modern world. What would you do to persuade those people that we need to conserve our nonrenewable resources?

B.   E.

Energy That Comes from Mines

THINK ABOUT WHAT YOU KNOW

How might your life be different if there were no electricity in your community?

STUDY THE VOCABULARY

turbine   shaft
peat   mining
anthracite   nuclear
bituminous   energy

FOCUS YOUR READING

Why are coal and nuclear energy valuable natural resources?

A. Coal, an Important Source of Energy

Uses of Coal You learned in Lesson 1 that coal is a fossil fuel, just as petroleum and natural gas are. But coal is a much different kind of fossil fuel. Coal is a kind of rock that gives off heat when it is burned. Because coal is a solid, it cannot be pumped from the ground. Instead, it must be dug out of mines and brought to the surface.

At one time, coal was the most important fossil fuel. It was the main fuel used for transportation. In the 1800s, steam engines fueled by coal were used to power trains and steamships. In the early 1900s, many people also used coal-burning furnaces to heat their homes and places of business.

Today, few homes still have coal furnaces. Trains and ships use other forms of energy, but coal is still an important source of energy. Coal is used to produce the heat needed to make iron and steel and for other kinds of manufacturing. But the most important use of coal today is to generate, or create, electricity.

To generate electricity, coal is burned to make the steam that drives large **turbines** (TUR bihnz). A turbine has parts that spin rapidly when steam passes across them. As the steam makes a turbine spin, it drives another machine called a generator. When the generator turns, it produces electricity. A little more than half of the electricity used in the United States today comes from burning coal.

Generators at Hoover Dam in Arizona produce electricity.
▶ Why, do you think, are there stairs going up to the generators?

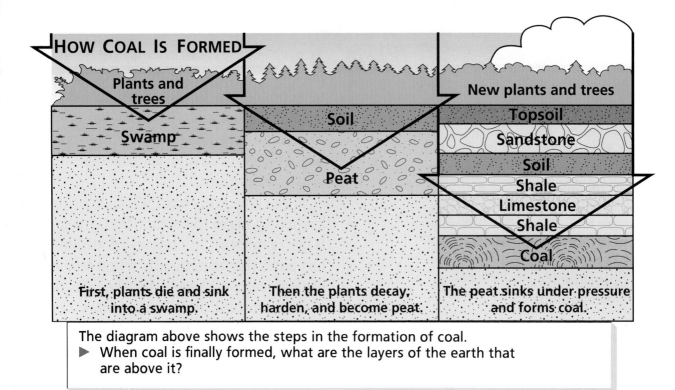

HOW COAL IS FORMED

Plants and trees

Swamp

First, plants die and sink into a swamp.

Soil

Peat

Then the plants decay, harden, and become peat.

New plants and trees

Topsoil

Sandstone

Soil

Shale

Limestone

Shale

Coal

The peat sinks under pressure and forms coal.

The diagram above shows the steps in the formation of coal.
► When coal is finally formed, what are the layers of the earth that are above it?

B. The Story of Coal

Formation Coal is formed from the remains of plants and trees that lived in swamps and marshes millions of years ago. When the trees died, they fell into the mud and water of the swamps, where they decayed. Gradually, mud and sand covered the layers of decayed plant material. Over millions of years, the buried plant material slowly became coal.

Coal is still forming in the earth. In some European countries, such as Ireland and Denmark, there are marshes that are full of a material that is called **peat**. The peat is made of partly decayed plant remains. Peat is the beginning of coal. If peat gets covered with mud or sand, and if it is left untouched for millions of years, coal will eventually be formed.

Today some people in Ireland and Denmark burn peat in open fireplaces to heat their homes and cook their food. But peat does not make a hot fire, so it is a poor source of energy.

Kinds of Coal There are two kinds of coal, and both are useful. **Anthracite** (AN thruh syt), or hard coal, burns hot and is used in many special kinds of manufacturing. **Bituminous** (bih TOO-muh nus) coal, or soft coal, is much more plentiful, so it is used more often. Bituminous is much dirtier than anthracite coal when it is burned and so it pollutes the air much more than anthracite coal does.

The United States has the largest amount of coal of any country in the world. The Soviet Union has the second largest amount of coal, and China is in third place.

344

C. Getting Coal from the Ground

Open-pit Mining You know that coal is taken from the ground by mining. If the coal is close to the surface of the ground, the miners simply dig away the rock or earth layer over the coal to get to it. This kind of mining is called open-pit mining, which you read about in Chapter 8.

Open-pit mining can leave ugly scars on the surface. In 1977 the United States government passed a law stating that mine owners must put back the soil and rock that was removed in open-pit mining. The land must be restored, as much as possible, to its original condition.

Shaft Mining If the coal lies far under the ground, a kind of mining called **shaft mining** is used. In this type of mining, long tunnels, or shafts, are dug through the rock to reach the coal. The coal is dug out of the rock, broken up, and taken out of the mine.

Once the coal reaches the surface of the ground, it is cleaned. This means the coal is first sorted into different sizes. Then it has to be washed and dried. Finally the coal is loaded onto trains, trucks, or barges. Much of the coal then goes to electric power companies. The power companies burn the coal to produce heat for running the machines that make electricity.

AN OPEN-PIT MINE

Benches

Coal

Coal is removed from an open-pit mine in layers that form a road up the sides of the pit.
▶ What are the layers called?

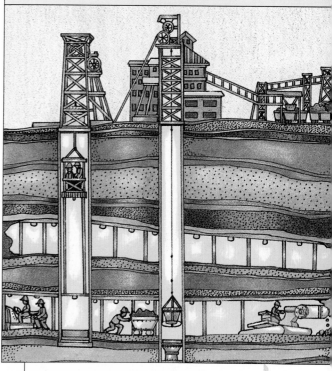

A SHAFT MINE

One way that coal is mined is through shaft mines.
▶ What are the two shafts in the diagram used for?

In Coal Country

By Judith Hendershot
Setting: Willow Grove, Ohio

In this excerpt from her book *In Coal Country*, Judith Hendershot describes how coal was mined in the community in which she lived many years ago.

*T**he coal was dragged out of the mine in small cars pulled by mules. Then it was sent up into a tall building called the tipple, where it was sorted and washed. The water that washed the coal ran into the creek, and the dust from the coal turned it black as night.*

Papa sometimes worked at the picking table on the tipple to sort out rocks from the good coal. After it was sorted, the good coal was dumped into railroad cars waiting under the tipple. The rest of the stone and dirt was hauled away to a gob pile. There were gob piles all over Willow Grove. The kids from the row ran to the tops of the piles to play king of the mountain. . . .

Trains moved the coal in cars from the mine to power plants and steel mills on the Ohio River. We watched from the porch swing as the engineer worked his levers to guide the train, blowing clouds of hot white steam on the tracks. One engine pushed and another pulled as many as one hundred cars at a time. The houses shook as the trains rumbled by.

Written and illustrated by Judith Hendershot

This nuclear plant provides power for the surrounding area.
► Is this plant in an urban or a rural area?

D. Nuclear Energy

Coal is not the only source of energy that comes from mines. Uranium is another energy-producing mineral that is found in rock buried deep under the ground. Uranium is like coal in another way, too. It is also a nonrenewable resource.

Uranium is not formed from the remains of animals and plants, as petroleum, natural gas, and coal are. It is a metal that is a part of the rocks that make up the earth.

The energy that comes from uranium is called **nuclear energy**. Nuclear energy, like energy from oil and coal, can be used to heat water to drive turbines and make electricity.

LESSON 2 REVIEW

THINK AND WRITE

A. Why is coal an important natural resource?

B. How is coal formed?

C. How is open-pit mining different from shaft mining?

D. How is uranium used as a source of energy?

SKILLS CHECK

MAP SKILL

Find Ireland and Denmark on the map on page 394. Which of these countries is an island? Which country borders on the North Sea?

Solar Electricity Solar energy can also be used to generate electricity. One way is to use mirrors to gather large amounts of sunlight and then aim that light at a container of water. When the water boils, it can be used to turn turbines that generate electricity.

Another way to use the sun to make electricity is with **solar cells**. Have you ever seen a calculator with a solar cell? It runs out of energy in a dark room, but as soon as it is exposed to sunlight, it works again. Solar cells can make the tiny amounts of electricity that are needed to run a calculator. But they can also be connected to each other to create enough energy to be used in the space program.

Solar Collectors Some scientists believe that in the future we will be able to build solar collectors in outer space. Imagine a satellite that sends beams of concentrated sunlight to the ground from its orbit in space. Such a satellite might one day be used to capture solar energy in space and send it to earth. This solar energy could heat water to make steam. The steam could drive turbines to generate electricity.

Other scientists think it might be possible to make electricity on the satellites themselves. This electricity could be beamed to receivers on earth and then sent through wires to people's homes. For now, however, this is only a wonderful dream.

All of the items shown in the photograph above are powered by solar energy.
▶ How many of these items can you identify?

C. Energy from the Wind

Windmills have captured the energy of the wind for centuries. Today in the United States and other parts of the world, windmills are used to make electricity. The wind turns the blades of a windmill, just as water or steam makes parts of a turbine move. The windmill turns a generator, making electricity.

Of course, the windmills only work when the wind blows, so ways must be found to store wind energy. Also, it would take hundreds of windmills to produce the same amount of energy that can be produced by a modern coal-fueled power station.

Finally, although the wind is free, windmills are not. It is so expensive to build and fix windmills that the electricity produced by them usually turns out to be more expensive than that provided by the local electric company.

Perhaps in the future, ways will be found to generate large amounts of electricity from windmills and to store that energy until it is needed. If that happens, you may see giant windmills on hilltops, on the roofs of buildings, and in other places where they can catch the wind to make electricity.

Electricity is produced when the wind turns the blades of these windmills.
▶ Are windmills a reliable source of electric power?

LESSON **3** REVIEW

THINK AND WRITE

A. How can running water be used to produce electricity?
B. What is solar energy used for?
C. Why can't windmills always be depended on?

SKILLS CHECK

WRITING SKILL

Imagine how a classroom might be heated and lighted in the year 2050. Write a paragraph describing what a classroom of the future might look like.

USING THE VOCABULARY

nonrenewable
   resource
conserve
acid rain
turbine
peat

anthracite
nuclear energy
recycle
solar cell
solar energy

On a separate sheet of paper, write the word or words from the list above that best complete each sentence.

1. Without mud- or sand-covered _____, coal could not form.
2. Once a _____ has been taken from the ground and used, it can never be replaced.
3. Water is a renewable energy source because we can _____ it.
4. Precipitation can be turned into unhealthy _____ by polluted air.
5. A nonrenewable mineral resource called uranium produces _____.
6. Of the two kinds of coal, _____ is cleaner and causes less pollution.
7. Making use of _____ would be one way to have clean energy.
8. Our supplies of natural resources would last much longer if people would learn to _____ them.
9. When steam makes a _____ spin, it drives a generator, which in turn produces electricity.
10. A calculator can run on the tiny amount of electricity made by a _____.

REMEMBERING WHAT YOU READ

On a separate sheet of paper, answer the questions in complete sentences.

1. Where do we get the energy we need to make our bodies move and work?
2. Name some different fossil fuels.
3. How might the greenhouse effect harm our earth?
4. What is the most important use of coal today?
5. What country has the world's second largest amount of coal?
6. In some ways, uranium is like coal. Name one way in which it is not.
7. What are the two great advantages of hydroelectric power?
8. What is the source of almost all of the earth's energy?
9. Why is it necessary to find a good way to store solar energy?
10. Why is electricity produced by wind so expensive?

TYING SCIENCE TO SOCIAL STUDIES

Learn about geothermal energy. Share what you learn with the class.

1. Find the meaning of the word *geothermal* in the dictionary.
2. Research the meaning of each of the word's parts—*geo-* and *thermal.*
3. Look in science books and an encyclopedia to learn how geothermal energy is formed and used.

THINKING CRITICALLY

On a separate sheet of paper, answer the following questions in complete sentences.

1. What way in which you use electricity would you find the hardest to give up? Why?
2. What might happen if Saudi Arabia stopped selling us petroleum?
3. Do you think all mine owners liked the law that requires them to restore the land after open-pit mining? Why or why not?
4. Does the electricity provided by building dams always make up for damage done to the land? Explain.
5. Would you rather work on better ways to store solar or wind energy? Explain why.

SUMMARIZING THE CHAPTER

Copy this graphic organizer on a separate sheet of paper. Under the main idea for each lesson, write four facts that support the idea.

CHAPTER THEME

Energy from natural resources is necessary to supply the power that runs almost every aspect of our modern world.

LESSON 1	LESSON 2	LESSON 3
Fossil fuels are important nonrenewable sources of energy.	Coal generates much of our electricity. Nuclear energy also produces electricity.	Clean, renewable sources of energy may one day provide most of the world's power.
1.	1.	1.
2.	2.	2.
3.	3.	3.
	4.	4.

14

LIVING IN OTHER LANDS

*M*any people in our country earn their living by farming, fishing, mining, and lumbering. Some people in other countries also earn their living in these ways.

Food from the Sea

THINK ABOUT WHAT YOU KNOW
How is the work of a farmer, a
fisher, and a logger alike?

STUDY THE VOCABULARY
geyser   **factory ship**
trawler

FOCUS YOUR READING
Why is fishing so important in
some parts of the world?

A. A Nation That Depends on Fish

Iceland is a small island nation in the North Atlantic Ocean. It is far north of the Equator. Find Iceland on the map on page 385.

Iceland, like the Hawaiian Islands, was created by volcanic eruptions. Over time, the lava and ashes of the volcanoes built up to form the island. Active volcanoes, hot springs, and **geysers** (GYE zurz) are found all across Iceland. A geyser is a spring that regularly sends up columns of hot steam and water.

Not much of the land in Iceland is good for growing crops, though there are some farmers who raise sheep and dairy cattle. More than one fifth of the people in Iceland earn their living by catching, cleaning, or canning fish. Each day about 900 fishing boats carry 6,000 fishers out into the rich fishing waters that surround the island.

B. A Fishing Town in Iceland

The little town of Heimaey is on a small island off the southern coast of Iceland. Heimaey is the port closest to the rich fishing waters off Iceland. The waters off Heimaey are the world's richest waters for codfish.

Let's spend a day with Eric Olafsson (OH lahf sawn). Eric lives in Heimaey with his father and mother and sister. His father is a cod fisherman, and he has his own **trawler**. A trawler is a special kind of fishing boat that has equipment to use nets called trawls for catching fish.

A Day at Sea Early one morning, before the sun rose, Eric crawled out of bed to join his father for the day's work on their fishing boat. After a hearty breakfast, Eric listened to the weather

Steam and water erupt from one of the many geysers in Iceland.
▶ Why would it be dangerous to stand close to a geyser?

357

report on the radio. Storms at sea can come up quickly. People's lives often depend on accurate weather reports.

After hearing the weather report, Eric and his father walked down to the dock. The three men who also work on the boat were already there.

Once aboard the trawler, the fishers checked the radio to be sure they could communicate with people on other boats or on the shore. They also checked the engine and other equipment. Then Eric's father cranked the engine. The trawler moved slowly out of the harbor into the open sea.

Soon Eric and his father noticed that the smooth ocean was being rippled by the heavy trawl filled with fish. The crew used an electric winch to pull the trawl back close to the boat.

The winch drew the net up over the side of the trawler and positioned it over a large wooden box. Then the net was loosened, and hundreds of cod dropped into the box. Eric helped shovel ice on top of the fish to keep them from spoiling in the sun.

When the box was completely filled, Eric's father turned the trawler back to the harbor and steered it right up to the fish-processing factory.

C. Processing the Catch

Sorting Out Fish The fish-processing factory begins its work as soon as the fish are delivered. Men with large long-handled forks separate the different kinds of fish. Then the cod are skinned, cleaned, and filleted (fih LAYD). *Fillet* means "to remove the bones."

The fillets of cod are packed into boxes. These boxes are frozen quickly and then packed into larger cartons. The cartons are stamped with the name of the country to which they will be sent by freighter.

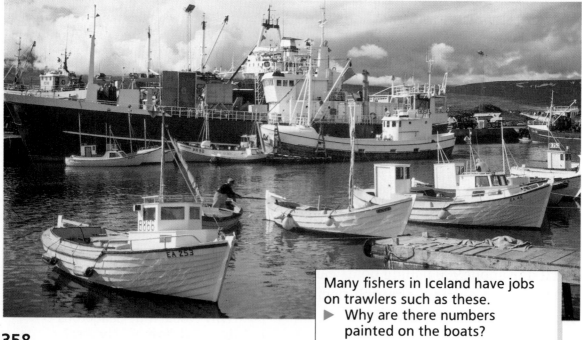

Many fishers in Iceland have jobs on trawlers such as these.
► Why are there numbers painted on the boats?

Exporting Fish Most of the cod caught in Iceland is frozen and exported. However, about one fifth of the cod is dried before it is exported to countries that do not have many fish.

The dried fish keep fresh for a long time without refrigeration, even in hot climates. Much of the Icelandic dried cod goes to countries in Africa and southern Europe, where few people have refrigerators or freezers.

D. High-Tech Fishing

New Ways of Fishing Scientists have found ways to use high-tech equipment to catch huge numbers of fish. Electronic devices are used to quickly find large schools of fish. Helicopters are also used to spot schools of fish. Nets have been made so strong that they can catch thousands of fish in a single haul.

Because very large trawlers are at sea for weeks at a time, there are living, sleeping, and eating quarters for the fishers. The ship's crew includes not only fishers but people who sort, clean, fillet, freeze, and package the fish.

Some of the codfish caught off Iceland are dried on wooden racks before they are exported.
► Why are the fish dried before they are exported?

These fishing ships have huge freezers on board in which the cartons of fish are stored. The ships are called **factory ships** because they are really floating fish-processing factories.

LESSON **1** *REVIEW*

THINK AND WRITE

A. Why do people in Iceland depend so much on fishing?
B. Why do fishers depend on radios?
C. Why is most of the fish caught near Iceland frozen before it is exported?
D. What high-tech methods does the fishing industry use now?

SKILLS CHECK

WRITING SKILL

Imagine that you are going to write a letter to Eric Olafsson, the boy you read about in this lesson. Make a list of questions that you would ask him about what it is like to live in a fishing town.

Forest Resources

THINK ABOUT WHAT YOU KNOW

If you were to walk through a forest in winter, what sights and sounds might you see and hear?

STUDY THE VOCABULARY

coniferous	**hibernate**
taiga	**cacao**

FOCUS YOUR READING

How are forests in northern regions different from forests in the tropics?

A. A Great Northern Forest Region

A Large Country What is the largest country in the world? If you answered "the Soviet Union," you are correct. The full name of the Soviet Union is *Union of Soviet Socialist Republics.* Many people refer to the country by its abbreviation, *U.S.S.R.*

The Soviet Union stretches across two continents — from Europe all the way across Asia. It is so large that the United States, Canada, and Mexico taken together could fit into the Soviet Union and still leave room to spare. The Soviet Union extends almost halfway around the world.

Forests One of the main natural resources of the Soviet Union is its forests. The largest unbroken stretch of forest in the world is in the northern part of the Soviet Union. The forests are mainly made up of **coniferous** (koh-NIHF ur us), or cone-bearing, trees.

The type of coniferous forest found in the northern Soviet Union is called the **taiga** (TYE guh). This taiga is the biggest forest in the world. You can

(left) A timber raft moves logs on the Vychegda River. (right) This Soviet village is nestled in the hills near Lake Baikal.

▶ Why, do you think, are the buildings in this village made of wood?

	United States	0	300	600 miles
	Soviet Union	0	300 600	kilometers

The Soviet Union is the largest country in the world. It is almost two and one half times as large as the United States.

► About how many miles is it across the widest part of the mainland United States?

travel miles and miles through the taiga without seeing a village or a road.

The trees often stand so close together that their thick branches block out the light. They make the forest floor so dark that no smaller plants can grow there. Some people refer to this kind of taiga as a "dark forest," and many used to think of it as a place of mystery.

A Harsh Climate The climate of the taiga is harsh. Summers are short. The taiga can be warm and dry for a couple of months, but there are stormy, gloomy days even in the summer. When the wind blows in from the Arctic Ocean, the days are chilly. You are reminded that summers are brief.

By September, signs of the approaching winter are all around. Birds fly overhead, heading for warmer climates to the south. The animals—which include deer, bears, and wolves—have grown thicker coats of fur. Some are beginning to **hibernate**. Animals that hibernate spend the winter sleeping in caves, tree trunks, or other shelters. Hibernation allows the

361

animals that live in a very harsh climate to survive the winter months.

Precipitation Snow usually covers the taiga by October. Ice begins to form around the edges of ponds and rivers. By the middle of the winter, the ground is frozen solid, and a layer of snow covers everything. In some parts of the taiga, such as the mountains of the far north, the temperature often drops as low as -75°F (-60°C).

B. The Taiga as a Resource

For centuries, the taiga of the Soviet Union has served as a rich natural resource for the people of that country. Until recent times, almost all buildings in the Soviet Union were made of wood. Even large palaces and great churches were built of wood. The people also used wood as fuel to heat their homes and cook their food.

Yet no matter how fast the timber is harvested, there seems to be no end

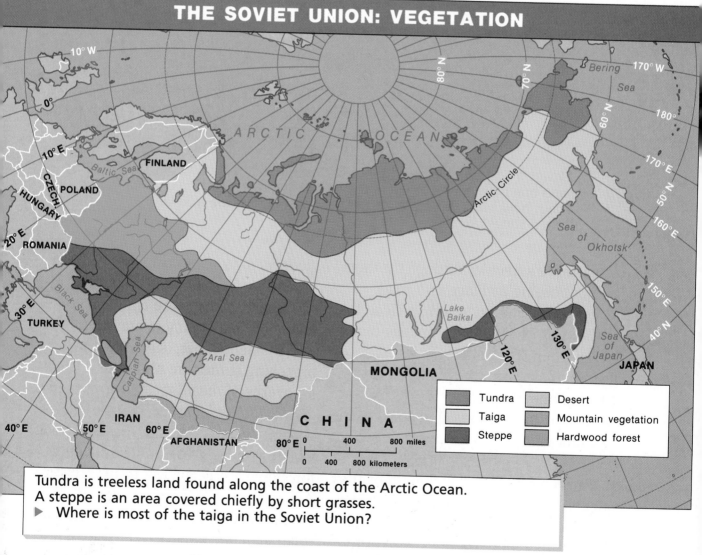

THE SOVIET UNION: VEGETATION

Legend	
Tundra	Desert
Taiga	Mountain vegetation
Steppe	Hardwood forest

Tundra is treeless land found along the coast of the Arctic Ocean.
A steppe is an area covered chiefly by short grasses.
▶ Where is most of the taiga in the Soviet Union?

362

to the huge expanse of forest. There are large areas of the taiga that have hardly been touched by loggers. Why is that so? The timber in the taiga is heavy and hard to move after it has been cut. And in most of the taiga, there are no railroads and few roads.

C. Exploring a Tropical Forest

A Rain Forest The taiga is just one of the major kinds of forests in the world. You read about the forests of the United States in Unit 2. Now let's look briefly at the forests of the tropics.

The main kind of forest found in the tropics is the rain forest. The largest rain forest in the world is in the basin of the Amazon River in South America. Let's make believe that we are going to visit the Amazon Basin.

In the Forest From an airplane, the forest looks like a great, green blanket that stretches as far as the eye can see. The blanket is not smooth. It looks as if many pillows were beneath it, making lumps. What looks like a lumpy, green blanket are the top branches and leaves of the tallest trees. This green blanket is called the canopy (KAN uh pee). It looks the same all year round. Much of the life of the rain forest is found in the canopy layer. Birds, insects, snakes, and monkeys live high above the ground.

In a rain forest, the canopy is so thick that sunlight can't get through. Below the canopy, plants can't grow well because they don't get sunlight. As a result, the ground remains almost clear of plants, and people can easily walk through the forest.

The Amazon River winds through a dense area of rain forest that is located near the city of Iquitos, Peru.
▶ What is the major resource that comes from the rain forest?

After cacao is picked from the trees, the beans, or seeds, are dried in large trays.
▶ What products are made from cacao beans?

D. A Rich Storehouse

Special Woods More and more people are going into the Amazon Basin today. They are drawn there by its rich natural resources. Some special woods, such as mahogany, teak, and ebony, grow only in tropical regions. These beautiful and expensive woods are used to make fine furniture.

Up to now, lumbering has been carried out only in a small way, close to the rivers. Millions of acres of forest have hardly been touched. Now modern machinery is making logging easier.

However, many people want laws passed to protect the rain forest.

Other Resources Timber is not the only thing of value in the forest. From the **cacao** (kuh KAY oh) tree come the seeds from which cocoa and chocolate are made.

On another kind of tree, Brazil nuts grow. Have you ever eaten a Brazil nut? The next time you go to a supermarket, look for these large nuts with rough, dark-brown shells.

LESSON 2 REVIEW

THINK AND WRITE

A. What is special about the taiga of the Soviet Union?

B. Why have trees never been cut in many parts of the taiga?

C. Why do few plants grow on the floor of a rain forest?

D. Why is the Amazon rain forest being explored today?

SKILLS CHECK

MAP SKILL

Find the Amazon River on the map of South America on page 390 of the Atlas. Name four countries in which a part of the Amazon River or its tributaries flows. Name three cities on the Amazon River or one of its tributaries.

Mineral Riches in the Americas

THINK ABOUT WHAT YOU KNOW
What do you think of when you hear about buried treasure?

STUDY THE VOCABULARY

explorer	bauxite
expedition	alloy

FOCUS YOUR READING
What are the chief mineral riches of the Latin American countries?

A. Voyages of Discovery

A Special Year In the history of the world, the year 1992 is special. That year marks exactly 500 years since Christopher Columbus sailed from Spain to the Caribbean Sea. It was a great voyage of discovery.

Leading the Way Christopher Columbus planned to sail west to reach a group of islands called the Indies, off the southeastern coast of Asia. He had hoped to find a water route between Spain and the Indies. The silks, spices, and precious stones of Asia could then be more easily transported to Spain where they could be sold. Spain would become a wealthy nation, and Columbus hoped to become a rich man.

What Columbus and his crew didn't know as they sailed west was that two giant continents—North America and South America—lay between Asia and Europe. It was these continents, not Asia, that Columbus found when he sailed west from Spain in 1492.

On August 3, 1492, Christopher Columbus set sail from Spain on his famous voyage of discovery.
► Which person do you think is Columbus?

The Granger Collection

359

"Little Steven" Soon other Spanish **explorers** came to the lands that Columbus found. An explorer is a person who travels in search of something new. One of the first explorers to travel through Florida, and later through parts of Arizona, New Mexico, and Texas, was a man named Estevanico (es tay vah NEE koh). His name means "Little Steven" in Spanish. In English he probably would have been called Stevie.

During his travels, Estevanico learned about Cíbola (SEE buh luh), the Seven Cities of Gold, from the Native Americans that he met. These fabulous cities were said to be located somewhere north of Mexico. The first explorers to find these cities would be rich beyond their wildest dreams.

Estevanico acted as a scout for an explorer who led an **expedition**, or trip, to search for the Seven Cities of Gold. We do not know if Estevanico ever reached the golden cities. We only know that he was killed near the place where people had hoped to find the Seven Cities of Gold.

B. Mineral Wealth in Modern Latin America

Metals and Gems Several countries of Latin America are famous for mineral wealth, such as gold, silver, and precious gems. Mexico is an important producer of precious metals. It has some of the world's biggest silver mines. These mines make Mexico the world's biggest producer of silver.

The finest emeralds in the world are found in Colombia, a country on the continent of South America. Emeralds are valuable green stones that are used in making jewelry.

THE WORLD: WHERE COPPER IS LOCATED

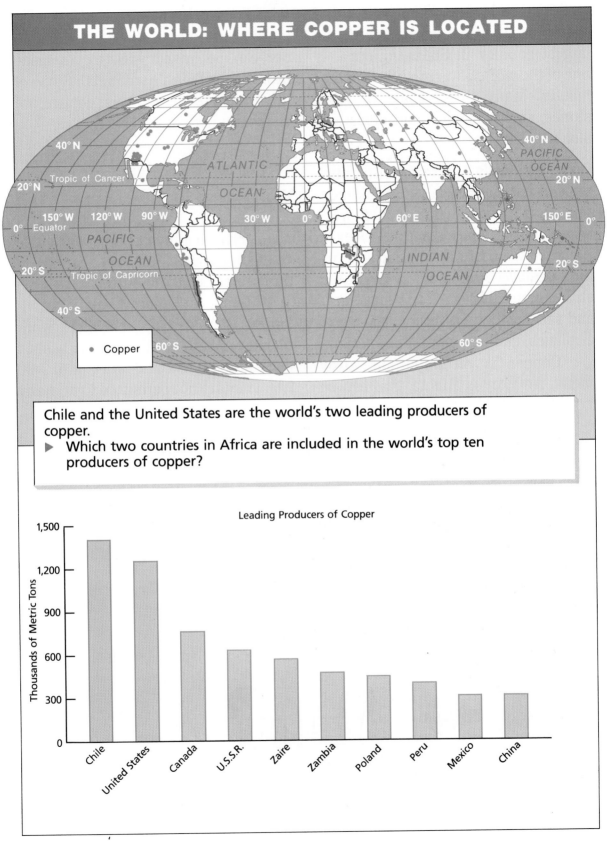

- Copper

Chile and the United States are the world's two leading producers of copper.
▶ Which two countries in Africa are included in the world's top ten producers of copper?

Leading Producers of Copper

	Thousands of Metric Tons

Chile · United States · Canada · U.S.S.R. · Zaire · Zambia · Poland · Peru · Mexico · China

Diamonds are among the most costly jewels in the world. Brazil, the largest country in South America, is one of the world's top producers of diamonds. Many other kinds of gemstones, such as rubies and opals, are also found in Brazil.

Other Minerals There are other minerals in Latin America that are important, too. These minerals include iron, copper, tin, and **bauxite** (BAWKS eyt). Bauxite is the ore from which aluminum is made. Aluminum is a light but strong metal that is used to make pots and pans, containers for foods, parts of airplanes, and many other products.

Copper is an important **alloy** metal. An alloy is a metal that can be mixed with other metals to make a new, more useful metal. For example, copper can be mixed with tin to make bronze, which is a hard metal. Some of the products made from copper are shown on the chart below.

C. Mining in Bolivia

Working in a Tin Mine Pedro's father works in a tin mine in Oruro (aw ROOR oh), a city on a high plateau in Bolivia (buh LIHV ee uh). Bolivia is a country in the western part of South America.

Mining tin is hard work, and conditions in the mines make the work seem even harder. Miners usually start work at 6:00 A.M. and work until 3:00 P.M. They are not permitted to take any

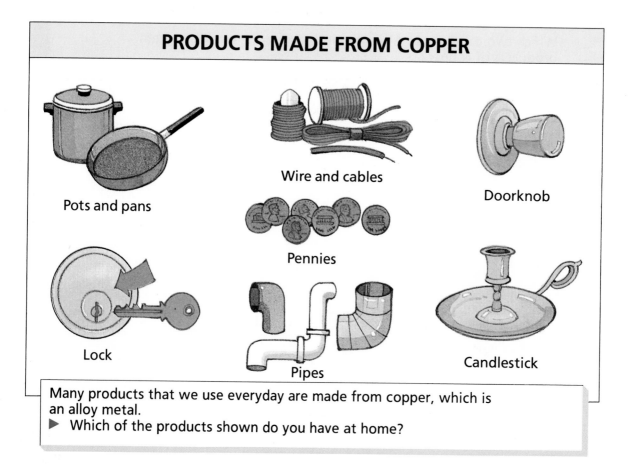

PRODUCTS MADE FROM COPPER

Pots and pans

Wire and cables

Doorknob

Pennies

Lock

Pipes

Candlestick

Many products that we use everyday are made from copper, which is an alloy metal.
▶ Which of the products shown do you have at home?

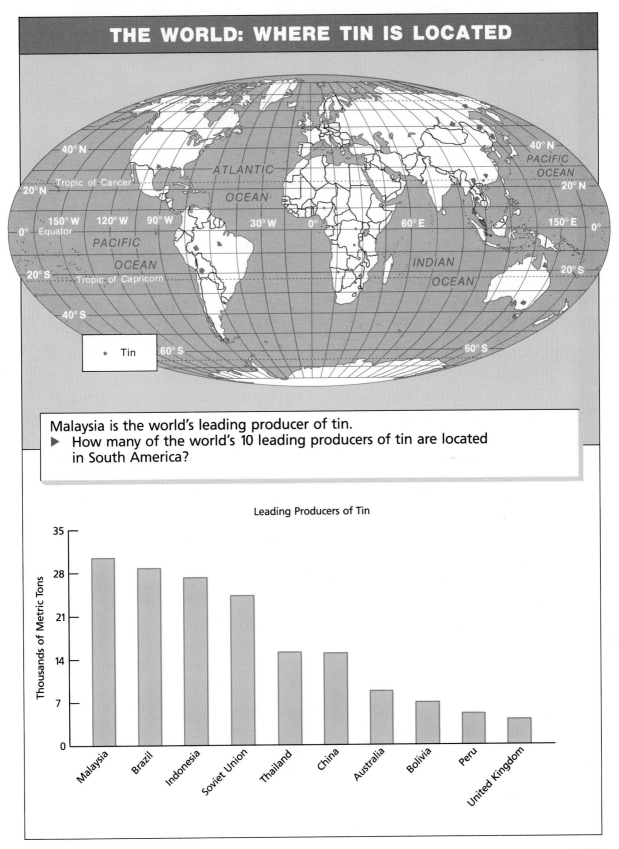

THE WORLD: WHERE TIN IS LOCATED

- Tin

Malaysia is the world's leading producer of tin.
▶ How many of the world's 10 leading producers of tin are located in South America?

Leading Producers of Tin

Thousands of Metric Tons

Malaysia, Brazil, Indonesia, Soviet Union, Thailand, China, Australia, Bolivia, Peru, United Kingdom

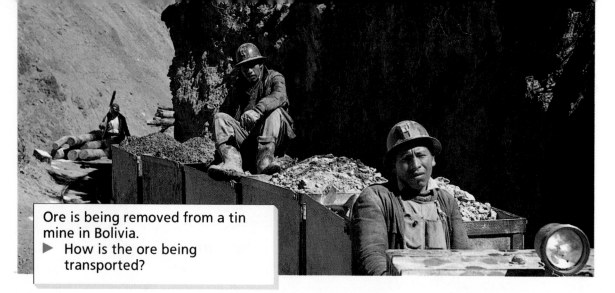

Ore is being removed from a tin mine in Bolivia.
▶ How is the ore being transported?

food into the mine, so they are unable to eat during the work day. The food would be spoiled by all the dust and dirt in the mine.

Living in Oruro Pedro's father earns only a few dollars each day. This is not enough to buy all the things that Pedro's family needs. They live in a small house that has only three rooms. The house doesn't have electricity or running water. Every day, Pedro carries large buckets of water from the public well to his house.

Pedro also goes to the grocery store every morning. He often has to join a long line of people who are waiting to get the groceries they need. The store where Pedro's family shops is owned by the mining company.

Sometimes when the line is very long, Pedro has to miss school. This makes his parents unhappy because they want him to get a good education. They hope that someday Pedro will have a job different from mining.

Many miners in Oruro have lost their jobs in recent years, and Pedro's father might lose his job, too. If that happens, the family might have to move to La Paz, the capital city of Bolivia. There, Pedro's father and mother might be able to find work. Pedro hopes that life in his city will improve, because he would rather continue to live in Oruro.

LESSON **3** *REVIEW*

THINK AND WRITE

A. Why is the year 1992 an important year to all Americans?

B. Why do we call Latin America a mineral-rich region?

C. What problems do people who work in the tin mines of Bolivia face every day?

SKILLS CHECK

THINKING SKILL
Christopher Columbus looked for an all-water route from Spain to the Indies, and he found the Americas. Today, astronauts look down on the earth from space. In the future, what surprises about our earth might astronauts find?

Japan—a Country with Few Natural Resources

THINK ABOUT WHAT YOU KNOW

Japan is famous for making automobiles and electronic equipment. Name as many Japanese products as you can.

STUDY THE VOCABULARY

kelp human resource

FOCUS YOUR READING

How do the Japanese people produce so many products with so few natural resources?

A. A Nation of Islands

A Crowded Place The island nation of Japan is located off the east coast of Asia. Four main islands and hundreds of smaller islands make up the country.

More than 123,000,000 people live in Japan. That's about one half the population of the United States. Can you imagine half of all the people in the United States living in an area the size of Montana? You can see that Japan is very densely populated.

Japan is also a mountainous country. About 200 of the mountains are volcanoes. Many of the volcanoes are active. Because there are so many mountains, it is hard for Japanese farmers to grow enough food to feed their people. Less than one seventh of the land is good for farming. The rest is too rocky and mountainous to farm.

Feeding the Nation In Japan people use terrace farming to grow rice, which is their main food. By using terrace farms, Japanese farmers can grow all the rice their country needs.

The Japanese people have also turned to the sea as a source of food. Like the people of Iceland, the Japanese catch and eat a lot of fish. They have more fishing boats than any other nation in the world.

The Japanese eat fish that has been cooked, fish that has been dried and salted, and even fish that is raw. Japanese fishing boats catch much more fish than their country needs. So Japan exports fish to the rest of the

Tea fields cover a hillside on the island of Honshu in Japan.
▶ Do you think this tea will be picked by hand or by machine?

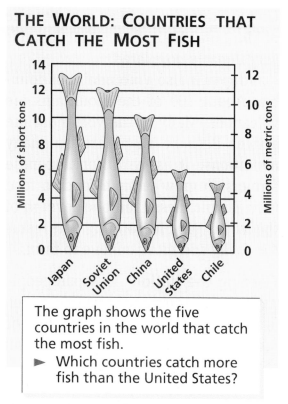

THE WORLD: COUNTRIES THAT CATCH THE MOST FISH

The graph shows the five countries in the world that catch the most fish.

► Which countries catch more fish than the United States?

world. Look at the bar graph on this page. About how much more fish is caught by Japanese fishers than by United States' fishers?

Fish is not the only product of the sea that the Japanese eat. They also enjoy **kelp**, or seaweed, which is made into everything from soup to biscuits. Still, Japan has to import much of its food from other countries.

B. A Country with Many Industries

Japan is one of the leading industrial nations in the world. What is amazing is that Japan has become an important exporter of industrial products in only about 30 years. Japan is now the world leader in the electronics

industry. Almost all of the televisions that Americans buy are made in Japan. And many Japanese calculators and radios are sold everywhere.

Millions of Japanese automobiles are found on the highways of the United States. Japan is also a leader in shipbuilding. Its shipyards build the largest ships in the world—the huge supertankers that carry oil to the industrial nations of the world.

C. Importing Natural Resources

A Lack of Coal and Oil You might think that Japan has been so successful in industry and trade because it has many natural resources. In fact, Japan lacks many natural resources that are necessary for industry.

One product that all industrial nations need to produce is steel. Steel is used in making many of the things Japan exports, including automobiles and ships. The main ingredient in steel is iron ore. Japan has almost no iron ore of its own. So it must import iron ore from other countries.

As you know, coal is also needed to make steel. Yet Japan has very little coal. Almost all of the coal used in Japanese steel plants must be imported. Much of the coal that Japan imports comes from mines in West Virginia and Pennsylvania.

Another product that every industrial nation uses a lot of every day is petroleum. Again, Japan produces almost none. Over 99 percent of Japan's petroleum is imported.

Forests More than half of Japan is covered with forests. Yet timber ranks second after petroleum on Japan's list of imports. Why, you might wonder, is that so? One reason for importing timber is that most of the forests in Japan are high in the mountains. Only about one fourth of the timber can be easily reached for cutting.

The second reason for importing timber is that much of Japan's forest land is protected from cutting by the government. The government tries to conserve, or save, a certain amount of the timber that is available for cutting. So Japan imports about half of the timber it needs. Much of the timber is imported from Canada.

D. Another Resource in Japan

Japan's People How, you might be asking yourself, has Japan been so successful when it has so few natural resources? Japan has one important kind of resource—a **human resource**. A human resource is people, especially people who use their knowledgde and skill to improve life for everyone.

The Japanese people are good at working together for a common goal. They take great pride in their work and encourage one another to work hard. Many factories display signs with this saying: "Only half right is always half wrong." What does this saying mean?

In Japan many workers have exercise breaks everyday.
► How, do you think, do these exercise breaks help the workers?

These Japanese children are enjoying an outing in a park near their school.
▶ What do you think they might be painting?

E. Going to School in Japan

When Japanese children begin school at age six, they can look forward to 12 hard years of school. Japanese students have classes until about three o'clock in the afternoon on weekdays, but they also go to school from eight to noon on Saturdays.

Grade-school students have one or two hours of homework every night. As students go into junior high and high school, they have more and more homework. In addition, most Japanese students take extra classes in the afternoons after school.

The most common subjects children study after school are math and English. Japanese children study English because English is the language used in international trade. Most Japanese companies want employees who are able to speak and write English.

Many American schools are trying to understand Japanese ways better. They hope to learn things from Japan.

LESSON **4** REVIEW

THINK AND WRITE

A. Why does Japan have to import so much food?

B. What are three important Japanese industries?

C. How does Japan get most of its natural resources?

D. What would you say is Japan's most important resource?

E. In what ways is school in Japan like your school?

SKILLS CHECK

WRITING SKILL

Reread section D on page 373. Then write two or three slogans to encourage workers or students to work together or to work harder.

USING THE VOCABULARY

geyser bauxite
trawler alloy
factory ship kelp
coniferous human
taiga resource
expedition

On a separate sheet of paper, write the word or words from the list above that best complete each sentence.

1. In Japan, _____ is made into many kinds of foods.
2. Without _____, we would not be able to have aluminum pots and pans.
3. A _____ sends up columns of hot steam and water.
4. The Soviet Union's large northern forests are filled mostly with _____, or cone-bearing, trees.
5. Copper is an _____ metal that can be mixed with tin to make bronze.
6. Many workers on a _____ are neither sailors nor fishers.
7. The Soviet Union's _____ is the world's biggest forest.
8. With their knowledge and skill, people are a great _____ and can improve life for everyone.
9. Estevanico went on an _____, hoping to find the Seven Cities of Gold.
10. A radio is standard equipment on a _____.

REMEMBERING WHAT YOU READ

On a separate sheet of paper, answer the questions in complete sentences.

1. How was Iceland formed?
2. What happens to most of the cod caught off Iceland?
3. Name two high-tech methods of locating huge numbers of fish.
4. How do the animals of the taiga protect themselves against the harsh winters?
5. How has the taiga for centuries served as a great natural resource?
6. In what layer of the rain forest is much of its wildlife found?
7. What country is the world's largest producer of silver?
8. In what Latin American countries are there large iron mines?
9. What kind of farming is used to grow the main food of Japan?
10. Why does Japan import a great deal of timber?

TYING LANGUAGE ARTS TO SOCIAL STUDIES

In this chapter you read that people are a great resource—a human resource. Write a short poem, story, or report about a person or kind of person you consider to be a great human resource. Remember, human resources are people who make life better for others.

THINKING CRITICALLY

On a separate sheet of paper, answer the following questions in complete sentences.

1. Describe one way in which high-tech fishing is good and one way in which it might be bad.
2. How might building railroads and more roads in the taiga change the way that the lumbering industry is carried out in the Soviet Union?
3. Why do many people want laws passed to protect the rain forest?
4. Why, do you think, does Pedro want to stay in Oruro rather than move to La Paz? Do you agree with him?
5. What might happen if other countries stopped selling iron ore to Japan?

SUMMARIZING THE CHAPTER

Copy this graphic organizer on a separate sheet of paper. Under the main idea for each lesson, write four facts that support the idea.

CHAPTER THEME Natural resources are important not only because they provide us with food, warmth, shelter, and energy but also because of the millions of products that are made from them.

LESSON 1

The people of Iceland depend for jobs, food, and national income on fish.

1. _____ 3. _____
2. _____ 4. _____

LESSON 3

Mexico and several countries of South America have important natural resources.

1. _____ 3. _____
2. _____ 4. _____

LESSON 2

One of the main natural resources of both the Soviet Union and the Amazon Basin is the forest land.

1. _____ 3. _____
2. _____ 4. _____

LESSON 4

Japan imports enough resources from other countries to allow it to become a leading industrial country.

1. _____ 3. _____
2. _____ 4. _____

COOPERATIVE LEARNING

In Unit 3 you learned about places that are far distant from the United States. Now you are going to work with some of your classmates to prepare a talk show that will have guests from at least three of these places—Puerto Rico, the Netherlands, Australia, Bolivia, and Japan.

REMEMBER TO:
- Give your ideas.
- Listen to others' ideas.
- Plan your work with the group.
- Present your project.
- Discuss how your group worked.

PROJECT

• Meet with your group and decide what you would like to know about people who live in those places. Listen to all the suggestions that are given. Select the topics that your group thinks would make an interesting talk show.

• Decide whether the program is going to be presented with props. If your group wants to have props, choose a group member to be responsible for making or getting the props.

• Work in pairs writing questions to ask each guest as well as answers for the questions. Make use of the classroom or school library to find the answers to questions that are not answered in Unit 3.

• Choose one group member to be the talk show host. The other members of the group will be the guests.

• Rehearse the talk show. This will help all the people in the group feel more comfortable with their parts.

PRESENTATION AND REVIEW

• Present the talk show for your classmates.

• Ask your classmates what they liked best about your talk show. What interesting facts did they learn from the talk show?

• Hold a meeting with your group to talk about your presentation. Decide whether you listened carefully enough to each other as you prepared the talk show. What advice would we give to a group that was going to prepare a talk show?

A. WHY DO I NEED THIS SKILL?

One thing sometimes causes something else to happen. For example, an earthquake in California in 1989 caused a bridge to collapse. We call this cause and effect. The cause of what happened was the earthquake. The effect was the collapse of the bridge. Identifying cause and effect relationships is part of thinking clearly. When you understand cause-and-effect relationships, you are better able to solve problems.

B. LEARNING THE SKILL

Read the following sentences.

It is warm in Puerto Rico year round. In the summer the average temperature is about 85°F (29°C), and in the winter the average temperature is about 73°F (23°C). These temperatures make it possible to grow crops all year long.

To find out whether there is a cause-and-effect relationship in what you have just read, ask yourself this question: What is special about farming in Puerto Rico? The answer is that crops are grown in Puerto Rico all year long. That is what is happening. That is the effect of something.

Then ask yourself this question: Why do crops grow in Puerto Rico all year long? Crops grow there because it is warm in Puerto Rico year-round. This is the cause.

C. PRACTICING THE SKILL

Read the following paragraph and then answer the questions below.

Long ago, it might have taken weeks or months to learn about something that happened in a far-off place. Today, news from many parts of the world reaches us within minutes. New technology has improved the ease and speed of communication. This makes our world seem much smaller than it used to seem. These improvements also help to bring people throughout the world closer together.

1. What are some of the changes that have taken place in communication?
2. In what ways has the world changed because of these changes in communication?
3. Which is the cause of the changes in communication?
4. What has been the effect of changes in ways of communicating?

D. APPLYING THE SKILL

The art on this page shows some of the ways that people communicate almost every day. Think how you might use one or two ideas to write a story showing a cause-and-effect relationship.

You might think about something that happened to you recently. Think about how you depended on communication in the situation.

Write two paragraphs about the event. In the first paragraph, describe what happened and explain what caused it. In the second paragraph, describe the effect the event had.

379

A. WHY DO I NEED THIS SKILL?

You cannot possibly remember all the information in every lesson you read in school. But if you can find the main ideas in the lessons you read, remembering will be easier. The main ideas of a lesson are the most important points in the lesson. Being able to find main ideas will also help you understand better what you read.

B. LEARNING THE SKILL

You already know that the lessons in this book are divided into sections. The letters A, B, C, and so on tell where each section of a lesson begins. In addition to a letter, each section has a title. The title tells you what the section is about.

Within the section there often are headings at the beginning of some of the paragraphs in the section. These headings tell you what the most important ideas in the section are. The sentences that follow the headings give you what are called details. Information about the main ideas in a paragraph are the details.

In the next column on this page, you will find a section taken from your textbook. Read the paragraphs carefully. Find the title of the section and the main heading. Find one important detail.

C. *From Zuider Zee to Polderlands*

Making More Land *If you look at the map on page 315, you can see that the Netherlands borders on the North Sea. The North Sea is the part of the Atlantic Ocean that is between the continent of Europe and the British Isles.*

A large, shallow bay once exded well into the Netherlands ʃrom the North Sea. The bay was called the Zuider Zee (ZYE dur Zee). In their search for more farmland, the Dutch decided to reclaim the Zuider Zee. Reclaim means "to bring back to a useful condition."

To help you understand how main ideas and details work together, there is a Main Idea Rocket on page 381. The rocket has a cone and three stages, or parts. Notice that the title of Section C that you just read is in the cone of the rocket. The heading for the first paragraph is in the first stage, or part, of the rocket. One main idea has been written under the first heading. There is space to write a heading in each of the other two stages of the rocket. There is also space to write details under each heading.

C. PRACTICING THE SKILL

On a sheet of paper, draw the Main Idea Rocket. Then turn to page 315 and begin to read Section C. When you have completed reading pages 315 and 316, fill in what is missing in the stages of the rocket. Fill in the headings and the important details. Remember that each stage has one main idea. The details in each stage explain or tell about the main idea. They make the main idea clear.

D. APPLYING THE SKILL

Draw a Main Idea Rocket to help you find the main ideas the next time you read something you want to remember. Be sure to look for the important details. Those details will help you to remember the main ideas.

FROM ZUIDER ZEE TO POLDERLANDS

Making More Land

The Dutch decided to reclaim the land.

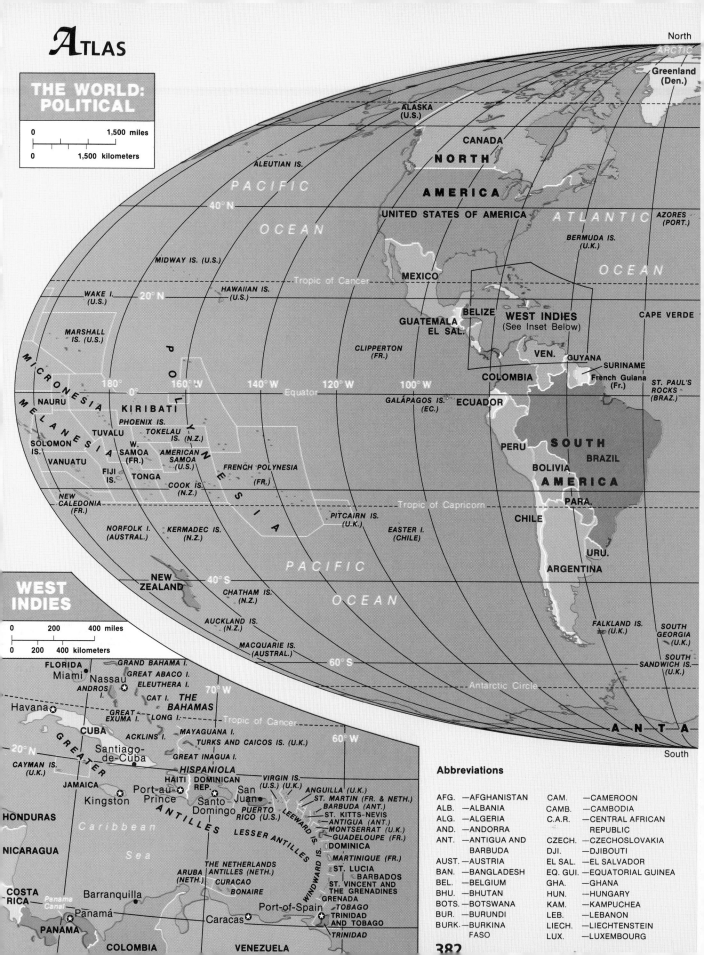

ATLAS

THE WORLD: POLITICAL

| 0 | 1,500 miles |
| 0 | 1,500 kilometers |

WEST INDIES

| 0 | 200 | 400 miles |
| 0 | 200 | 400 kilometers |

North
ARCTIC
Greenland (Den.)

ALASKA (U.S.)
CANADA
NORTH
AMERICA
UNITED STATES OF AMERICA
ATLANTIC
AZORES (PORT.)
BERMUDA IS. (U.K.)
OCEAN

PACIFIC
OCEAN
40° N

MEXICO
BELIZE
WEST INDIES
(See Inset Below)
CAPE VERDE

MIDWAY IS. (U.S.)
Tropic of Cancer
WAKE I. (U.S.)
20° N
HAWAIIAN IS. (U.S.)
GUATEMALA
EL SAL.
VEN.
GUYANA
SURINAME
French Guiana (Fr.)
ST. PAUL'S ROCKS (BRAZ.)

MARSHALL IS. (U.S.)
CLIPPERTON (FR.)
COLOMBIA

MICRONESIA
P
O
L
Y
N
E
S
I
A
180°
0°
160° W
140° W
Equator
120° W
100° W
GALÁPAGOS IS. (EC.)
ECUADOR
MELANESIA
NAURU
KIRIBATI
PERU
SOUTH
BRAZIL

PHOENIX IS.
TUVALU
TOKELAU IS. (N.Z.)
BOLIVIA
AMERICA
SOLOMON IS.
W. SAMOA (FR.)
AMERICAN SAMOA (U.S.)
VANUATU
FIJI IS.
TONGA
FRENCH POLYNESIA (FR.)
PARA.

COOK IS. (N.Z.)
Tropic of Capricorn
CHILE

NEW CALEDONIA (FR.)
PITCAIRN IS. (U.K.)
EASTER I. (CHILE)
URU.
NORFOLK I. (AUSTRAL.)
KERMADEC IS. (N.Z.)
ARGENTINA

PACIFIC
OCEAN
NEW ZEALAND
40° S
CHATHAM IS. (N.Z.)
FALKLAND IS. (U.K.)
SOUTH GEORGIA (U.K.)
AUCKLAND IS. (N.Z.)
MACQUARIE IS. (AUSTRAL.)
60° S
SOUTH SANDWICH IS. (U.K.)
Antarctic Circle
A N T A
South

FLORIDA
Miami
GRAND BAHAMA I.
GREAT ABACO I.
ELEUTHERA I.
Nassau
ANDROS I.
CAT I.
THE BAHAMAS
Havana
GREAT EXUMA I.
LONG I.
Tropic of Cancer
CUBA
70° W
Santiago-de-Cuba
ACKLINS I.
MAYAGUANA I.
TURKS AND CAICOS IS. (U.K.)
60° W
20° N
GREAT INAGUA I.
GREATER
HISPANIOLA
CAYMAN IS. (U.K.)
HAITI
DOMINICAN REP.
VIRGIN IS. (U.S.) (U.K.)
JAMAICA
Port-au-Prince
San Juan
ANGUILLA (U.K.)
ST. MARTIN (FR. & NETH.)
Kingston
Santo Domingo
PUERTO RICO (U.S.)
BARBUDA (ANT.)
ST. KITTS-NEVIS
ANTIGUA (ANT.)
HONDURAS
ANTILLES
LESSER ANTILLES
MONTSERRAT (U.K.)
GUADELOUPE (FR.)
Caribbean
DOMINICA
NICARAGUA
Sea
MARTINIQUE (FR.)
ST. LUCIA
BARBADOS
THE NETHERLANDS ANTILLES (NETH.)
ST. VINCENT AND THE GRENADINES
ARUBA (NETH.)
CURACAO
GRENADA
COSTA RICA
BONAIRE
TOBAGO
Panama Canal
Barranquilla
Port-of-Spain
TRINIDAD AND TOBAGO
PANAMÁ
Panamá
Caracas
TRINIDAD
PANAMA
COLOMBIA
VENEZUELA

Abbreviations

AFG.	—AFGHANISTAN	CAM.	—CAMEROON
ALB.	—ALBANIA	CAMB.	—CAMBODIA
ALG.	—ALGERIA	C.A.R.	—CENTRAL AFRICAN
AND.	—ANDORRA		REPUBLIC
ANT.	—ANTIGUA AND	CZECH.	—CZECHOSLOVAKIA
	BARBUDA	DJI.	—DJIBOUTI
AUST.	—AUSTRIA	EL SAL.	—EL SALVADOR
BAN.	—BANGLADESH	EQ. GUI.	—EQUATORIAL GUINEA
BEL.	—BELGIUM	GHA.	—GHANA
BHU.	—BHUTAN	HUN.	—HUNGARY
BOTS.	—BOTSWANA	KAM.	—KAMPUCHEA
BUR.	—BURUNDI	LEB.	—LEBANON
BURK.	—BURKINA	LIECH.	—LIECHTENSTEIN
	FASO	LUX.	—LUXEMBOURG

382

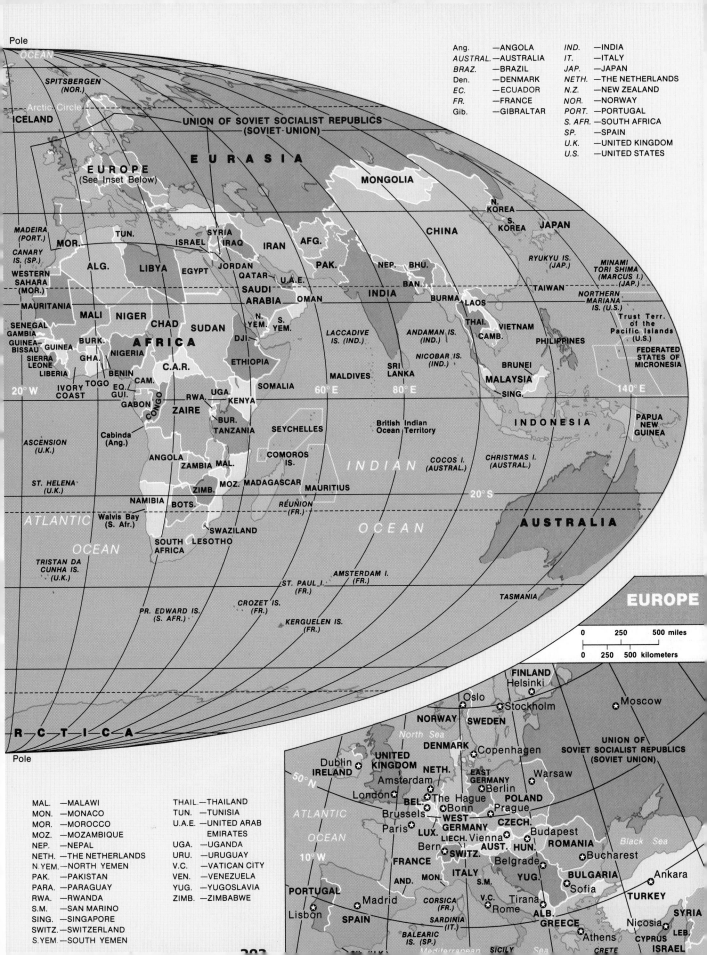

Pole

OCEAN

SPITSBERGEN
(NOR.)

Arctic Circle

ICELAND

UNION OF SOVIET SOCIALIST REPUBLICS
(SOVIET UNION)

EUROPE
(See Inset Below)

E U R A S I A

MONGOLIA

N.
KOREA
S.
KOREA

JAPAN

MADEIRA
(PORT.)

TUN.

SYRIA

CHINA

CANARY
IS. (SP.)

MOR.

ISRAEL

IRAQ

IRAN

AFG.

RYUKYU IS.
(JAP.)

MINAMI
TORI SHIMA
(MARCUS I.)
(JAP.)

WESTERN
SAHARA
(MOR.)

ALG.

LIBYA

EGYPT

JORDAN

QATAR

PAK.

NEP.

BHU.

TAIWAN

NORTHERN
MARIANA
IS. (U.S.)

U.A.E.

BAN.

Trust Terr.
of the
Pacific Islands
(U.S.)

MAURITANIA

SAUDI
ARABIA

OMAN

INDIA

BURMA

LAOS

MALI

NIGER

CHAD

SUDAN

N.
YEM.

S.
YEM.

THAI.

VIETNAM

CAMB.

FEDERATED
STATES OF
MICRONESIA

SENEGAL

GAMBIA

BURK.

AFRICA

NIGERIA

DJI.

LACCADIVE
IS. (IND.)

ANDAMAN IS.
(IND.)

PHILIPPINES

GUINEA-
BISSAU

GUINEA

GHA.

C.A.R.

ETHIOPIA

NICOBAR IS.
(IND.)

BRUNEI

SIERRA
LEONE

BENIN

SRI
LANKA

MALAYSIA

LIBERIA

IVORY
COAST

TOGO

EQ.
GUI.

CAM.

MALDIVES

SING.

20° W

GABON

RWA.

UGA.

KENYA

SOMALIA

60° E

80° E

140° E

PAPUA
NEW
GUINEA

CONGO

ZAIRE

BUR.

TANZANIA

SEYCHELLES

I N D O N E S I A

Cabinda
(Ang.)

ASCENSION
(U.K.)

ANGOLA

ZAMBIA

MAL.

COMOROS
IS.

British Indian
Ocean Territory

I N D I A N

COCOS I.
(AUSTRAL.)

CHRISTMAS I.
(AUSTRAL.)

ST. HELENA
(U.K.)

ZIMB.

MOZ.

MADAGASCAR

MAURITIUS

NAMIBIA

BOTS.

RÉUNION
(FR.)

20° S

A U S T R A L I A

ATLANTIC

Walvis Bay
(S. Afr.)

SWAZILAND

O C E A N

OCEAN

SOUTH
AFRICA

LESOTHO

TRISTAN DA
CUNHA IS.
(U.K.)

AMSTERDAM I.
(FR.)

ST. PAUL I.
(FR.)

PR. EDWARD IS.
(S. AFR.)

CROZET IS.
(FR.)

KERGUELEN IS.
(FR.)

TASMANIA

R — C — T — I — C — A

Pole

Ang.	—ANGOLA	IND.	—INDIA
AUSTRAL.	—AUSTRALIA	IT.	—ITALY
BRAZ.	—BRAZIL	JAP.	—JAPAN
Den.	—DENMARK	NETH.	—THE NETHERLANDS
EC.	—ECUADOR	N.Z.	—NEW ZEALAND
FR.	—FRANCE	NOR.	—NORWAY
Gib.	—GIBRALTAR	PORT.	—PORTUGAL
		S. AFR.	—SOUTH AFRICA
		SP.	—SPAIN
		U.K.	—UNITED KINGDOM
		U.S.	—UNITED STATES

MAL.	—MALAWI	THAIL.	—THAILAND
MON.	—MONACO	TUN.	—TUNISIA
MOR.	—MOROCCO	U.A.E.	—UNITED ARAB
MOZ.	—MOZAMBIQUE		EMIRATES
NEP.	—NEPAL	UGA.	—UGANDA
NETH.	—THE NETHERLANDS	URU.	—URUGUAY
N.YEM.	—NORTH YEMEN	V.C.	—VATICAN CITY
PAK.	—PAKISTAN	VEN.	—VENEZUELA
PARA.	—PARAGUAY	YUG.	—YUGOSLAVIA
RWA.	—RWANDA	ZIMB.	—ZIMBABWE
S.M.	—SAN MARINO		
SING.	—SINGAPORE		
SWITZ.	—SWITZERLAND		
S.YEM.	—SOUTH YEMEN		

EUROPE

| 0 | 250 | 500 miles |
| 0 | 250 | 500 kilometers |

FINLAND
Helsinki

Oslo

Stockholm

Moscow

NORWAY

SWEDEN

North Sea

DENMARK

Copenhagen

UNION OF
SOVIET SOCIALIST REPUBLICS
(SOVIET UNION)

Dublin

UNITED
KINGDOM

NETH.

EAST
GERMANY

Warsaw

IRELAND

Amsterdam

Berlin

London

BEL.

The Hague

POLAND

ATLANTIC

Brussels

Bonn

WEST
GERMANY

Prague

CZECH.

Paris

LUX.

LIECH.

Vienna

Budapest

OCEAN

10° W

50° N

FRANCE

Bern

SWITZ.

AUST.

HUN.

ROMANIA

Bucharest

Belgrade

AND.

MON.

ITALY

S.M.

YUG.

BULGARIA

Ankara

PORTUGAL

V.C.

Tirana

Sofia

Lisbon

Madrid

CORSICA
(FR.)

Rome

ALB.

TURKEY

SYRIA

SPAIN

SARDINIA
(IT.)

GREECE

Nicosia

LEB.

BALEARIC
IS. (SP.)

SICILY

Athens

CYPRUS

ISRAEL

Mediterranean   Sea

CRETE

ASIA

ARCTIC OCEAN

Barrow

ALASKA (U.S.)

Bering Sea

Fairbanks

Anchorage

Beaufort Sea

Dawson

Thule

Greenland (Den.)

ICELAND

Pond Inlet

Baffin Bay

Gulf of Alaska

Juneau

Port Radium

Great Bear Lake

Arctic Circle

Godthaab

150° W

50° N

Great Slave Lake

Labrador Sea

Churchill

Hudson Bay

PACIFIC

Edmonton

Goose Bay

Vancouver

C A N A D A

Victoria

Calgary

OCEAN

Seattle

Seven Islands

Gander St. John's

Portland

Regina

Lake Winnipeg

Columbia R.

Spokane

40° N

Quebec

Halifax

Winnipeg

Missouri R.

Montreal

130° W

Great Lakes

Minneapolis

St. Paul

Ottawa

Great Salt Lake

Milwaukee

Toronto

San Francisco

Salt Lake City

Omaha

Detroit

Buffalo

Boston

Denver

Chicago

Cleveland

New York

UNITED STATES OF AMERICA

Los Angeles

Pittsburgh

Philadelphia

30° N

Kansas City

Cincinnati

Baltimore

San Diego

St. Louis

Washington

Phoenix

Ohio R.

Norfolk

Arkansas R.

ATLANTIC

El Paso

Memphis

GUADALUPE I. (MEX.)

BERMUDA IS. (U.K.)

Dallas

Atlanta

Mississippi R.

OCEAN

Houston

San Antonio

New Orleans

Gulf of California

Abbreviations

Den. —DENMARK
FR. —FRANCE
NETH. —THE NETHERLANDS
MEX. —MEXICO
U.K. —UNITED KINGDOM
U.S. —UNITED STATES

Monterrey

GRAND BAHAMA I.

Miami

GREAT ABACO I.

M E X I C O

Gulf of Mexico

Nassau

ELEUTHERA I.

CAT I.

THE BAHAMAS

Tropic of Cancer

ANDROS I.

Havana

GREAT EXUMA I.

LONG I.

Guadalajara

CUBA

ACKLINS I.

MAYAGUANA I.

PUERTO RICO (U.S.)

Mexico City

Santiago-de-Cuba

GREAT INAGUA I.

VIRGIN IS. (U.S.&U.K.)

Orizaba

CAYMAN IS. (U.K.)

DOMINICAN REPUBLIC

HAITI

NORTH AMERICA: POLITICAL

Belmopan

JAMAICA

Port-au-Prince

Santo Domingo

ANTIGUA & BARBUDA

GUATEMALA

BELIZE

Kingston

ST. KITTS-NEVIS

GUADELOUPE (FR.)

⊗ National capitals

Guatemala

HONDURAS

Caribbean Sea

DOMINICA

MARTINIQUE (FR.)

• Other cities

San Salvador

Tegucigalpa

NETH. ANTILLES (NETH.)

ST. LUCIA

EL SALVADOR

NICARAGUA

ST. VINCENT AND THE GRENADINES

0   250   500 miles

ARUBA (NETH.)

GRENADA

0   250   500 kilometers

Managua

San José

Panama Canal

TRINIDAD AND TOBAGO

384

COSTA RICA

Panamá

SOUTH AMERICA

0°

Equator

100° W

90° W

PANAMA

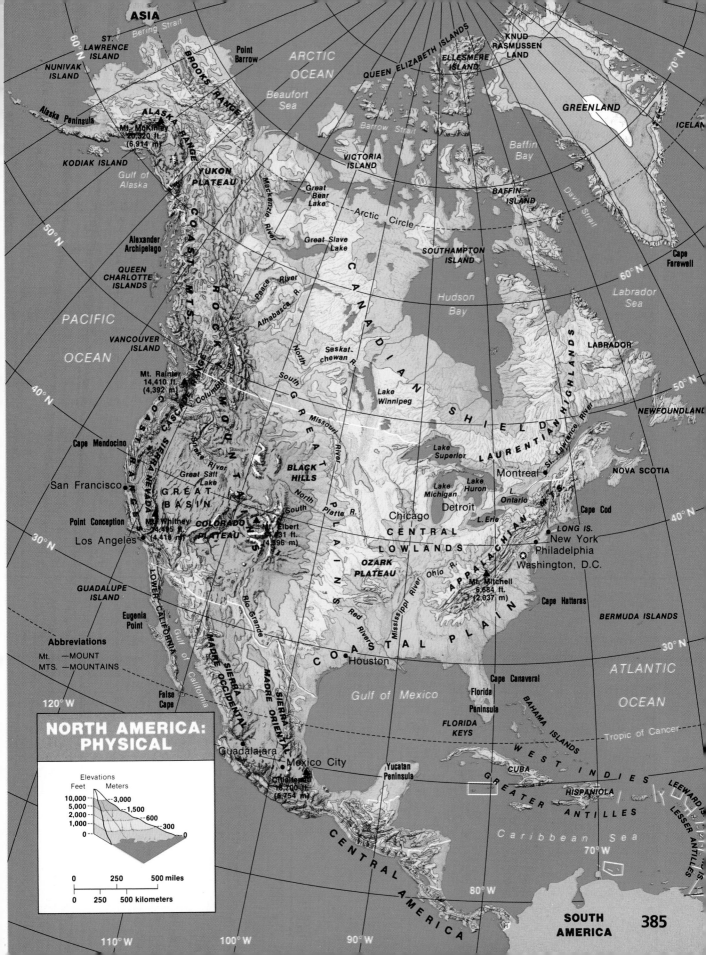

CANADA

6 A.M.

Seattle
WASHINGTON
Olympia
Spokane

Mountain Time Zone

7 A.M.

Central Time Zone

8 A.M.

45° N

Portland
Columbia   River
Salem
Eugene

Great Falls
Helena ⊛
MONTANA
Missouri   River
Billings

Grand Forks
NORTH DAKOTA
Bismarck ⊛
Fargo

OREGON

IDAHO
Boise ⊛
Snake
River
Idaho Falls
Pocatello

WYOMING
Casper

SOUTH DAKOTA
Rapid City
Pierre ⊛
Sioux Falls

NEVADA

Great
Salt
Lake

Sacramento ⊛
Reno
Carson City
West Valley
Salt Lake
City ⊛
Provo

Laramie
Cheyenne ⊛

NEBRASKA
Grand Island
Omaha ⊛
Lincoln

Oakland
San Francisco
San Jose

UTAH

Denver ⊛ Aurora
COLORADO
Colorado
Springs

Topeka ⊛

Fresno

35° N

CALIFORNIA
Las
Vegas
Colorado   River

KANSAS
Wichita

Los Angeles   Anaheim
Long Beach   Riverside
Santa Ana

ARIZONA
Albuquerque
Santa Fe ⊛

Tulsa
OKLAHOMA
Oklahoma City ⊛

San Diego

Phoenix ⊛
Mesa

NEW MEXICO

Lawton
Red   River

30° N
120° W

Tucson

Las Cruces
El Paso

Arlington
Fort Worth   Dallas
Brazos   River

TEXAS

PACIFIC

OCEAN

HAWAII
Kailua
Pearl City Honolulu ⊛
4 A.M.

ARCTIC   OCEAN

Alaska Time Zone

5 A.M.

Pacific
Time Zone

Austin ⊛

U.S.S.R.

20° N
PACIFIC
OCEAN

Yukon

6 A.M.
CANADA

MEXICO

Houston

0   100 miles
0   100 kilometers
160° W   155° W

Fairbanks

ALASKA

Rio
Grande

San Antonio

Corpus
Christi

180°

55° N

0   200 miles
0   200 kilometers

Anchorage

Juneau ⊛

4 A.M.
170° W

PACIFIC   OCEAN
150° W   140° W

386

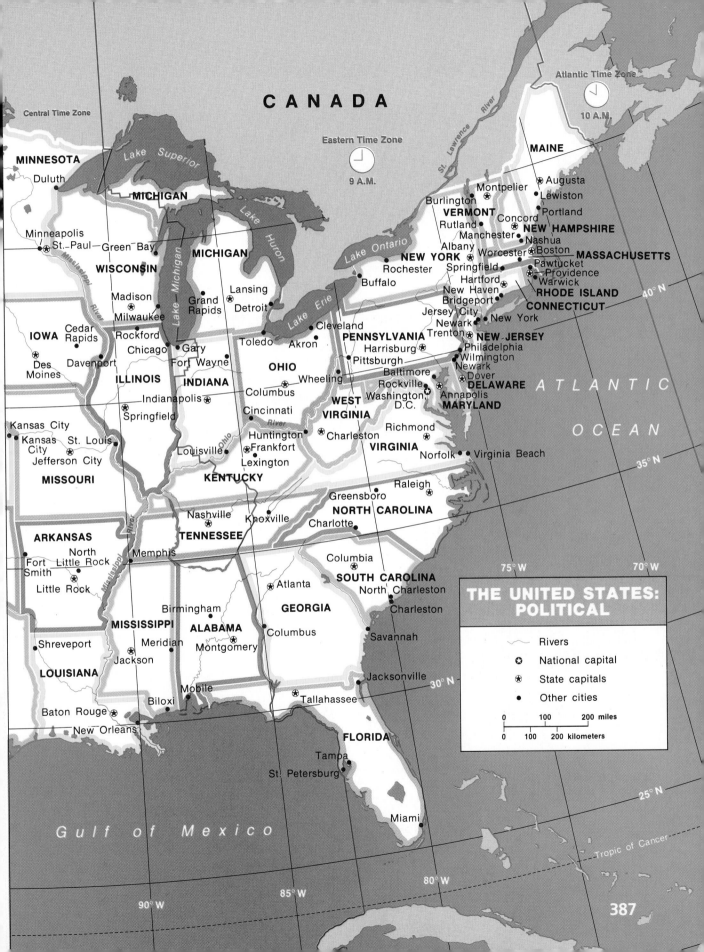

CANADA

Central Time Zone

MINNESOTA
Duluth

Lake Superior

MICHIGAN

Minneapolis
St. Paul — Green Bay
WISCONSIN

Lake Huron

MICHIGAN

Madison
Milwaukee
IOWA
Cedar Rapids
Rockford
Chicago — Gary
Davenport
Des Moines
Fort Wayne
ILLINOIS **INDIANA**
Indianapolis
Springfield

Kansas City
Kansas City
St. Louis
Jefferson City
MISSOURI

Eastern Time Zone
9 A.M.

Lake Michigan

Grand Rapids
Lansing
Detroit

Lake Erie

Cleveland
Akron
Toledo

OHIO
Columbus
Cincinnati

WEST VIRGINIA
Huntington
Charleston
Louisville
Frankfort
Lexington
KENTUCKY

PENNSYLVANIA
Harrisburg
Pittsburgh
Wheeling

St. Lawrence River

Atlantic Time Zone
10 A.M.

MAINE

Augusta
Montpelier
Lewiston
Burlington
Portland
VERMONT
Concord
Rutland
NEW HAMPSHIRE
Manchester
Nashua
Albany
Worcester
Boston
NEW YORK
MASSACHUSETTS
Rochester
Springfield
Pawtucket
Buffalo
Hartford
Providence
New Haven
Warwick
Bridgeport
RHODE ISLAND
Jersey City
CONNECTICUT
Newark
New York
Trenton
NEW JERSEY
Philadelphia
Wilmington
Newark
Baltimore
Dover
Rockville
DELAWARE
Washington, D.C.
Annapolis
MARYLAND

40° N

A T L A N T I C

O C E A N

Richmond

Charleston
VIRGINIA
Norfolk
Virginia Beach

35° N

Raleigh
Greensboro
NORTH CAROLINA
Nashville
Knoxville
Charlotte
TENNESSEE

ARKANSAS
North Little Rock
Fort Smith
Memphis
Little Rock

Columbia
SOUTH CAROLINA
North Charleston
Charleston

75° W   70° W

Atlanta
Birmingham
GEORGIA
MISSISSIPPI
ALABAMA
Columbus
Meridian
Montgomery
LOUISIANA
Jackson
Shreveport

Savannah

Jacksonville
30° N

THE UNITED STATES: POLITICAL

	Rivers
⊛	National capital
⊛	State capitals
•	Other cities

| 0 | 100 | 200 miles |
| 0 | 100 | 200 kilometers |

Mobile
Biloxi
Baton Rouge
New Orleans

Tallahassee

FLORIDA

Tampa
St. Petersburg

25° N

Miami

Gulf of Mexico

Tropic of Cancer

90° W   85° W   80° W

387

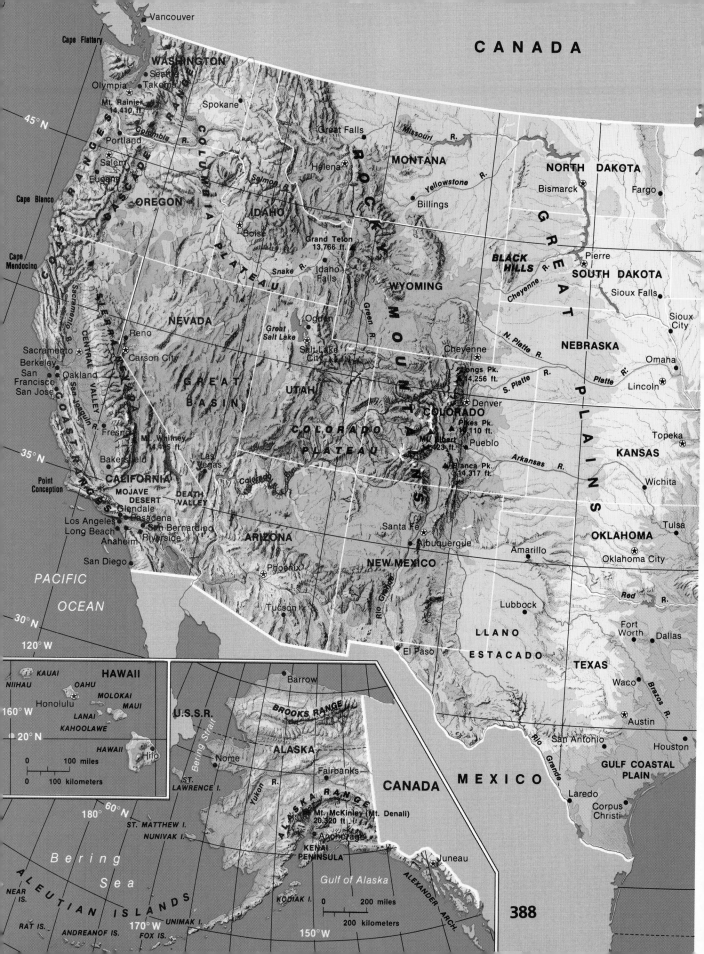

CANADA

45° N

Vancouver
Cape Flattery
WASHINGTON
Olympia • Seattle • Tacoma
Mt. Rainier 14,410 ft.
Spokane
Portland
Salem
Eugene
OREGON
Cape Blanco
Cape Mendocino

COAST RANGES
CASCADE RANGE
COLUMBIA PLATEAU
Columbia R.
Salmon R.

Great Falls
Missouri R.
MONTANA
Helena ⭐
Billings
Yellowstone R.

NORTH DAKOTA
Bismarck ⭐
Fargo

Pierre ⭐
SOUTH DAKOTA
BLACK HILLS
Cheyenne R.
Sioux Falls
Sioux City

G R E A T

IDAHO
Boise ⭐
Grand Teton 13,766 ft.
Snake R.
Idaho Falls
Green R.
WYOMING

ROCKY MOUNTAINS

NEVADA
Reno
Carson City ⭐
Sacramento
Berkeley
San Francisco
Oakland
San Jose
SIERRA NEVADA
CENTRAL VALLEY
San Joaquin R.
Fresno

GREAT BASIN

Ogden
Great Salt Lake
Salt Lake City
UTAH

Cheyenne ⭐
Longs Pk. 14,256 ft.
Denver ⭐
Pikes Pk. 14,110 ft.
Mt. Elbert 14,423 ft.
Pueblo
COLORADO
Blanca Pk. 14,317 ft.
Arkansas R.

N. Platte R.
S. Platte R.
NEBRASKA
Platte R.
Lincoln
Omaha

35° N

Mt. Whitney 14,495 ft.
Bakersfield
CALIFORNIA
Point Conception
MOJAVE DESERT
DEATH VALLEY
Las Vegas

COLORADO PLATEAU
Colorado R.

Santa Fe ⭐
Albuquerque ⭐

Topeka ⭐
KANSAS
Wichita

Tulsa
OKLAHOMA
Oklahoma City ⭐

P L A I N S

PACIFIC OCEAN

120° W

Los Angeles
Glendale Pasadena
Long Beach San Bernardino
Anaheim Riverside
San Diego

Phoenix ⭐
ARIZONA

Tucson

NEW MEXICO

El Paso

Amarillo

Lubbock

LLANO ESTACADO

Fort Worth Dallas
TEXAS
Waco

Red R.

Brazos R.

30° N

HAWAII
KAUAI
NIIHAU OAHU
Honolulu MOLOKAI
LANAI MAUI
KAHOOLAWE
20° N
HAWAII
Hilo
0   100 miles
0   100 kilometers

160° W

Barrow

BROOKS RANGE

U.S.S.R.
Bering Strait
Nome
ST. LAWRENCE I.
ALASKA
Yukon R.
Fairbanks
ALASKA RANGE
Mt. McKinley (Mt. Denali) 20,320 ft.
Anchorage
KENAI PENINSULA

CANADA

MEXICO

Rio Grande

San Antonio
Laredo

GULF COASTAL PLAIN

Corpus Christi

Houston

180°

60° N

ST. MATTHEW I.
NUNIVAK I.

Bering Sea

ALEUTIAN ISLANDS
NEAR IS.
RAT IS.
ANDREANOF IS.
170° W
UNIMAK I.
FOX IS.
150° W

KODIAK I.

Gulf of Alaska

ALEXANDER ARCH.
Juneau ⭐

0   200 miles
0   200 kilometers

388

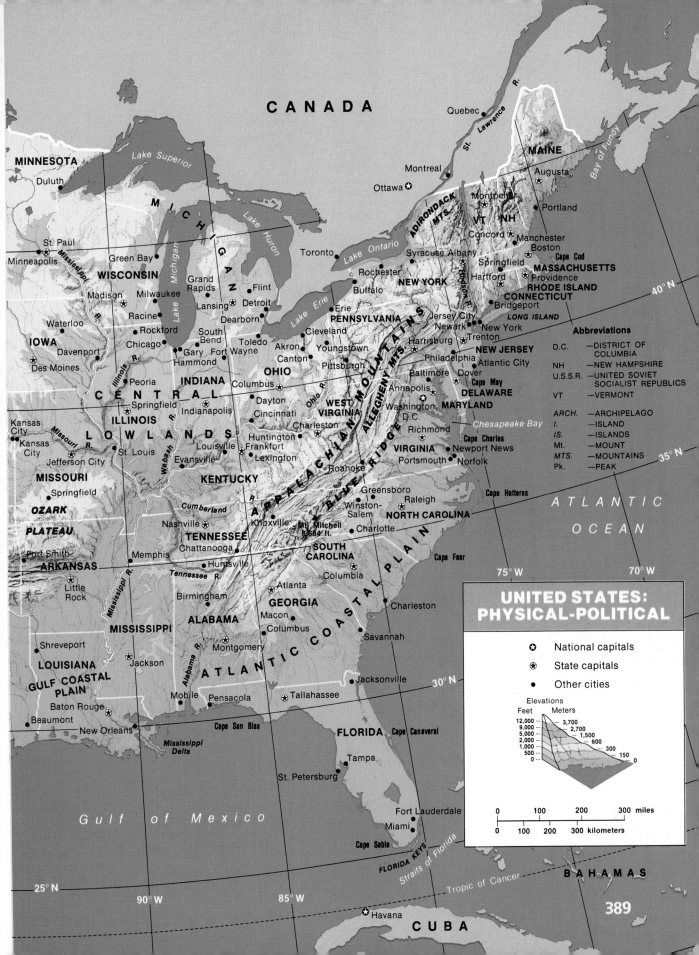

CANADA

Quebec ●

St. Lawrence R.

MINNESOTA
Duluth ●

Lake Superior

M I C H I G A N

Lake Michigan

Lake Huron

Montreal ●

Ottawa ☉

MAINE

Augusta ✇

Montpelier ✇

VT **NH**

Portland ●

ADIRONDACK MTS.

Concord ✇ Manchester ●
Boston ●

MASSACHUSETTS

Cape Cod

● St. Paul
Minneapolis ●

Green Bay ●

Madison ✇
WISCONSIN

Milwaukee ●

Racine ●

Grand
Rapids ●

Lansing ✇

Flint ●

Detroit ●

Dearborn ●

Toronto ●

Lake Ontario

Rochester ●

Buffalo ●

Syracuse ● Albany ✇

NEW YORK

Erie ●

Lake Erie

Springfield ●
Hartford ✇

Providence ✇

RHODE ISLAND

CONNECTICUT
Bridgeport ●

LONG ISLAND

40° N

Waterloo ●

Rockford ●

Chicago ●

IOWA
Davenport ●

Des Moines ✇

South
Bend ●

Gary Fort Wayne ●
Hammond ●

Peoria ●

INDIANA

Cleveland ●

Akron ● Youngstown ●

Canton ●

Toledo ●

OHIO

Columbus ✇

Pittsburgh ●

PENNSYLVANIA

Harrisburg ✇

Philadelphia ●

APPALACHIAN MOUNTAINS

ALLEGHENY MTS.

Jersey City ●
Newark ●
Trenton ✇

New York ●

NEW JERSEY
Atlantic City ●

Baltimore ●
Dover ✇

Cape May

Abbreviations

D.C. —DISTRICT OF
COLUMBIA

NH —NEW HAMPSHIRE

U.S.S.R. —UNITED SOVIET
SOCIALIST REPUBLICS

VT —VERMONT

Kansas
City ●

Kansas
City ●

C E N T R A L

L O W L A N D S

Springfield ✇

ILLINOIS

Indianapolis ✇

Dayton ●

Cincinnati ●

Ohio R.

**WEST
VIRGINIA**

Charleston ✇

Annapolis ✇
Washington, ✇
D.C.

MARYLAND

Richmond ✇

Chesapeake Bay

Cape Charles

DELAWARE

ARCH. —ARCHIPELAGO

I. —ISLAND

IS. —ISLANDS

Mt. —MOUNT

MTS. —MOUNTAINS

Pk. —PEAK

Missouri R.

Jefferson City ✇

St. Louis ●

Wabash R.

Louisville ●

Frankfort ✇

Lexington ●

Huntington ●

Newport News ●
Portsmouth ●

VIRGINIA

Norfolk ●

35° N

MISSOURI

Springfield ●

OZARK

PLATEAU

Evansville ●

KENTUCKY

Cumberland R.

A P P A L A C H I A N

Roanoke ●

Greensboro ●

Raleigh ✇

BLUE RIDGE

Winston-
Salem ●

NORTH CAROLINA

Cape Hatteras

A T L A N T I C

O C E A N

Fort Smith ●

ARKANSAS

Little
Rock ✇

Memphis ●

Nashville ✇

TENNESSEE

Chattanooga ●

Tennessee R.

Huntsville ●

Knoxville ●

Mt. Mitchell
R 684 ft.

Charlotte ●

**SOUTH
CAROLINA**

Columbia ✇

A T L A N T I C   C O A S T A L   P L A I N

Cape Fear

75° W

70° W

**UNITED STATES:
PHYSICAL-POLITICAL**

Atlanta ✇

Birmingham ●

ALABAMA

Macon ●

GEORGIA

Columbus ●

Charleston ●

☉ National capitals

✇ State capitals

● Other cities

MISSISSIPPI

Shreveport ●

LOUISIANA

**GULF COASTAL
PLAIN**

Jackson ✇

Alabama R.

Montgomery ✇

Savannah ●

Jacksonville ●

30° N

Elevations

Feet   Meters

12,000 — 3,700
9,000 — 2,700
5,000 — 1,500
2,000 — 600
1,000 — 300
500 — 150
0 — 0

Baton Rouge ●
Beaumont ●

New Orleans ●

Mobile ●

Cape San Blas

Mississippi
Delta

Pensacola ●

Tallahassee ✇

FLORIDA Cape Canaveral

0   100   200   300 miles

0 100 200 300 kilometers

G u l f   o f   M e x i c o

Tampa ●

St. Petersburg ●

Fort Lauderdale ●

Miami ●

25° N

Cape Sable

FLORIDA KEYS

Straits of Florida

90° W

85° W

Tropic of Cancer

BAHAMAS

389

☉ Havana

CUBA

Barranquilla
Cartagena
Maracaibo
Valencia
Caracas
Barquisimeto
Cúcuta
San Cristóbal
Medellín
Bucaramanga
Bogotá
Cali

VENEZUELA
GUYANA
Georgetown
Paramaribo
SURINAME
Cayenne
French Guiana (Fr.)

COLOMBIA

MALPELO I. (COL.)

River
Orinoco

Quito
ECUADOR
Guayaquil
Iquitos

0°
Equator

Belém
São Luis
Manaus
River
Amazon

Fortaleza

PERU

BRAZIL

Trujillo

10°S

Callao
Lima
Cuzco
Lake Titicaca
Arequipa

Recife
Maceió

Salvador

BOLIVIA
La Paz

Sucre

Brasília
(Federal District)

Belo Horizonte

PACIFIC

20°S

Chuquicamata

PARAGUAY

Rio de Janeiro
São Paulo
Niterói
Santos

OCEAN

Antofagasta

Asunción

Curitiba

Tropic of Capricorn

SAN FELIX I. *SAN AMBROSIO I.*
(CHILE) *(CHILE)*

Tucumán

C
H
I
L
E

Paraná
River

ATLANTIC

Pôrto Alegre

Córdoba
Santa
Fe
Paraná

URUGUAY

30°S

Valparaiso
Santiago

Rosario
Buenos Aires
La Plata

Montevideo

OCEAN

JUAN FERNÁNDEZ IS.
(CHILE)
Concepción

ARGENTINA

Rio de la Plata

Bahía Blanca
Mar del Plata

40°S

50°S
390

FALKLAND IS. (U.K.)
(MALVINAS IS.)

Strait of
Magellan

Punta Arenas

90°W   80°W   70°W   60°W   50°W   40°W   30°W

10°N

SOUTH AMERICA: POLITICAL

⊛ National capitals
• Other cities

0   500 miles
0   500 kilometers

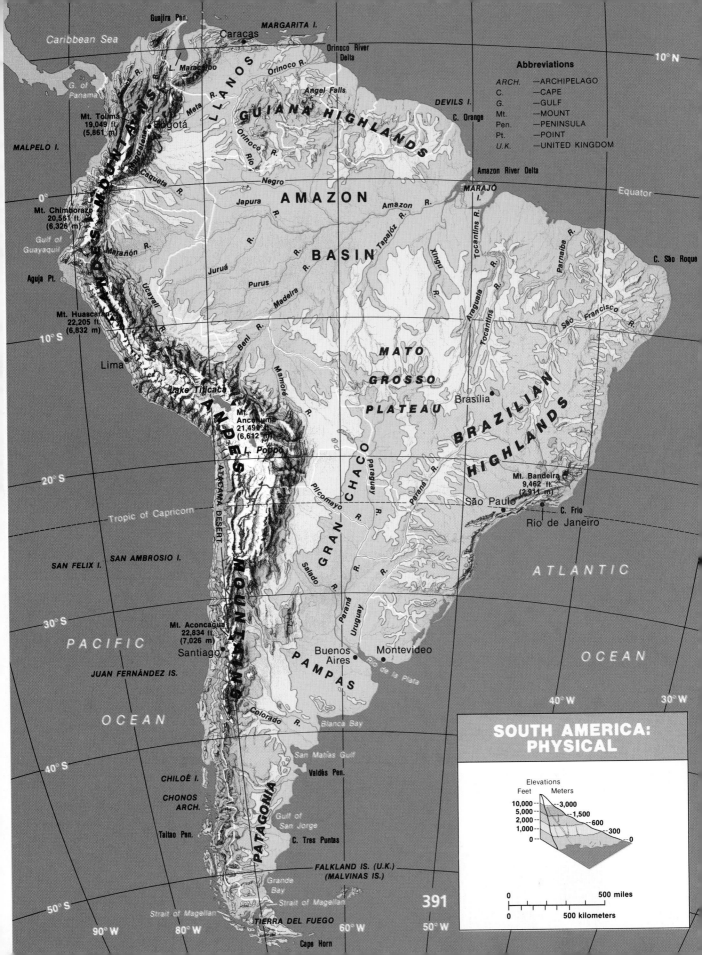

Caribbean Sea

Guajira Pen.

MARGARITA I.

Caracas

Orinoco River Delta

G. of Panama

L. Maracaibo

LLANOS

Orinoco R.

Angel Falls

GUIANA HIGHLANDS

DEVILS I.

C. Orange

10° N

Mt. Tolima
19,049 ft.
(5,861 m)

Bogotá

Meta R.

MALPELO I.

Magdalena R.

Caqueta R.

Orinoco R.

Rio Negro

Amazon River Delta

MARAJÓ I.

Equator

0°

Mt. Chimborazo
20,561 ft.
(6,326 m)

Japura R.

AMAZON

Amazon R.

C. São Roque

Gulf of Guayaquil

Marañón R.

Juruá R.

BASIN

Tapajóz R.

Xingu R.

Tocantins R.

Parnaiba R.

Aguja Pt.

Ucayali R.

Purus R.

Madeira R.

Araguaia R.

Tocantins R.

São Francisco R.

Mt. Huascarán
22,205 ft
(6,832 m)

10° S

Lima

Beni R.

Mamoré R.

MATO

GROSSO

PLATEAU

Brasília

BRAZILIAN

Lake Titicaca

ANDES

Mt. Ancohuma
21,490 ft
(6,612 m)

L. Poopó

Paraguay R.

HIGHLANDS

Mt. Bandeira
9,462 ft.
(2,911 m)

GRAN CHACO

Parana R.

São Paulo

20° S

ATACAMA DESERT

Tropic of Capricorn

Pilcomayo R.

São Paulo

C. Frio

Rio de Janeiro

SAN FELIX I.

SAN AMBROSIO I.

MOUNTAINS

Salado R.

Parana R.

ATLANTIC

30° S

PACIFIC

Mt. Aconcagua
22,834 ft.
(7,026 m)

Santiago

PAMPAS

Paraná R.

Uruguay R.

Buenos Aires

Montevideo

OCEAN

JUAN FERNÁNDEZ IS.

Rio de la Plata

OCEAN

Colorado R.

Blanca Bay

40° W

30° W

San Matias Gulf

Valdés Pen.

40° S

CHILOÉ I.

CHONOS ARCH.

PATAGONIA

Gulf of San Jorge

Taitao Pan.

C. Tres Puntas

Grande Bay

50° S

Strait of Magellan

Strait of Magellan

TIERRA DEL FUEGO

90° W

80° W

60° W

50° W

Cape Horn

Abbreviations

ARCH. —ARCHIPELAGO
C. —CAPE
G. —GULF
Mt. —MOUNT
Pen. —PENINSULA
Pt. —POINT
U.K. —UNITED KINGDOM

SOUTH AMERICA: PHYSICAL

Elevations

Feet — Meters

10,000 — 3,000
5,000 — 1,500
2,000 — 600
1,000 — 300
0 — 0

0   500 miles

0   500 kilometers

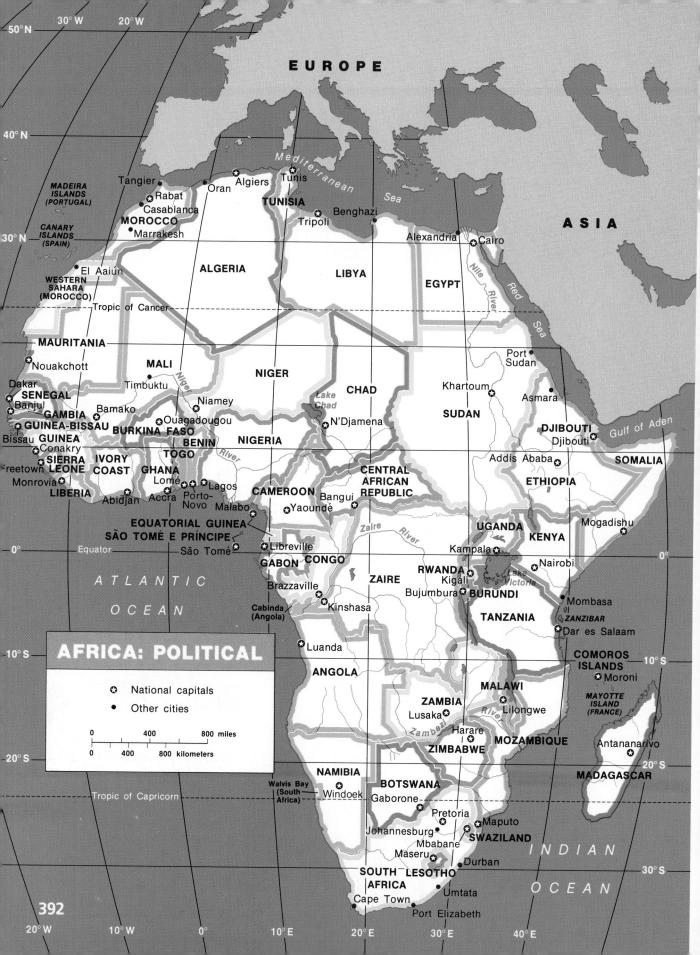

EUROPE

ASIA

MADEIRA
ISLANDS
(PORTUGAL)

CANARY
ISLANDS
(SPAIN)

Tangier
Rabat
Casablanca
MOROCCO
Marrakesh

Oran

Algiers

TUNISIA
Tunis

Benghazi
Tripoli

Mediterranean
Sea

Alexandria
Cairo

El Aaiún

WESTERN
SAHARA
(MOROCCO)

ALGERIA

LIBYA

EGYPT

Nile River

Red Sea

Tropic of Cancer

MAURITANIA

Nouakchott

MALI

Timbuktu

NIGER

CHAD

Lake
Chad

Khartoum

Asmara

Port
Sudan

Dakar
SENEGAL
Banjul
GAMBIA
GUINEA-BISSAU
Bissau GUINEA
Conakry
SIERRA IVORY
Freetown LEONE COAST
Monrovia
LIBERIA

Bamako

Niamey

Ouagadougou

BURKINA FASO

BENIN

NIGERIA
TOGO
GHANA
Lomé
Abidjan Accra Porto-
Novo

Niger River

Lagos

N'Djamena

SUDAN

DJIBOUTI
Djibouti

CAMEROON

Malabo
EQUATORIAL GUINEA
SÃO TOMÉ E PRÍNCIPE
São Tomé
GABON
CONGO

Bangui

Yaoundé

CENTRAL
AFRICAN
REPUBLIC

Addis Ababa

ETHIOPIA

SOMALIA

Mogadishu

Libreville

Equator

Brazzaville

Cabinda
(Angola)

ZAIRE

Zaire River

Kinshasa

RWANDA
Kigali
Bujumbura
BURUNDI

UGANDA
Kampala

Lake
Victoria

KENYA

Nairobi

Mombasa
ZANZIBAR
Dar es Salaam

ATLANTIC

OCEAN

Luanda

ANGOLA

TANZANIA

COMOROS
ISLANDS
Moroni

MAYOTTE
ISLAND
(FRANCE)

AFRICA: POLITICAL

⊛ National capitals
• Other cities

0   400   800 miles
0   400   800 kilometers

ZAMBIA
Lusaka

MALAWI

Lilongwe

Zambezi River

Harare

ZIMBABWE

MOZAMBIQUE

Antananarivo

MADAGASCAR

NAMIBIA

Walvis Bay
(South
Africa)

Windoek

BOTSWANA
Gaborone

Pretoria

Johannesburg
Maputo
SWAZILAND
Mbabane
Maseru
LESOTHO
Durban

INDIAN

OCEAN

SOUTH
AFRICA
Cape Town
Umtata
Port Elizabeth

AFRICA: PHYSICAL

ATLANTIC OCEAN

IRELAND
Glasgow
Dublin
UNITED KINGDOM
Bergen
London
North Sea
NORWAY
Oslo
Narvik
ARCTIC OCEAN
SPITSBERGEN (NOR.)
NORTH LAND
40° N
MADEIRA IS. (PORT.)
Lisbon
PORTUGAL
Madrid
SPAIN
ANDORRA
Valencia
Barcelona
Marseille
Nice
BALEARIC IS. (SP.)
CORSICA
SARDINIA
The Hague
Brussels
Amsterdam
Paris
BELG.
LUXEMBOURG
FRANCE
SWITZ.
LIECH.
MONACO
ITALY
SAN MARINO
Rome
Naples
Palermo
SICILY
MALTA
Valletta
Bordeaux
NETH.
Hamburg
Bonn
W. GER.
Munich
Bern
Milan
DENMARK
Göteborg
Stockholm
Copenhagen
E. GER.
Berlin
Hannover
Prague
CZECH.
AUSTRIA
Vienna
Budapest
HUNGARY
YUGOSLAVIA
Belgrade
Tirana
ALBANIA
Sofia
BULGARIA
GREECE
Athens
CRETE (GR.)
Mediterranean Sea
Danube River
SWEDEN
FINLAND
Helsinki
Tallinn
Kaliningrad
Riga
POLAND
Wroclaw
Warsaw
ROMANIA
Bucharest
Odessa
UKRAINE
Kharkov
Istanbul (Constantinople)
Izmir
Ankara
TURKEY
Black Sea
Barents Sea
Murmansk
Archangel
Leningrad
Moscow
Kiev
NOVAYA ZEMLYA
Yenisei R.
UNION OF SOVIET
(SOVIET UNION)
Perm
Kazan
Saratov
Ufa
Kuibyshev
Sverdlovsk
Chelyabinsk
Magnitogorsk
Orenburg
Omsk
Tomsk
Novosibirsk
Volga R.
Volgograd
Krasnodar
Ob River

Nicosia
CYPRUS
LEBANON
Beirut
ISRAEL
Jerusalem
SYRIA
Damascus
Amman
JORDAN
IRAQ
Baghdad
Basra
Abadan
Kuwait
KUWAIT
SAUDI ARABIA
Riyadh
Manama
BAH.
QATAR
Doha
Abu Dhabi
UNITED ARAB EMIRATES
Empty Quarter
Mecca
Red Sea
Euphrates R.
Tigris R.
Tehran
IRAN
Baku
Caspian Sea
Aral Sea
TURKESTAN
Tashkent
Urumqi
SINKIANG
Kabul
AFGHANISTAN
Islamabad
Lahore
JAMMU AND KASHMIR
TIBET
PAKISTAN
Karachi
Hyderabad
Indus R.
Delhi
New Delhi
NEPAL
Katmandu
Ganges R.
Ahmadabad
INDIA
Masqat
OMAN

N. YEMEN
San'a
S. YEMEN
Aden
Madinat ash Sha'b
SOCOTRA (S. YEMEN)
Arabian Sea
Bombay
Hyderabad
LACCADIVE IS. (IND.)
Madras
10° N
AFRICA

Persian Gulf
50° E
60° E
70° E
80° E

SRI LANKA
Colombo
MALDIVES
Male
0°
Equator
INDIAN OCEAN
10° S

Abbreviations

BAH. —BAHRAIN
BELG. —BELGIUM
CZECH. —CZECHOSLOVAKIA
E. GER. —EAST GERMANY
LIECH. —LIECHTENSTEIN
NETH. —THE NETHERLANDS
SWITZ. —SWITZERLAND
W. GER. —WEST GERMANY

GR. —GREECE
IND. —INDIA
NOR. —NORWAY
PORT. —PORTUGAL
SP. —SPAIN
U.K. —UNITED KINGDOM
U.S. —UNITED STATES
U.S.S.R. —UNION OF SOVIET
SOCIALIST REPUBLICS

394

NEW
SIBERIAN
IS.

S I B E R I A

Bering Sea

40° N

30° N

Magadan

Kamtchatka
Peninsula

Yakutsk

Lena R.

Sea of
Okhotsk

S O C I A L I S T   R E P U B L I C S

SAKHALIN

KURIL IS. (U.S.S.R.)

ALEUTIAN IS.
(U.S.)

20° N

Krasnoyarsk

Amur R.

Khabarovsk

Irkutsk

MANCHURIA

Harbin

Vladivostok

Sapporo

Ulan Bator

MONGOLIA

INNER
MONGOLIA

Fushun
Shenyang

N. KOREA

Pyongyang

Sea
of
Japan

JAPAN

Tokyo
Yokohama

Kyōto   Nagoya
Kōbe   Ōsaka

Great Wall

Dalian

Seoul   Pusan
S. KOREA

Beijing
Tianjin

He

Kitakyūshū

CHINA

Taiyuan

Qingdao

Lanzhou

Huang

Nanjing   Shanghai

East
China
Sea

RYUKYU IS. (JAPAN)

PACIFIC

10° N

Xi'an

Wuhan

Chengdu

Chang Jiang

Chongqing

Taipei

TAIWAN

Tropic of Cancer

OCEAN

Lhasa

BHUTAN

Thimbu

Brahmaputra R.

Kunming

Guangzhou

Hong Kong
(U.K.)

Macao
(Port.)

FEDERATED STATES OF MICRONESIA

0°

BANGLADESH

Dacca   Mandalay

Calcutta

BURMA

Hanoi

LAOS

Mekong R.

Hue
Da Nang

South
China
Sea

Manila

PHILIPPINES

Equator

Rangoon

Vientiane

THAILAND

VIETNAM

Bay
of
Bengal

Bangkok

CAMBODIA

Phnom
Penh

Ho Chi Minh
City

Davao

ANDAMAN
IS. (IND.)

Bandar
Seri
Begawan

Djajapura

Lae

IRIAN
JAYA

PAPUA NEW GUINEA

NICOBAR
IS. (IND.)

BRUNEI

Manado

NEW GUINEA

Port Moresby

M A L A Y S I A

BORNEO

CELEBES

Coral Sea

Medan

Kuala
Lumpur

Samarinda

Arafura Sea

SUMATRA

Pontianak
Bandjermasin

Ujung
Pandang

I N D O N E S I A

TIMOR

Palembang

JAVA

Jakarta   Surabaja
Bandung

395

A U S T R A L I A

90° E

100° E

EURASIA: POLITICAL

✪ National capitals

• Other cities

0   400   800 miles

0   400   800 kilometers

ATLANTIC
OCEAN

MADEIRA
ISLANDS

BRITISH ISLES

London

North
Sea

SCANDINAVIA

LAPLAND

SPITSBERGEN

ARCTIC OCEAN

NORTH
LAND

Paris

Hamburg

Stockholm

Kola
Peninsula

NOVAYA ZEMLYA

Barents
Sea

Kara Sea

Taymir

Madrid

Iberian
Peninsula

Berlin

Baltic
Sea

Arctic

Circle

Yamal
Peninsula

Yenisey
River

BALEARIC
IS.

Milan

BALTIC PLAINS

Leningrad

NORTH EUROPEAN PLAIN

Dvina R.

URAL MOUNTAINS

Ob
River

WEST

CORSICA

Po R.

Vistula
River

N.

Ob

SIBERIAN

SARDINIA

Rome

Danube
River

Dnieper River

Moscow

Volga
River

Kama River

SICILY

Tyrrhenian
Sea

Adriatic Sea

River

Bucharest

Don R.

Volga River

Ural River

Irtysh
River

Ob
River

PLAIN

ALTAI

MALTESE
ISLANDS

Ionian
Sea

Balkan
Peninsula

Aegean Sea

Istanbul

Black
Sea

CAUCASUS

KIRGIZ
STEPPE

Ishim River

KAZAKH

UPLANDS

CRETE

ASIA MINOR

Caspian
Sea

TURAN LOWLAND

Arai
Sea

Sir Darya

Lake
Balkhash

CYPRUS

Mediterranean
Sea

EMBURZ MTS.

Amu
Darya

TIEN SHAN

TARIM
BASIN

Abbreviations

Mt.   —MOUNT
MTS. —MOUNTAINS

SYRIAN
DESERT

Baghdad

Euphrates
River

Tigris R.

ZAGROS MOUNTAINS

Tehran

PLATEAU
OF
IRAN

KUNLUN

PLATEAU

TIB.

MESOPOTAMIA

HINDU KUSH

Mt. Everest
29,028 ft.
(8,932 m)

HEJAZ

Red

AFRICA

Arabian

Persian Gulf

HIMALAYA

Indus River

Sutlej River

Ganges River

INDIAN
DESERT

Delhi

GANGES
PLAIN

Peninsula

Karachi

Gulf of Oman

Sea

HADHRAMAUT

Gulf of Aden

Arabian Sea

DECCAN

Bombay

Godavari R.

PLATEAU

WESTERN GHATS

EASTERN GHATS

10° N

Madras

LACCADIVE
ISLANDS

SRI
LANKA

0°

Equator

MALDIVES

INDIAN

396

OCEAN

50° E

60° E

70° E

80° E

EURASIA: PHYSICAL

Elevations
Feet / Meters

10,000	3,000
5,000	1,500
2,000	600
1,000	300
0	0

Land below sea level

0 — 400 — 800 miles

0 — 400 — 800 miles

Physical feature labels:

Laptev Sea
NEW SIBERIAN ISLANDS
Peninsula
CENTRAL SIBERIAN PLATEAU
SIBERIA
CHERSKI RANGE
VERKHOYANSK RANGE
KOLYMA RANGE
CENTRAL RANGE
ALEUTIAN ISLANDS
Bering Sea
Kamchatka Peninsula
Sea of Okhotsk
Lena River
Aldan River
Amur River
SAKHALIN
KURIL ISLANDS
HOKKAIDŌ
Lower Tunguska R.
Angara River
Lake Baikal
Shilka River
Shika River
Amur River
GREAT KHINGAN MTS.
MANCHURIA PLAIN
Harbin
HONSHŪ
Sea of Japan
SAYAN MTS.
Yenisei River
MONGOLIAN PLATEAU
Shenyang
Tokyo
Mt. Fujiyama 12,388 ft. (3,812 m)
Kyōto
THE GOBI
Great Wall
Beijing
Dalian
Korea Strait
SHIKOKU
Tianjin
Yellow Sea
KYŪSHŪ
NAN SHAN
NORTH CHINA PLAIN
Huang He
Shanghai
East China Sea
OF
TIBET
Chang Jiang
OKINAWA
RYUKYU ISLANDS
Brahmaputra R.
Chongqing
BOHEA HILLS
Philippine Sea
PACIFIC
Calcutta
Irrawaddy R.
Salween R.
Mekong River
Xi River
Guangzhou
Hong Kong
TAIWAN
Luzon Strait
PHILIPPINE ISLANDS
OCEAN
HAINAN
LUZON
Manila
SAMAR
ADMIRALTY ISLANDS
NEW IRELAND
Bay of Bengal
Ganges R.
South China Sea
MINDORO
PANAY
NEGROS
MINDANAO
NEW BRITAIN
ANDAMAN ISLANDS
Gulf of Siam
Indochina Peninsula
Ho Chi Minh City
PALAWAN
Celebes Sea
HALMAHERA
MOLUCCAS
NEW GUINEA
SNOW MTS.
Andaman Sea
NATUNA ISLANDS
BURU
CERAM
ARU ISLANDS
Coral Sea
NICOBAR ISLANDS
Strait of Malacca
BORNEO
CELEBES
Arafura Sea
SUMATRA
MENTAWAI ISLANDS
BANGKA
SUNDA ISLANDS
Java Sea
FLORES
TIMOR
SUMBAWA
SUMBA
Jakarta
JAVA
BALI
LOMBOK
AUSTRALIA

90° E   100° E

40° N   30° N

Tropic of Cancer

10° N

0°

397

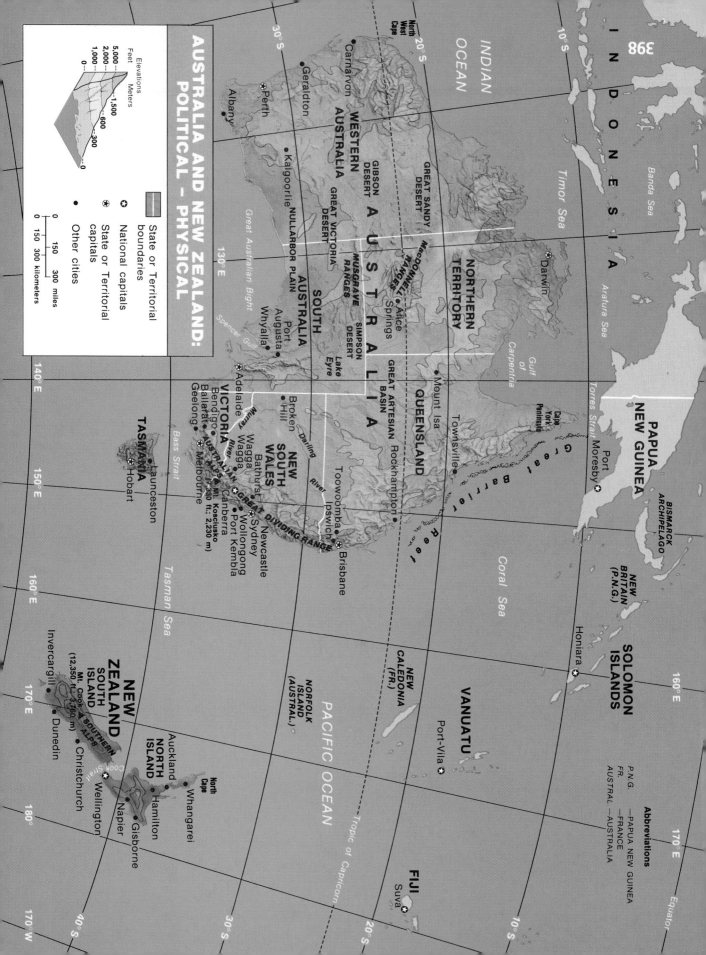

AUSTRALIA AND NEW ZEALAND: POLITICAL - PHYSICAL

Elevations
Feet Meters
5,000 — 1,500
2,000 — 600
1,000 — 300
0 — 0

State or Territorial boundaries
✪ National capitals
⊛ State or Territorial capitals
• Other cities

0   150   300 miles
0   150   300 kilometers

Abbreviations
P.N.G. — PAPUA NEW GUINEA
FR. — FRANCE
AUSTRAL. — AUSTRALIA

INDONESIA

Banda Sea

Timor Sea

Arafura Sea

INDIAN OCEAN

North West Cape

Carnarvon
Geraldton
Albany
⊛ Perth
Kalgoorlie

WESTERN AUSTRALIA

GIBSON DESERT
GREAT SANDY DESERT
GREAT VICTORIA DESERT

A U S T R A L I A

NULLARBOR PLAIN
Great Australian Bight

NORTHERN TERRITORY

Darwin

MUSGRAVE RANGES
MacDONNELL RANGES
Alice Springs
SIMPSON DESERT

SOUTH AUSTRALIA

Lake Eyre

GREAT ARTESIAN BASIN

QUEENSLAND

Gulf of Carpentaria

Cape York Peninsula

Mount Isa
Townsville
Rockhampton
Toowoomba
Ipswich
Brisbane

Port Augusta
Whyalla
Spencer Gulf

⊛ Adelaide
Broken Hill
Murray River
Darling River

VICTORIA
Bendigo
Ballarat
Geelong
Melbourne

NEW SOUTH WALES
Wagga Wagga
Bathurst
✪ Canberra
AUSTRALIAN CAPITAL TERRITORY
Mt. Kosciusko 7,330 ft: 2,230 m
GREAT DIVIDING RANGE
Newcastle
Sydney
Wollongong
Port Kembla

Bass Strait

TASMANIA
Launceston
⊛ Hobart

Tasman Sea

Great Barrier Reef

Coral Sea

PAPUA NEW GUINEA

BISMARCK ARCHIPELAGO

NEW BRITAIN (P.N.G.)

Port Moresby
Torres Strait

SOLOMON ISLANDS

Honiara ✪

VANUATU

Port-Vila ✪

NEW CALEDONIA (FR.)

NORFOLK ISLAND (AUSTRAL.)

PACIFIC OCEAN

FIJI
Suva ✪

NEW ZEALAND

NORTH ISLAND
North Cape
Whangarei
Auckland
Hamilton
Gisborne
Napier
⊛ Wellington
Cook Strait

SOUTH ISLAND
SOUTHERN ALPS
Mt. Cook (12,350 ft: 3,760 m)
Christchurch
Dunedin
Invercargill

Tropic of Capricorn

Equator

10°S
20°S
30°S
40°S

10°E
130°E
140°E
150°E
160°E
170°E
180°
170°W

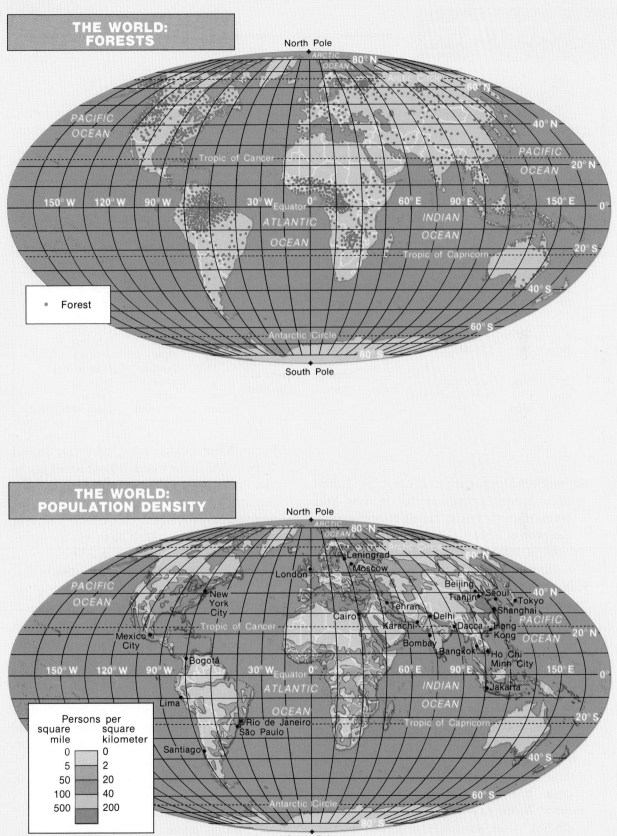

THE WORLD: FORESTS

North Pole

ARCTIC
OCEAN

80° N

Arctic Circle

60° N

PACIFIC
OCEAN

40° N

PACIFIC
OCEAN

Tropic of Cancer

20° N

150° W   120° W   90° W   30° W   Equator   0°   60° E   90° E   150° E   0°

ATLANTIC

INDIAN

OCEAN

OCEAN

Tropic of Capricorn

20° S

40° S

- Forest

60° S

Antarctic Circle

80° S

South Pole

THE WORLD: POPULATION DENSITY

North Pole

ARCTIC
OCEAN

80° N

Arctic Circle

Leningrad

60° N

Moscow

London

PACIFIC
OCEAN

Beijing

40° N

New
York
City

Tianjin   Seoul

Tokyo

Tehran

Shanghai

Cairo

Delhi

Tropic of Cancer

Karachi

Dacca   Hong
Kong

PACIFIC
OCEAN

20° N

Mexico
City

Bombay

Bangkok

Bogotá

Ho Chi
Minh City

150° W   120° W   90° W   30° W   Equator   0°   60° E   90° E   150° E   0°

Lima

ATLANTIC

Jakarta

INDIAN

OCEAN

OCEAN

Rio de Janeiro

Tropic of Capricorn

20° S

São Paulo

Persons per		
square mile		square kilometer
0		0
5		2
50		20
100		40
500		200

Santiago

40° S

60° S

Antarctic Circle

80° S

South Pole

399

Some words in this book may be new to you or difficult to pronounce. Those words have been spelled phonetically in parentheses. The syllable that receives stress in a word is shown in small capital letters.

For example: **Chicago** (shuh KAH goh)

Most phonetic spellings are easy to read. In the following Pronunciation Key, you can see how letters are used to show different sounds.

PRONUNCIATION KEY

a	after	(AF tur)	ye	lie	(lye)	ch	chicken	(CHIHK un)
ah	father	(FAH thur)	oh	flow	(floh)	g	game	(gaym)
ai	care	(kair)	oi	boy	(boi)	ing	coming	(KUM ing)
aw	dog	(dawg)	oo	rule	(rool)	j	job	(jahb)
ay	paper	(PAY pur)	or	horse	(hors)	k	came	(kaym)
						ng	long	(lawng)
e	letter	(LET ur)	ou	cow	(kou)	s	city	(SIH tee)
ee	eat	(eet)	yoo	few	(fyoo)	sh	ship	(shihp)
			u	taken	(TAY kun)	th	thin	(thihn)
				matter	(MAT ur)	thh	feather	(FETHH ur)
ih	trip	(trihp)	uh	ago	(uh GOH)	y	yard	(yahrd)
eye	idea	(eye DEE uh)				z	size	(syz)
y	hide	(hyd)				zh	division	(duh VIHZH un)

A

Adirondack Mountains (ad uh RAHN dak MOUNT unz). Mountain range located in New York State. Highest peak is Mount Marcy, with an elevation of 5,344 ft (1,629 m). p. 103.

Africa (AF rih kuh). The earth's second largest continent. p. 5.

Albany (AWL buh nee). Capital of New York. Located on the Hudson River. (43°N/74°W) p. 98.

Albuquerque (AL buh kur kee). Most populated city in New Mexico. Located on the Rio Grande. (35°N/107°W) p. 186.

Alice Springs (AL ihs springz). Town situated practically in the center of the continent of Australia. (24°S/134°E) p. 326.

Allegheny Mountains (al uh GAY nee MOUNT unz). Part of the Appalachian Mountains, extending from Pennsylvania to Virginia and West Virginia. p. 103.

Amazon Basin (AM uh zahn BAYS un). Area drained by the Amazon River and its tributaries. p. 391.

Amazon River (AM uh zahn RIHV ur). Second longest river in the world. It flows across northern Brazil and into the Atlantic Ocean at the Equator. p. 390.

American River (uh MER ih kun RIHV ur). River in north central California. It flows into the Sacramento River at Sacramento. p. 239.

American Samoa (uh MER ih kun suh MOH uh). Group of islands in the Pacific Ocean. (14°S/170°W) p. 286.

Anchorage (ANG kur ihj). Most populated city in Alaska. Located on Cook Inlet, an arm of the Pacific Ocean. (61°N/150°W) p. 236.

Antarctica (ant AHRK tih kuh). The earth's third smallest continent. p. 5.

Appalachian Mountains (ap uh LAY chun MOUNT unz). Chain of mountains stretching from Canada to Alabama. The highest peak is Mount Mitchell, at 6,684 ft (2,037 m). pp. 388–389.

Arctic Circle (AHRK tihk SUR kul). Line of latitude located at 66½° north latitude. p. 6.

Arctic Ocean (AHRK tihk OH shun). Large body of salt water north of the Arctic Circle. p. 5.

Arkansas River (AHR kun saw RIHV ur). River that rises in central Colorado and flows into the Mississippi River in southern Arkansas. p. 212.

Aroostook River (uh ROOS tuk RIHV ur). Rises in northern Maine and flows northeast into the St. John River in Canada. p. 78

Asia (AY zhuh). The earth's largest continent. p. 5.

Atacama Desert (ah tah KAH mah DEZ urt). Dry area in northern Chile. Major source of nitrates. p. 391.

Athens (ATH unz). City located about 60 mi (97 km) northeast of Atlanta, Georgia. (34°N/ 83°W) p. 14.

Atlanta (at LAN tuh). Capital of and most populated city in Georgia. (34°N/84°W) p. 14.

Atlantic Coastal Plain (at LAN tihk KOHS tul playn). Large plain located along the Atlantic Ocean from Maine to Florida. pp. 388–389.

Atlantic Ocean (at LAN tihk OH shun). Large body of salt water separating North America and South America from Europe and Africa. p. 5.

Austin (AWS tun). Capital of Texas. Located near the western edge of the Gulf Coastal Plain. (30°N/98°W) p. 186.

Australia (aw STRAYL yuh). The earth's smallest continent. Also the name of the country located on the continent. p. 5.

B

Baltimore (BAWL tuh mor). Most populated city in Maryland. Located on Chesapeake Bay. (39°N/ 77°W) p. 98.

Barre (BAR ee). City in north central Vermont, with large granite quarries and stoneworks. (44°N/73°W) p. 74.

Baton Rouge (BAT un roozh). Capital of Louisiana, located on the Mississippi River. (30°N/ 91°W) p. 124.

Bering Sea (BER ing see). Part of the North Pacific Ocean. Bounded on the east by the mainland of Alaska and on the south and southeast by the Aleutian Islands. p. 6.

Birmingham (BUR ming ham). Most populated city in Alabama. One of the nation's leading iron- and steel-producing centers. (34°N/ 87°W) p. 124.

Black Hills (blak hihlz). Mountainous region rich in gold and other minerals. Located in southeastern South Dakota and northeastern Wyoming. p. 385.

Blue Ridge Mountains (bloo rihj MOUNT unz). Eastern range of the Appalachian Mountains, stretching from northern West Virginia into northern Georgia. p. 128.

Boston (BAWS tun). Capital of and most populated city in Massachusetts. Located on Massachusetts Bay. (42°N/71°W) p. 74.

Brussels (BRUS ulz). Capital of Belgium. Headquarters of European Community. (51°N/ 4°E) p. 307.

Buffalo (BUF uh loh). City in New York. Located on Lake Erie and the Niagara River. (43°N/ 79°W) p. 98.

C

Canada (KAN uh duh). A country in the northern part of North America. p. 6.

Cape Canaveral (kayp kuh NAV ur ul). National Space Center. Site of launchings for space flights. Located on Florida's eastern coast. (28°/81°W) p. 128.

Cape May (kayp may). City in southern New Jersey. A famous resort. (39°N/75°W) pp. 386–387.

Caribbean Sea (kar uh BEE un see). Part of the Atlantic Ocean, bounded by South America on the south; Central America on the west; and Cuba, Puerto Rico, and other islands on the north and east. p. 6.

Cascade Range (kas KAYD raynj). Mountains that extend from northern California through Oregon and Washington and into Canada. The highest peak is Mount Rainier, at 14,408 ft (4,392 m). p. 239.

Catskill Mountains (KATS kihl MOUNT unz). Part of the Appalachian Mountains. Located in New York, west of the Hudson River. p. 103.

Central Plains (SEN trul playnz). Large plains area in the middle of the United States, between the Appalachian and the Rocky mountains. p. 159.

Central Valley (SEN trul VAL ee). One of the most important farming areas in the United States. Located between the Sierra Nevada and the Coastal Ranges. p. 239.

Charleston (CHAHRLS tun). Port city in South Carolina. (33°N/80°W) p. 124.

Charlotte Amalie (SHAHR lut uh MAHL yuh). Capital of the United States Virgin Islands, in the Caribbean Sea. Located on the island of St. Thomas. (18°N/65°W) p. 278.

Chesapeake Bay (ches uh PEEK bay). Inlet of the Atlantic Ocean, in Maryland and Virginia. p. 124.

Chicago (shuh KAH goh). One of eight cities in the United States with a population of more than 1 million people. Located in Illinois, on the southern tip of Lake Michigan. (42°N/88°W) p. 156.

Cleveland (KLEEV lund). Second most populated city in Ohio. Located on Lake Erie, at the mouth of the Cuyahoga River. (42°N/82°W) p. 156.

Coastal Ranges (KOHS tul raynj ihz). Mountains along the Pacific coast of North America that extend from California through Oregon and Washington and into Canada. p. 239.

Cologne (kuh LOHN). Large city and river port in West Germany. (51°N/7°E) p. 307.

Colorado Plateau (kal uh RAD oh pla TOH). Large high area located in the southern part of the Mountain West region. p. 212.

Colorado River (kal uh RAD oh RIHV ur). River that rises in the Rocky Mountains in northern Colorado and flows into the Gulf of California, in Mexico. p. 210.

Colorado Springs (kaluh RAD oh springz). City in Colorado. Location of the United States Air Force Academy. (39°N/105°W) p. 210.

Columbia (kuh LUM bee uh). Capital of South Carolina. Located in the west central part of the state. (34°N/81°W) p. 124.

Columbia River (kuh LUM bee uh RIHV ur). River that rises in the Rocky Mountains in Canada and flows into the Pacific Ocean along the Washington-Oregon boundary. p. 236.

Columbus (kuh LUM bus). Capital of and most populated city of Ohio. Located on the Scioto River. (40°N/83°W) p. 156.

Connecticut River (kuh NET uh kut RIHV ur). Longest river in the New England region. Rises in northern New Hampshire and flows into Long Island Sound. p. 78.

D

Dallas (DAL us). One of the eight cities in the United States with a population of more than 1 million people. Located in Texas, on the Trinity River. (33°N/97°W) p. 186.

Death Valley (deth VAL ee). Low valley located at the northern edge of the Mojave Desert. It is 282 ft (86 m) below sea level. p. 239.

Delaware Bay (DEL uh wer bay). Arm of the Atlantic Ocean, between New Jersey and Delaware. p. 98.

Delaware River (DEL uh wer RIHV ur). River that rises in the Catskill Mountains, in New York, and flows into the Atlantic Ocean at Delaware Bay. p. 98.

Denver (DEN vur). Capital of and most populated city in Colorado. Located at the base of the Rocky Mountains where they join the Great Plains. (40°N/105°W) p. 210.

Des Moines (duh MOIN). Capital of Iowa. Located on the Des Moines River. (42°N/94°W) p. 156.

Detroit (dih TROIT). One of eight cities in the United States with a population of more than 1 million people. Located on the Detroit River, in Michigan, near Lake Erie. (42°N/83°W) p. 156.

Dublin (DUB lun). City in central Georgia. (33°N/83°W) p. 14.

Duluth (duh LOOTH). Port city in Minnesota. Located at the western end of Lake Superior. (47°N/92°W) p. 156.

E

Eastern Hemisphere (EES turn HEM ih sfihr). The half of the earth east of the Prime Meridian. Includes Australia and most of Europe, Africa, and Asia. p. 12.

Equator (ee KWAYT ur). Line drawn on maps that circles the earth halfway between the two poles. The Equator is labeled 0° latitude. p. 11.

Erie Canal (IHR ee kuh NAL). Canal between the cities of Buffalo and Albany, in New York State. p. 102.

Eugene (yoo JEEN). Industrial city in western Oregon, on the Willamette River. (43°N/123°W) p. 19.

Europe (YOOR up). The earth's second smallest continent. p. 5.

Everglades (EV ur glaydz). Large swamp located in southern Florida. p. 128.

F

Federated States of Micronesia (FED ur ay ted stayts uv mye kruh NEE zhuh). Islands in the western Pacific Ocean, between 1° and 20° north latitude and 131° and 177° east longitude. p. 286.

Florida Keys (FLOR uh duh keez). Chain of islands, about 150 miles (241 km) long, that stretches southwest around the tip of Florida from Virginia Key, near Miami, to Key West. p. 128.

G

Galveston Bay (GAL vihs tun bay). Inlet of Gulf of Mexico. p. 186.

Gary (GER ee). Large industrial city in Indiana. Located on the southern end of Lake Michigan. One of the most important steel-making centers in the United States. (42°N/87°W) p. 156.

Grand Canyon (grand KAN yun). Largest canyon in the United States. Located along the Colorado River in Arizona. (36°N/113°W) p. 189.

Great Basin (grayt BAYS un). Large high region located between the Rocky Mountains on the east and the Cascade Range and Sierra Nevada on the west. p. 212.

Great Dividing Range (grayt duh VYD ing raynj). Mountain area of Australia. Extends from north to south near most of the eastern coast. Forms the western limit of the coastal plain. p. 398.

Great Lakes (grayt layks). Five large lakes in central North America. Except for Lake Michigan, which is entirely in the United States, the lakes are on the Canada–United States boundary. p. 156.

Great Plains (grayt playnz). Large plains area in the western part of the Central Plains. Stretches from Montana and North Dakota to Texas. p. 159.

Great Salt Lake (grayt sawlt layk). Lake located in Utah. An inland lake with no streams flowing out of it. (41°N/113°W) p. 212.

Great Smoky Mountains (grayt SMOH kee MOUNT unz). Part of the Appalachian Mountains. Located in western North Carolina and eastern Tennessee. p. 128.

Greenland (GREEN lund). Largest island in the world, excluding the continent of Australia. Located off the northeastern coast of North America. p. 6.

Green Mountains (green MOUNT unz). Part of the Appalachian Mountains. Located in Vermont. Mount Mansfield, at 4,393 ft (1,339 m), is the highest point. p. 78.

Groton (GRAHT un). City in Connecticut. Located on Long Island Sound. Site of large submarine shipbuilding base. (41°N/72°W) p. 74.

Guam (qwahm). An island in the western Pacific, belonging to the United States. (13°N/145°E) p. 286.

Gulf Coastal Plain (gulf KOHS tul playn). Large flat area located along the Gulf of Mexico from Florida to Texas. p. 128.

Gulf of California (gulf uv kal uh FOR nyuh). Arm of the Pacific Ocean, extending into northwestern Mexico. p. 384.

Gulf of Mexico (gulf uv MEKS ih koh). Body of salt water surrounded by the United States, Mexico, and Cuba. p. 6.

H

Haarlem (HAHR lum). Major city in the Netherlands, a country in Europe. (52°N/5°E) p. 315.

Hartford (HAHRT furd). Capital of and most populated city in Connecticut. (42°N/73°W) p. 74.

Hawaii (huh WAH ee). Largest of all the Hawaiian Islands. Also the name given to the state that includes all the Hawaiian Islands. p. 236.

High Point (hye point). City in the Piedmont section of North Carolina. (36°N/80°W) p. 124.

Honolulu (hahn uh LOO loo). Capital of and most populated city in Hawaii. Located on the island of Oahu. (21°N/158°W) p. 236.

Houston (hyoos tun). City in Texas. Located near the Gulf of Mexico. One of the eight cities in the United States with a population of over 1 million people. (30°N/95°W) p. 186.

Hudson River (HUD sun RIHV ur). River that rises in Adirondack Mountains, in New York, and flows south into New York Harbor at New York City. p. 98.

I

Iceland (EYE slund). Island between the North Atlantic and Arctic oceans. A quarter of the land is lowland and is only partly habitable. (65°N/18°W) p. 385.

Indianapolis (ihn dee uh NAP uh lihs). Capital of and most populated city in Indiana. (40°N/86°W) p. 156.

Indian Ocean (IHN dee un OH shun). Body of water surrounded by Asia, Australia, Africa, and Antarctica. p. 5.

Interior Lowlands (ihn TIHR ee ur LOH lundz). Eastern part of the Central Plains, including the states of Ohio, Indiana, Michigan, Wisconsin, Iowa, and Missouri. p. 159.

J

Jacksonville (JAK sun vihl). Most populated city in Florida. (30°N/82°W) p. 124.

Juneau (JOO noh). Capital of Alaska. Located on the Alaskan panhandle. (58°N/134°W) p. 236.

K

Kansas City, Kansas (KAN zus SIHT ee, KAN-zus). City in Kansas. Located on the western side of the Missouri River. (39°N/95°W) p. 156.

Kansas City, Missouri (KAN zus SIHT ee mih-ZOOR ee). City in Missouri. Located on the eastern side of the Missouri River. (39°N/95°W) p. 156.

Kansas River (KAN zus RIHV ur). Major river of Kansas. Empties into the Missouri River at Kansas City. p. 159.

L

La Grange (luh graynj). City in western Georgia. (33°N/85°W) p. 14.

Lake Erie (layk IHR ee). Lake located on the border between Canada and the United States. Second smallest of the Great Lakes. Has coastline in Michigan, Ohio, Pennsylvania, and New York. p. 98.

Lake Huron (layk HYOOR ahn). Lake located along the boundary between Canada and the United States. Second largest of the five Great Lakes. United States portion of the lake is in Michigan. p. 159.

Lake Michigan (layk MIHSH ih gun). Lake located in the United States. Third largest of the five Great Lakes. Has coastline in Michigan, Wisconsin, Illinois, and Indiana. p. 159.

Lake Ontario (layk ahn TER ee oh). Lake located along the border between Canada and the United States. Smallest of the five Great Lakes. United States' portion of the lake is in New York. The only one of the Great Lakes that does not have a coastline in Michigan. p. 98.

Lake Superior (layk suh PIHR ee ur). Lake located along the boundary between Canada and the United States. Largest of the five Great Lakes. Has coastline in Minnesota, Wisconsin, and Michigan. p. 159.

Lanai (lah NAH ee). One of the islands of Hawaii. Famous for its pineapple plantations. p. 239.

London (LUN dun). Capital of and the most populated city in the United Kingdom. Located on the Thames River. (52°N/0° longitude) p. 394.

Long Island (lawng EYE lund). Island located between Long Island Sound on the north and the Atlantic Ocean on the south. p. 98.

Long Island Sound (lawng EYE lund sound). Body of water between the southern coast of Connecticut and the north shore of Long Island, in the state of New York. p. 103.

Los Angeles (laws AN juh lus). City in southern California, on the Pacific Ocean. One of eight cities in the United States with a population of more than 1 million. (34°N/118°W) p. 236.

M

Marshall Islands (MAHR shul EYE lundz). Group of atolls and reefs in the western Pacific Ocean. p. 286.

Mediterranean Sea (med ih tuh RAY nee un see). Large body of water surrounded by Europe, Africa, and Asia. It is the largest enclosed sea in the world. p. 392.

Memphis (MEM fihs). Most populated city in Tennessee. One of the 20 most populated cities in the United States. Located along the Mississippi River. (35°N/90°E) p. 124.

Mexico (MEKS ih koh). A country in North America, south of the United States. p. 6.

Mexico City (MEKS ih koh SIHT ee). Capital of Mexico. The most populated city in North America. (19°N/99°W) p. 384.

Miami (mye AM ee). Large city in the state of Florida. Located on the Atlantic Ocean. (26°N/80°W) p. 124.

Minneapolis (mihn ee AP ul ihs). Most populated city in Minnesota. Located on Mississippi River. (45°N/93°W) p. 156.

Mississippi River (mihs uh SIHP ee RIHV ur). Chief river of North American and second longest river in the United States. Rises in northern Minnesota and flows into the Gulf of Mexico near New Orleans, in Louisiana. p. 124.

Missouri River (mih ZOOR ee RIHV ur). Longest river in the United States. Rises in western Montana and flows into the Mississippi River near St. Louis, Missouri. p. 156.

Mohawk River (MOH hawk RIHV ur). Largest branch of the Hudson River, in east central part of New York State. p. 98.

Mojave Desert (moh HAH vee DEZ urt). Desert in California. Located between the Sierra Nevada and the Colorado River. p. 239.

Montpelier (mahnt PEEL yur). Capital of Vermont. Located in the central part of the state, on the Winooski River. (44°N/73°W) p. 74.

Mount Elbert (mount EL burt). Highest peak in Rocky Mountains. Located in Colorado, it has an elevation of 14,433 ft (4,399 m). (39°N/106°W) p. 212.

Mount McKinley (mount muh KIHN lee). Highest peak in North America, with an elevation of 20,320 ft (6,194 m). (64°N/150°W) p. 239.

Mount Mitchell (mount MIHCH ul). Highest peak in the Appalachian Mountains, with an elevation of 6,684 ft (2,037 m). Located in the Black Mountains, in North Carolina. (36°N/82°W) p. 385.

Mount St. Helens (mount saynt HEL unz). Volcanic peak. Located in the Cascade Range in the southern part of the state of Washington. Has an elevation of 9,671 ft (2,948 m). (46°N/122°W) p. 239.

Mount Washington (mount WAWSH ing tun). Mountain peak located in the White Mountains of New Hampshire. Has an elevation of 6,288 ft (1,917 m). Located in the White Mountains of New Hampshire. (44°N/71°W) p. 78.

Mount Whitney (mount HWIHT nee). Located in the Sierra Nevada mountain range. Is the highest peak in the United States outside of Alaska. (37°N/118°W) p. 239.

N

New Orleans (noo OR lee unz). Most populated city in Louisiana. Located on the Mississippi River. One of the busiest ports in the United States. (30°N/90°W) p. 124.

New York City (noo york SIHT ee). One of eight cities in the United States with a population of more than 1 million people. Located at the mouth of the Hudson River, in the state of New York. (41°N/74°W) p. 98.

Niagara Falls (nye AG uh ruh fawlz). Famous waterfalls located between Canada and the western part of New York State. (43°N/79°W) p. 103.

North America (north uh MER ih kuh). The earth's third largest continent. p. 5.

Northern Hemisphere (NOR thurn HEM ih sfihr). The half of the earth that is north of the Equator. p. 11.

Northern Mariana Islands (NOR thurn mer ee-AN uh EYE lundz). Group of islands in the Pacific Ocean, between 12° and 21° north longitude and between 144° and 146° east longitude. p. 286.

North Pole (north pohl). Most northern place on the earth. p. 10.

North Sea (north see). Part of the Atlantic Ocean, between Great Britain and the continent of Europe. p. 315.

O

Oahu (oh AH hoo). Third largest island in Hawaii. The island on which Honolulu is located. (22°N/158°W) p. 239.

Ogden (AHG dun). City in the state of Utah. Located north of Salt Lake City. (41°N/112°W) p. 210.

Ohio River (oh HYE oh RIHV ur). River formed at Pittsburgh, Pennsylvania, by the joining of the Allegheny and the Monongahela rivers. Flows into the Mississippi River at Cairo, Illinois. Forms part of the boundary of five states. p. 98.

Oklahoma City (oh kluh HOH muh SIHT ee). Capital of and most populated city in Oklahoma. (35°N/98°W) p. 186.

Olympia (oh LIHM pee uh). Capital of the state of Washington. Located on Puget Sound. (47°N/123°W) p. 236.

Omaha (OH muh haw). Most populated city in the state of Nebraska. Located in the eastern part of the state, on the Missouri River. (41°N/96°W) p. 156.

P

Pacific Ocean (puh SIHF ihk OH shun). The earth's largest body of water. It stretches from the Arctic Circle to Antarctica and from the western coast of North America to the eastern coast of Asia. p. 5.

Pago Pago (PAHNG oh PAHNG oh). Capital of American Samoa. Important United States naval base. (14°S/171°W) p. 286.

Panama Canal (PAN uh mah kuh NAL). Canal that crosses the Isthmus of Panama. Connects the Caribbean Sea and the Pacific Ocean. p. 384.

Paris (PAR ihs). National capital of and most populated city in France, a country in Europe. Located on the Seine River. (49°N/2°E) p. 307.

Pawtucket (puh TUK iht). Fourth largest city in Rhode Island. First cotton-spinning mill in the United States was located here. (42°N/71°W) p. 74.

Persian Gulf (PUR zhun gulf). Body of water in southwestern Asia, between Iran and the Arabian Peninsula. (27°N/51°E) pp. 394–395.

Philadelphia (fihl uh DEL fee uh). One of eight cities in the United States with a population of more than 1 million. Located in Pennsylvania, at a point where the Delaware and Schuylkill rivers join. (40°N/75°W) p. 98.

Phoenix (FEE nihks). Capital of and most populated city in Arizona. Located on the Salt River. (33°N/112°W) p. 186.

Piedmont Plateau (PEED mahnt pla TOH). Land area between the Atlantic Coastal Plain and the Appalachian Mountains. p. 128.

Pittsburgh (PIHTS burg). Second most populated city in Pennsylvania. Located where the Monongahela and the Allegheny rivers join to form the Ohio River. (40°N/80°W) p. 98.

Portland (PORT lund). Most populated city in Oregon. Located on the Willamette River, near the point where the Willamette joins the Columbia River. (46°N/123°W) p. 236.

Prime Meridian (prym muh RIDH ee un). 0° line of longitude. It divides the earth into the Eastern Hemisphere and the Western Hemisphere. p. 12.

Providence (PRAHV uh duns). Capital of Rhode Island. Located at the head of the Providence River. (42°N/71°W) p. 74.

Prudhoe Bay (PROOD oh bay). Small bay on the Beaufort Sea. Located in northern Alaska. p. 251.

Pueblo (PWEB loh). City in Colorado. Located on the Arkansas River. (38°N/105°W) p. 210.

Puerto Rico (PWER tuh REE koh). Island of the West Indies. It forms part of the boundary between the Atlantic Ocean and the Caribbean Sea. p. 278.

R

Raleigh (RAWL ee). Capital city of North Carolina. Located in the east central part of the state. (36°N/79°W) p. 124.

Red Sea (red see). Large body of water separating part of eastern Africa from Asia. p. 392.

Reno (REE noh). Second most populated city in Nevada. (40°N/120°W) p. 210.

Rio Grande (REE oh grand). River that rises in the Rocky Mountains in Colorado. It empties into the Gulf of Mexico near Brownsville, Texas. It forms the boundary between Texas and Mexico. p. 189.

The page reference in each entry tells where the term is first used in the text.

A

acid rain (AS ihd rayn). A mixture of acid and rain water that falls to the earth. p. 340.

adobe (uh DOH bee). A mixture of straw and clay shaped into blocks and sun-dried into hard bricks. p. 205.

alloy (AL oi). A mixture of two or more metals. p. 368.

ambassador (am BAS uh dor). The highest representative of a government working and living in another country. p. 273.

ancient (AYN chunt). Belonging to times long past. p. 55.

anthracite (AN thruh syt). Hard coal. p. 344.

aqueduct (AK wuh dukt). A structure of pipes or an artificial channel used to transport water over a distance. p. 245.

atlas (AT lus). A collection of maps. p. 4.

atoll (A tawl). A ring-shaped coral island completely or nearly enclosing a body of water. p. 287.

axis (AK sihs). An imaginary line running through the earth between the North Pole and the South Pole.

B

barge (bahrj). A flat-bottomed boat used for transporting raw materials and other freight. p. 102.

bar graph (bahr graf). A kind of graph that uses bars to show information. p. 83.

barter (BAHRT ur). Trade by exchanging goods for other goods without using money. p. 302.

basin (BAYS un). A region drained by a river and its tributaries. p. 213.

bauxite (BAWKS yt). The ore from which aluminum is made. p. 368.

bilingual (bye LING gwel). Able to speak two languages equally well. p. 281.

bituminous (bih TOO muh nus). Soft coal that is used in making steel. p. 344.

blizzard (BLIHZ urd). A snowstorm with high winds. p. 218.

bog (bahg). A low marshy place. p. 82.

boom town (boom toun). A town that grew very quickly. p. 251.

boundary (BOUN duh ree). A line that separates one place from another. The border of a state or country. p. 10.

brand (brand). An identification mark burned into an animal's hide. p. 218.

butte (byoot). A small steep-sided hill. p. 188.

C

cacao (kuh KAY oh). A tropical tree and the seeds from which cocoa and chocolate are made. p. 364.

cactus (KAK tus). A plant of many varieties and sizes that grows in the desert. p. 193.

canal (kuh NAL). A waterway made by people. p. 102.

cannery (KAN ur ee). A food-processing factory. p. 170.

canyon (KAN yun). A very deep valley with steep sides, formed by running water that cuts into the ground over thousands of years. p. 40.

cardinal direction (KAHRD un ul duh REK shun). One of the four main directions, known as north, south, east, and west, used to locate a place on a map or globe. p. 8.

cash crop (kash krahp). A crop that is raised to be sold rather than to be used by the grower. p. 134.

cassava (kuh SAH vuh). A tropical plant with a large root that can be eaten or from which flour is made. p. 319.

causeway (KAWZ way). A bridge made by building up earth in strips until it is above water. p. 147.

census (SEN sus). A government count of the number of people in a country. p. 112.

citrus fruit (SIH trus froot). An edible fruit with a firm thick skin and a pulpy flesh with a sweet-sour taste. Oranges, lemons, and grapefruits are citrus fruits. p. 132.

climate (KLYE mut). The kind of weather a place has over a long period of time. p. 35.

coast (kohst). The land along the edge of an ocean or sea. p. 40.

colony (KAHL uh nee). A group of people who leave their own country to settle in another land, but who remain loyal to their own country. p. 93.

commerce (KAHM urs). The buying and selling of goods and services. p. 90.

compass rose (KUM pus rohz). A drawing on a map, used to show directions. p. 9.

coniferous (koh NIHF ur us). Having cones. Almost all coniferous trees are called evergreen trees. p. 360.

conserve (kun SURV). To use something carefully. p. 337.

continent (KAHN tuh nunt). A very large area of land. There are seven continents—North America, South America, Europe, Africa, Asia, Australia, and Antarctica. p. 5.

Continental Divide (kahn tuh NENT ul duh-VYD). High ridges separating rivers or streams flowing toward the east from those flowing toward the west. In the United States the Continental Divide is in the Rocky Mountains. p. 214.

contour line (KAHN toor lyn). A line on a map showing height above sea level. All places along the same contour line have approximately the same height. p. 22.

coral (KOR ul). A hard, chalky, rocklike material consisting of the skeleton or shell of polyps. p. 287.

crop rotation (krahp roh TAY shun). The varying from year to year of the crops grown in the same field to keep the soil from losing its fertility. p. 165.

D

delta (DEL tuh). Land made up of mud and sand and carried by some rivers downstream where it settles at the river's mouth. p. 40.

desalination (dee sal uh NAY shun). A process whereby the salt is removed from sea water, making it fresh water. p. 283.

desert (DEZ urt). A region with very little rainfall and few plants. p. 31.

diagram (DYE uh gram). A special kind of drawing that explains how something works or why something happens. p. 36.

dike (dyk). A wall or bank built to control or hold back the water of a river or a sea. p. 313.

dingo (DIHNG goh). A wild dog found in Australia. p. 330.

dock (dahk). A long platform built on the shore or out from the shore where ships can be loaded or unloaded. p. 110.

domestic trade (doh MES tihk trayd). The trade that takes place within a country. p. 305.

drought (drout). A long period of dryness with little or no rain. p. 164.

E

economy (ih KAHN uh mee). The production, distribution, and use of resources, goods, and services. p. 161.

elevation (el uh VAY shun). The height of something, often in relation to sea level. p. 22.

embassy (EM buh see). The building where an ambassador of a foreign country lives and works. p. 273.

emigrate (EM ih grayt). To leave one country for the purpose of settling in another. p. 281.

environment (en VYE run munt). All the things around us, such as water, land, animals, plants, and air. p. 31.

Equator (ee KWAYT ur). The imaginary line halfway between the North Pole and the South Pole, dividing the earth into the Northern Hemisphere and the Southern Hemisphere. Its latitude is 0°. p. 11.

erosion (ee ROH zhun). The wearing away of the earth's surface by wind, running water, ice, or waves. p. 164.

ethnic neighborhood (ETH nihk NAY bur hood). A part of a community that is settled by people who speak the same language and have the same customs. p. 93.

executive ● hydroelectricity

executive (eg ZEK yoo tihv). The part of government that has the power and duty to see that laws are carried out. p. 118.

explorer (ek SPLOR ur). A person who travels in search of something new. p. 366.

expedition (eks puh DIHSH un). A journey undertaken for a special purpose, such as exploration. p. 366.

export (eks PORT). **1.** Something that is sent to another country, usually for sale there. **2.** To send something to another country for sale. p. 110.

extraterrestrial (eks truh tuh RES tree ul). Anything that exists, happens, or comes from outside the earth. p. 148.

F

factory ship (FAK tuh ree shihp). A ship with equipment and people who can process, freeze, and package the fish that the ship takes in. p. 359.

fall line (fawl lyn). A line of small rapids and waterfalls that marks the change in elevation between plateaus and plains. p. 142.

famine (FAM ihn). A very great shortage of food. p. 93.

feedlot (FEED laht). A large fenced-in pen where livestock are kept and fattened before being slaughtered. p. 168.

fertile (FURT ul). Condition of soil rich in minerals needed by plants for good growth. p. 106.

fossil fuel (FAHS ul FYOO ul). Fuel that was formed over millions of years from the remains of once-living things. p. 338.

freeway (FREE way). An express highway with limited entrances and exits on which no toll is charged. p. 259.

freight (frayt). Goods that a ship or a train carries. p. 295.

G

geography (jee AHG ruh fee). The study of the earth and how people use it. p. 30.

geyser (GYE zur). A fountain of steam and water that has been heated by hot lava and forced above the ground by volcanic gases. p. 357.

ghost town (gohst toun). A community from which people have departed but where buildings still stand. p. 220.

globe (glohb). A model of the earth. p. 4.

grain elevator (grayn EL uh vayt ur). A large building where grain is stored and cleaned before it is shipped. p. 172.

grid (grihd). A system of crossing lines or boxes on a map or globe. Crossing latitude and longitude lines form a grid. p. 15.

growing season (GROH ing SEE zun). The time of the year when crops can be grown. p. 37.

gulf (gulf). A part of an ocean or a sea that pushes inland. p. 41.

H

harvest (HAHR vihst). The gathering of crops of any kind. p. 177.

hemisphere (HEM ih sfihr). One half of a sphere, or ball; half of the earth. p. 12.

heritage (HER ih tihj). What is handed on to people from the past, such as beliefs and customs. p. 259.

hibernate (HYE bur nayt). To spend the winter in a sleeping state in a sheltered place as some animals do. p. 361.

high technology (hye tek NAHL uh jee). The most up-to-date knowledge and tools that do jobs that were once done by people. p. 89.

human resources (HYOO mun REE sors ihz). A term used when referring to people and especially when referring to the employment of their knowledge and skills. p. 373.

humidity (hyoo MIHD uh tee). The amount of moisture in the air. p. 105.

hurricane (HUR ih kayn). A violent storm with heavy rains and high winds. p. 125.

hydroelectricity (hye droh ee lek TRIH siht ee). Electricity produced by the power of rapidly moving water. p. 144.

I

igloo (IHG loo). A small dwelling that is often shaped like a dome and is built of blocks of hard snow. p. 257.

immigrant (ihm uh grunt). A person who comes to a country with the purpose of making a home there. p. 60.

import (IHM port). **1.** Something that is brought into a country, usually for sale there. **2.** To bring in goods to a country, usually for sale there. p. 110.

industry (IHN dus tree). Manufacturing of goods. p. 47.

inland (IHN lund). Land away from the ocean. p. 125.

intermediate direction (ihn tur MEE dee iht duh-REK shun). Directions between two of the main or cardinal directions, such as southwest. p. 10.

international trade (ihn tur NASH uh nul trayd). Trade that takes place between or among countries. p. 305.

interstate highway (ihn tur stayt hye way). A major road that goes from one state to another. p. 228.

irrigation (ihr uh GAY shun). The watering of crops or other plants, usually through pipes, canals, or ditches. p. 163.

island (EYE lund). A body of land completely surrounded by water. p. 41.

J

jackeroo (jak uh ROO). A person who works on a sheep station in Australia. p. 330.

judicial (joo DIHSH ul). The part of government that is in charge of deciding the meaning of laws. p. 118.

K

kayak (KYE ak). A small skin-covered canoe large enough for only one passenger. p. 256.

kelp (kelp). Seaweed used for a variety of foods, such as vegetables, soups, and biscuits. p. 372.

kernel (KUR nul). The part of any grain that is used for food. p. 325.

key (kee). The place on a map where symbols are explained. p. 16.

L

lake (layk). A body of water completely surrounded by land. p. 41.

landform (LAND form). A feature of the earth's surface created by nature. Mountains, hills, plateaus, and plains are all landforms. p. 34.

landscape (LAND skayp). The natural environment and the things people have built on it. p. 58.

latitude (LAT uh tood). Distance north or south of the earth's Equator, measured in degrees. The lines that measure latitude run east and west on a map or globe. p. 11.

lava (LAH vuh). Melted rock that is very hot. p. 240.

legend (LEJ und). The part of a map that tells what the symbols on the map stand for. *Key* is another word for legend on a map. p. 16.

legislative (LEJ ihs layt ihv). The part of government that makes laws. p. 118.

lei (lay). In Hawaii, a garland of flowers generally worn around the neck. p. 258.

line graph (lyn graf). A graph that shows information by means of a line. A line graph usually shows how things change over a period of time. p. 117.

livestock (LYV stahk). Farm animals, such as cows, pigs, and sheep. p. 174.

location (loh KAY shun). Where something is on the earth. p. 30.

locomotive (loh kuh MOHT ihv). An engine on wheels that moves railroad trains. p. 293.

longitude (LAHN juh tood). The distance east or west of the Prime Meridian, measured in degrees. Lines of longitude on a map or globe run from the North Pole to the South Pole. p. 12.

luau (LOO ou). A Hawaiian-style dinner with performances by singers and dancers. p. 258.

manufacture • ore

M

manufacture (man yoo FAK chur). To make a finished product from raw material. p. 46.

map (map). A special kind of drawing that can show different parts of the earth. p. 4.

meat-packing industry (MEET pak ing IHN dustree). The industry that prepares meat for the food market. p. 169.

megalopolis (meg uh LAHP uh lihs). A group of cities so close to one another that they seem to form a continuous city. p. 114.

mesa (MAY suh). A hill with steep sides. p. 188.

metropolitan area (me troh PAHL ih tun ER ee-uh). An area made up of a large city or several large cities and surrounding towns, smaller cities, and other communities. p. 90.

migration (mye gray shun). The movement of people from one place to another. p. 62.

mill (mihl). A building in which special machines process raw materials into useful products by various methods. p. 88.

milling (MIHL ing). The grinding of grain, cutting of metal, or other processes that prepare a product for use. p. 170.

mineral (MIHN ur ul). A substance obtained by mining or digging in the earth. p. 60.

mint (mihnt). A place where the government makes coins. p. 230.

mission (mihsh un). A small church and settlement where missionaries taught people about Christianity. p. 204.

model (MAHD ul). A small copy of a real thing. p. 4.

monsoon (mahn SOON). Seasonal wind that blows from the land to the water in one season and from the water to the land in the other. p. 323.

monument (MAHN yoo munt). Something such as a building, tower, or statue that is built to honor a person or an event. p. 119.

mountain (MOUNT un). A piece of land that rises sharply from the land around it. p. 42.

mountain range (MOUNT un raynj). A line of mountains. p. 53.

N

natural resource (NACH ur ul REE sors). Something that is provided by nature and that is useful to people. p. 46.

natural vegetation (NACH ur ul vej uh TAY shun). The plants that grow naturally in a region untouched by people. p. 37.

navigable (nav ih guh bul). Able to be traveled by ships and boats. p. 298.

nonrenewable resource (nahn rih NOO un bul REE sors). A resource that cannot be replaced by nature or by people. p. 337.

North Pole (north pohl). The northernmost place on the surface of the earth. The North Pole is located in the Arctic Ocean. p. 8.

nuclear energy (NOO klee ur EN ur jee). The energy that is stored in the center of an atom and that can be used to make electricity. p. 347.

O

ocean (OH shun). A very large body of salt water. There are four oceans — the Pacific, Atlantic, Indian, and Arctic. p. 5.

offshore field (AWF shor feeld). A petroleum field located at the bottom of the sea, a distance away from the coast. p. 197.

oil refinery (oil rih FYN ur ee). A factory where crude oil, or petroleum, is purified. p. 197.

oil rig (oil rihg). A platform held up by legs fastened to the bottom of the sea. p. 198.

oil shale (oil shayl). A rock with a tarlike substance that contains tiny drops of oil. p. 223.

oil tanker (oil TANGK ur). A big ship with large tanks used for shipping oil. p. 199.

open-pit mining (OH pun piht MYN ing). Mining carried out by stripping the soil from the surface rather than by tunneling into the earth. Also called strip mining. p. 223.

orange grove (OR ihnj grohv). An orchard with orange trees. p. 132.

orchard (OR churd). A field of fruit trees planted in a straight row. p. 107.

ore (or). A material containing one or more minerals. p. 60.

ore carrier (or KAR ee ur). A large ship built for carrying ore. p. 172.

outback (OUT bak). The hot dry lands in the middle and the western part of Australia. p. 327.

P

paddock (PAD uk). A large fenced-in area where sheep graze. p. 330.

paddy (PAD ee). A rice field, particularly a field in which irrigated rice is raised. p. 321.

panhandle (PAN han dul). A narrow strip of land extending from a larger land area. p. 188.

pasture (pas chur). A grassy field where animals can feed. p. 174.

peat (peet). Decayed moss and plants used as fuel and fertilizers. p. 344.

peninsula (puh nihn suh luh). A piece of land almost surrounded by water and connected to a larger body of land. p. 42.

pesticide (PES tuh syd). A chemical used to prevent insects and disease from destroying crops. p. 194.

petrochemical industry (pe troh KEM ih kul IHN-dus tree). The industry that produces chemicals or synthetic materials from petroleum or natural gas. p. 143.

petroleum (puh TROH lee um). An oily liquid found in the earth from which gasoline and many other products are made. p. 197.

pie graph (pye graf). A graph in the form of a circle, used to show the parts of a whole. p. 7.

pioneer (pye uh nihr). A person who does something first, such as settling a new place, making it easier for others to follow. p. 157.

plain (playn). A wide area of flat or gently rolling land that is often treeless. p. 42.

plantain (PLAN tihn). A kind of large banana. p. 276.

plantation (plan TAY shun). A large farm on which one main crop is grown. p. 132.

plateau (pla TOH). A raised, level piece of land that covers a large area. p. 43.

polder (pohl dur). Land reclaimed from water, usually by pumping the water out of the area enclosed by dikes. p. 315.

pollution (puh LOO shun). The act of making the air, land, and water dirty. p. 340.

population density (pahp yoo LAY shun DEN suh-tee). The average number of people per unit of an area, such as a square mile or square kilometer, in a country or state. p. 112.

prairie (PRER ee). An area of level or rolling grassland with few trees. p. 157.

precipitation (pree sihp uh TAY shun). Moisture that falls on the earth's surface in the form of rain, snow, sleet, hail, fog, or mist. p. 35.

Prime Meridian (prym muh RIHD ee un). The longitude line from which other longitudes are measured. The Prime Meridian is numbered 0°. p. 12.

produce (PRAH doos). Fresh fruit and vegetables on sale at a market. p. 106.

promontory (PRAHM un tor ee). High land that juts out into water along a coastline. p. 76.

prospector (PRAH spek tur). A person who explores an area in search of minerals such as gold. p. 220.

pueblo (PWEB loh). A Native American village in the southwestern United States. Also a dwelling in such a village. p. 204.

Q

quarry (KWAWR ee). A place from which materials such as marble, stone, slate, or limestone are cut, dug, or blasted. p. 88.

R

rain forest (rayn FOR ihst). A forest with a thick growth of trees and heavy rainfall. p. 320.

ranch (ranch). A large farm with grazing land for raising cattle, sheep, or horses. p. 196.

rapids (RAP ihdz). Part of a river's course where the water rushes quickly, often over rocks that are near the surface. p. 142.

raw material • suburb

raw material (raw muh TIHR ee ul). Material in its natural state that can be used to make finished products. p. 46.

reclaim (ree KLAYM). To return something to useful condition. p. 315.

recycle (ree SYE kul). To use again and again, as a supply of water. p. 350.

region (REE jun). An area of land whose parts have one or more common characteristics. p. 55.

relief map (rih LEEF map). A map that shows the elevation of land on the earth's surface. p. 23.

renewable resource (rih NOO uh bul REE sors). A resource that can be replaced by nature or by people. p. 337.

reservation (rez ur VAY shun). Land set aside by the government for a special purpose, for example, for use by Native Americans. p. 191.

reservoir (REZ ur vwahr). A collection and storage place for water. Reservoirs look like small lakes. p. 144.

roundup (ROUND up). The gathering together of all the cattle or sheep on a ranch at certain times. p. 218.

rural area (ROOR ul ER ee uh). An area in the country as opposed to the city. p. 59.

S

scale (skayl). A way of showing distance or size on a map. p. 16.

sea level (see LEV ul). The base from which the elevation of the earth's land is measured. p. 22.

semidesert (sem ih DEZ urt). An area not quite as dry as a desert but with less rain and vegetation than a plain. p. 214.

service (SUR vihs). A kind of work that helps people. p. 48.

shaft mining (shaft MYN ing). Mining done by digging straight down to the level of the material that is to be removed. p. 345.

shearing (SHIHR ing). The term used for cutting off a sheep's thick winter wool. p. 330.

shifting agriculture (SHIHFT ing AG rih kul chur). Agriculture practiced in areas with poor soil. Farmers move every year or two, clearing new land for crops by cutting and burning the natural vegetation. p. 319.

slash-and-burn-farming (slash un BURN FAHRM-ing). A term for the cutting, slashing, drying, and burning of trees and plants that clears the land and enriches the soil for crops. p. 320.

smelter (SMELT ur). A place for the process of separating a metal from other materials in its ore. p. 224.

solar cell (SOH lur sel). A part of a solar battery that can change sun energy to electric energy. p. 352.

solar energy (SOH lur EN ur jee). Energy that comes from the sun. p. 351.

sound (sound). A channel of water connecting two large bodies of water or separating an island from the mainland. p. 76.

South Pole (south pohl). The southernmost place on the surface of the earth. The South Pole is located on the continent of Antarctica. p. 9.

specialize (SPESH ul yz). To work at only one kind of task. p. 302.

specialty crop (SPESH ul tee krahp). A type of crop that brings in more money than other crops raised on the same amount of land. p. 83.

sphere (sfihr). An object that is round like a ball. The earth is a sphere. p. 4.

standard of living (STAN durd uv LIHV ing). A measure of how well people live in a country. p. 304.

station (STAY shun). In Australia, a big sheep or cattle ranch. p. 326.

stockyard (STAHK yahrd). A large yard where livestock is kept for a short time before being shipped or slaughtered. p. 179.

strip cropping (strihp KRAHP ing). The planting of crops in long strips between rows of thick grass. p. 164.

suburb (SUB urb). A community near a city, where many people have their homes. p. 59.

sugarcane (SHOOG ur kayn). A plant with a tall stalk that is used to make sugar. p. 247.

supertanker (SOO pur tangk ur). A huge ship fitted with tanks for transporting oil. p. 297.

surplus (SUR plus). Amount over and above what is needed. p. 306.

swamp (swahmp). Low, spongy land, often covered with water. p. 147.

symbol (SIHM bul). Something used on a map that stands for real things and places on the earth's surface. p. 16.

synthetic (sihn THET ihk). Made artificially by a chemical process. p. 141.

T

taiga (TYE guh). A coniferous forest region that stretches across northern Europe, Asia, and North America. p. 360.

temperature (TEM pur uh chur). The amount of heat and cold as measured on a given scale, such as the Fahrenheit or Celsius scale. p. 35.

terrace (TER us). Flat shelf of land cut into the side of a hill or mountain to make places where crops can be grown. p. 56.

textile (TEKS tyl). Having to do with cloth. Also fibers and yarns woven into cloth. p. 88.

timber (TIHM bur). Standing or cut trees that can be used for building. p. 47.

time line (tym lyn). A line that shows facts about time. p. 92.

tourism (TOOR ihz um). The industry that serves people who travel for pleasure. p. 111.

tourist (TOOR ihst). A person who makes a trip for pleasure. p. 111.

trade wind (trayd wind). Wind that blows over the ocean in one direction, usually toward the Equator. p. 278.

transcontinental railroad (trans kahn tuh NENT ul RAYL rohd). Train system that goes across a continent. p. 226.

trawler (TRAWL ur). A fishing boat used for commercial fishing. p. 357.

tree farm (tree fahrm). An area where hundreds of trees, usually pines, are planted in long, straight rows, just like farm crops. p. 141.

tributary (TRIHB yoo ter ee). A stream or river that flows into a larger stream or river or into a lake. p. 102.

tropics (TRAHP ihks). The region extending on either side of the Equator from about 23° north latitude to about 23° south latitude. p. 320.

truck farm (truk fahrm). A farm that raises fruits and vegetables that are sent by trucks to nearby markets. p. 106.

tundra (tun druh). A cold treeless area found in the Arctic region. p. 251.

turbine (TUR bihn). A machine that turns rapidly from the pressure of steam or water. p. 343.

typhoon (TYE foon). A tropical storm occurring in the region of the Philippine Islands and the China Sea. p. 285.

V

valley (VAL ee). A long, low area, usually between hills and mountains or along a river. p. 43.

veterinarian (vet ur uh NER ee un). A doctor who takes care of the health of animals. p. 48.

vineyard (VIHN yurd). A place where grapes are grown. p. 107.

volcanic island (vahl KAN ihk eye lund). An island formed by volcanic eruptions that have piled lava high above the surface of the water. p. 287.

volcano (vahl KAY noh). An opening in the earth, usually at the top of a cone-shaped hill, out of which steam and melted or hot rock may pour from time to time. p. 240.

W

weather (WETHH ur). The condition of the air at a certain time in a given place. p. 35.

wheat belt (wheet belt). A region of a country or continent where mostly wheat is grown. p. 55.

wilderness (WIHL dur nihs). An area that is more or less in its natural state. p. 99.

wood pulp (wood pulp). A mixture of ground wood and chemicals used to make paper. p. 86.

INDEX

A

Acid rain, 340
Adelaide, Australia, 326, 328
Adirondack Mountains, 101
Africa, 5, 31, 32, 62, 297, 298, 309, 338, 359
Aircraft industry, 254
Airplanes, 295, 299
Alabama, 77, 126, 127, 130, 134
Alaska, 10, 57, 58, 188, 211, 213, 238, 246, 251, 253, 255, 256
Albany, New York, 102
Albuquerque, New Mexico, 202
Alice Springs, Australia, 326, 328
Allegheny Mountains, 101, 102
Allen, Joseph, 53
Aluminum, 144, 368
Amazon Basin, 363–364
Amazon River, 363
Ambassadors, 273
American River, 250
American Samoa, 288–289
Anchorage, Alaska, 246
Anglo culture, 204, 205
Antarctica, 5, 34, 62, 108, 342
Anthracite, 344
Appalachian Mountains, 77, 101, 127, 129, 135, 142, 145, 148, 161, 213
Aqueducts, 245
Arctic Ocean, 5, 57, 246, 251
Arizona, 54, 187, 188, 190, 191, 192, 193, 199, 200, 203, 204, 366
Arkansas, 126, 131, 135
Arkansas River, 214
Asia, 5, 7, 56, 62, 309, 321, 338, 360, 365
Atacama Desert, 36
Atlanta, Georgia, 130, 145–146
Atlantic Coastal Plain, 102, 106, 114, 127, 130, 131, 142
Atlantic Ocean, 5, 32, 57, 75, 76, 85, 99, 100, 101, 102, 109, 126, 138, 142, 160, 162, 214, 299, 315, 357
Atlas, 4
Atolls, 287
Austin, Texas, 190
Australia, 5, 7, 62, 326–333
Automobiles, 173, 295, 297, 372
Axis of Earth, 36–37
Aztecs, 303

B

Baltimore, Maryland, 109, 110, 114
Barges, 102, 298, 307
Bar graphs, 83
Barre, Vermont, 91
Bartering, 302–303
Basins, 191, 213
Bath, Maine, 89
Baton Rouge, Louisiana, 143
Bauxite, 368
Bays, 5, 100, 138–139, 315
Beef cattle, 168–169, 179, 195, 203, 218, 247, 327
Belgium, 306, 307
Bering Sea, 57
Bingham Canyon, 221, 223
Bird's-eye view, 20–21
Birmingham, Alabama, 142, 143
Bituminous coal, 344
Black Hills, 173
Blizzards, 218
Blue Ridge Mountains, 127, 149
Bogs, 82–83
Bolivia, 368, 370
Boom towns, 251
Boston, Massachusetts, 75, 90, 93, 113, 114
Boundary lines, 10
Brands, 218
Brazil, 368
Brazil nuts, 364
Brussels, Belgium, 306–307
Buffalo, New York, 102, 109, 111
By the Shores of Silver Lake, 157–158

C

Cacao, 364
Cactuses, 193
Cairo, Egypt, 13
California, 44, 53, 200, 211, 226, 237, 238, 243, 244, 245, 250, 252, 254, 305
  gold rush, 250–251
Canada, 57, 63, 76, 77, 100, 111, 129, 160, 190, 213, 309, 360, 373
Canals, 102, 298, 307
Canaveral, Cape, 148
Canneries, 170, 230, 253, 255
Capitol, 117–118
Cardinal directions, 8–9
Caribbean Sea, 43, 276, 278, 283, 298, 365
Carver, George Washington, 134, 136, 137
Cascades, 238
Cassava, 319–320
Catskill Mountains, 101, 102
Causeways, 147
Census, 112
Central Plains, 158, 160
Central Valley, 243, 244
Charleston, South Carolina, 126
Charlotte Amalie, U. S. Virgin Islands, 282
Chesapeake Bay, 100, 109, 110, 138
Chicago, Illinois, 178, 294
China, 63, 303, 344
Cities, 58–59
  See also names of individual cities.
Citrus fruits, 132, 194
Climate, 35–36, 37, 55, 79–80, 81, 83, 105, 130–131, 132, 162–164, 192, 213, 216, 244, 245, 246–247, 278–279, 361–362
Climographs, 163
Coal, 108, 142, 143, 288–289, 305, 337–340, 343–345, 372
Coal mining, 108–109, 142, 345
Coastal Ranges, 238
Colleges and universities, 90
Cologne, West Germany, 306

Colombia, 366
Colonies, 93
Colorado, 188, 190, 200, 211, 213, 214, 217, 219, 221, 223
Colorado Plateau, 190–191, 192
Colorado River, 187, 190, 192, 194, 200, 213
Columbia River, 243, 298
Columbia, South Carolina, 142
Columbus, Christopher, 299, 365, 366
Commerce, 90
Common Market, 307–308
Communities, 58–59
Compass rose, 9
Complete Book of Marvels, 237
Computers, 89, 90, 255
Congress, 117–118, 277
Coniferous trees, 360
Connecticut, 76, 77, 79, 89, 90
Connecticut River, 77
Constitution of the United States, 118
Continental Divide, 214
Continents, 5, 7
Contour lines, 22, 23
Cooper, Peter, 293
Copper, 199, 221, 223, 224, 368
Coral islands, 287
Corn, 82, 106, 135, 165–166, 167, 169, 204, 217, 288, 319
Corn belt, 165, 169
Coronado, Francisco, 195, 204
Cotton, 132, 139, 141, 194, 245
Countries, 7, 10
Cow towns, 179
Cranberries, 82–83
Crop rotation, 165
Crops. *See* Farming and names of individual crops.
Cuba, 57

D

Dairy belt, 167
Dairy farming, 81–82, 107, 167, 174, 176–177, 315–316, 357
Dallas, Texas, 190, 202
Dams, 144, 200, 245, 254, 350

Death Valley, 244
Defense industry, 89
Delaware, 99, 102, 105, 106, 111, 278
Delaware Bay, 102, 111, 115
Delaware River, 102, 111, 115
Delmarva Peninsula, 106
Denmark, 307
Denver, Colorado, 213, 229–231
Department of Defense Dependents School system, 274–275
Desalination, 283
Deserts, 31, 32, 36, 191, 192, 193, 214, 244, 327
Des Moines, Iowa, 170
Detroit, Michigan, 172–173, 295
Diagrams, 36–37
Dikes, 313–315
Dingoes, 330, 332
Directions, 8–10
Distance, map and earth, 16, 18
District of Columbia, 99
Domestic trade, 305
Douglas firs, 253
Drought, 164
Duluth, Minnesota, 172, 173
Durban, South Africa, 13
Dust Bowl, 164

E

Earhart, Amelia, 53–54
Earning a living, ways of, 44–47
Earth
  axis of, 36–37
  bird's-eye view of, 20–21
  contours and elevation of, 22–23
  distance, 16, 18
  globe as model of, 4
  path of around sun, 36–37
  shape of, 4
East (direction), 8, 9
Eastern Hemisphere, 12
Economy, 161
Egypt, 298, 301
Elbert, Mount, 213
Electricity, 85, 144, 199, 200, 343, 345, 347, 350, 352, 353
Elevation, 22–23
Embassies, 273

Energy
  definition of, 337
  fossil fuels used for, 338, 340, 341, 342, 343–345
  nuclear, 199, 202, 347
  solar, 351–352
  water power used for, 350
  of the wind, 353
England, 75, 88
Environment, 31
  damage to the, 340, 342
  people and their, 39
Equator, 11–12, 36, 288, 357
Erie Canal, 102, 298
Erie, Lake, 100, 102
Erosion, 164–165
Eskimos. *See* Inuit.
Estevanico, 366
Estimation, 13, 15
Ethnic neighborhoods, 93
Eurasia, 5
Europe, 5, 62, 297, 306, 315, 338, 359, 360, 365
European Community, 307–308
Everglades, 147
Executive branch of government, 118
Explorers, 366
Exports, 110, 305
Exxon Valdez, 252

F

Factory ships, 359
Fall line, 142
Farming, 37, 44–45, 55, 313–333
  in African rain forest, 318–320
  in American Samoa, 289
  in Australia, 326–333
  beef cattle, 168–169, 179, 195, 203, 218, 247, 327
  citrus, 132, 194
  corn, 82, 106, 135, 165–166, 167, 169, 204, 217, 288, 319
  cotton, 132, 139, 141, 194, 245
  cranberry, 82–83
  crop rotation in, 165
  dairy, 81–82, 107, 167, 174, 176–177, 315–316, 357
  in East Asia, 321–325
  flower, 316–317

on Guam, 288
irrigation in, 163–164, 193, 194–195, 200, 245
in Japan, 371
in Middle Atlantic region, 106–107
mixed, 135
in Mountain West region, 216–219
in the Netherlands, 313–317
in New England, 81–83
in North Central region, 161, 162, 163–164
in Pacific West region, 244–245, 246–247
peach, 134–135
peanut, 132, 134
pineapple, 246, 281
potato, 82, 131, 135, 217, 245, 246
poultry, 106, 135, 316
in Puerto Rico, 281
rice, 131, 170, 194, 321–325
sheep, 218, 219, 326, 327, 328, 330, 357
slash-and-burn, 319, 320
in Southeast region, 130, 131–132, 134–135
in Southwest region, 193–196
soybean, 168
strip cropping in, 164–165
sugar beet, 217, 245
sugarcane, 247, 281, 288
tobacco, 135
truck, 106
in United States of America, 59–60
vegetable, 82, 106, 131, 135, 170, 194, 245, 246, 316
wheat, 14, 164, 165, 166, 170, 172, 217, 245, 305, 327
Federated States of Micronesia, 288
Feedlots, 168–169
Finger Lakes, 107
Fish and fishing, 84–85, 109, 138–139, 253–254, 255, 289, 357–359, 371–372
Fish ladders, 254

Florida, 126, 127, 130, 131, 132, 146–148, 190, 278, 366
Florida Keys, 127
Food processing, 254–255
  See also Canneries and Meat-packing industry.
Ford, Henry, 295
Forests
  in Amazon Basin, 363–364
  in Japan, 373
  in Mountain West region, 225
  in New England, 86
  in Pacific West region, 252–253
  in Southeast region, 141
  in Southwest region, 193
  in Soviet Union, 360–363
Fossil fuels, 338, 340, 343–345
Four Corners, 190
France, 306, 307
Frankfurt, West Germany, 274–275
Free Associated State, 277
Freeways, 259
Freight, 295
Fruits, 106, 107, 132, 134–135, 194, 245, 246

G

Galveston Bay, 199
Gary, Indiana, 172
Gemstones, 143, 366, 368
Geography, 30
  and people, 38
  themes of, 30, 33, 39, 47, 57, 58
Georgia, 126, 130, 134–135, 145
Geysers, 357
Ghost towns, 220
Globe, 4
Gold, 173, 221, 250–251, 366
Gold rush, 250–251
Government
  executive branch of, 118
  judicial branch of, 118
  legislative branch of, 118
  of Puerto Rico, 277
  state, 91

United States, 112
Grain elevators, 172
Grand Canyon, 40, 187, 188, 190
Granite, 88, 91
Graphs, 7, 83, 117, 142–143, 163
Great Basin, 213, 218, 229
Great Britain, 282, 307
Great Dividing Range, 327
Great Lakes, 100, 102, 160, 172
    See also names of individual lakes.
Great Plains, 160, 163, 164, 166, 172, 173, 179, 190, 192, 213, 229
Great Salt Lake, 214, 229
Great Salt Lake Desert, 214
Great Smoky Mountains, 127, 148–149
Greece, 307
Greenhouse effect, 340, 342
Green Mountains, 76, 77, 88, 91
Greenwich, England, 12
Grid, using a, 15
Groton, Connecticut, 89
Growing season, 37, 81, 82, 130–131, 167
Guam, 287–288
Gulf Coastal Plain, 127, 130, 131, 190, 194, 198
Gulf of Alaska, 57
Gulf of California, 200, 214
Gulf of Mexico, 41, 57, 126, 127, 129, 130, 138, 143, 190, 197, 198, 199, 214

H
Haarlem, Netherlands, 317
Halliburton, Richard, 187, 237
Hartford, Connecticut, 77, 90–91
Hatshepsut, 301
Hawaii, 10, 35–36, 41, 53, 58, 130, 238, 240, 246, 247, 257–258, 285, 306
Heimaey, Iceland, 357
Hemispheres, 12
High Point, North Carolina, 141

High-tech industries, 89, 90
High technology, 89
Honolulu, Hawaii, 238, 254, 258, 287
Hoover Dam, 200
House of Representatives, 118
Houston, Texas, 190, 197, 198, 199, 201
Hudson River, 101–102, 298
Human resources, 373
Humidity, 105
Huron, Lake, 172
Hurricane Hugo, 125, 284
Hurricanes, 125
Hydroelectricity, 144, 200, 350

I
Iceland, 357, 371
Idaho, 211, 214, 217, 225
Igloos, 257
IJsselmeer, 315
Illinois, 143, 160, 161, 162, 165, 167, 170, 229
Immigrants, 60, 62, 93, 259, 260
Imports, 110, 305
India, 63
Indiana, 160, 162, 165, 167, 170
Indian Ocean, 5, 323
Indonesia, 55, 316
Industries, 47, 86, 88–89, 90, 91, 92, 109, 111, 139, 141, 142, 143, 169, 170, 172–173, 198–199, 201–202, 224–225, 254–255, 276, 281, 282, 288, 372
Insurance, 90–91, 202
Interior Lowlands, 158, 160
Intermediate directions, 10
International trade, 305–309
Interstate highways, 228
Inuit, 256
Iowa, 160, 161, 165, 167
Ireland, 93, 307, 344
Iron ore, 109, 143, 172, 368, 372
Irrigation, 163–164, 193, 194–195, 200, 245
Irving, Washington, 101
Islands, 100, 127, 240, 257, 276–289
Italy, 307

J
Jackeroos, 330
Japan, 321, 371–374
Jefferson Memorial, 119
Jefferson, Thomas, 119
Johnson, Lyndon B., Space Center, 201
Judicial branch of government, 118
Juneau, Alaska, 246

K
Kangaroos, 332
Kansas, 160, 168, 179
Kansas City, Kansas, 170
Kansas City, Missouri, 170
Kansas River, 170
Kelp, 372
Kennedy, John F., Space Center, 148
Kentucky, 126, 129, 130, 135, 142, 143
Kernels, rice, 325
Key, 16, 22
Kilauea, 240
Kitty Hawk, North Carolina, 299

L
Lakes, 5, 76, 85, 100, 107, 160
    See also names of individual lakes.
Lakes Plain, 102
Lake Superior, 172
Lanai, Hawaii, 246
Landforms, 34, 40–43, 55
La Paz, Bolivia, 370
Las Vegas, Nevada, 214
Latin America, 55
Latitude, 11–12, 13, 15
Lava, 240, 287
Lead, 108, 173
Leadville, Colorado, 220
Legend, 16
Legislative branch of government, 118
Limestone, 143
Lincoln, Abraham, 119
Lincoln Memorial, 119
Line graphs, 117
Little Prince, The, 29, 30, 31
Livestock, 174, 179, 195–196, 218–219
    See also Beef cattle, Dairy farming, Poultry, Sheep.
Location, 30
Locomotives, 293, 294,

295
London, England, 299
Long Island, 100
Long Island Sound, 76, 77
Longitude, 12, 13, 15
Long, Stephen H., 145
Los Angeles, California, 259, 326
Louisiana, 126, 127, 131, 143
Luxembourg, 306, 307

M
Maine, 76, 79, 82, 84, 85, 86, 305
Manufacturing, 46
    in Mountain West region, 224–225
    in New England, 85
    in North Central region, 161, 172–173
    in Pacific West region, 254–255
    in Southeast region, 139, 141–144
    in Southwest region, 201–202
Maps, 4
    contour lines and elevation on, 22
    distance on, 16, 18
    latitude and longitude on, 11–13, 15
    physical, 23
    relief, 23
    scale on, 16, 18
    symbols on, 16, 32–33
Marcy, Mount, 101
Market gardens, 316
Marshall Islands, 288
Marshall, James, 250
Maryland, 99, 101, 105, 306
Massachusetts, 45, 75–76, 77, 79, 82, 84, 89, 195
Massachusetts Bay, 76
May, Cape, 111
McKinley, Mount, 42, 238
Mead, Lake, 200
Meat-packing industry, 169
Mediterranean Sea, 55, 298, 303
Megalopolis, 114
Memphis, Tennessee, 130
Menhaden, 84
Metric system, 19
Metropolitan area, 90

Mexico, 57, 188, 190, 195, 200, 204, 213, 303, 340, 360, 366
Miami, Florida, 130, 146–147
Michigan, 44, 158, 160, 211
Michigan, Lake, 158, 172, 178
Micronesia, islands of, 288–289
Middle Atlantic region, 64, 99–119, 127, 131
cities of, 113–115, 117–119
climate of, 105
farming in, 106–107
fishing in, 109
industry in, 109, 111
location and boundaries of, 99–100
minerals and mining in, 108–109
physical features of, 101–102
population of, 112–113
shipping in, 110
tourism in, 111
variety in, 99
Migration, 62
See also Movement.
Mills and milling, 85, 88–89, 109, 139, 141, 142, 170, 172, 230, 247, 253, 330
Minerals, 60, 88, 91, 108, 109, 142, 143, 172, 173, 197–199, 201, 220–224, 250–251, 252, 281, 282, 288–289, 297, 305, 337–340, 343–345, 366, 368, 370, 372
Mining, 108–109, 142, 172–173, 220–221, 223–224, 251, 345, 368, 369
Minneapolis, Minnesota, 170
Minnesota, 44, 129, 146, 158, 160, 165, 167, 172
Mints, 230
Missions, 204, 259
Mississippi, 126, 127, 130, 131
Mississippi River, 129, 146, 157, 160, 161, 170, 298
Missouri, 160, 161, 165, 173
Missouri River, 161, 214

Mitchell, Mount, 127
Mohawk River, 102
Mojave Desert, 244
Money, used in trade, 303–304
Monsoons, 323
Montana, 161, 211, 213, 217, 218, 221, 225, 371
Montpelier, Vermont, 91
Monuments, 119
Mormons, 229
Mountain ranges, 53, 191, 213
See also names of individual ranges.
Mountain West region, 64, 211–231
cities of, 214, 226, 228–231
farming in, 216–219
industry in, 224–225
location and climate of, 216
mining in, 220–224
physical features of, 213–214
size and population of, 211, 213
Movement, 47, 60, 62–63
Mystic, Connecticut, 91–92

N

National Earthquake Information Center (NEIC), 230
Native Americans, 59, 191, 199, 203, 204, 253, 303
Natural gas, 143, 337
Natural resources, 45–46, 357–374
air, 46
conserving, 337–338
fish, 357–359
forests, 337, 360–364
in Japan, 371–374
land, 46
nonrenewable, 337
people as, 373
renewable, 337
See also Forests, Minerals, Soil, and Water.
Natural vegetation, 37–38, 55, 192–193
Navajo Reservation, 191
Nebraska, 160, 165, 168
Netherlands, 306, 307, 313–317
Nevada, 200, 211, 213,

221
New England region, 64, 75–93, 99, 114, 127, 131, 139, 238
cities in, 90
climate of, 79–80, 81
early settlers in, 75
farming in, 81–83
fishing in, 84–85
forests in, 86
industry in, 86, 88–89, 90, 91, 92
location of, 75–76
name of, 75
physical features of, 76–77
size and population of, 79, 90
water as natural resource in, 85
New Hampshire, 76, 77, 79
New Jersey, 45, 83, 99, 102, 105, 106, 111, 316
New Mexico, 54, 188, 190, 191, 192, 193, 199, 202, 203, 204, 366
New Orleans, Louisiana, 13, 39, 146
New York, 44, 76, 99, 100, 101, 102, 105, 106, 107, 108, 111, 293
New York City, 105, 110, 114–115, 226, 299, 306, 326
Niagara Falls, 102, 111
Nonrenewable resources, 337
North America, 5, 55, 57, 102, 111, 129, 162, 193, 214, 238, 244, 365
North Carolina, 44, 45, 126, 127, 130, 134, 135, 141, 143, 148
North Central region, 64, 157–179, 218
cities of, 178–179
climate of, 162–164
farming in, 161, 162, 163–164
industry in, 170, 172–173
location of, 158, 161
minerals in, 172–173
physical features of, 158, 160–161
population of, 178–179
North Dakota, 160
North (direction), 8, 9
Northern Hemisphere, 12, 36, 37, 326

Northern Mariana Islands, 288
North Pole, 8, 11, 12, 36
North Sea, 306, 307, 315
North Slope, 251
Nuclear energy, 199, 202, 347

O

Oahu, 238
Oceans, 5
Offshore oil fields, 197–198
Ogden, Utah, 226
Ohio, 160, 162, 165, 170
Ohio River, 129, 160
Oil. *See* Petroleum.
Oil refineries, 197
Oil rigs, 198
Oil shale, 223–224
Oil spill, 252
Oil tankers, 199, 340
Oklahoma, 188, 190, 192, 193, 197, 201, 216
Oklahoma City, Oklahoma, 201
Omaha, Nebraska, 169
Ontario, Lake, 100, 298
Open-pit mining, 223, 345
Oranges, 132
Orchards, 107, 135, 245
Oregon, 238, 243, 244, 245, 252, 255
Ores, 60, 172
Oruro, Bolivia, 368, 370
Outback, 327
Oysters, 109, 139

P

Pacific islands, 285–289
Pacific Ocean, 5, 57, 58, 162, 238, 240, 245, 254, 257, 285, 287–288, 297–298, 327
Pacific West region, 64, 237–260
cities of, 258, 259–260
climate of, 244, 245, 246
farming in, 244–245, 246–247
fishing in, 253–254
industry in, 254–255
location of, 238
natural resources of, 250–254
physical features of, 238, 240, 243
ways of life in, 256–258
Paddies, 321, 323, 324
Paddocks, 330

Pago Pago, American Samoa, 288–289
Panama Canal, 298
Panhandles, 188
Paper industry, 86, 141, 142, 225, 253
Paris, France, 306
Patterns as part of geography, 56
Pawtucket, Rhode Island, 88
Peaches, 134–135
Peanuts, 132–134
Peat, 344
Pennsylvania, 99, 100, 101, 102, 105, 106, 107, 108, 109, 197, 372
Persian Gulf, 297
Pesticides, 194–195
Petrochemical industry, 143, 198–199, 224, 281, 282
Petroleum, 143, 197–199, 201, 223–224, 251–252, 281, 282, 297, 337, 338, 340, 372
Pharmaceutical industry, 276, 281
Philadelphia, Pennsylvania, 109, 114, 115, 117
Phoenix, Arizona, 201
Physical map, 23
Pictographs, 142–143
Piedmont Plateau, 127, 134–135, 142, 145
Pie graphs, 7
Pilgrims, 75, 195
Pineapples, 246, 281
Pioneers, 157
Pittsburgh, Pennsylvania, 109
Plains, 102, 134, 190
  See also names of individual plains.
Plantains, 276
Plantations, 132, 258, 281
Plateaus, 190
Platypuses, 332–333
Polders, 315
Pollution, 230–231, 340
Polynesia and Polynesian culture, 257–258
Population
  density, 112–113
  of United States, 112
Portland, Oregon, 255
Ports, 115, 146, 178, 251, 259, 260, 307

Portugal, 307
Potatoes, 82, 131, 135, 217, 245, 246
Poultry, 106, 135, 316
Precipitation, 35–36, 38, 163, 340
  See also Climate.
President of the United States, 118
Prime Meridian, 12
Prince William Sound, 251, 252
Produce, 106
Promontories, 76
Promontory Point, 226
Prospectors, 220
Providence, Rhode Island, 75
Prudhoe Bay, 251
Pueblos, 204
Puerto Rico, 276–281, 284
Punt, 301

Q
Quarries, 88, 91

R
Railroads, 293–294, 295, 306
Rainfall. *See* Precipitation.
Rain forests, 320, 363–364
Raleigh, North Carolina, 142
Ranches, 196, 205, 218–219, 326, 328, 330
Rapids, 142
Raw materials, 46–47, 86, 139, 141, 145, 260
Recycling, 350
Red Sea, 298
Redwoods, 252–253
Regions, 30, 55, 63–64
  Middle Atlantic, 64, 99–119, 127, 131
  Mountain West, 64, 211–231
  New England, 64, 75–93, 99, 114, 127, 131, 139, 238
  North Central, 64, 157–179, 218
  Pacific West, 64, 237–260
  Southeast, 64, 99, 125–149
  Southwest, 64, 187–205, 214
Relief map, 23

Renewable resources, 337
Reno, Nevada, 214
Research centers, 224–225
Reservations, 191, 204
Reservoirs, 144, 200, 245
Rhode Island, 75, 79, 278
Rice, 131, 170, 194, 321–325
Rio Grande, 188, 192
Rip Van Winkle, 101
Rivers, 5, 76, 77, 85, 101–102, 129, 142, 143–144, 160–161, 213–214, 245, 250, 298, 363
  See also names of individual rivers.
Rocky Mountains, 190, 192, 213, 214, 216, 218, 219, 220, 226, 229, 230
Roundup, 218
Rural areas, 59

S
Sacramento, California, 243
Sahara, 31, 32
St. Croix, U. S. Virgin Islands, 282, 283
Saint-Exupéry, Antoine de, 29
St. Helens, Mount, 240
St. John, U. S. Virgin Islands, 282, 283
St. Lawrence River, 100, 298
St. Lawrence Waterway, 160
St. Louis, Missouri, 32, 157, 161
St. Paul, Minnesota, 170
St. Thomas, U. S. Virgin Islands, 282
Salem, Oregon, 243, 255
Salmon, 253–254, 255
Salt Lake City, 214, 221, 224, 229
San Antonio, Texas, 190, 204
San Diego, California, 259
San Francisco Bay, 260
San Francisco, California, 251, 255, 259, 260
San Juan, Puerto Rico, 281
Santa Fe, New Mexico, 204

Saudi Arabia, 297, 338
Savage, James, 237
Savannah, Georgia, 13, 15
Scale, map, 16, 18
Schuylkill River, 115
Sea level, 22
Seas, 5
Seasons, 36–37, 326
Seattle, Washington, 254
Semidesert, 214
Senate, 118
Sequoias, 252, 253
Services and service workers, 48–49, 111
Shaft mining, 345
Shearing, 330
Sheep, 218, 219, 326, 327, 328, 330, 357
Shifting agriculture. *See* Slash-and-burn farming.
Shipbuilding, 86, 110, 254, 258, 259, 372
Shipping industry, 110, 146, 199, 260, 297–298
Sierra Nevada, 213, 238, 245
Silicon Valley, 255
Silver, 199, 220, 221, 366
Slash-and-burn farming, 319, 320
Slater, Samuel, 88
Smelters, 224, 230
Snake River, 214
Soil, 37, 38, 83, 106, 132, 164–165, 320
Solar cells, 352
Solar collectors, 351, 352
Solar energy, 351–352
Sound, 76
South (direction), 8, 9
South America, 5, 36, 55, 62, 109, 193, 309, 363, 365, 366, 368
South Carolina, 126, 135, 141
South Dakota, 160, 173
Southeast region, 64, 99, 125–149
  cities of, 145–147
  climate of, 130–131
  farming in, 130, 131–132, 134–135
  fishing in, 138–139
  industry in, 139, 141
  location of, 126–127
  natural wonders in, 148–149
  physical features of, 127, 129, 142

vacation spots in, 147–148
Southern Hemisphere, 12, 36, 37, 326
South Pole, 9, 11, 12, 36
Southwest region, 64, 187–205, 214
  borders of, 188
  cities of, 201–202
  climate of, 192
  cultures of, 203–205
  farming in, 193–196
  importance of water to, 200
  industry in, 198–199, 201–202
  minerals and metals in, 199
  physical features of, 188, 190–191
  population of, 188
  settlers in, 195–196, 204–205
  sizes and shapes of states of, 188
  vegetation of, 192–193
Soviet Union, 63, 344, 360–363
Soybeans, 168
Spain, 204, 277, 281, 287, 307, 365
Spanish culture, 204–205, 259, 281
Spanish language, 55
Specialization, 302, 304
Specialty crops, 83
Sphere, 4, 12
Standard of living, 304
States, 7, 10, 277
  See also names of individual states.
Stations, 326, 328, 330
Steel industry, 109, 142, 143, 172, 372
Stockyards, 179, 218, 230
Strip cropping, 164–165
Submarine building, 89
Suburbs, 59, 114
Suez Canal, 298
Sugar beets, 217, 245
Sugarcane, 247, 281, 288
Sun
  Earth's path around, 36–37
  as source of energy, 351–352
Supertankers, 297
Supreme Court, 118
Surplus goods, 306
Sutter, John, 250
Swamps, 147

Sydney, Australia, 326
Symbols on a map, 16, 32–33
Synthetic fibers, 141

T
Table, reading a, 62
Taiga, 360–363
Tariffs, 308
Temperature, 35, 37, 38, 163
  See also Climate.
Tennessee, 126, 130, 143, 144, 145, 148
Tennessee River, 129, 144
Tennessee Valley Authority (TVA), 144
Terraces, 56, 323, 371
Texas, 188, 190, 191, 192, 193, 194, 195, 197, 198, 211, 216, 218, 251, 366
Textile industry, 88–89, 139, 141, 142, 282
Timber, 47, 86, 141, 253, 297, 362–363, 364, 373
Time lines, 92
Tin, 368, 370
Tobacco, 135
Tomatoes, 82, 106, 131, 170, 245
Tom Sawyer Abroad, 32–33
Tom Thumb, 293, 294
Tourism and tourists, 111, 258, 281, 282, 288, 289
Trade
  bartering in, 302–303
  domestic, 305
  early, 301–303
  international, 305–309
  money used in, 303–304
  specialization and, 302
Trade winds, 278–279
Trans-Alaska Pipeline, 251
Transcontinental railroad, 226, 294
Transportation, 145, 178, 226, 228, 230
  by airplane, 295, 299
  early forms of, 293
  by railroads, 293–294, 295, 306
  by roads, 306
  by stagecoach, 293–294
  by water, 297–298, 306–307

Trawlers, 357, 358, 359
Tree farms, 141
Trenton, New Jersey, 112
Tributary, 102
Tropics, 320, 363
Truck farms, 106
Tucson, Arizona, 204
Tundra, 251
Turbines, 343, 347, 350
Turquoise, 199
Twain, Mark, 32
Typhoons, 285

U
United States of America, 7, 10
  changes in the land in, 59–60
  commonwealth of, 277
  communities in, 58–59
  landscapes of, 58–59
  location of, 57–58
  movement of people and goods in, 60, 62–63, 293–300
  regions of, 63–64, 75–93, 99–119, 125–149, 157–179, 187–205, 211–231, 237–260
U. S. Virgin Islands, 282–284
Uranium, 199, 202, 347
Utah, 188, 190, 191, 200, 211, 213, 214, 221, 223, 229

V
Valdez, Alaska, 251
Valleys, 243
Vegetables, 82, 106, 131, 135, 170, 194, 245, 246, 316
Vermont, 76, 77, 79, 81, 86, 87
Veterinarian, 48
Vietnam, 321
Virginia, 44, 99, 106, 126, 131, 134, 135, 149
Virgin Islands, 282
  See also U. S. Virgin Islands.
Volcanic islands, 287
Volcanoes, 240, 282, 289, 357, 371

W
Walt Disney World, 148
Washington, 44, 214, 238, 240, 244, 245, 253,

255
Washington, D.C., 99–100, 113, 114, 117–119, 164
Washington, George, 119
Washington Monument, 119
Washington, Mount, 77, 238
Water
  for drinking, 160, 200
  for farming, 160, 163–164, 200
  pollution of, 195
  for power, 85, 143–144, 200
  shortage of, 283
  for transportation, 85, 160
Waterfalls, 85, 102, 142
Weather, 35
West (direction), 8, 9
Western Hemisphere, 12
West Germany, 306, 307
West Virginia, 126, 129, 130, 372
Whaling industry, 91–92
Wheat, 14, 164, 165, 166, 170, 172, 217, 245, 305, 327
Wheat belt, 55, 166
Wheeler Peak, 190
White House, 118, 164
White Mountains, 77, 238
Wichita, Kansas, 179
Wilder, Laura Ingalls, 157–158
Wildlife, 38, 332–333, 361–362
Willamette River, 243
Willamette Valley, 243, 245, 255
Wilmington, Delaware, 110, 113, 114
Wind energy, 353
Wisconsin, 160, 161, 167, 174
Wood pulp, 86, 141, 225
Wright, Orville and Wilbur, 299
Wyoming, 211, 214, 218, 219, 223, 224, 225

Y
Young, Brigham, 229
Yukon River valley, 251

Z
Zinc, 108, 143, 173
Zuider Zee, 315

CREDITS

Cover: D.C. Lowe/AllStock

Contributing artists: Anthony Accardo: 61; Alex Bloch: 313; Suzanne Clee: 242; Len Ebert: 84, 168, 254; Dan Fiore: 87, 133, 171; Simon Galkin: 140, 269; Bob Jackson: 240, 318–319; Manissa Lipstein: 345, 348; Laurie Marks: 336; Kathy Mitchell: 284; Nancy Murga: 331; T. Oughton: 342; Susan Sanford: 279, 287.

Graphs: Richard Puder Design/JAK Graphics, Ltd.

Maps: Maryland Cartographics, Inc.

Time lines: Maryland Cartographics, Inc.

Photographs: *All photographs by Silver Burdett & Ginn (SB&G) unless otherwise noted.*

Table of contents: iii; Kunio Owaki/The Stock Market. iv: Larry Hamill. vi: Bob Thomason/Leo deWys, Inc.

Map Handbook 2, 4: Robert Harding Photo Library. 8: Historical Pictures Service, Chicago. 15: John Scowen/FPG. 16: Randa Bishop/After Image, Inc. 17: *t.–b.:* Alan Oddie/Photo Edit; Paul Conklin/Photo Edit; Craig Anderson/Stockfile; Alan Oddie/Photo Edit; Coal Mining Assoc.; Wendell Metzen/Bruce Coleman; 21: Spencer Swanger/TOM STACK & ASSOCIATES. 22: William Waterfall/The Stock Market.

Unit 1 opener 26: *t.l.* F. Salaff/FPG; *b.l.* Grant Heilman Photography; *t.r.* Kunio Owaki/The Stock Market.

Chapter 1 28: SuperStock; *inset:* TSW-Click, Chicago. 29: Christian Science Museum, Boston. 30: Patsy Davidson/Image Works. 31: Marmel Studios/The Stock Market. 33: *t.* James Blank/After Image, Inc.; *b.* David R. Frazier. 34: Kevin Schafer/AllStock, Inc. 36: Bill Binzen/The Stock Market. 38: *l.* Charis Harvey/TSW-Click, Chicago; *t.r.* Rod Williams/Bruce Coleman; *m.r.* TOM STACK & ASSOCIATES; *b.r.* Gerry Ellis/Ellis Wildlife Collection. 39: Nathan Benn/AllStock, Inc. 40: *t.* Cameron Davidson/Bruce Coleman; *m.* Steve Vidler/Leo deWys, Inc. 41: *t.* SuperStock; *b.* Dan McCoy/Rainbow. 42: *t.l.* Dr. E.R. Degginger; *m.l., b.l.* Harald Sund. 43: *t.* Grant Heilman Photography; *b.* Robert Harding Picture Library. 44: The Bettmann Archive. 45: © Reneee Lynn/Photo Researchers, Inc. 46: David R. Frazier. 47: *l.* J. Barry O'Rourke/The Stock Market; *r.* Charles Krebs/AllStock, Inc. 48: *l.* Will & Deni McIntyre/Photo Researchers, Inc; *m.* © Blair Seitz/Photo Researchers, Inc.; *r.* Photri. 49: *l.* Michal Heron; *r.* Richard Hutchings/Info Edit.

Chapter 2 52: Roy Bishop/Stock, Boston. 53: The Bettmann Archive. 54: *t.* N. Renandeau/Leo deWys, Inc.; *b.* Wolfgang Kaehler. 56: David Austen/TSW-Click, Chicago. 58: John Penisten/The Travel Image. 59: Ken Dequaine/Third Coast Stock Source.

Unit 2 opener 73: *t.* Larry Hamill.

Chapter 3 76: Jacob Mosser/Positive Images. 77: Craig Blouin. 78: F. Sieb/H. Armstrong Roberts. 79: Gabe Palmer/The Stock Market. 81: Grant Heilman Photography. 82: *l.* Sarah Putnam/The Picture Cube; *r.* Martin Rogers/Stock, Boston. 85: Robert Frerck/TSW-Click, Chicago. 86: Larry Kolvoord/TexaStock. 88: Luis Villota/The Stock Market. 90: Brownie Harris/The Stock Market. 91: Carolyn L. Bates/f/Stop Pictures, Inc. 93: Jeffrey Dunn.

Chapter 4 101: Animals Animals/© Mischeal P. Gadomski. 103: © Thomas D. Friedman/Photo Researchers, Inc. 105: Brent Petersen/The Stock Market. 106: *l.* J.T. Miller/The Stock Market; *r.* Index Stock International. 107: Augustus Upitis/SuperStock. 108: TSW-Click, Chicago. 109: Charles Harbutt/Actuality, Inc. 110: Phil Degginger. 111: Bruce Byers/FPG. 115: R. Kord/H. Armstrong Roberts. 117: Steve Vidler/Leo deWys, Inc. 118: *l.* David Ball/The Stock Market; *r.* Chip Hires/Gamma-Liaison. 119: *l.* Mark Antman/Image Works; *r.* James Blank/The Stock Market.

Chapter 5 127: Terry Oning/FPG. 128: © Kent & Donna Dannen/Photo Researchers, Inc. 129: TOM STACK & ASSOCIATES. 135: Charles McNulty/TSW-Click, Chicago. 136: National Parks Service. 137: Culver Pictures. 138: *l.* © Richard Frear/Photo Researchers, Inc. 139: © 1991 Bill Weems/Woodfin Camp & Associates. 141: Ron Sherman/Bruce Coleman; *inset:* Timothy O'Keefe/TOM STACK & ASSOCIATES. 142: Paul Reitmire/Southern Stock Photos. 145: Tony Linck/SuperStock. 146: Bob Daemmrich/Image Works. 147: Fridmar Damm/Leo deWys, Inc.; *l. inset* Stan Osolinski/TSW Click, Chicago; *r. inset* Animals Animals/© Fred Whitehead. 148: NASA. 149: The Stock Market.

Chapter 6 159: © Kent & Donna Dannen/Photo Researchers, Inc. 161: Gary Irving/TSW-Click, Chicago. 162: George Mars Cassidy/TSW-Click, Chicago. 164: J.G. Zimmerman/FPG. 166: Julian Calder/TSW-Click, Chicago. 167: Ken Dequaine/Third Coast Stock Source. 169: Walsh Bellville/Frozen Images. 170: E. Dahl/FPG. 172: © 1991 Cotton Coulson/Woodfin Camp & Associates. 173: George Schwartz/FPG. 174: Buck Miller/Third Coast Stock Source. 176: David R. Frazier. 177: Jon Yeager/Frozen Images. 178: G. Kufrin/FPG. 179: *l.* Arni Katz; *r.* Perry Murphy/Unicorn Stock.

Chapter 7 188: M. Long/Visual Images. 189: © Joe Munroe/Photo Researchers, Inc. 190: Shostal Associates/SuperStock. 191: *l.* Michal Heron; *r.* Terry E. Eiler/Stock, Boston. 193: *t.* Ken Ross/Viesti Associates; *b.* © Garry D. McMichael/Photo Researchers, Inc. 195: Aldus Archive/Syndication International. 196: Richard Stockton/The Stockhouse, Inc. 197: J. Howard/FPG. 199: Shostal Associates/SuperStock. 200: FPG. 202: Scott Berner/Nawrocki Stock Photos. 204: Joe Viesti. 205: Steve Vidler/Leo deWys, Inc.

Chapter 8 212: Michael Suber/Taurus Photos, Inc. 213: David Lokey/Comstock. 214: *l.* John Gerlach/DRK Photos; *r.* Grant Heilman Photography. 217: David R. Frazier. 218: © Junebug Clark/Photo Researchers, Inc. 219: David R. Frazier. 220: Peter French/Bruce Coleman. 223: *l.* © Jim Richardson/West Light; *r.* P. Degginger/H. Armstrong Roberts. 224: Jess Allen/The Stock Solution. 225: David Hiser. 226: The Bettmann Archive. 229: Glen Thomas Brown/The Stock Solution. 230: Cameraman International.

Chapter 9 238: Margaret Berg/Berg & Associates. 241: © 1991 Roger Werths/Woodfin Camp & Associates. 243: David Falconer/David Frazier Library. 244: P. Degginger/H. Armstrong Roberts. 246: Grant Heilman Photography. 247: Werner Stoy/Camera Hawaii. 248–249: Courtesy Northwest Harvest. 252: Michael Baytoff/Black Star; *inset* TOM STACK & ASSOCIATES. 256: Clark Mishler/The Stock Market. 258: FourByFive, Inc. 259: TSW-Click, Chicago. 260: C. Lujen.

Unit 3 opener 266: *t.* SuperStock; *m.* TSW-Click, Chicago; *b.* Bob Thomason/Leo deWys, Inc.

Chapter 10 272: Ray Pfortner/Peter Arnold, Inc. 273: Shostal Associates/SuperStock. 275: *l.* Stock, Boston; *r.* Comnet/Leo deWys, Inc. 276: Claudio Ferrer/TSW-Click, Chicago. 277: *l.* James P. Rowan/TSW-Click, Chicago; *r.* Pedro Coll/The Stock Market. 281: Robert Frerck/TSW-Click, Chicago. 282: Michael Bertan/TSW-Click, Chicago. 283: Robert Frerck/TSW-Click, Chicago. 285: Steve Vidler/Leo deWys, Inc. 289: Tom Mebbia/TSW-Click, Chicago. 288: N. Devore/Bruce Coleman.

Chapter 11 Phylane Norman/Nawrocki Stock Photos. 297: Aerocamera/Leo deWys, Inc. 299: Charles Palek/TOM STACK & ASSOCIATES. 303: Guildhall Art Gallery/The Bridgeman Art Library. 304: *l.* David L. Denemark/Third Coast Stock Source; *r.* © Lawrence Migdale/Photo Researchers, Inc. 305: Glen Ellen/Grant Heilman Photography. 306: © Gianni Tortosi/Photo Researchers, Inc. 308: Neil Beer/TSW-Click, Chicago. 309: Steve Vidler/Leo deWys, Inc.

Chapter 12 312: M. Thonig/AllStock, Inc. 314: M. Thonig/H. Armstrong Roberts. 316: FourByFive, Inc. 317: Ted Cordingley; *inset* © 1991 Mike Yamashita/Woodfin Camp & Associates. 320: SuperStock. 321: Hoa Qui/Viesti Associates. 323: SuperStock; *inset* Tom Lankes/TexaStock. 324: Ken Straiton/The Stock Market. 325: Steve Vidler/Leo deWys, Inc. 327: Jan Taylor/Bruce Coleman; *inset* Rod Allin/TOM STACK & ASSOCIATES. 328: Robin Smith/SuperStock. 330: *l.* Robert Frerck/Odyssey Productions; *r.* Robert Frerck/TSW-Click, Chicago. 333: John Cancalosi/TOM STACK & ASSOCIATES; *inset* Robin Smith/SuperStock.

Chapter 13 338: David R. Frazier. 343: Grant Heilman Photography. 347: Bruce Coleman. 350: Carlos Elmer/SuperStock. 352: *t.l.* © Larry Mulvehill/Photo Researchers, Inc.; *b.l.* John Lazenby/f/Stop Pictures, Inc.; *m.* Manuel Dos Passos/Bruce Coleman; *t.r.* Craig Davis/Sygma; *b.r.* SuperStock. 353: Comstock.

Chapter 14 356, 357: Kurt Scholz/SuperStock. 358: M. Koene/H. Armstrong Roberts. 359: Hubertus Kanus/SuperStock. 360: *l.* Tass/Sovfoto; *r.* © George Holton/Photo Researchers, Inc. 363: Steve Vidler/Leo deWys, Inc. 364: Fridmar Damm/Leo deWys, Inc.; *inset* SuperStock. 366: Alan Pitcairn/Grant Heilman Photography. 370: Ted Gruen/Bruce Coleman. 371: Jean Paul Nacivet/Leo deWys, Inc. 373: Diego Goldberg/Sygma. 374: Nara Kofukuji/Bruce Coleman.

A B C D E F G H I J—RRD—96 95 94 93 92 91 90